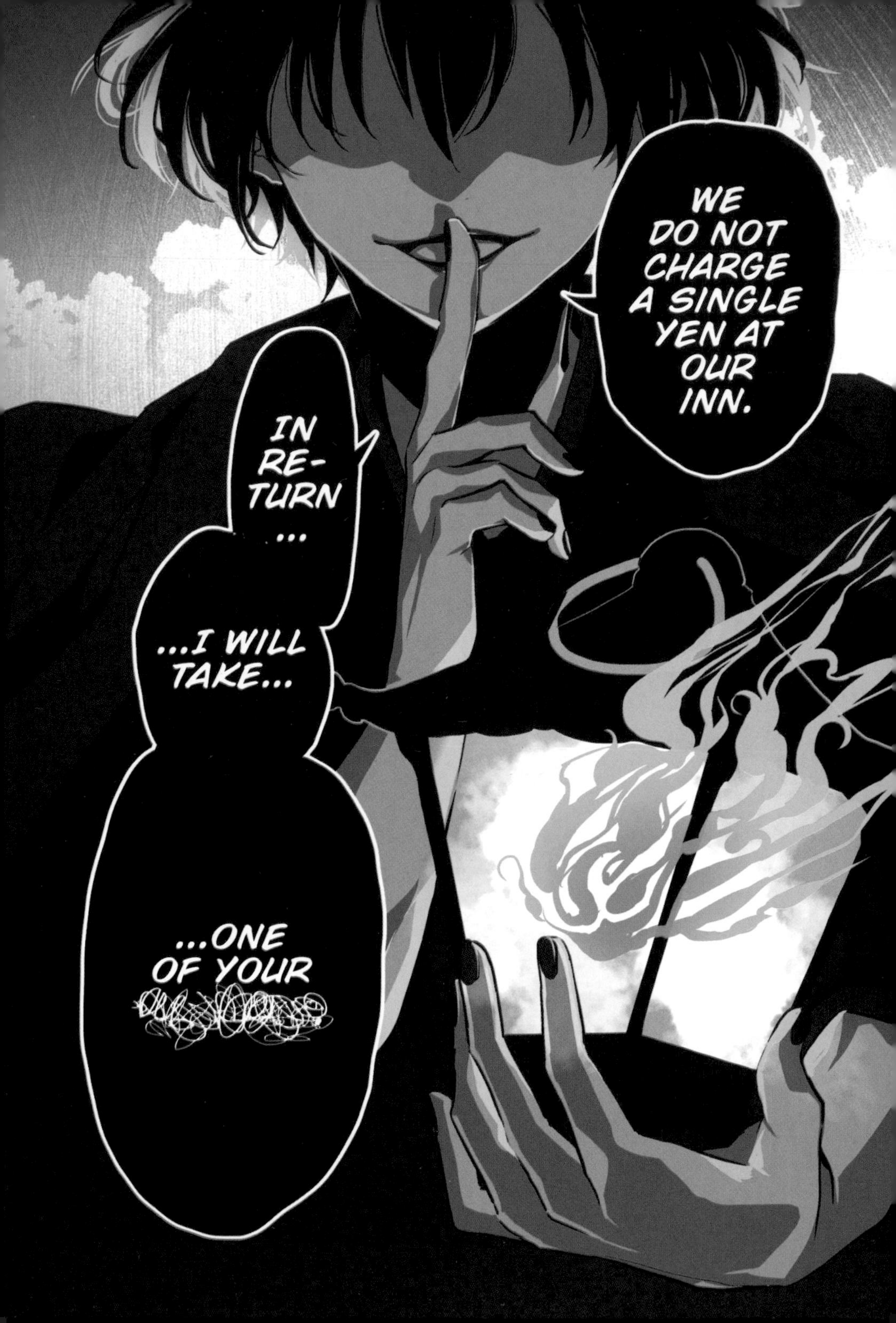
WE DO NOT CHARGE A SINGLE YEN AT OUR INN.
IN RE-TURN...
...I WILL TAKE...
...ONE OF YOUR

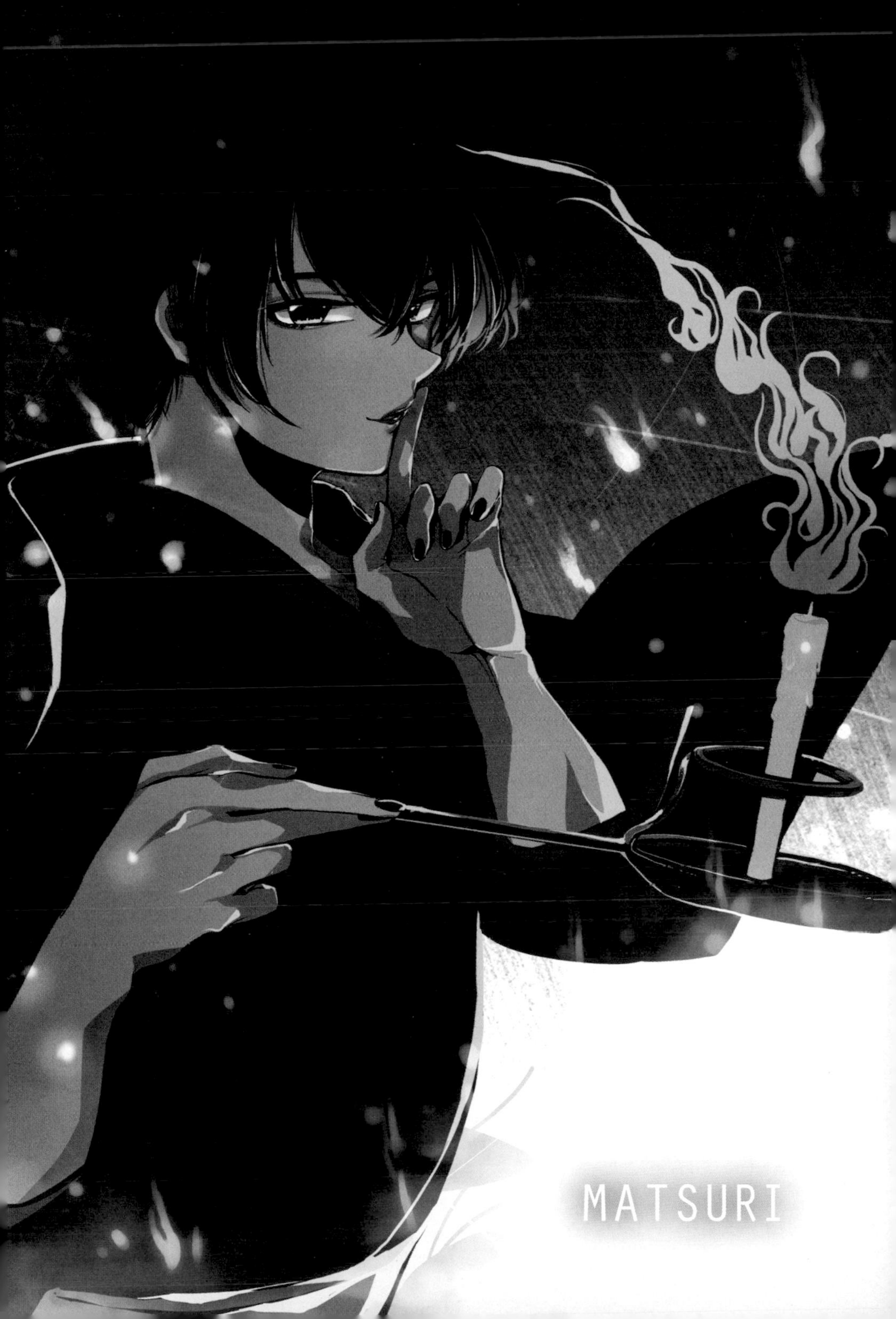
MATSURI

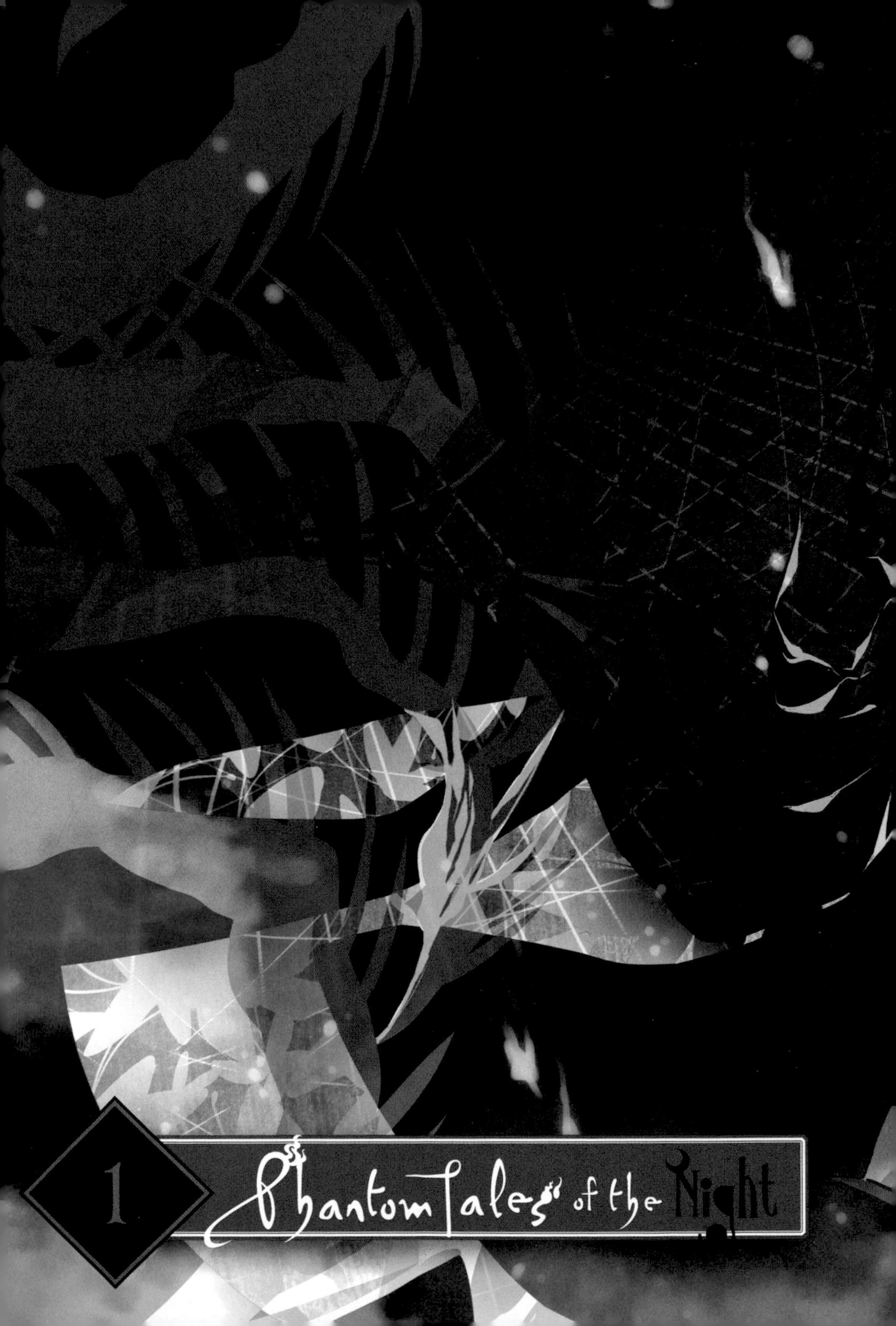
1
Phantom Tales of the Night

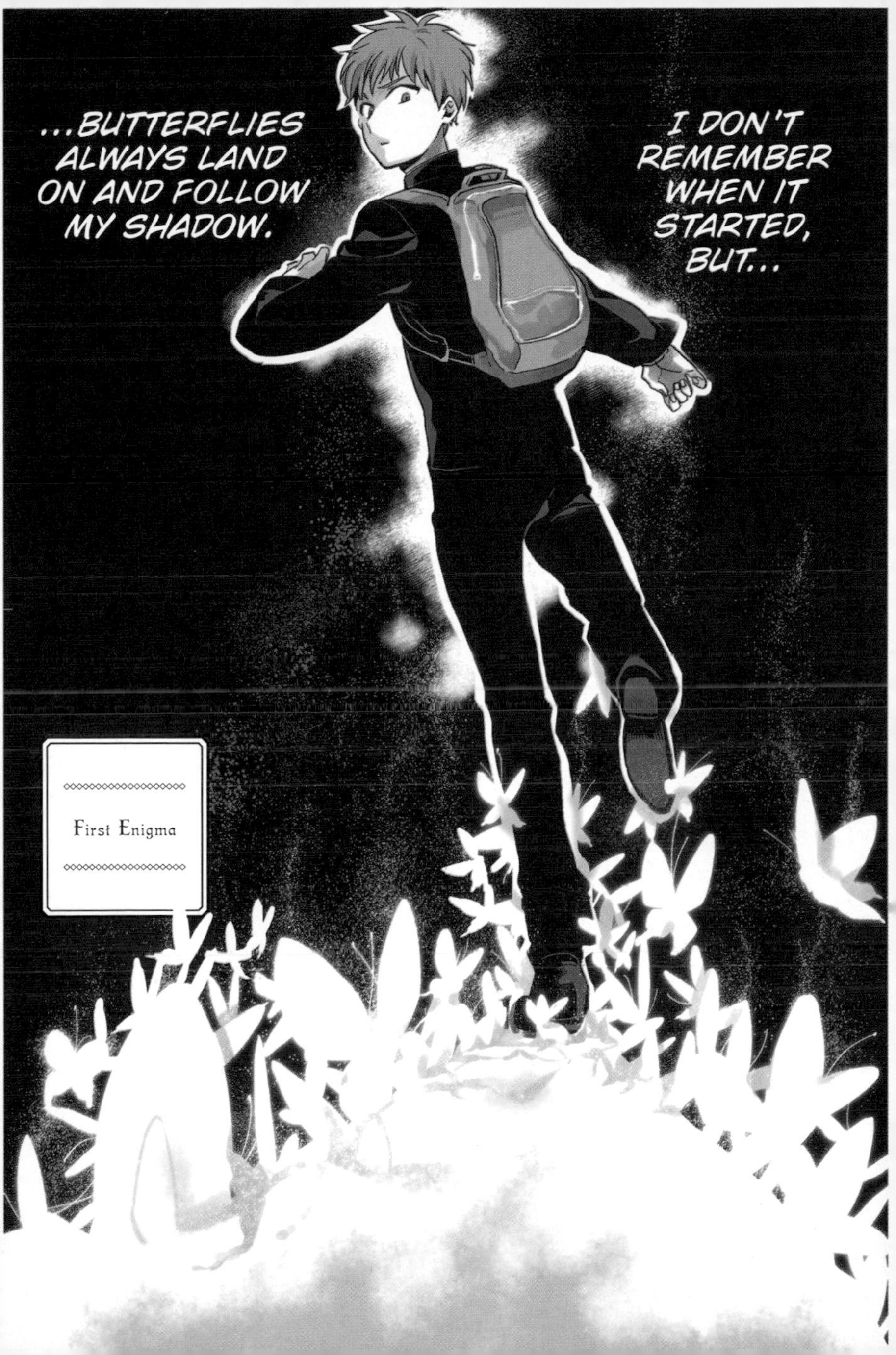
I DON'T REMEMBER WHEN IT STARTED, BUT...
...BUTTERFLIES ALWAYS LAND ON AND FOLLOW MY SHADOW.
First Enigma

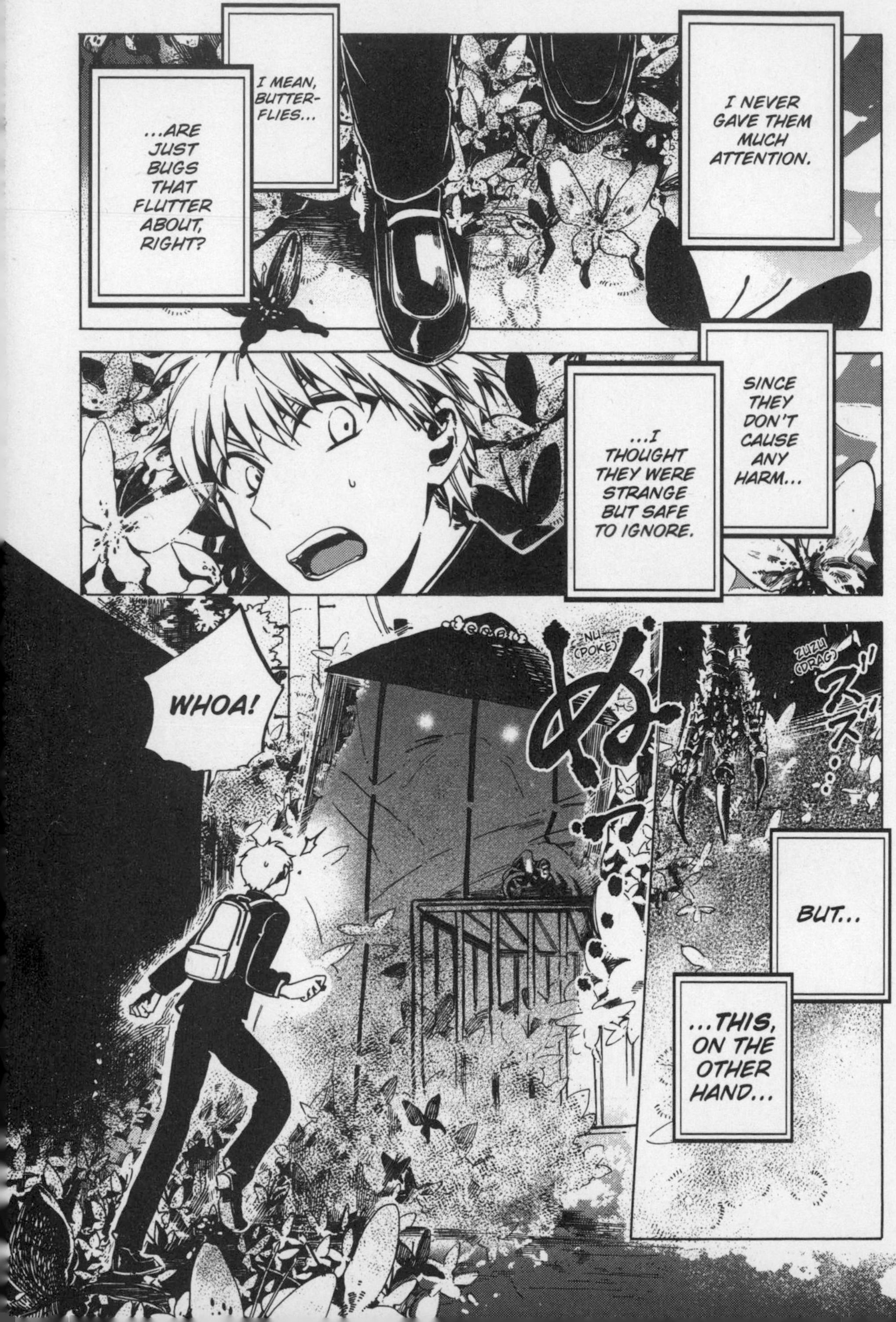
I NEVER GAVE THEM MUCH ATTENTION.
I MEAN, BUTTER-FLIES...
...ARE JUST BUGS THAT FLUTTER ABOUT, RIGHT?
SINCE THEY DON'T CAUSE ANY HARM...
...I THOUGHT THEY WERE STRANGE BUT SAFE TO IGNORE.
ZUZU (DRAG)
NU (POKE)
WHOA!
BUT...
...THIS, ON THE OTHER HAND...

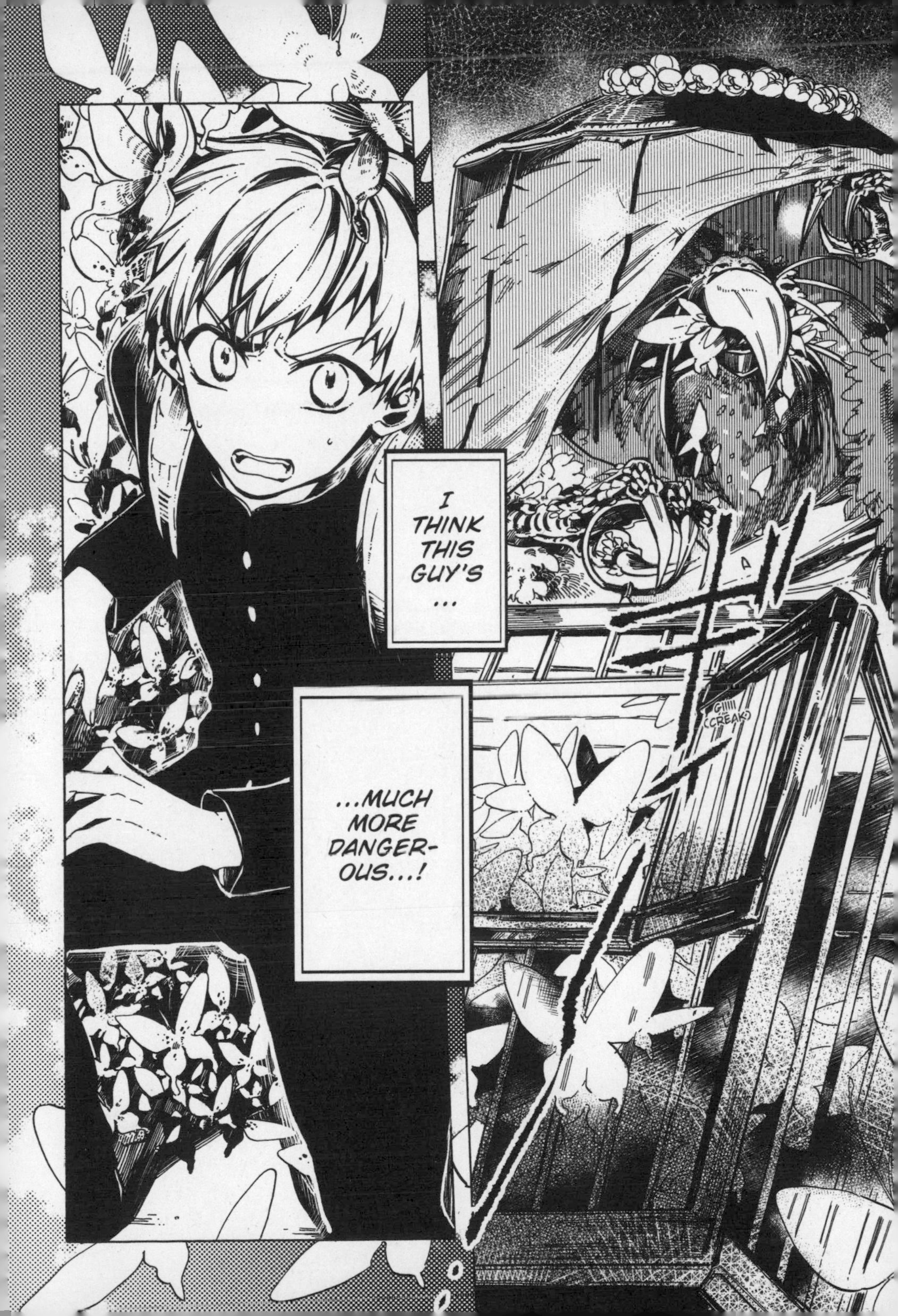
I THINK THIS GUY'S ...
GIIII (CREAK)
...MUCH MORE DANGER-OUS...!

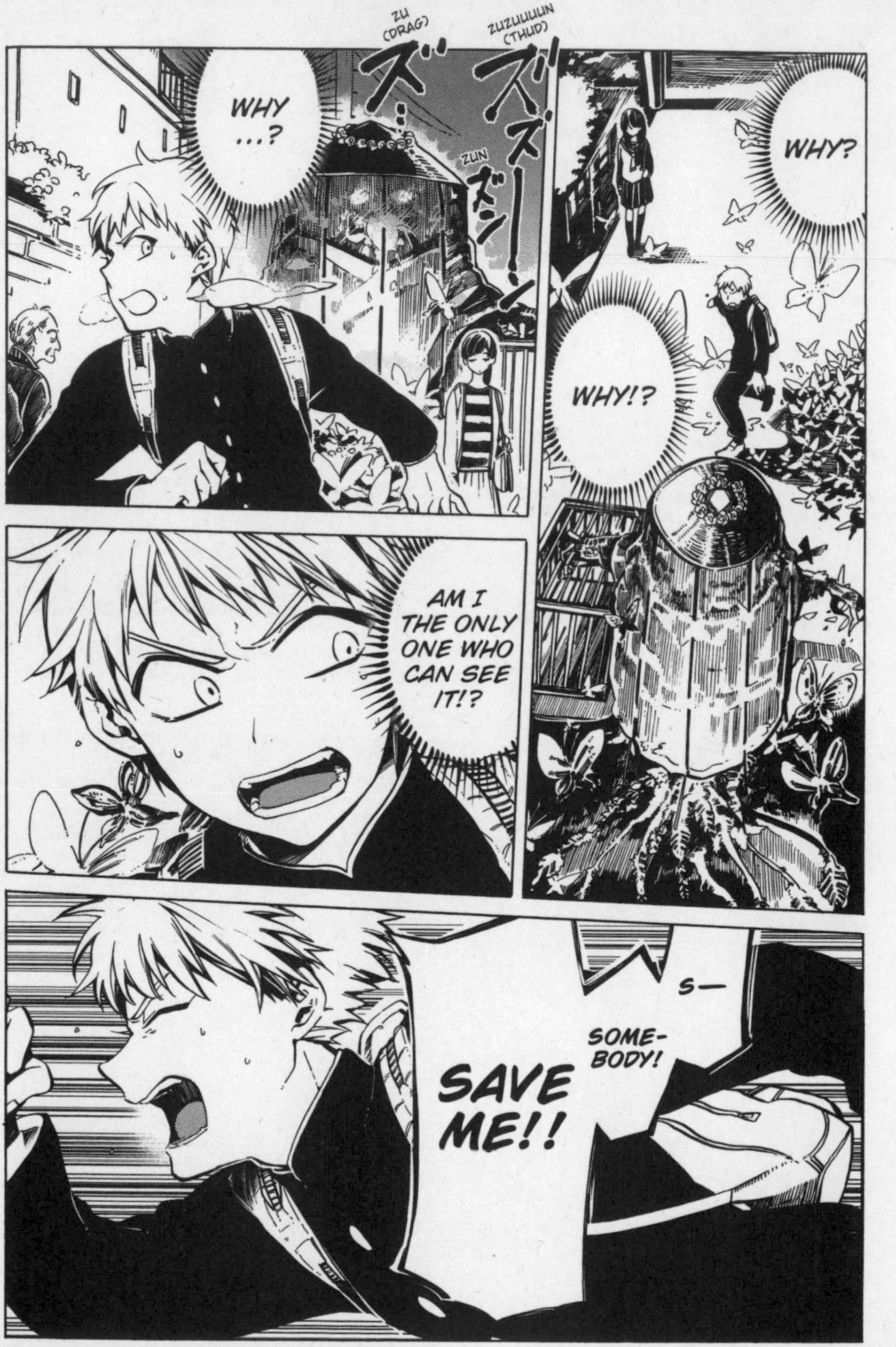
WHY?
WHY!?
ZUZUUUUUN (THUD)
ZU (DRAG)
WHY ...?
ZUN
AM I THE ONLY ONE WHO CAN SEE IT!?
S—
SOME-BODY!
SAVE ME!!

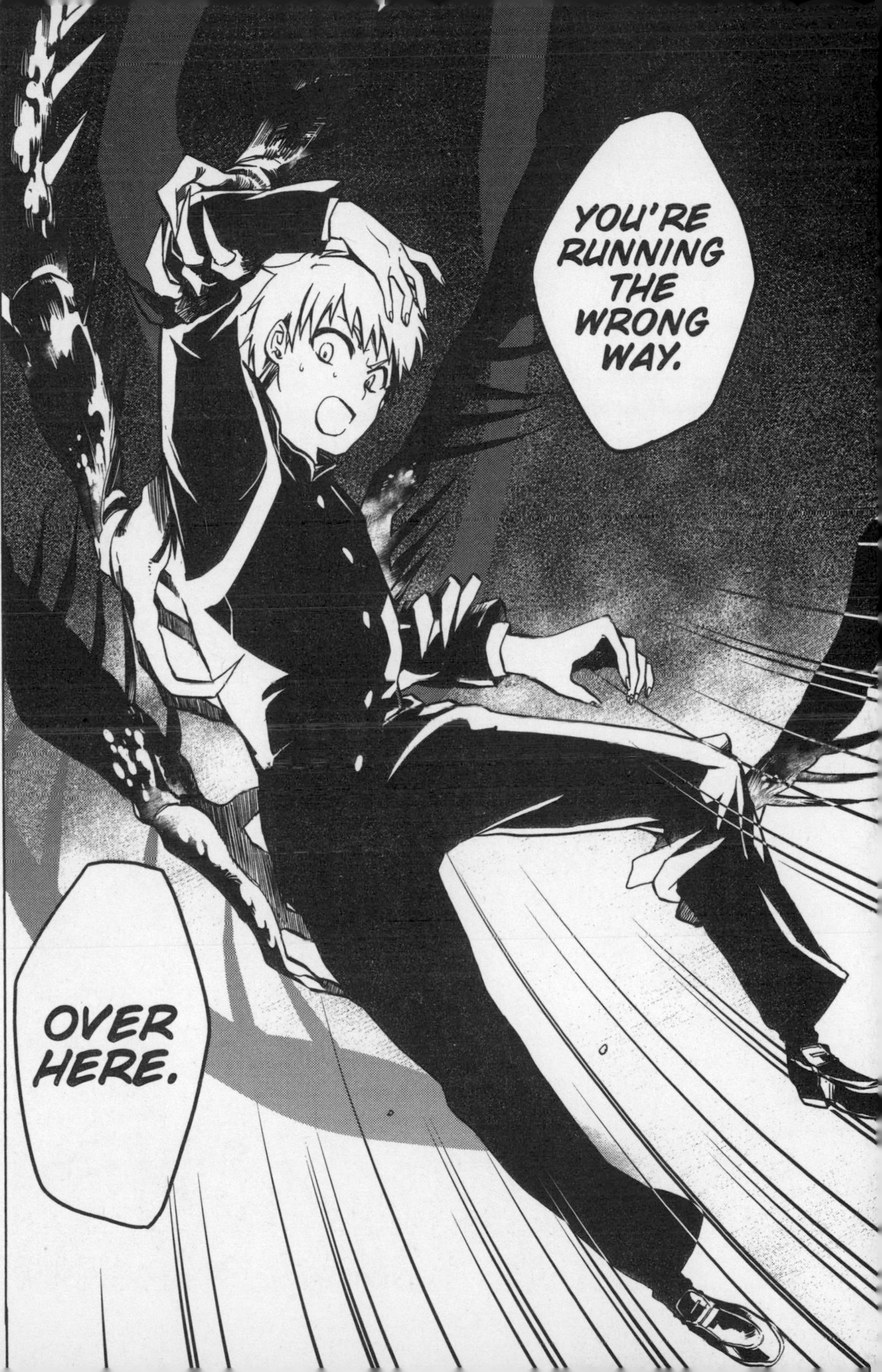
YOU'RE RUNNING THE WRONG WAY.
OVER HERE.

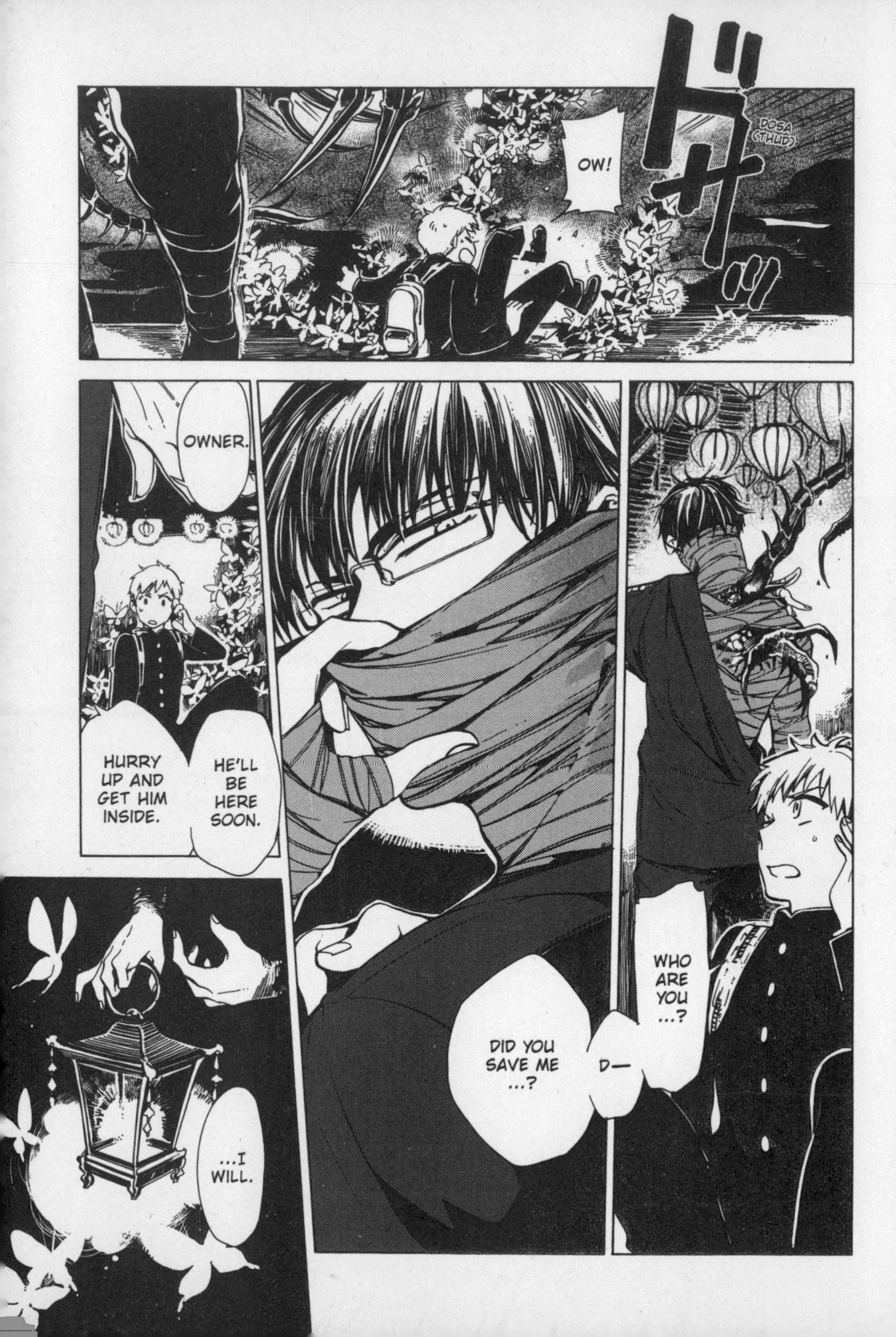
DOSA (THUD)
OW!
WHO ARE YOU ...?
D—
DID YOU SAVE ME ...?
OWNER.
HE'LL BE HERE SOON.
HURRY UP AND GET HIM INSIDE.
...I WILL.

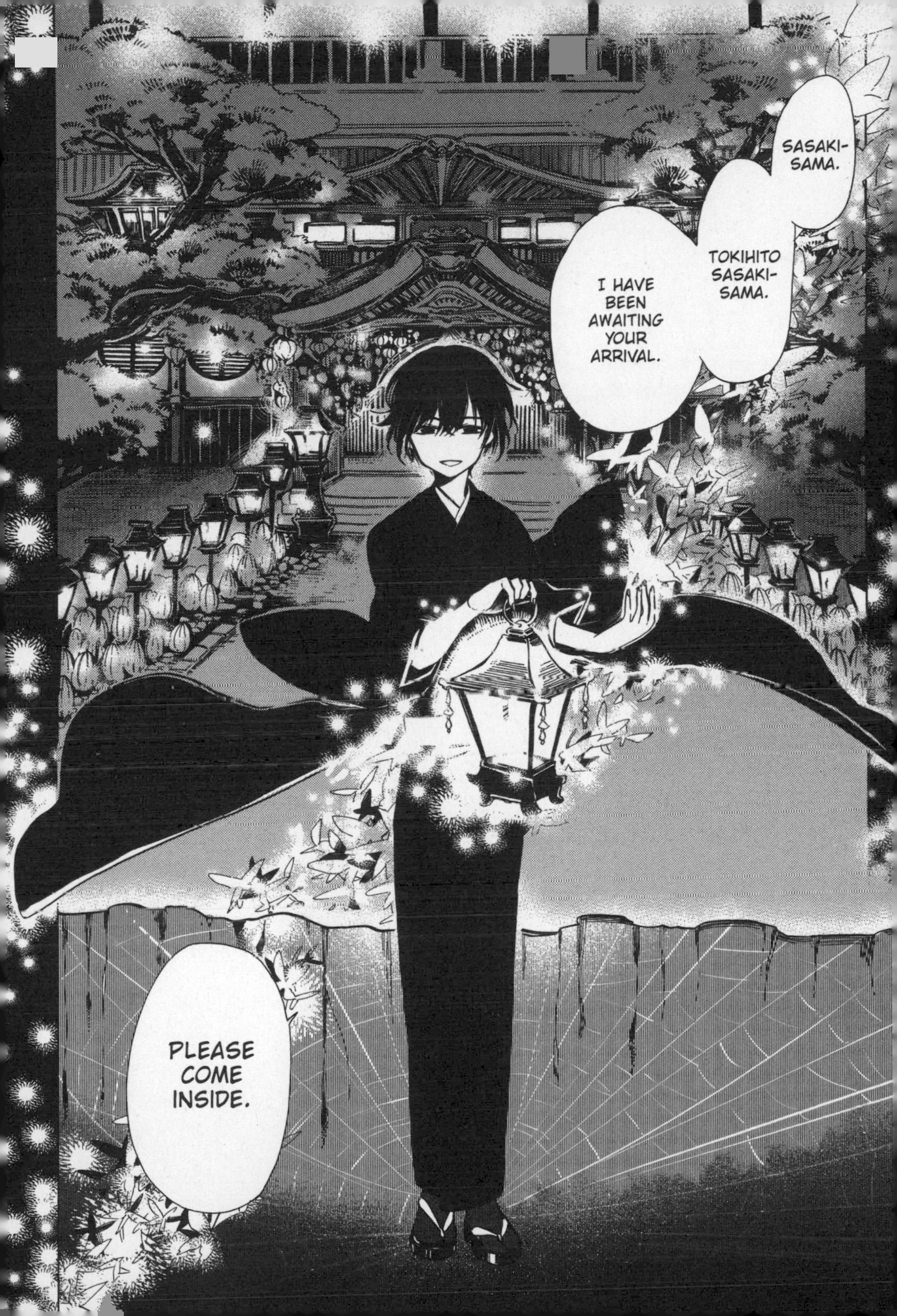
SASAKI-SAMA.
TOKIHITO SASAKI-SAMA.
I HAVE BEEN AWAITING YOUR ARRIVAL.
PLEASE COME INSIDE.

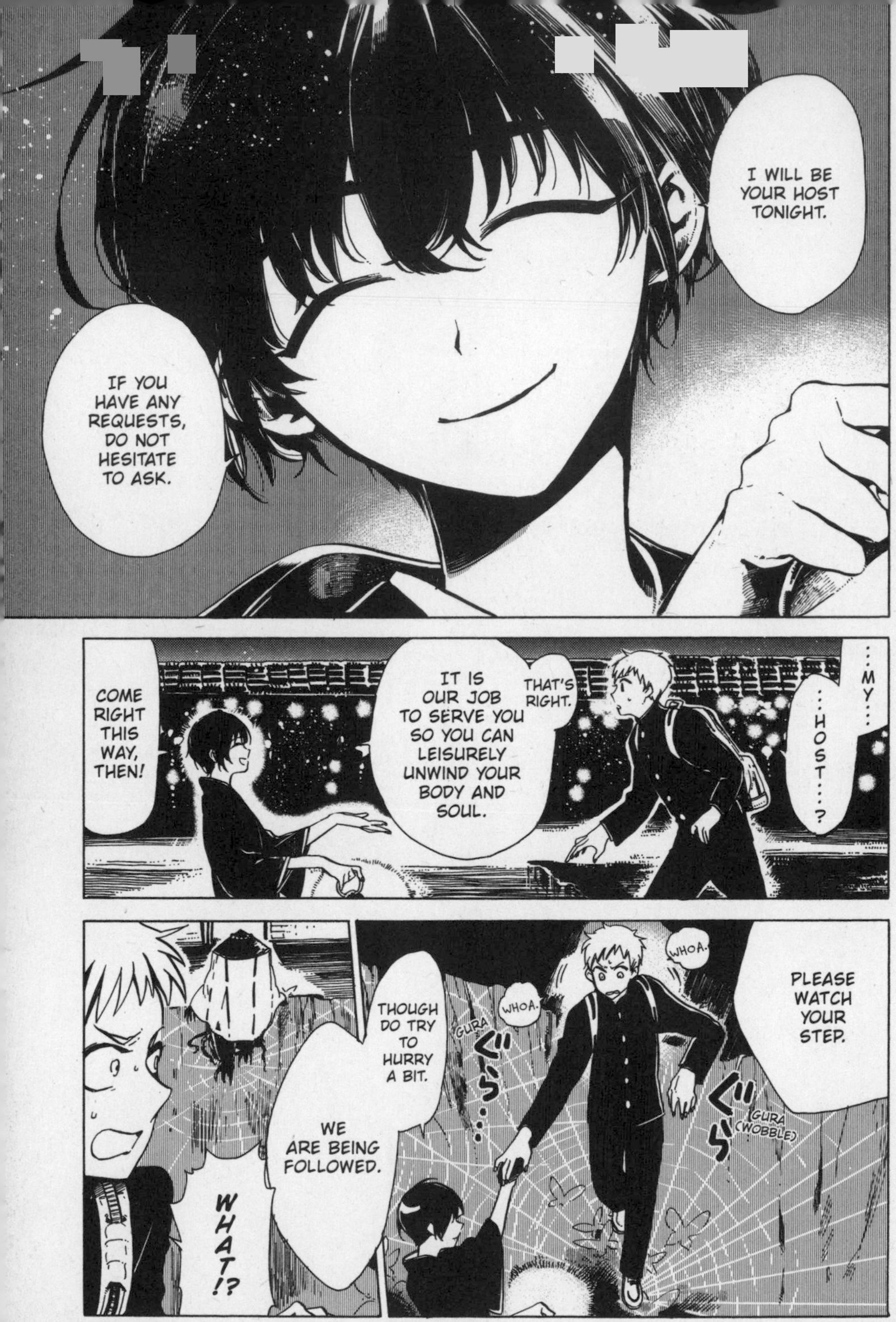
I WILL BE YOUR HOST TONIGHT.
IF YOU HAVE ANY REQUESTS, DO NOT HESITATE TO ASK.
...MY... ...HOST...?
THAT'S RIGHT.
IT IS OUR JOB TO SERVE YOU SO YOU CAN LEISURELY UNWIND YOUR BODY AND SOUL.
COME RIGHT THIS WAY, THEN!
PLEASE WATCH YOUR STEP.
WHOA.
ぐら
GURA (WOBBLE)
WHOA.
GURA
ぐら...
THOUGH DO TRY TO HURRY A BIT.
WE ARE BEING FOLLOWED.
WHAT!?

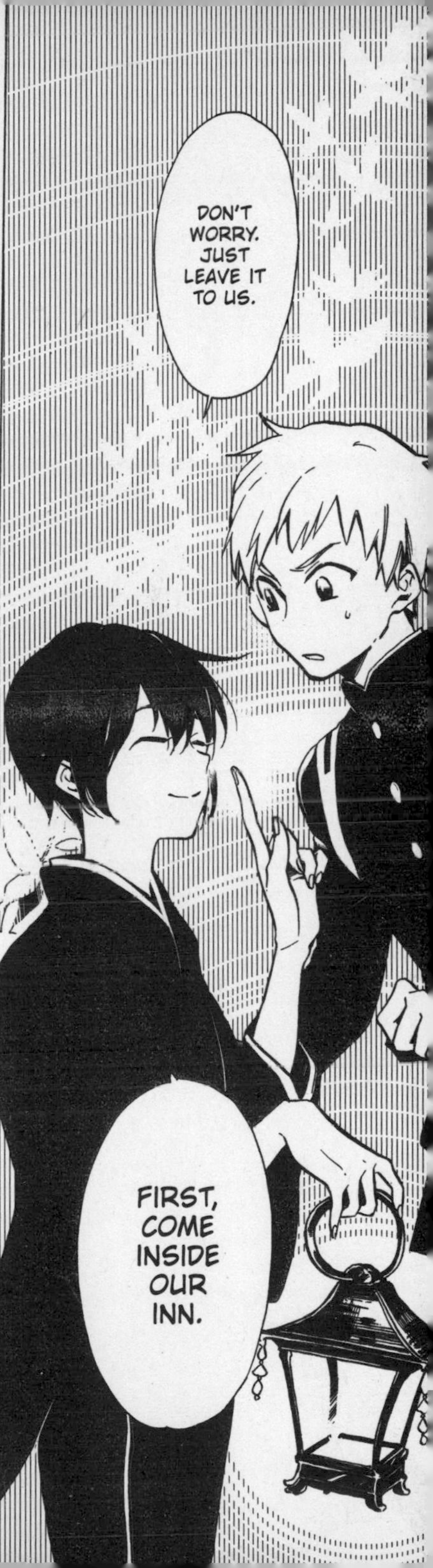
DON'T WORRY. JUST LEAVE IT TO US.
FIRST, COME INSIDE OUR INN.

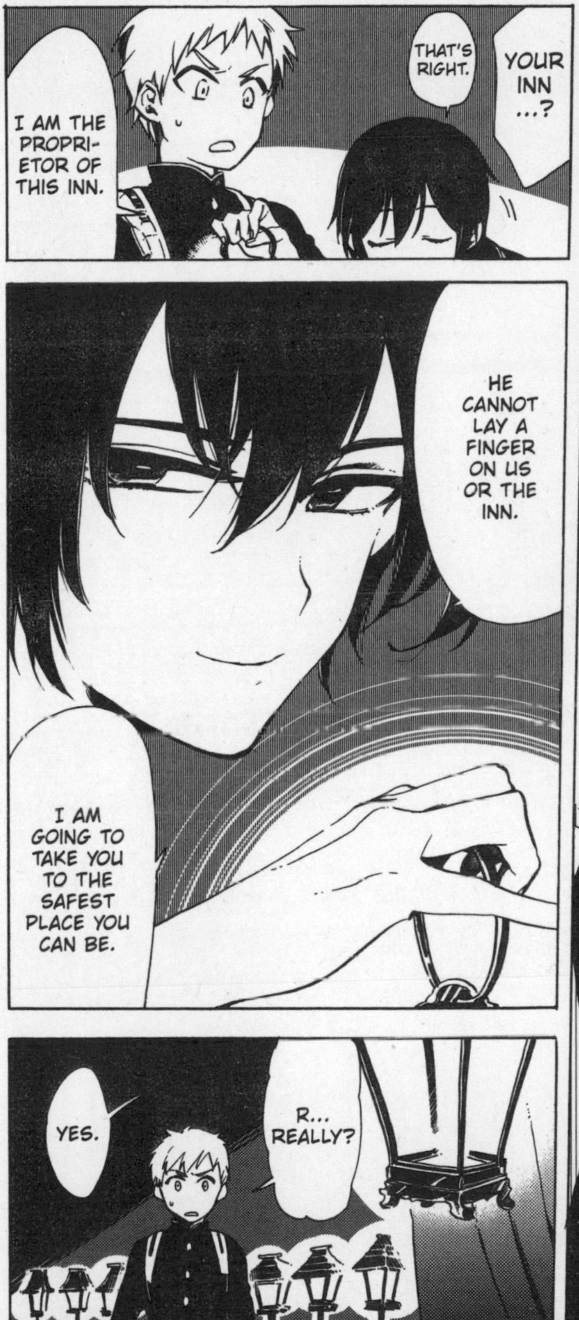
YOUR INN ...?
THAT'S RIGHT.
I AM THE PROPRI-ETOR OF THIS INN.
HE CANNOT LAY A FINGER ON US OR THE INN.
I AM GOING TO TAKE YOU TO THE SAFEST PLACE YOU CAN BE.
R... REALLY?
YES.

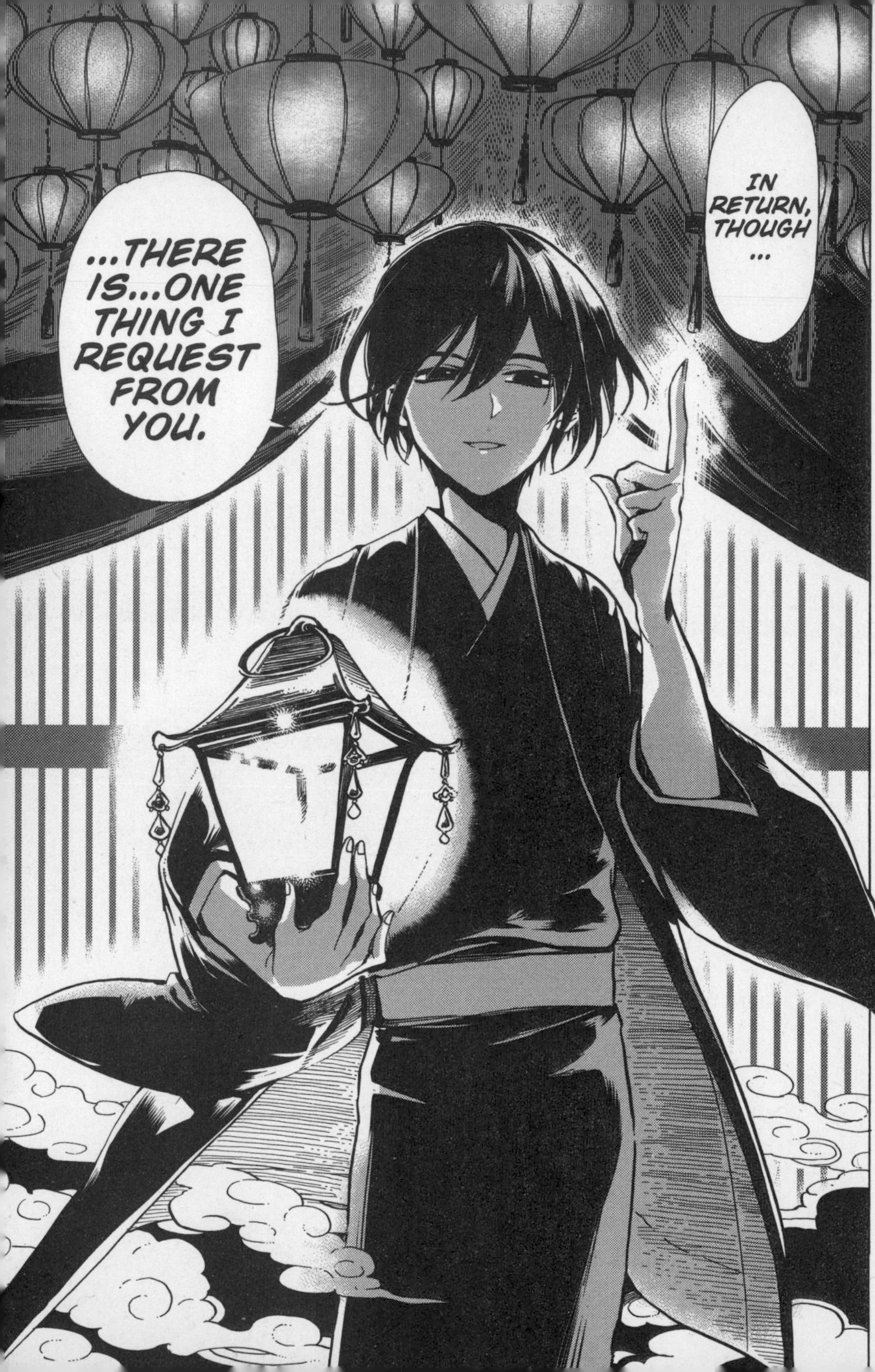
IN RETURN, THOUGH...
...THERE IS...ONE THING I REQUEST FROM YOU.

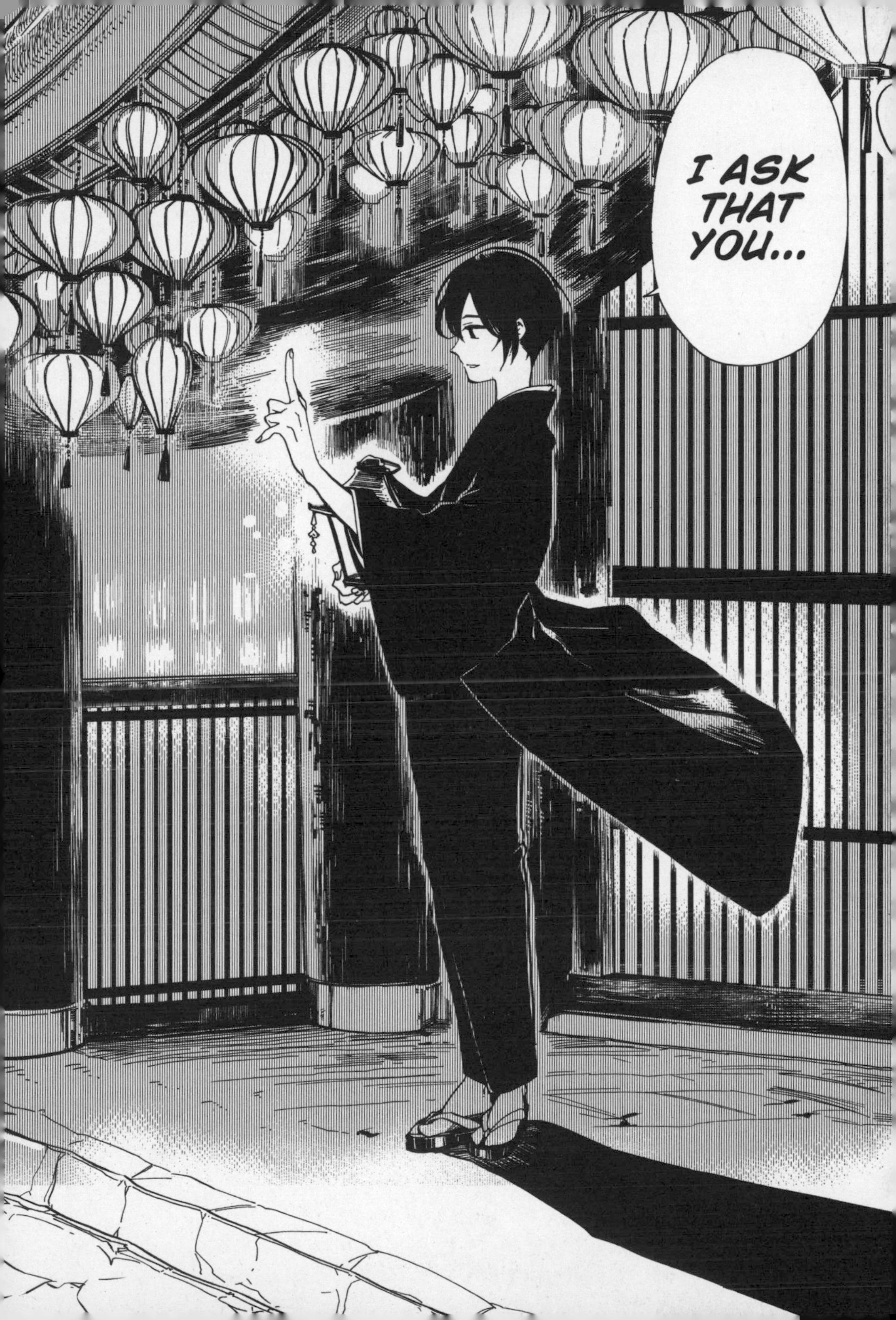
I ASK THAT YOU...

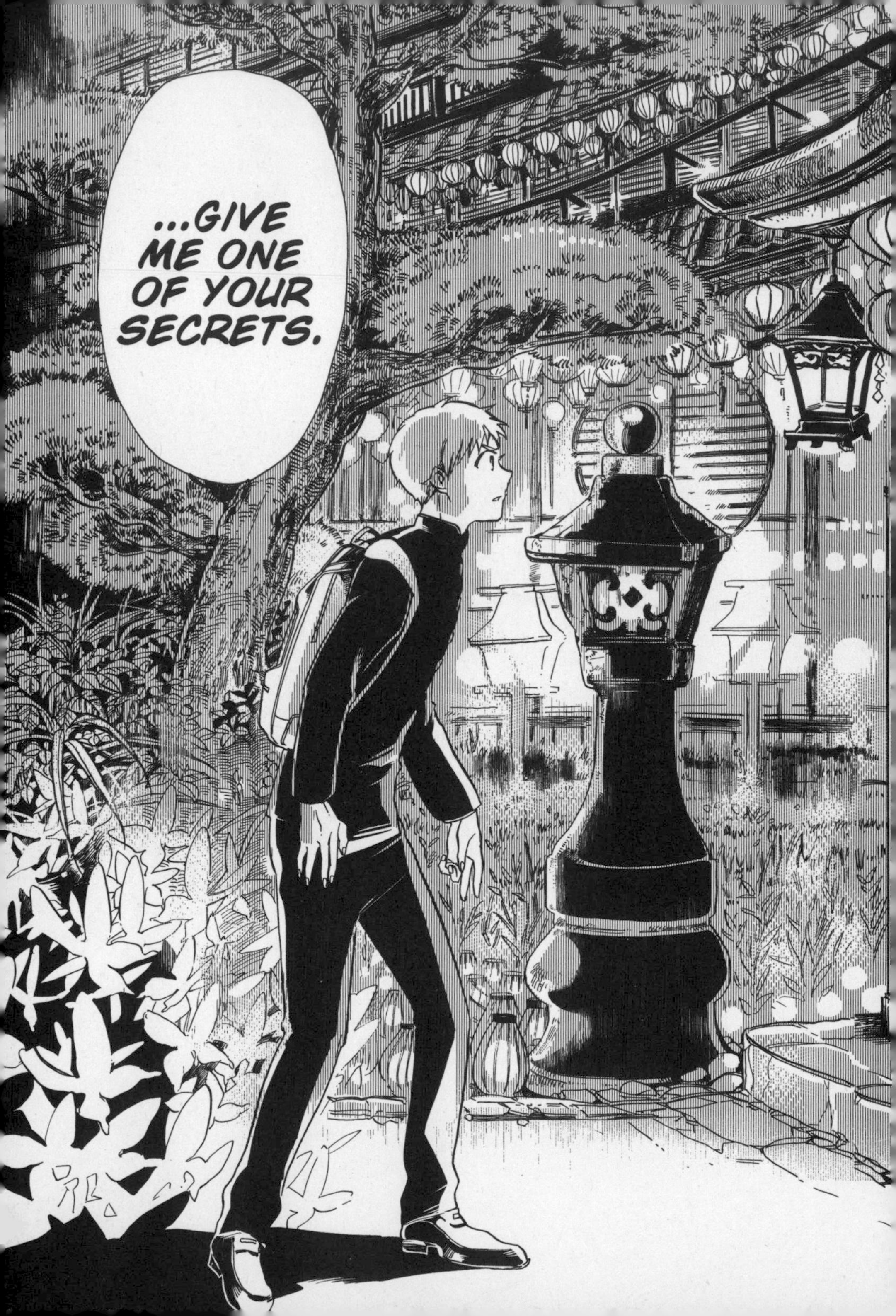
...GIVE ME ONE OF YOUR SECRETS.

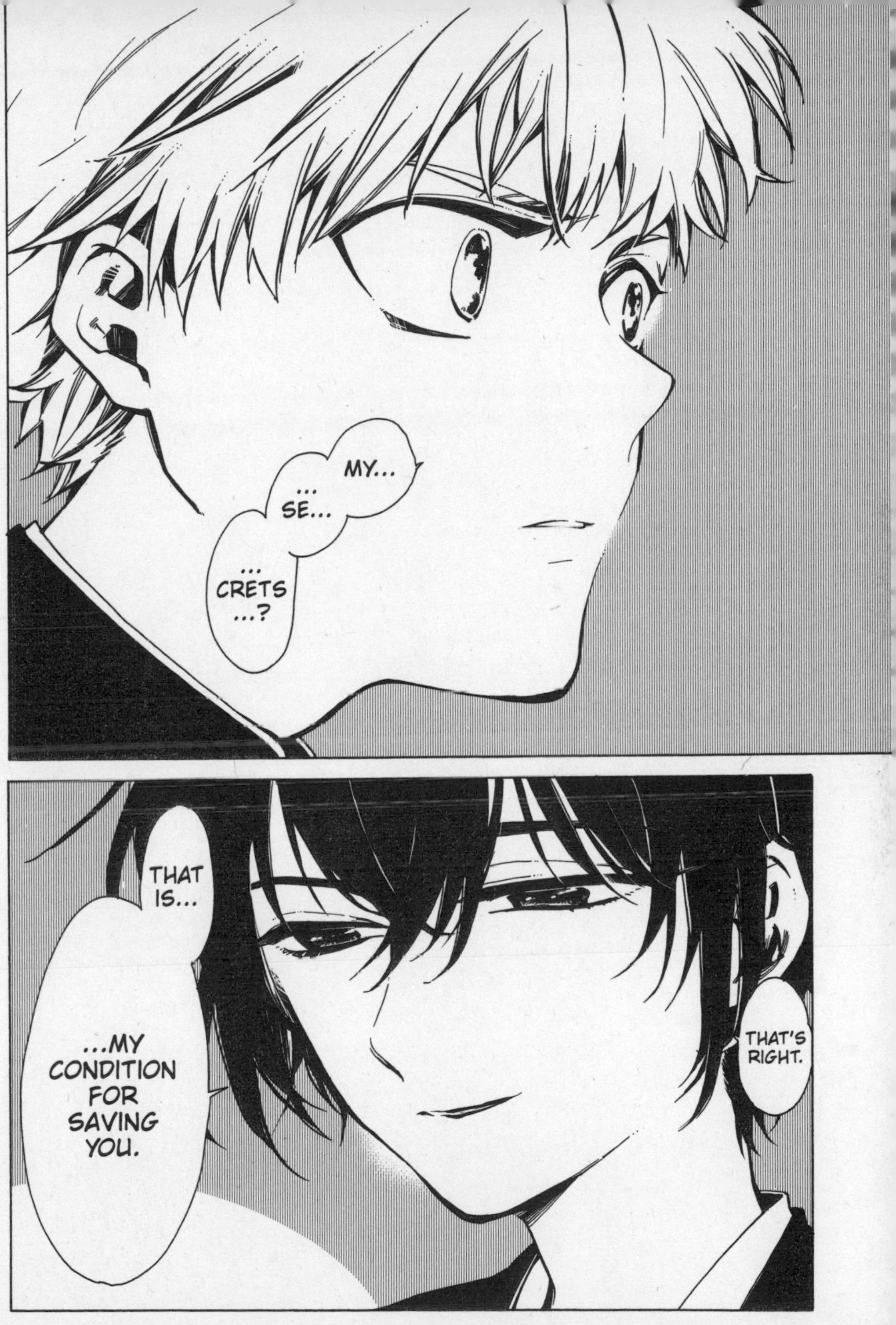
MY...
...SE...
...CRETS...?
THAT'S RIGHT.
THAT IS...
...MY CONDITION FOR SAVING YOU.

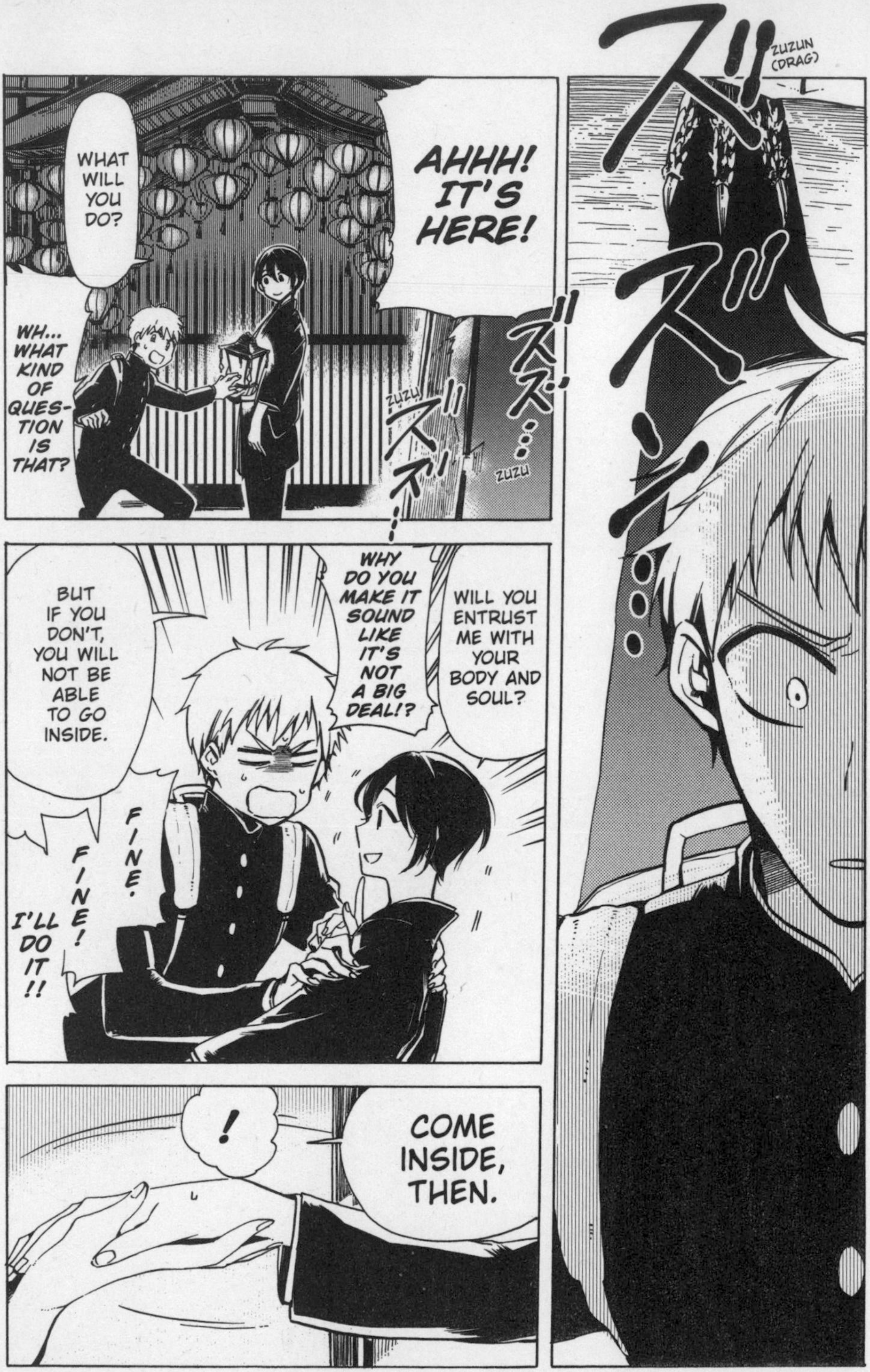
ZUZUN (DRAG)
AHHH! IT'S HERE!
WHAT WILL YOU DO?
WH... WHAT KIND OF QUESTION IS THAT?
ZUZU
ZUZU
WILL YOU ENTRUST ME WITH YOUR BODY AND SOUL?
WHY DO YOU MAKE IT SOUND LIKE IT'S NOT A BIG DEAL!?
BUT IF YOU DON'T, YOU WILL NOT BE ABLE TO GO INSIDE.
FINE. FINE! I'LL DO IT!!
COME INSIDE, THEN.
!

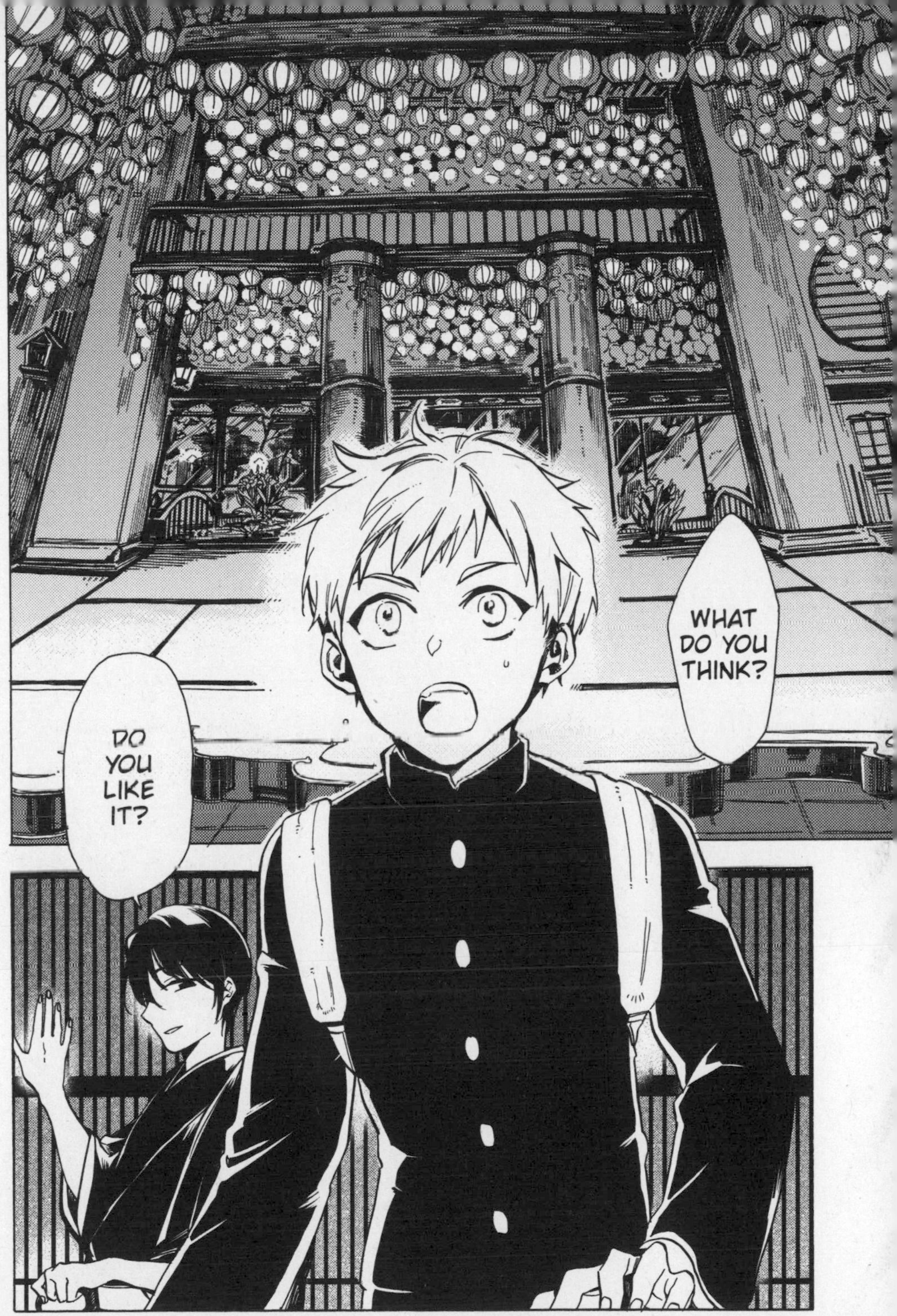
WHAT DO YOU THINK?
DO YOU LIKE IT?

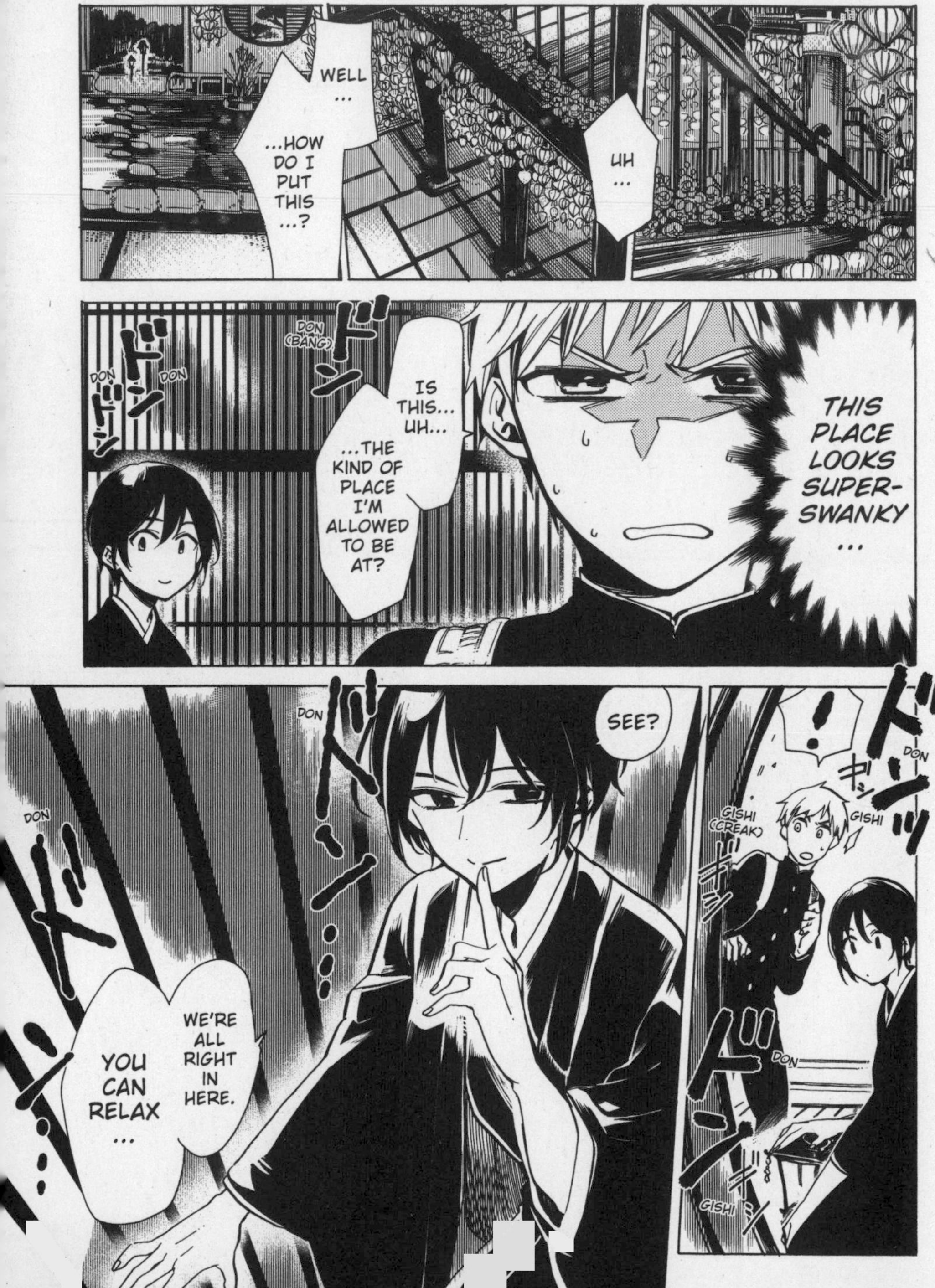
UH ...
WELL ...
...HOW DO I PUT THIS ...?
THIS PLACE LOOKS SUPER-SWANKY ...
DON (BANG)
IS THIS... UH...
...THE KIND OF PLACE I'M ALLOWED TO BE AT?
DON
DON
!
DON
GISHI (CREAK)
GISHI
DON
GISHI
SEE?
DON
DON
WE'RE ALL RIGHT IN HERE.
YOU CAN RELAX ...

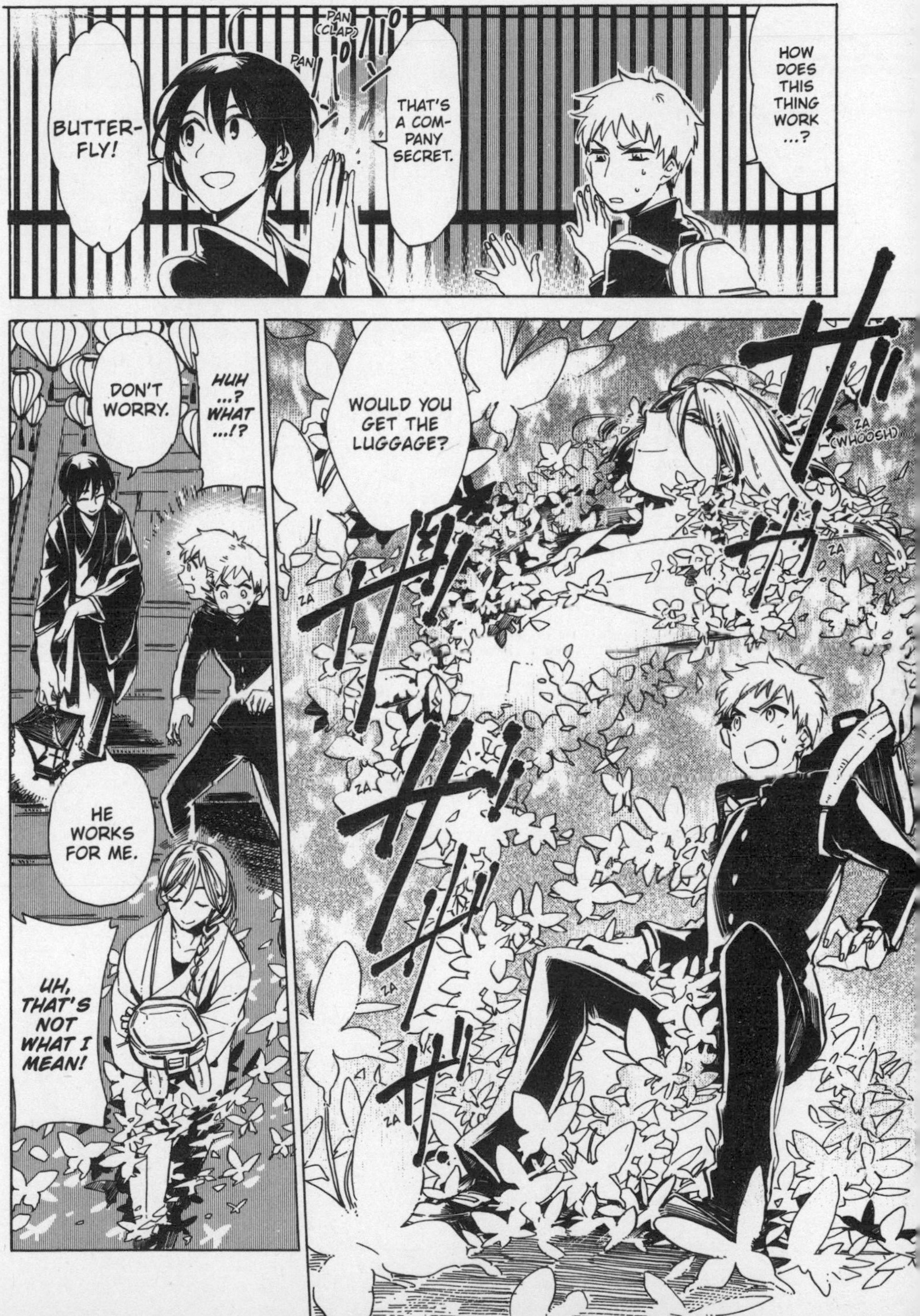
HOW DOES THIS THING WORK...?
THAT'S A COMPANY SECRET.
PAN (CLAP)
PAN
BUTTER-FLY!
WOULD YOU GET THE LUGGAGE?
ZA (WHOOSH)
ZA
ZA
ZA
ZA
ZA
HUH...? WHAT...!?
DON'T WORRY.
HE WORKS FOR ME.
UH, THAT'S NOT WHAT I MEAN!

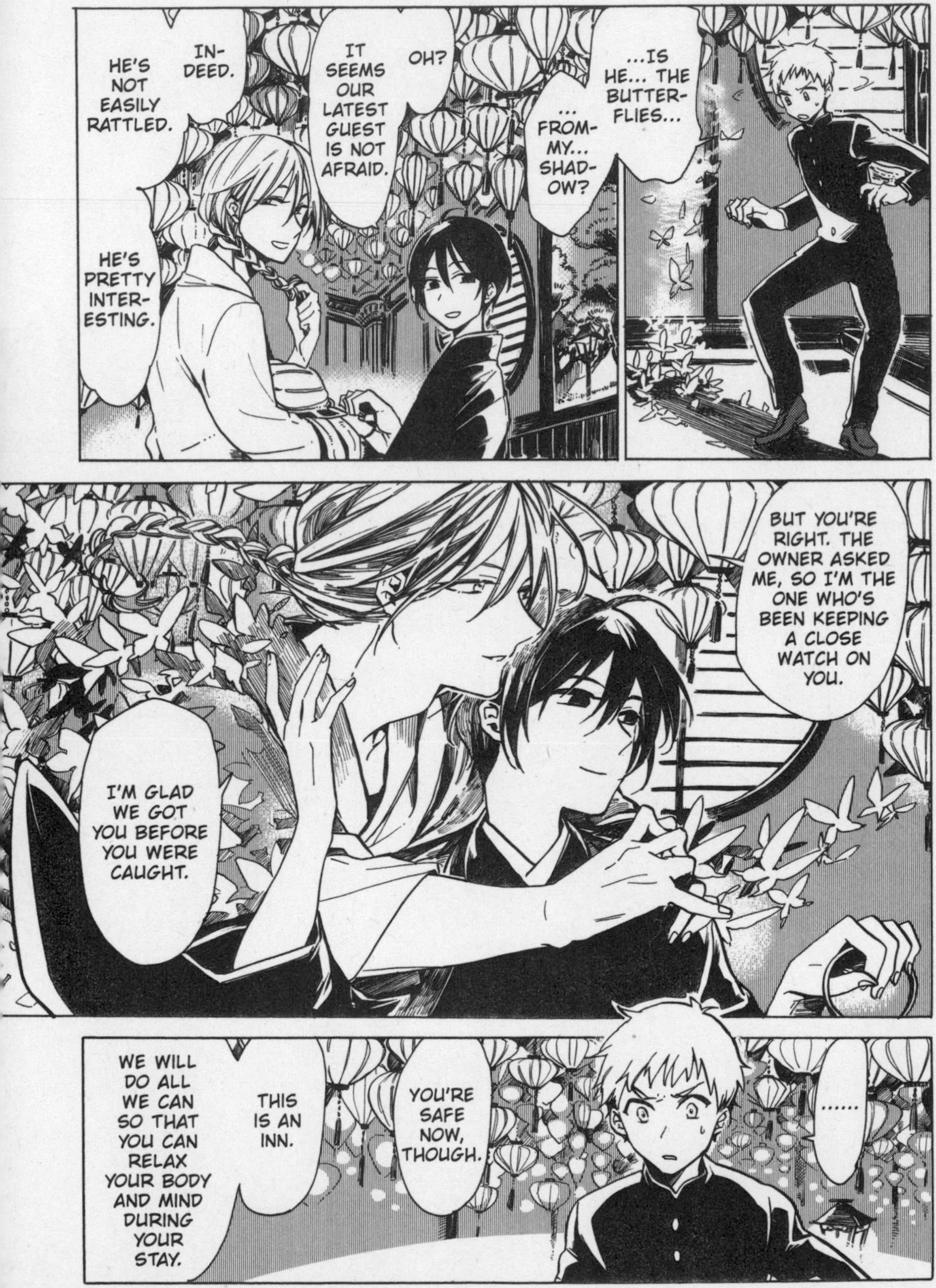

...IS HE... THE BUTTERFLIES...
...FROM MY... SHADOW?
OH?
IT SEEMS OUR LATEST GUEST IS NOT AFRAID.
IN-DEED.
HE'S NOT EASILY RATTLED.
HE'S PRETTY INTERESTING.
BUT YOU'RE RIGHT. THE OWNER ASKED ME, SO I'M THE ONE WHO'S BEEN KEEPING A CLOSE WATCH ON YOU.
I'M GLAD WE GOT YOU BEFORE YOU WERE CAUGHT.
......
YOU'RE SAFE NOW, THOUGH.
THIS IS AN INN.
WE WILL DO ALL WE CAN SO THAT YOU CAN RELAX YOUR BODY AND MIND DURING YOUR STAY.

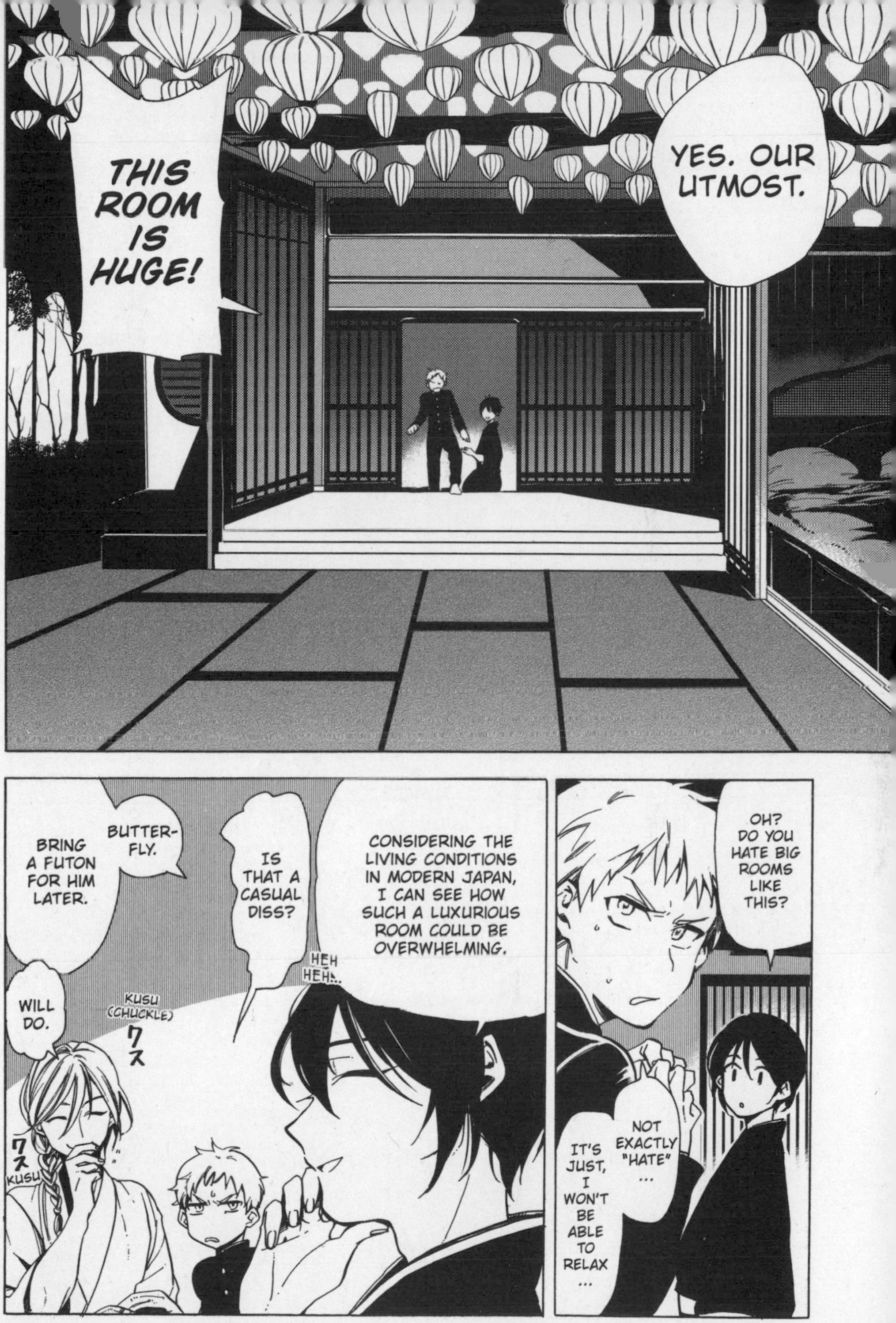
THIS ROOM IS HUGE!
YES. OUR UTMOST.
OH? DO YOU HATE BIG ROOMS LIKE THIS?
NOT EXACTLY "HATE"...
IT'S JUST, I WON'T BE ABLE TO RELAX...
CONSIDERING THE LIVING CONDITIONS IN MODERN JAPAN, I CAN SEE HOW SUCH A LUXURIOUS ROOM COULD BE OVERWHELMING.
HEH HEH...
IS THAT A CASUAL DISS?
BUTTER-FLY.
BRING A FUTON FOR HIM LATER.
KUSU (CHUCKLE)
クス
WILL DO.
クス
KUSU

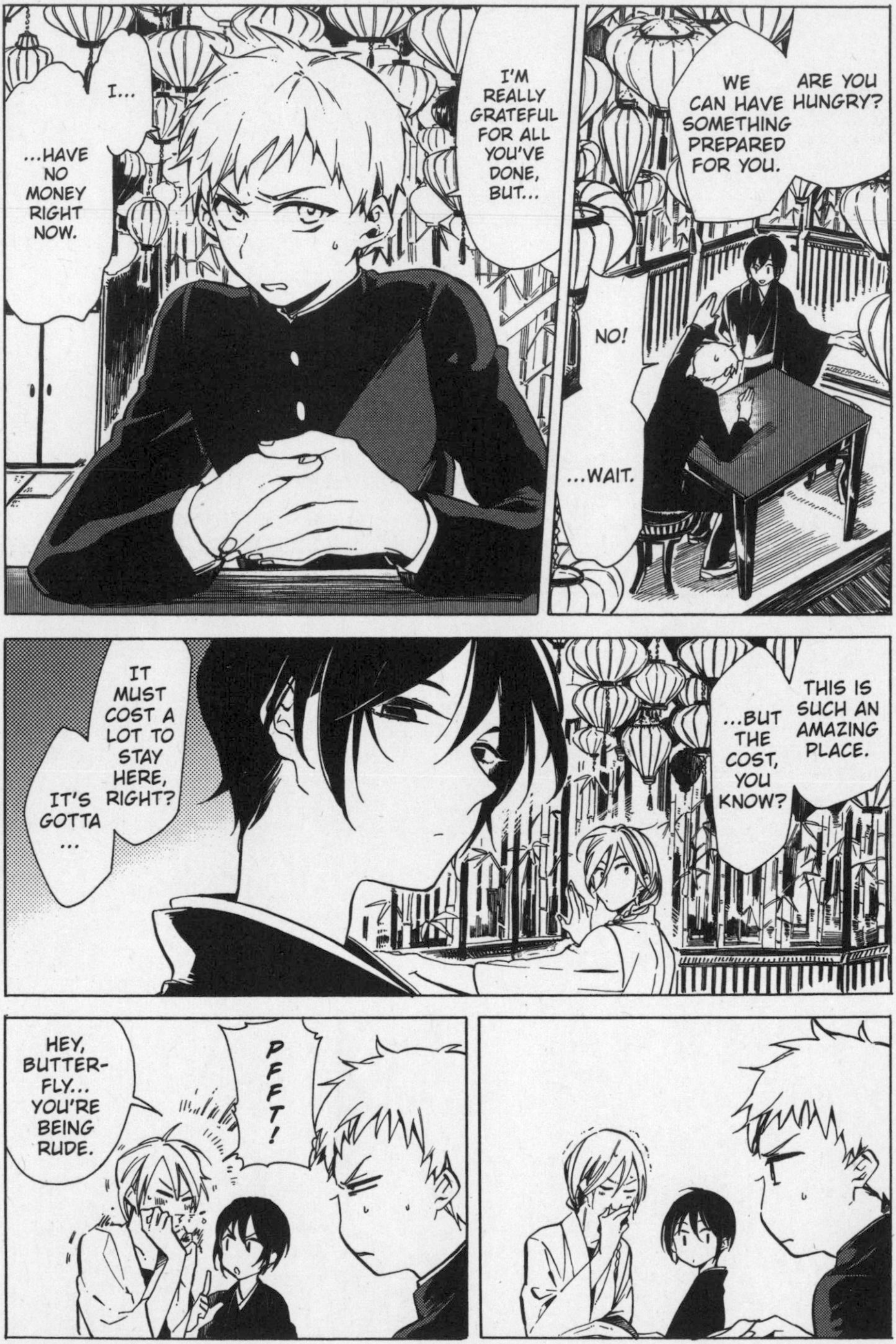
ARE YOU HUNGRY?
WE CAN HAVE SOMETHING PREPARED FOR YOU.
NO!
...WAIT.
I'M REALLY GRATEFUL FOR ALL YOU'VE DONE, BUT...
I...
...HAVE NO MONEY RIGHT NOW.
THIS IS SUCH AN AMAZING PLACE.
...BUT THE COST, YOU KNOW?
IT MUST COST A LOT TO STAY HERE, RIGHT?
IT'S GOTTA ...
PFFT!
HEY, BUTTER-FLY... YOU'RE BEING RUDE.

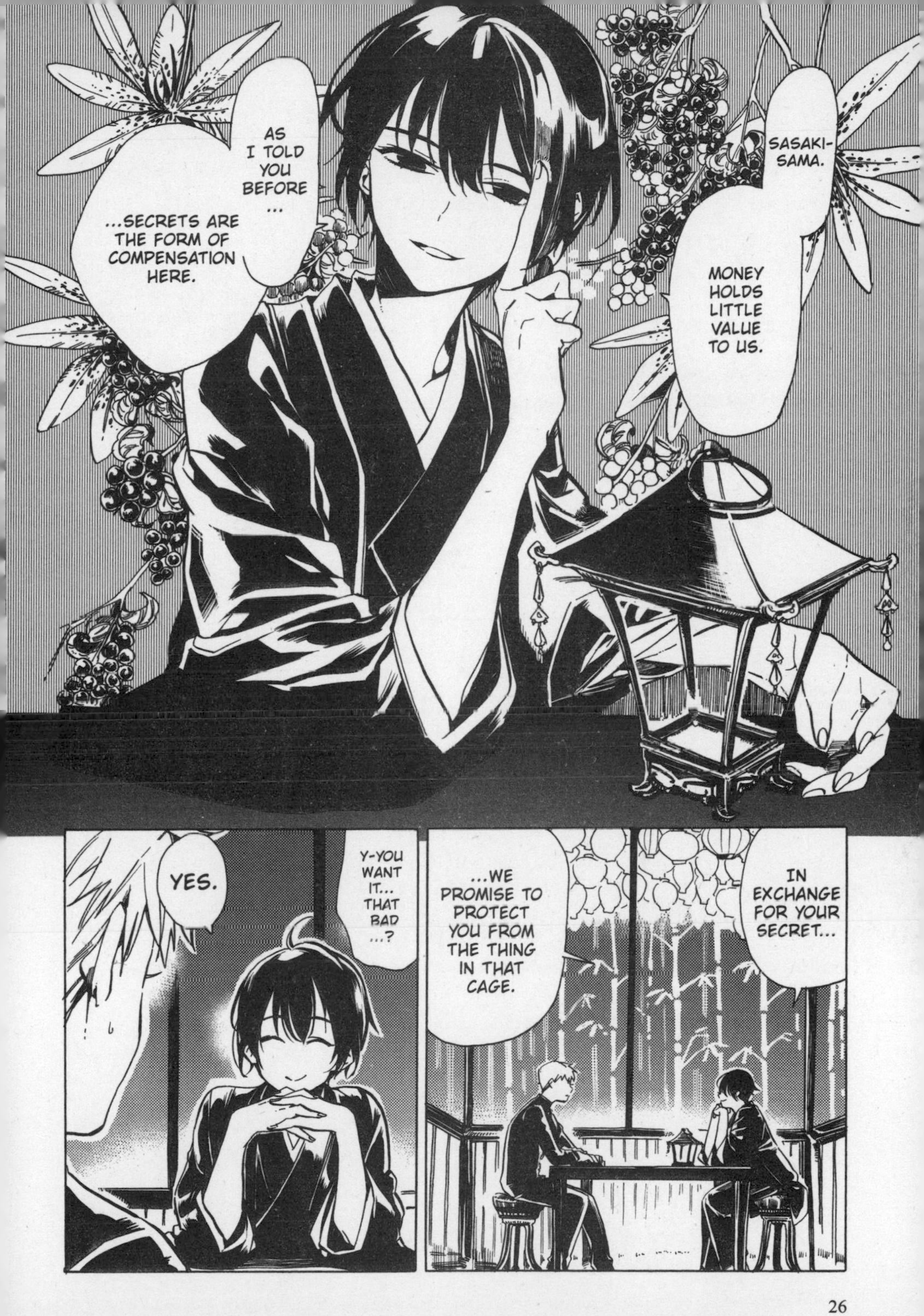
SASAKI-SAMA.
MONEY HOLDS LITTLE VALUE TO US.
AS I TOLD YOU BEFORE...
...SECRETS ARE THE FORM OF COMPENSATION HERE.
IN EXCHANGE FOR YOUR SECRET...
...WE PROMISE TO PROTECT YOU FROM THE THING IN THAT CAGE.
Y-YOU WANT IT... THAT BAD...?
YES.

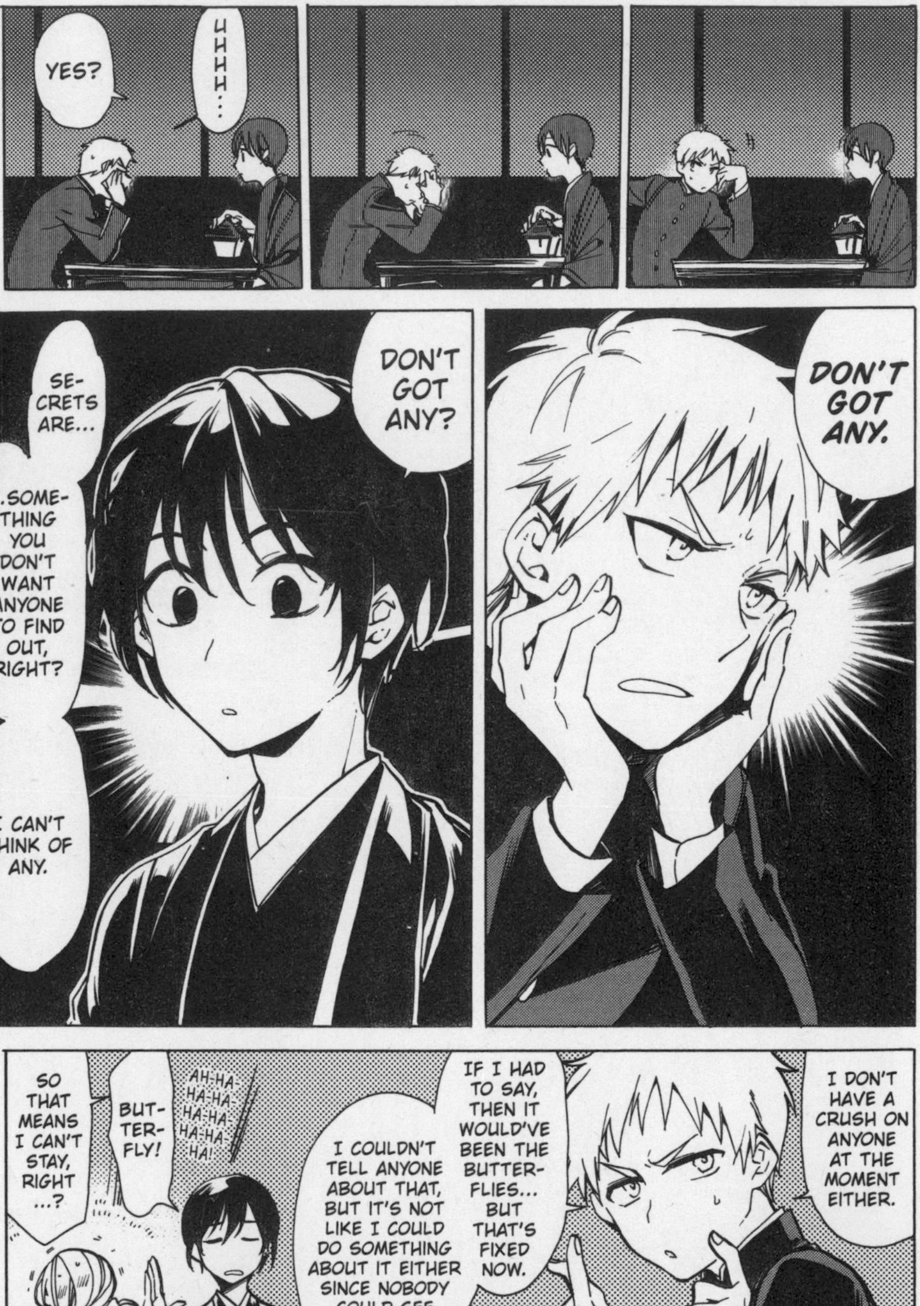
UHHH...
YES?
DON'T GOT ANY.
DON'T GOT ANY?
SECRETS ARE...
...SOMETHING YOU DON'T WANT ANYONE TO FIND OUT, RIGHT?
I CAN'T THINK OF ANY.
I DON'T HAVE A CRUSH ON ANYONE AT THE MOMENT EITHER.
IF I HAD TO SAY, THEN IT WOULD'VE BEEN THE BUTTERFLIES... BUT THAT'S FIXED NOW.
I COULDN'T TELL ANYONE ABOUT THAT, BUT IT'S NOT LIKE I COULD DO SOMETHING ABOUT IT EITHER SINCE NOBODY COULD SEE THEM.
AH-HA-HA-HA-HA-HA-HA-HA!
BUTTERFLY!
SO THAT MEANS I CAN'T STAY, RIGHT...?

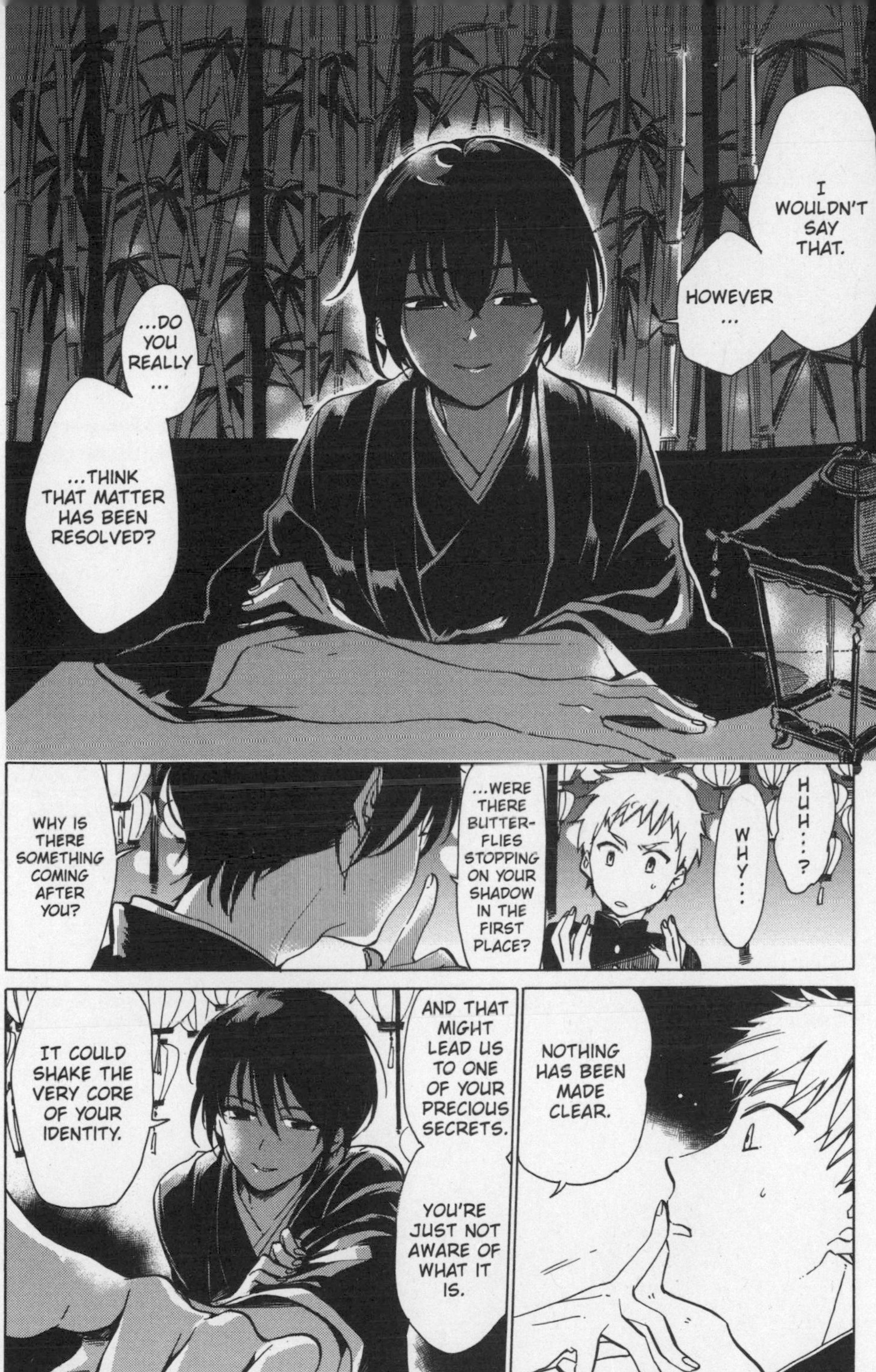
I WOULDN'T SAY THAT.
HOWEVER ...
...DO YOU REALLY ...
...THINK THAT MATTER HAS BEEN RESOLVED?
HUH...?
WHY...
...WERE THERE BUTTERFLIES STOPPING ON YOUR SHADOW IN THE FIRST PLACE?
WHY IS THERE SOMETHING COMING AFTER YOU?
NOTHING HAS BEEN MADE CLEAR.
YOU'RE JUST NOT AWARE OF WHAT IT IS.
AND THAT MIGHT LEAD US TO ONE OF YOUR PRECIOUS SECRETS.
IT COULD SHAKE THE VERY CORE OF YOUR IDENTITY.

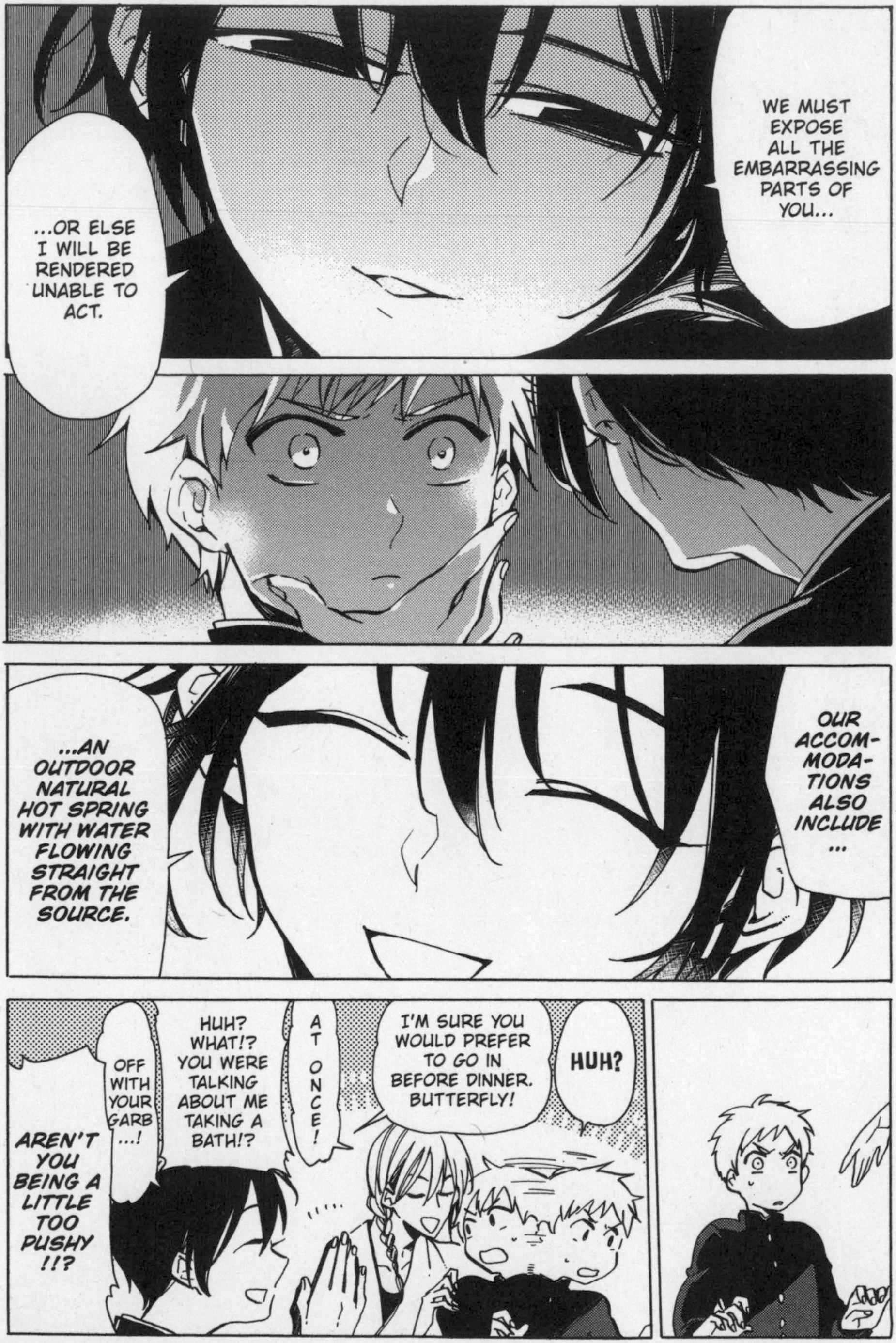
WE MUST EXPOSE ALL THE EMBARRASSING PARTS OF YOU...
...OR ELSE I WILL BE RENDERED UNABLE TO ACT.
OUR ACCOMMODATIONS ALSO INCLUDE...
...AN OUTDOOR NATURAL HOT SPRING WITH WATER FLOWING STRAIGHT FROM THE SOURCE.
HUH?
I'M SURE YOU WOULD PREFER TO GO IN BEFORE DINNER. BUTTERFLY!
AT ONCE!
HUH? WHAT!? YOU WERE TALKING ABOUT ME TAKING A BATH!?
OFF WITH YOUR GARB...!
AREN'T YOU BEING A LITTLE TOO PUSHY!!?

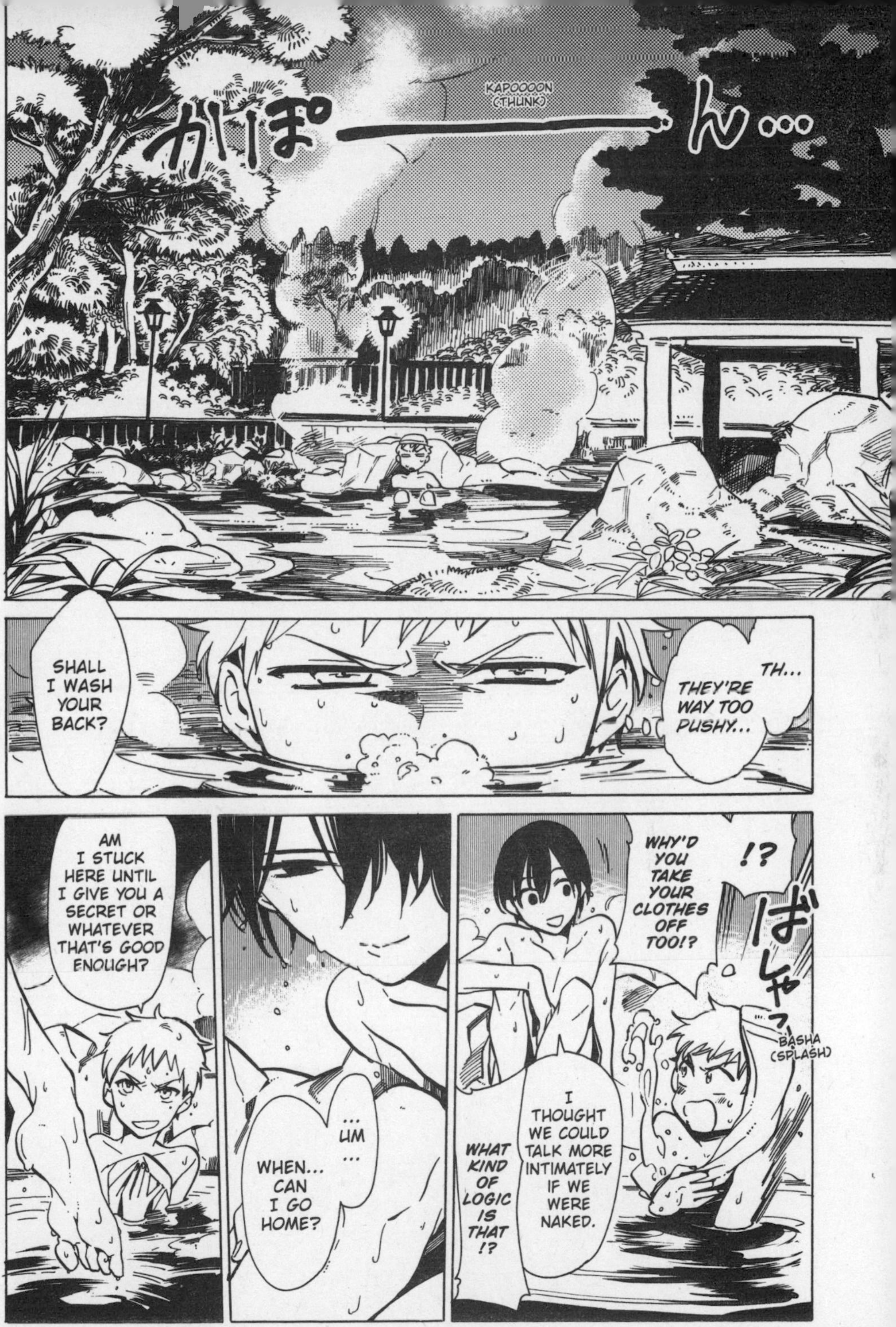
かぽーーーん…
KAPOOOON (THUNK)
TH... THEY'RE WAY TOO PUSHY...
SHALL I WASH YOUR BACK?
!?
ばしゃっ
BASHA (SPLASH)
WHY'D YOU TAKE YOUR CLOTHES OFF TOO!?
I THOUGHT WE COULD TALK MORE INTIMATELY IF WE WERE NAKED.
WHAT KIND OF LOGIC IS THAT!?
...UM...
WHEN... CAN I GO HOME?
AM I STUCK HERE UNTIL I GIVE YOU A SECRET OR WHATEVER THAT'S GOOD ENOUGH?

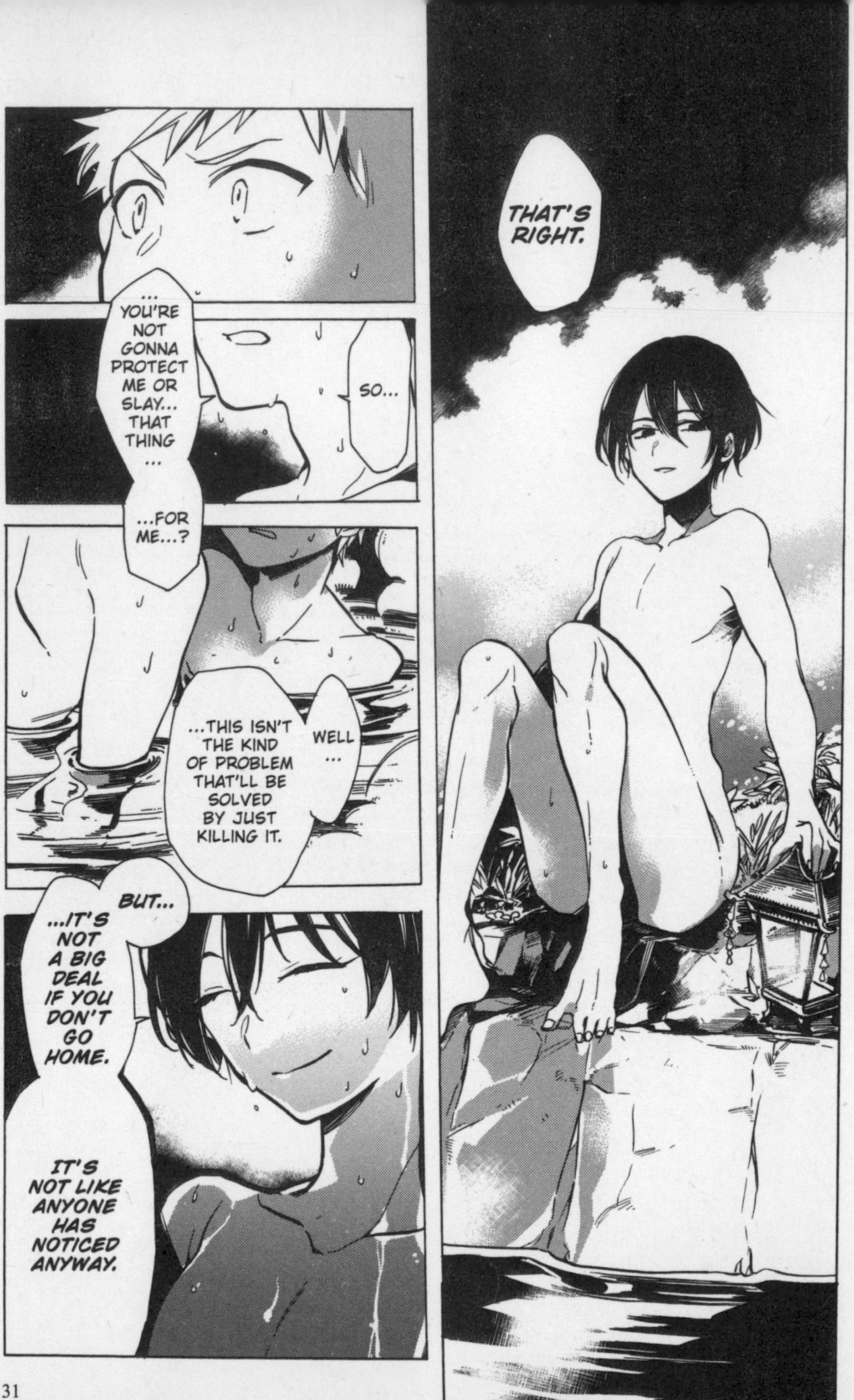
THAT'S RIGHT.
SO...
... YOU'RE NOT GONNA PROTECT ME OR SLAY... THAT THING ...
...FOR ME...?
WELL ...
...THIS ISN'T THE KIND OF PROBLEM THAT'LL BE SOLVED BY JUST KILLING IT.
BUT...
...IT'S NOT A BIG DEAL IF YOU DON'T GO HOME.
IT'S NOT LIKE ANYONE HAS NOTICED ANYWAY.

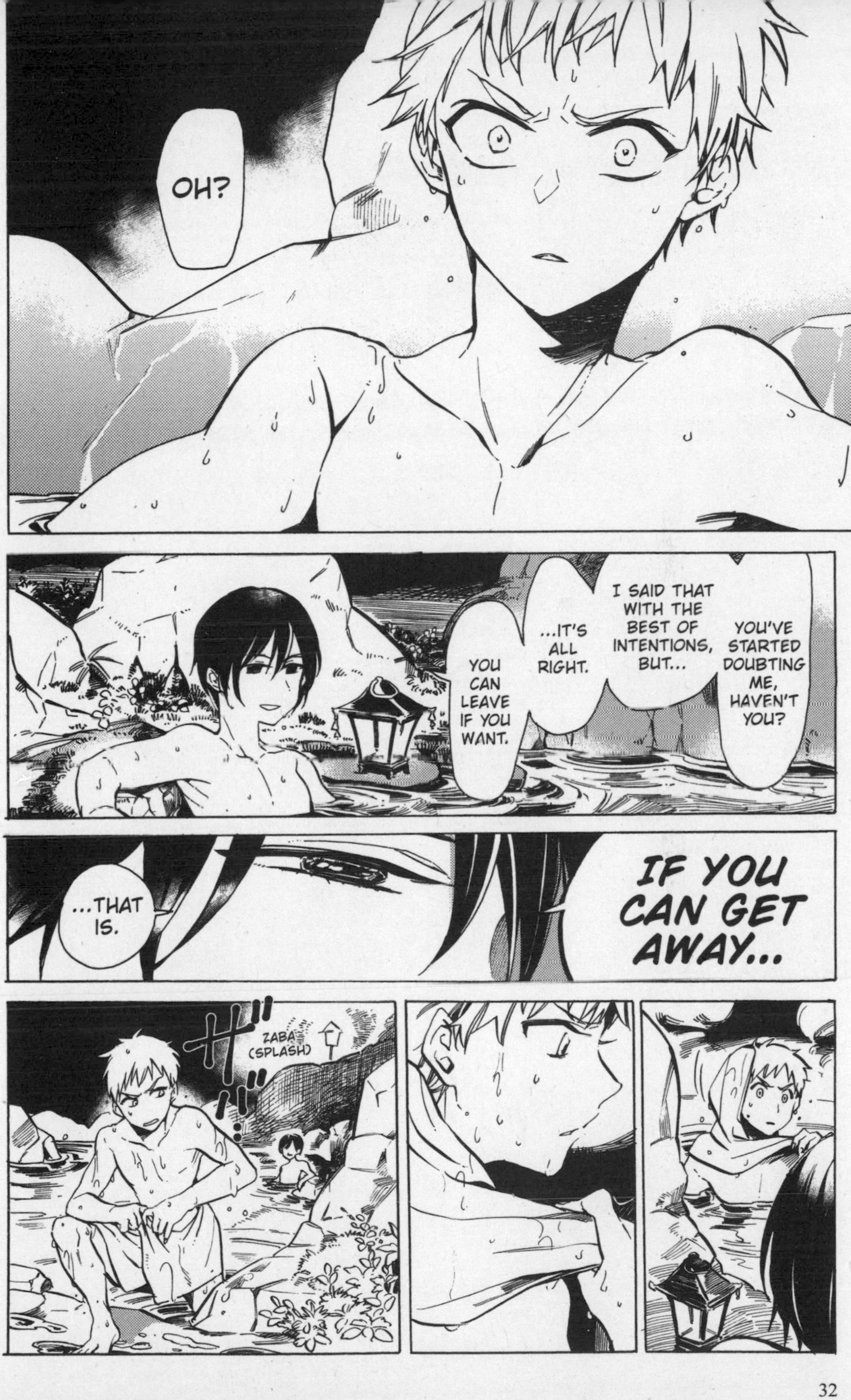
OH?
YOU'VE STARTED DOUBTING ME, HAVEN'T YOU?
I SAID THAT WITH THE BEST OF INTENTIONS, BUT...
...IT'S ALL RIGHT.
YOU CAN LEAVE IF YOU WANT.
IF YOU CAN GET AWAY...
...THAT IS.
ZABA (SPLASH)

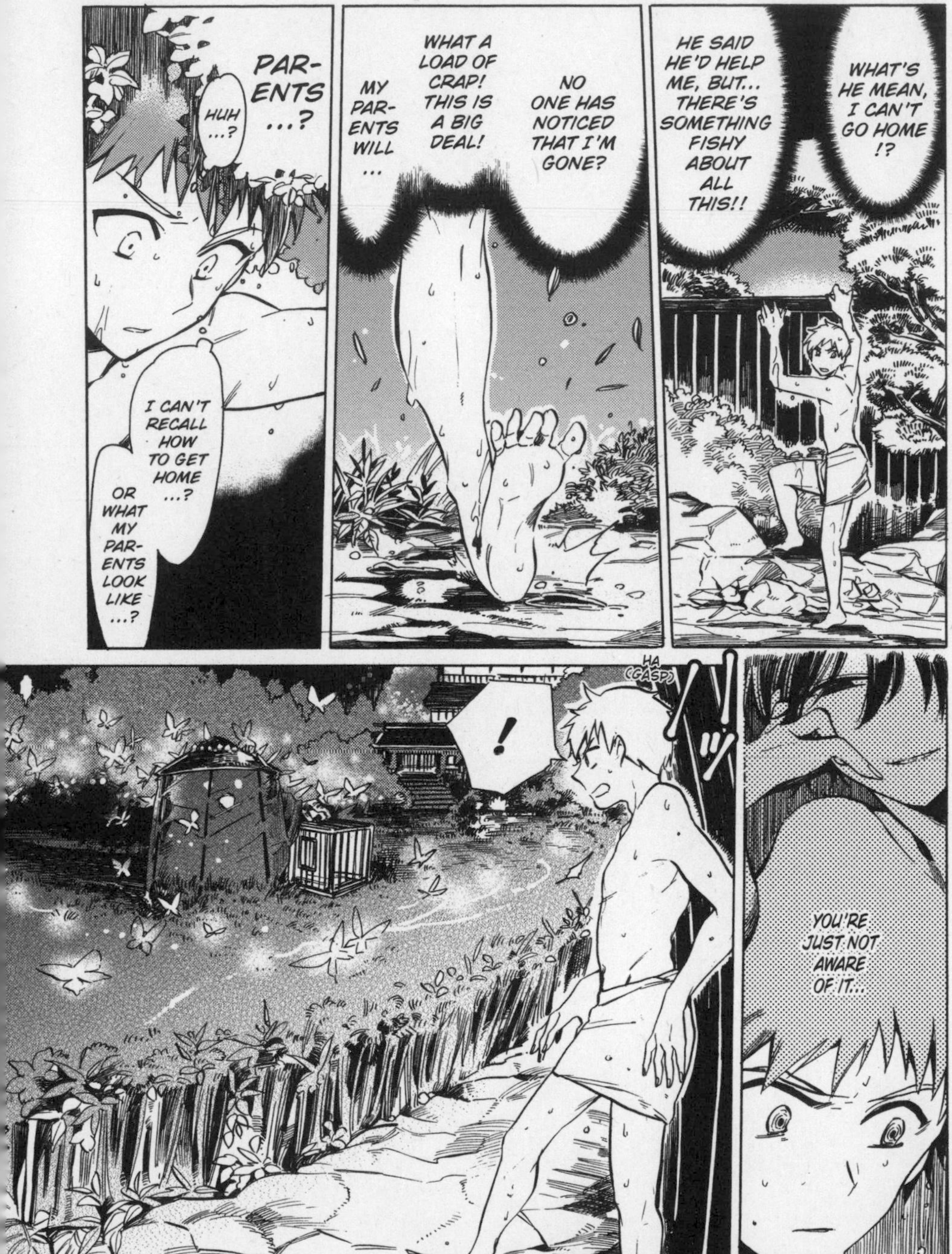
WHAT'S HE MEAN, I CAN'T GO HOME!?
HE SAID HE'D HELP ME, BUT... THERE'S SOMETHING FISHY ABOUT ALL THIS!!
NO ONE HAS NOTICED THAT I'M GONE?
WHAT A LOAD OF CRAP! THIS IS A BIG DEAL!
MY PARENTS WILL...
PARENTS...?
HUH...?
I CAN'T RECALL HOW TO GET HOME...?
OR WHAT MY PARENTS LOOK LIKE...?
YOU'RE JUST NOT AWARE OF IT...
HA (GASP)
!

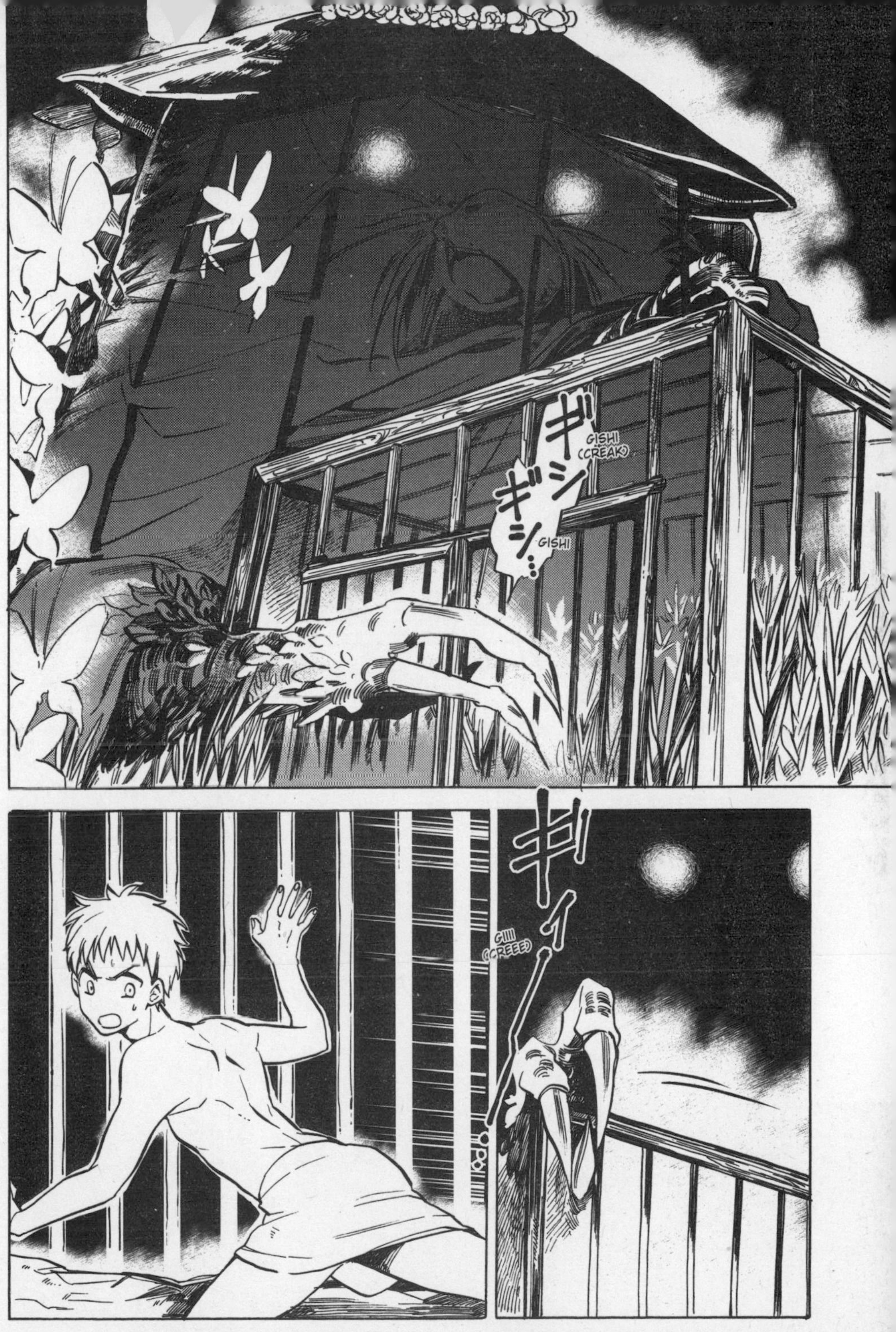
ギシ
GISHI (CREAK)
ギシ…
GISHI
ギイ
GIIII (CREEE)

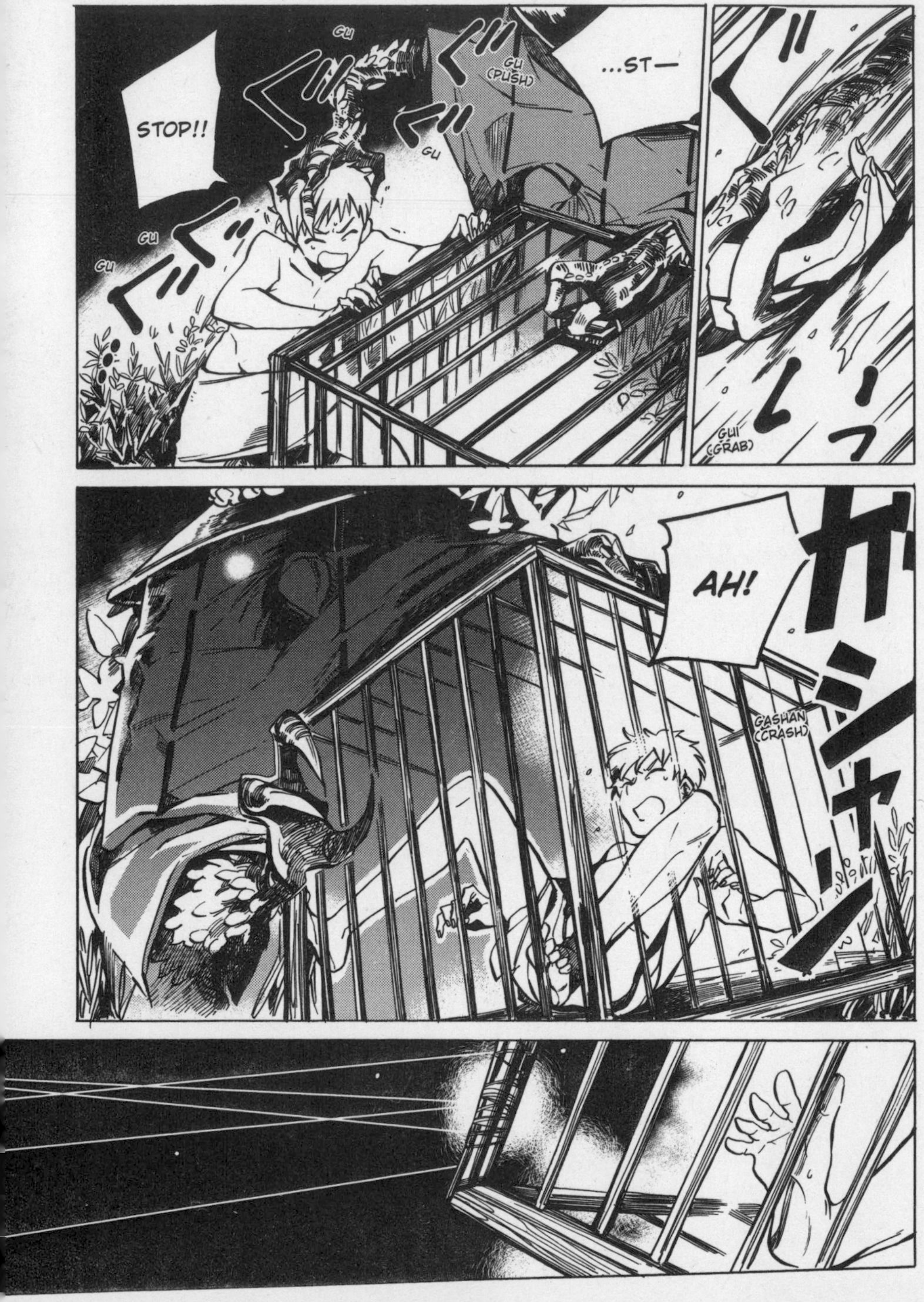
GUI (GRAB)
...ST—
GU (PUSH)
GU
GU
STOP!!
GU
GU
AH!
GASHAN (CRASH)

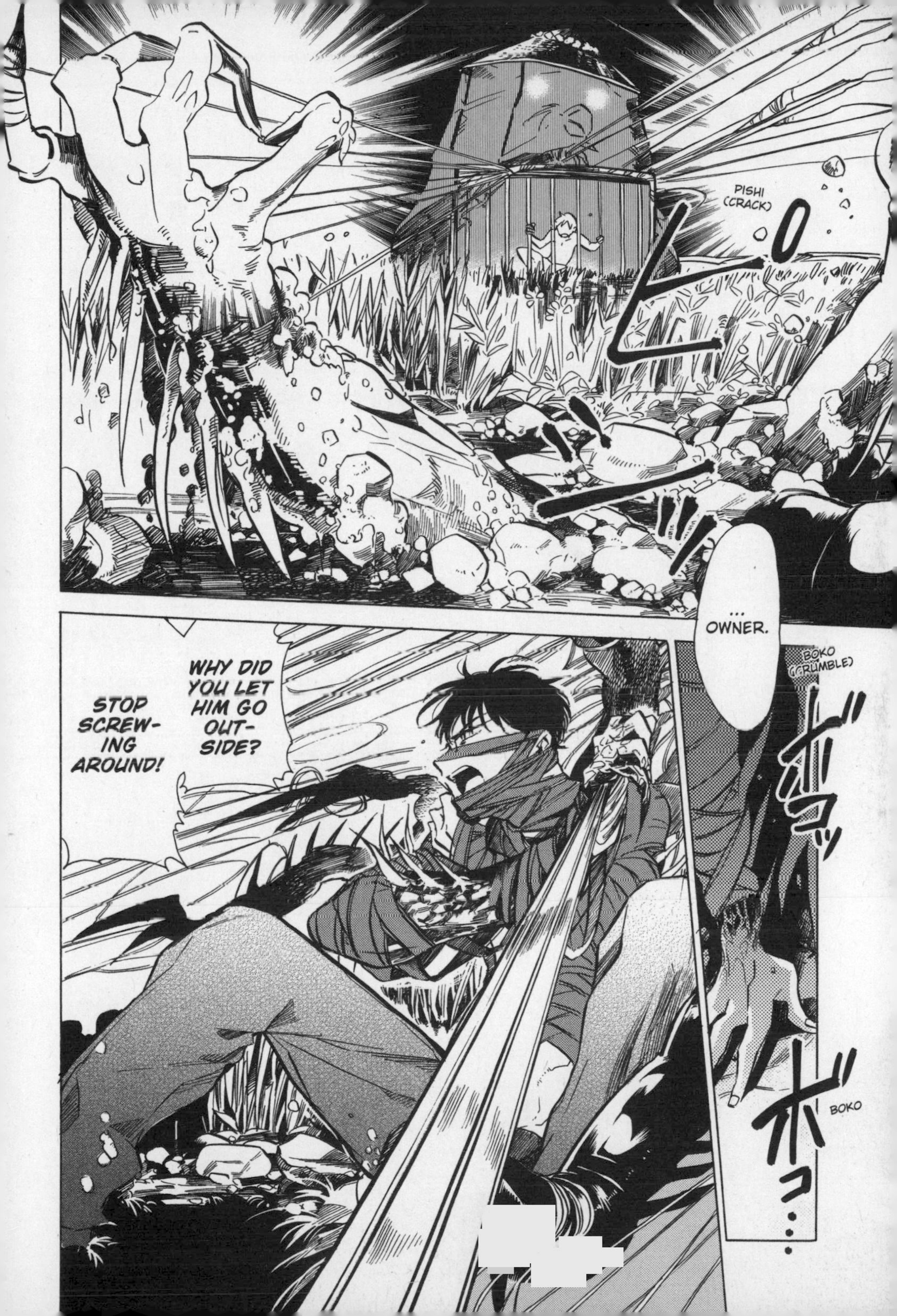
PISHI (CRACK)
... OWNER.
BOKO (CRUMBLE)
WHY DID YOU LET HIM GO OUT-SIDE?
STOP SCREW-ING AROUND!
BOKO

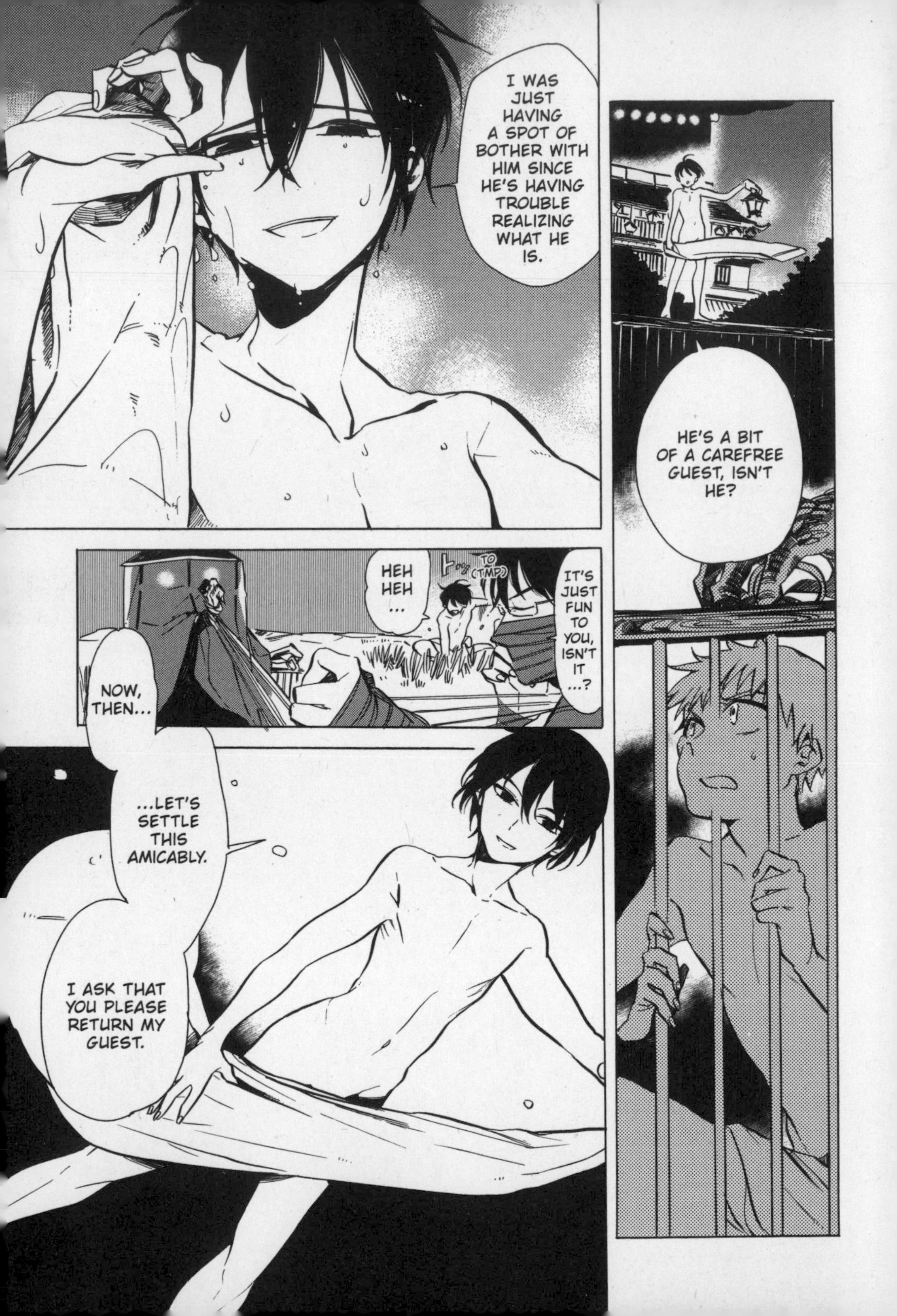
HE'S A BIT OF A CAREFREE GUEST, ISN'T HE?
I WAS JUST HAVING A SPOT OF BOTHER WITH HIM SINCE HE'S HAVING TROUBLE REALIZING WHAT HE IS.
IT'S JUST FUN TO YOU, ISN'T IT...?
TO (TMP)
HEH HEH...
NOW, THEN...
...LET'S SETTLE THIS AMICABLY.
I ASK THAT YOU PLEASE RETURN MY GUEST.
...

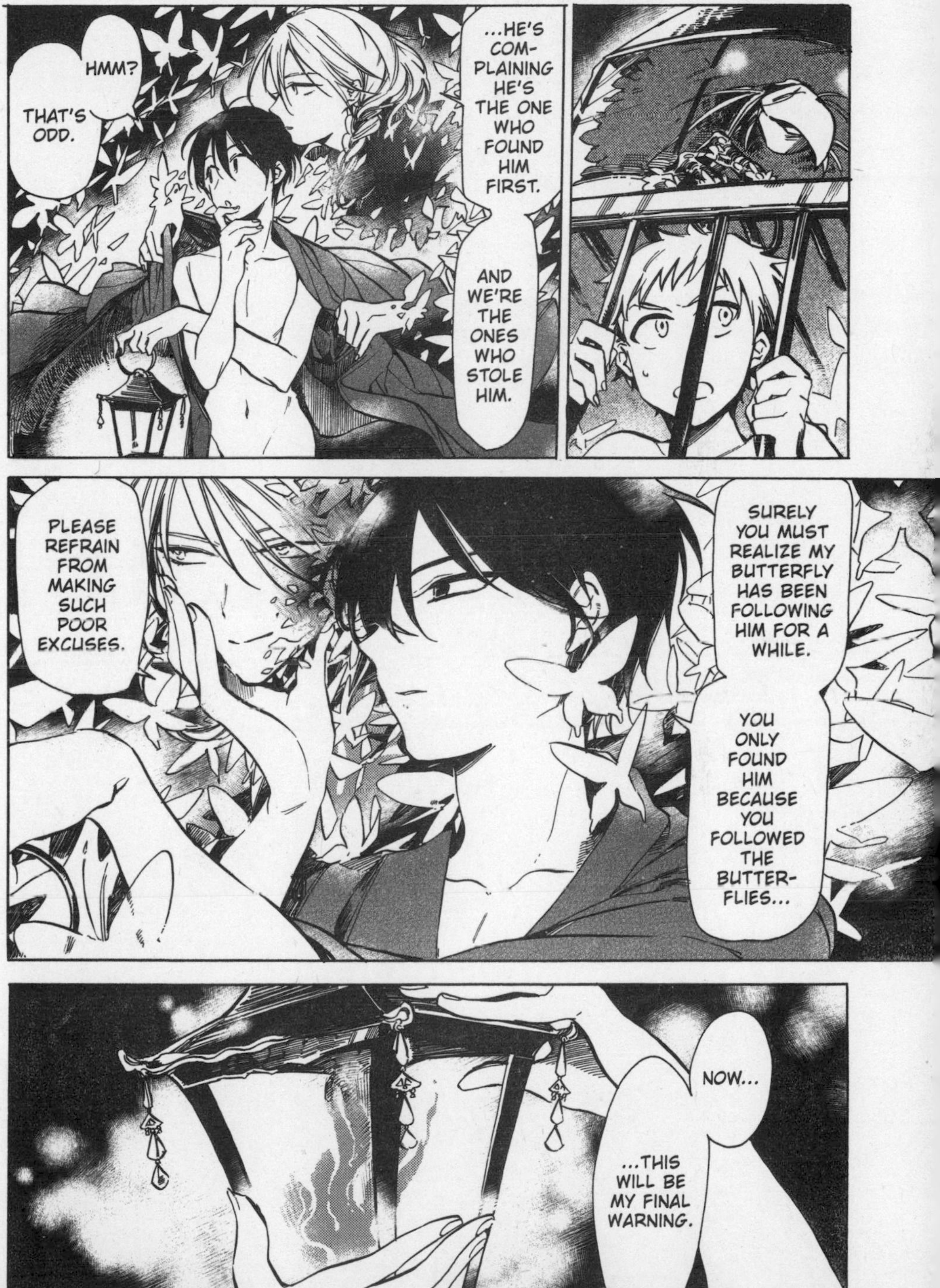
...HE'S COMPLAINING HE'S THE ONE WHO FOUND HIM FIRST.
AND WE'RE THE ONES WHO STOLE HIM.
HMM?
THAT'S ODD.
SURELY YOU MUST REALIZE MY BUTTERFLY HAS BEEN FOLLOWING HIM FOR A WHILE.
YOU ONLY FOUND HIM BECAUSE YOU FOLLOWED THE BUTTERFLIES...
PLEASE REFRAIN FROM MAKING SUCH POOR EXCUSES.
NOW...
...THIS WILL BE MY FINAL WARNING.

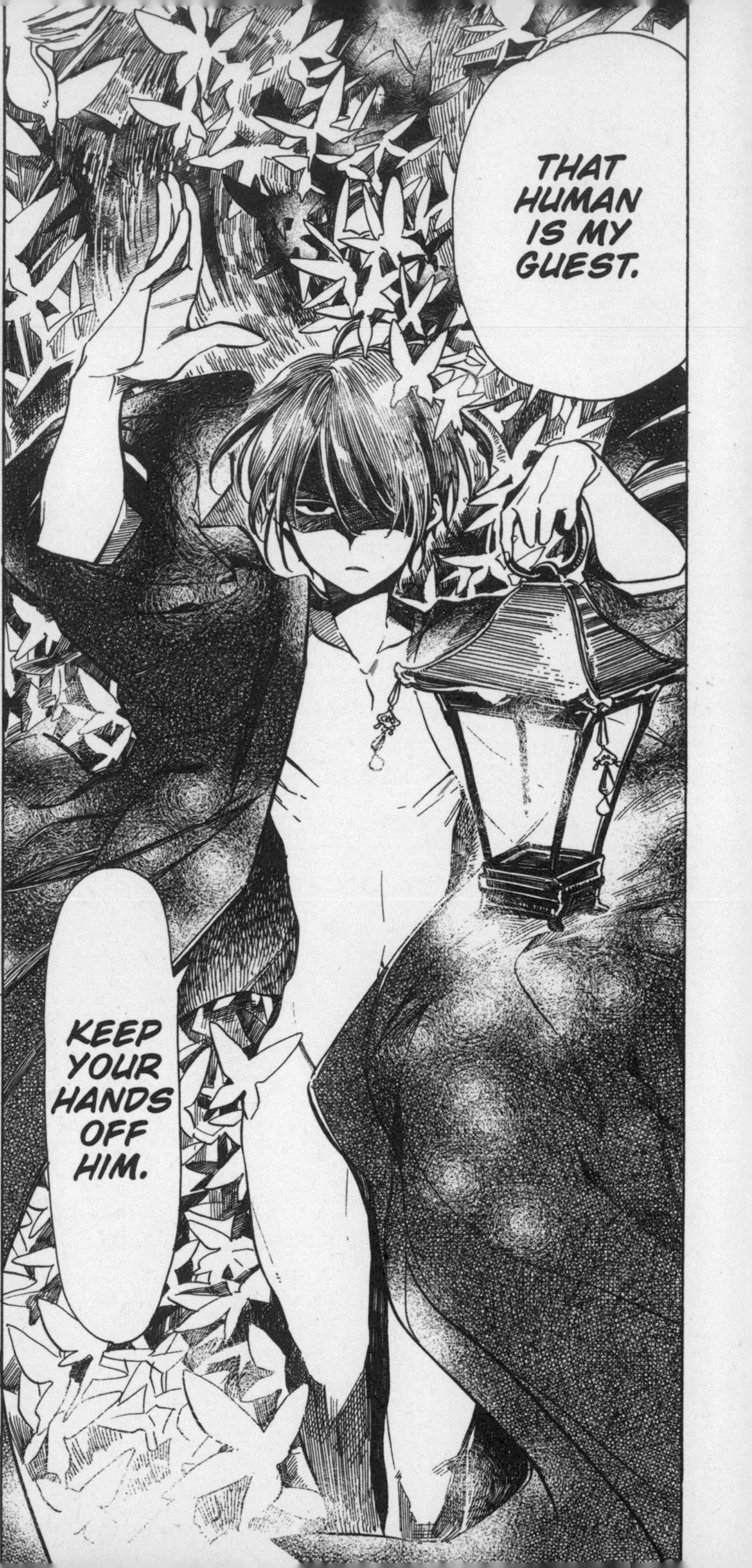
THAT HUMAN IS MY GUEST.
KEEP YOUR HANDS OFF HIM.
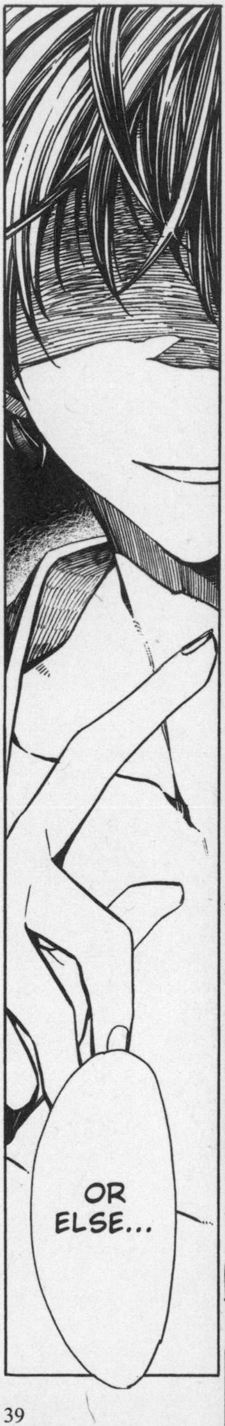
OR ELSE...

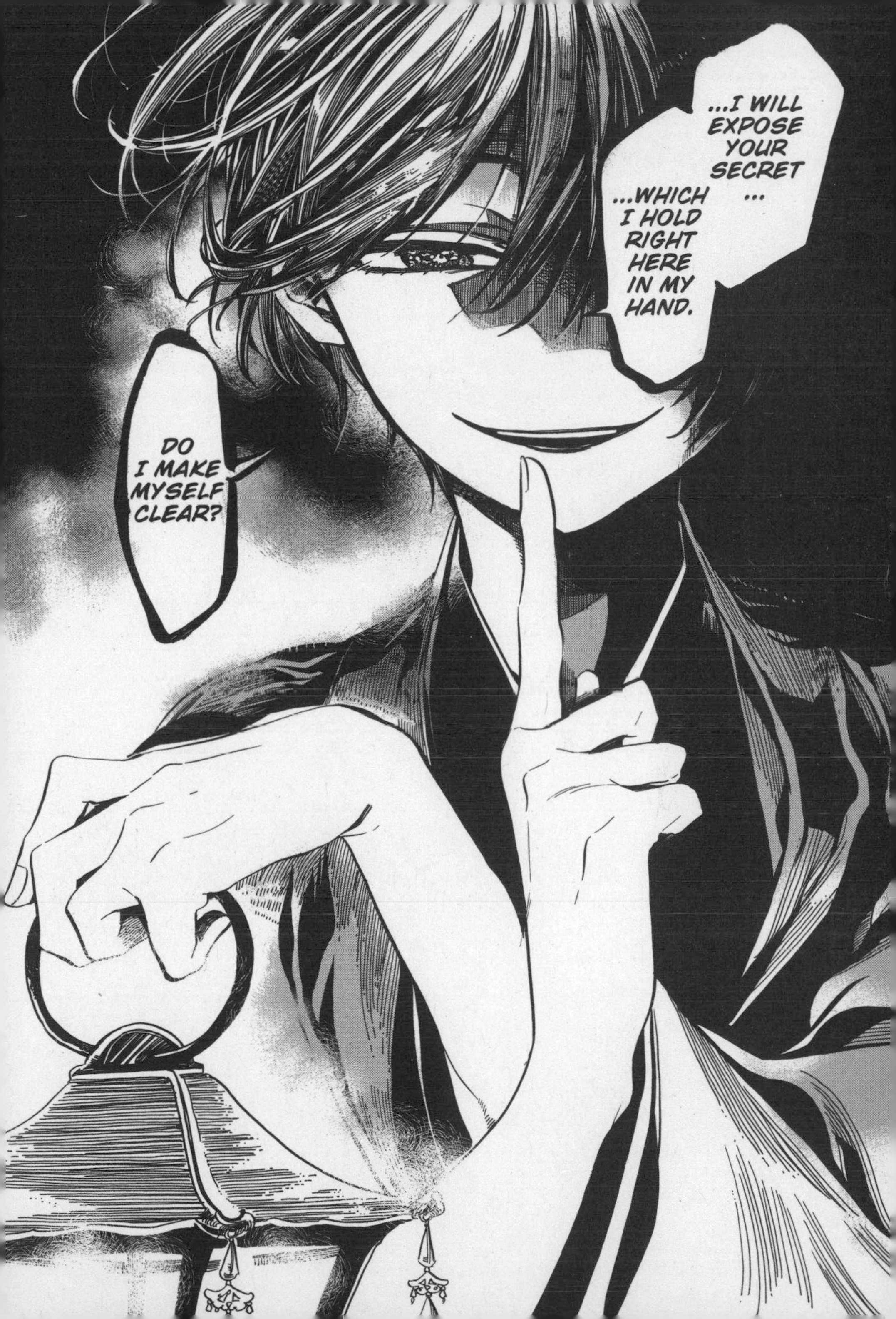
...I WILL EXPOSE YOUR SECRET ... ...WHICH I HOLD RIGHT HERE IN MY HAND.
DO I MAKE MYSELF CLEAR?

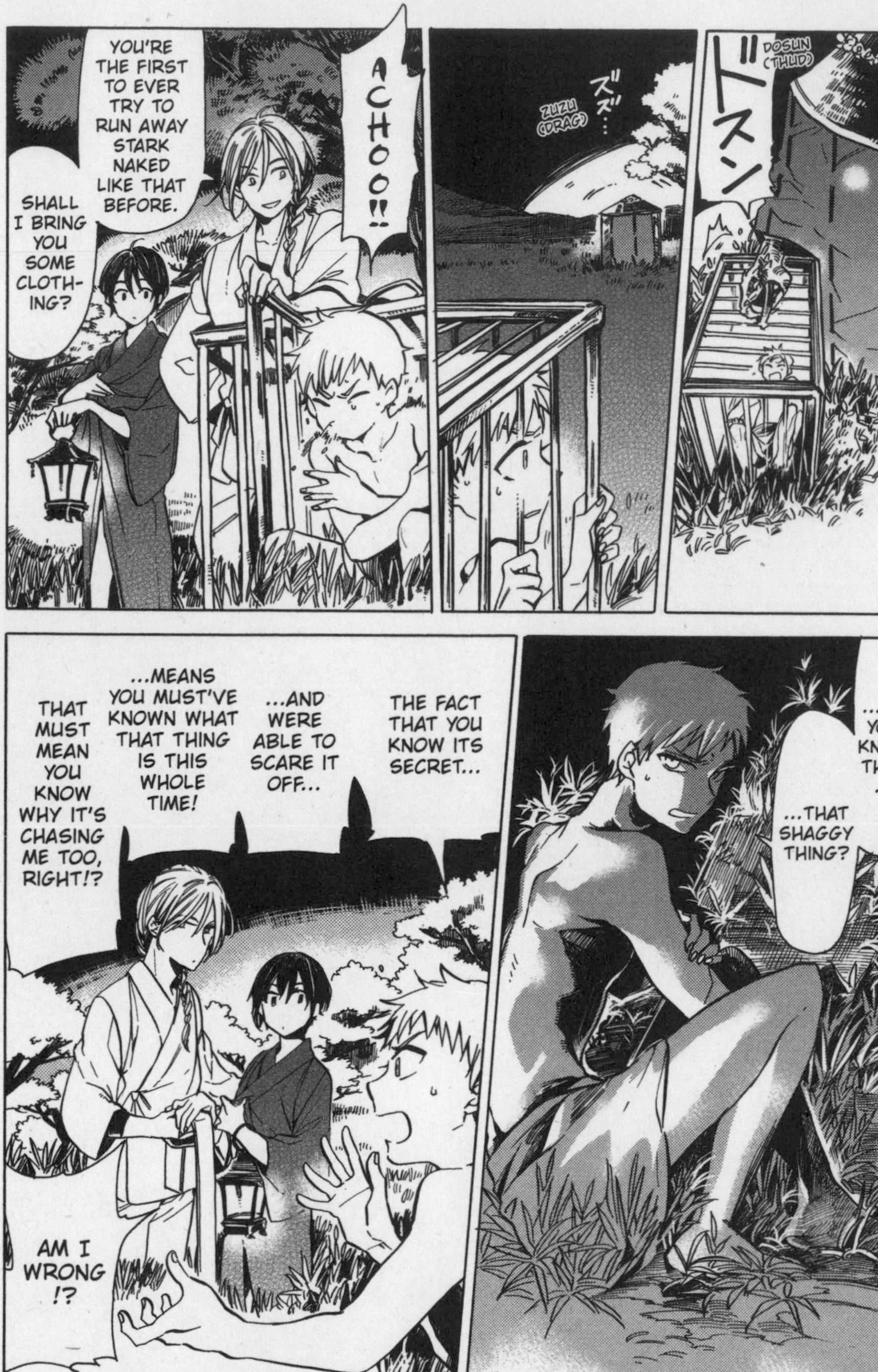
DOSUN (THUD)
ドスン
ズズ…
ZUZU (DRAG)
ACHOO!!
YOU'RE THE FIRST TO EVER TRY TO RUN AWAY STARK NAKED LIKE THAT BEFORE.
SHALL I BRING YOU SOME CLOTHING?
...DO YOU KNOW THAT ...
...THAT SHAGGY THING?
THE FACT THAT YOU KNOW ITS SECRET...
...AND WERE ABLE TO SCARE IT OFF...
...MEANS YOU MUST'VE KNOWN WHAT THAT THING IS THIS WHOLE TIME!
THAT MUST MEAN YOU KNOW WHY IT'S CHASING ME TOO, RIGHT!?
AM I WRONG !?

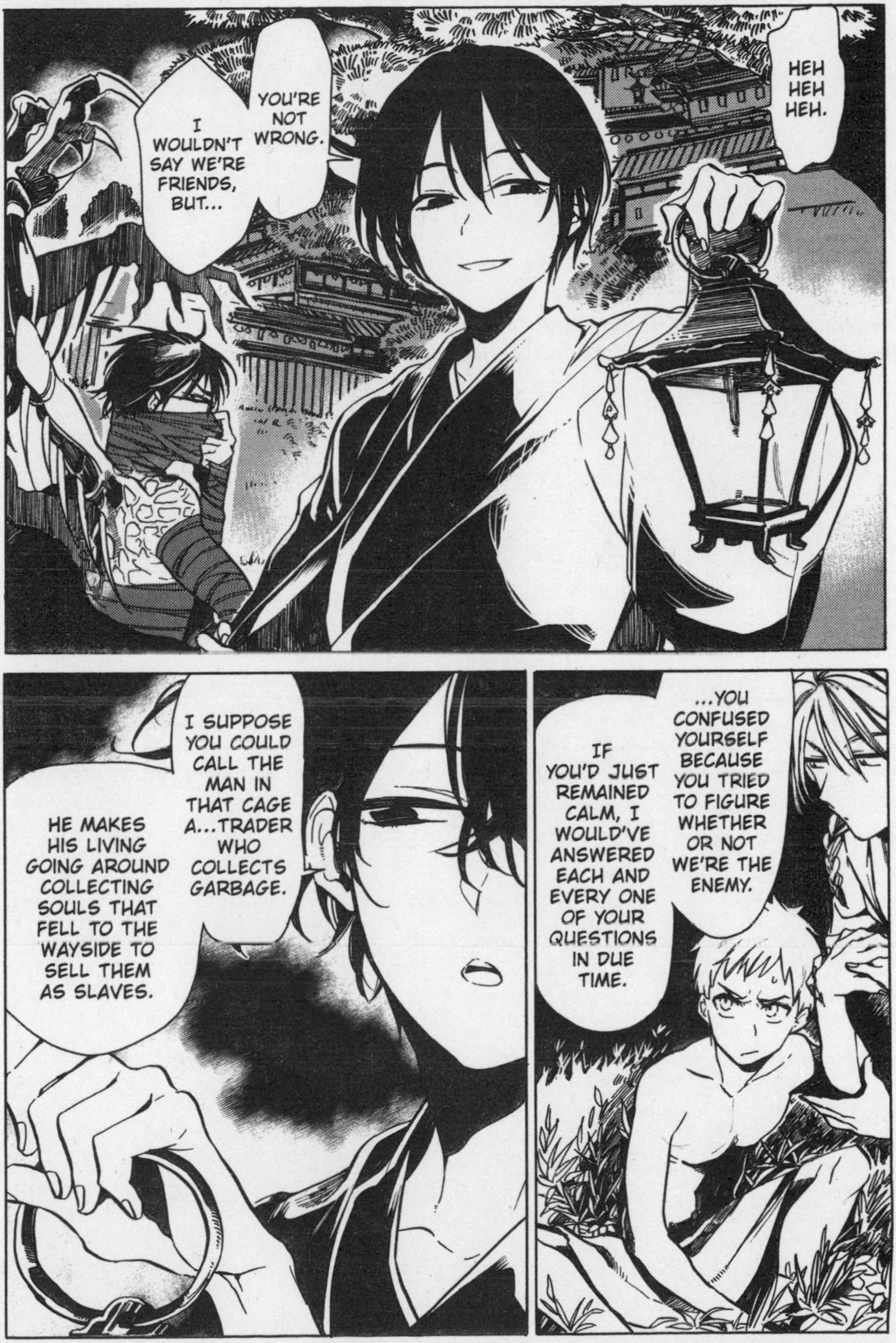
HEH HEH HEH.
YOU'RE NOT WRONG.
I WOULDN'T SAY WE'RE FRIENDS, BUT...
...YOU CONFUSED YOURSELF BECAUSE YOU TRIED TO FIGURE WHETHER OR NOT WE'RE THE ENEMY.
IF YOU'D JUST REMAINED CALM, I WOULD'VE ANSWERED EACH AND EVERY ONE OF YOUR QUESTIONS IN DUE TIME.
I SUPPOSE YOU COULD CALL THE MAN IN THAT CAGE A...TRADER WHO COLLECTS GARBAGE.
HE MAKES HIS LIVING GOING AROUND COLLECTING SOULS THAT FELL TO THE WAYSIDE TO SELL THEM AS SLAVES.

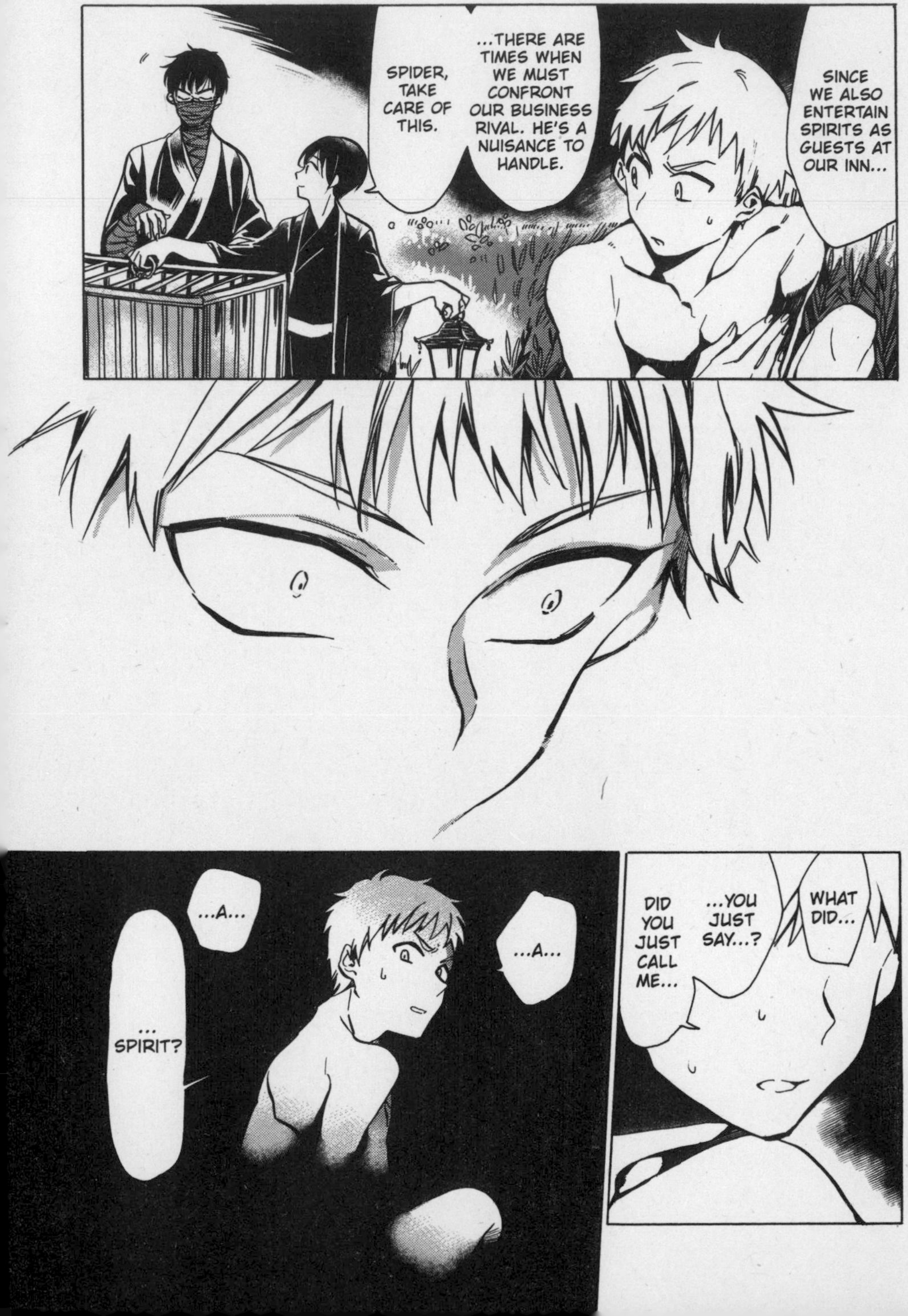
SINCE WE ALSO ENTERTAIN SPIRITS AS GUESTS AT OUR INN...
...THERE ARE TIMES WHEN WE MUST CONFRONT OUR BUSINESS RIVAL. HE'S A NUISANCE TO HANDLE.
SPIDER, TAKE CARE OF THIS.
WHAT DID...
...YOU JUST SAY...?
DID YOU JUST CALL ME...
...A...
...A...
... SPIRIT?

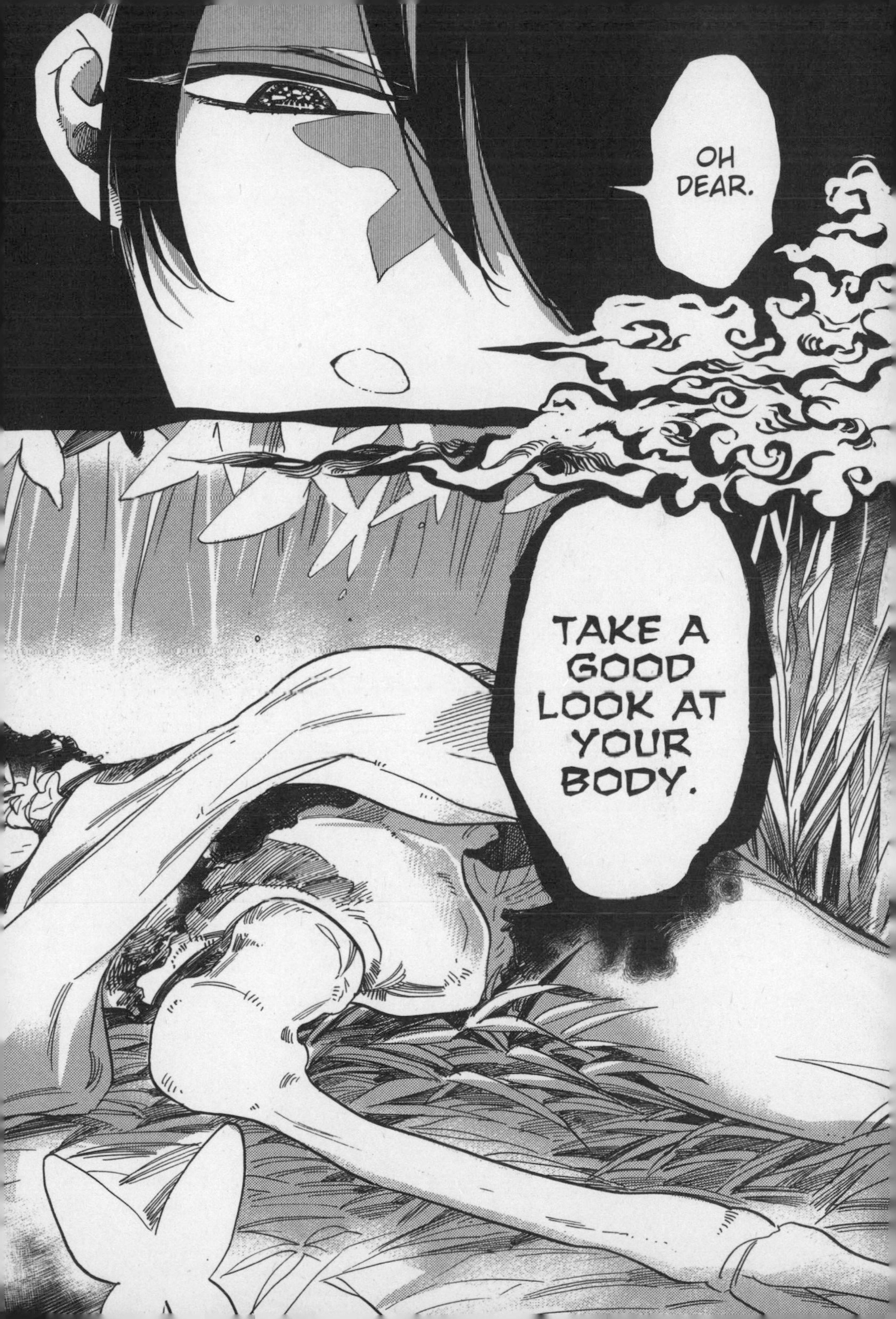
OH DEAR.
TAKE A GOOD LOOK AT YOUR BODY.

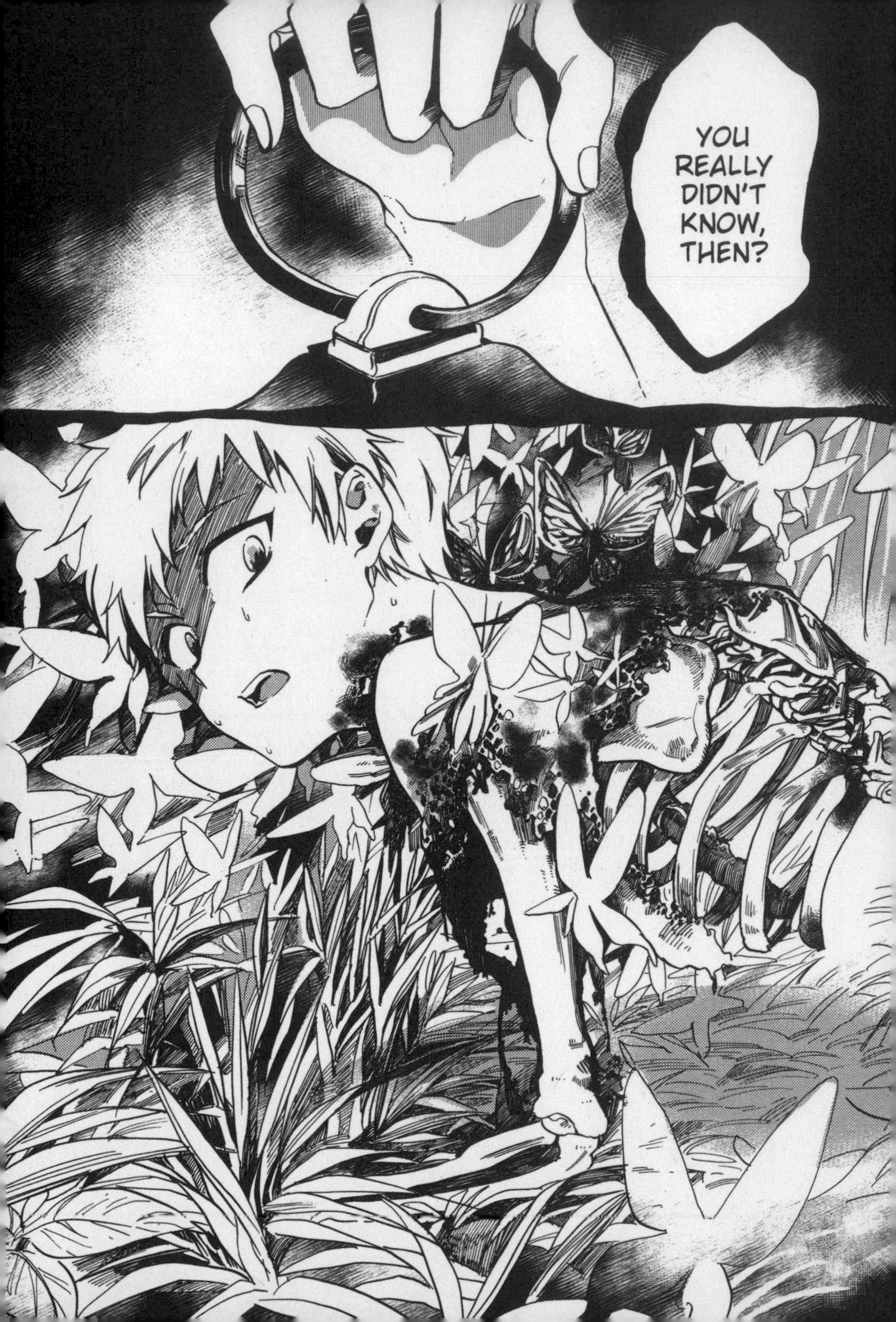
YOU REALLY DIDN'T KNOW, THEN?

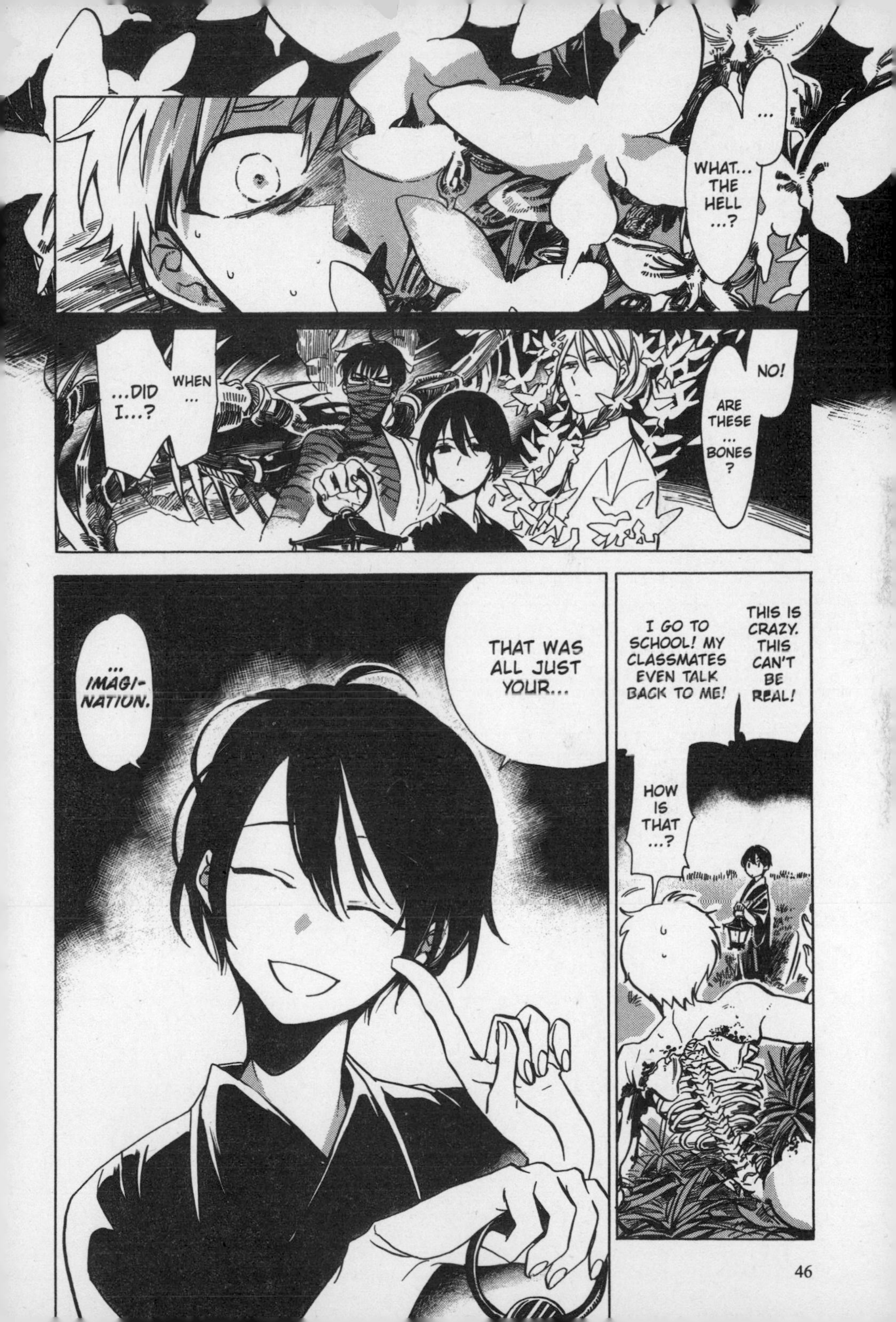
...
WHAT... THE HELL ...?
NO!
ARE THESE ... BONES ?
WHEN ...
...DID I...?
THIS IS CRAZY. THIS CAN'T BE REAL!
I GO TO SCHOOL! MY CLASSMATES EVEN TALK BACK TO ME!
HOW IS THAT ...?
THAT WAS ALL JUST YOUR...
... IMAGI-NATION.

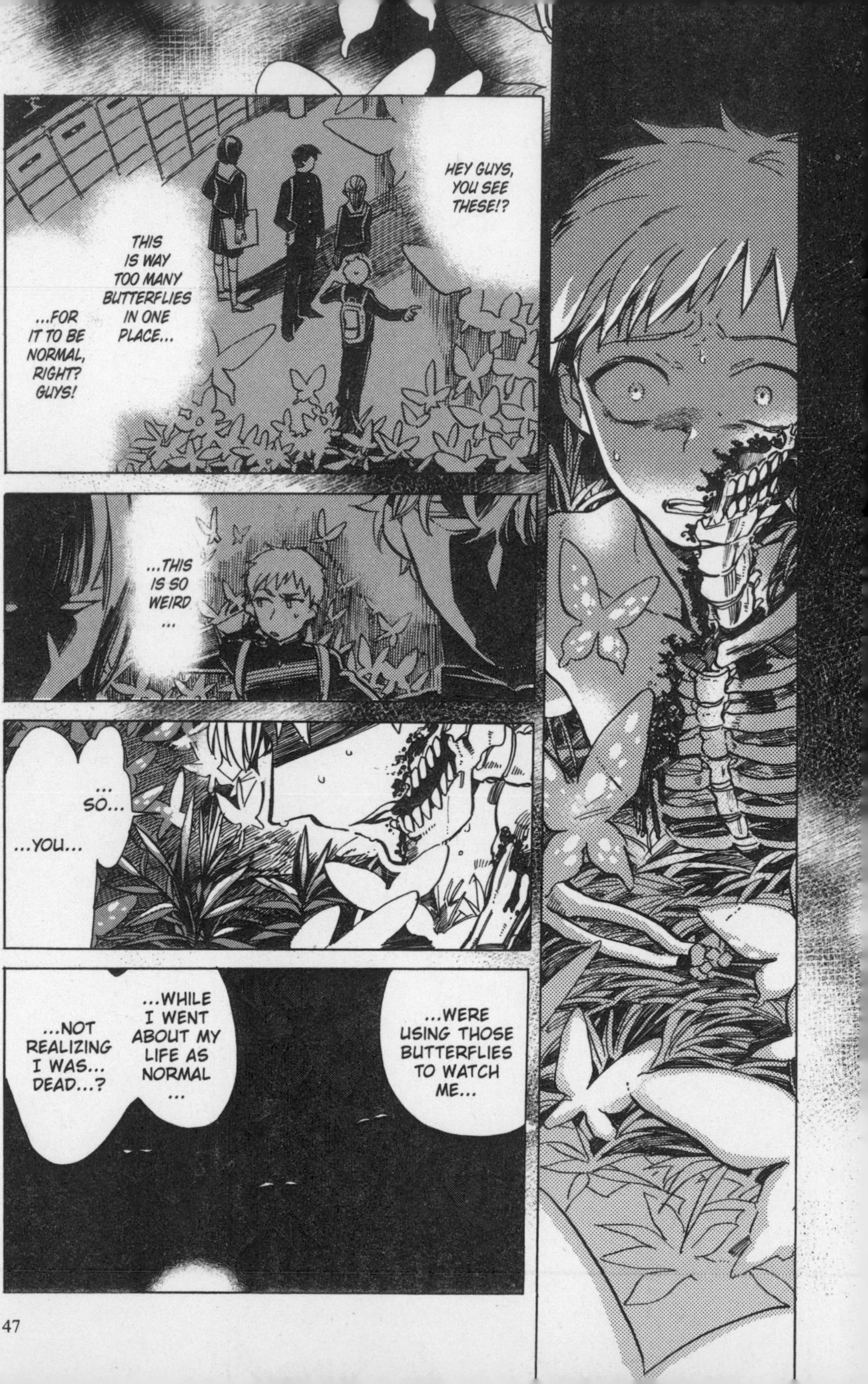
HEY GUYS, YOU SEE THESE!?
THIS IS WAY TOO MANY BUTTERFLIES IN ONE PLACE...
...FOR IT TO BE NORMAL, RIGHT? GUYS!
...THIS IS SO WEIRD ...
... SO...
...YOU...
...WERE USING THOSE BUTTERFLIES TO WATCH ME...
...WHILE I WENT ABOUT MY LIFE AS NORMAL ...
...NOT REALIZING I WAS... DEAD...?

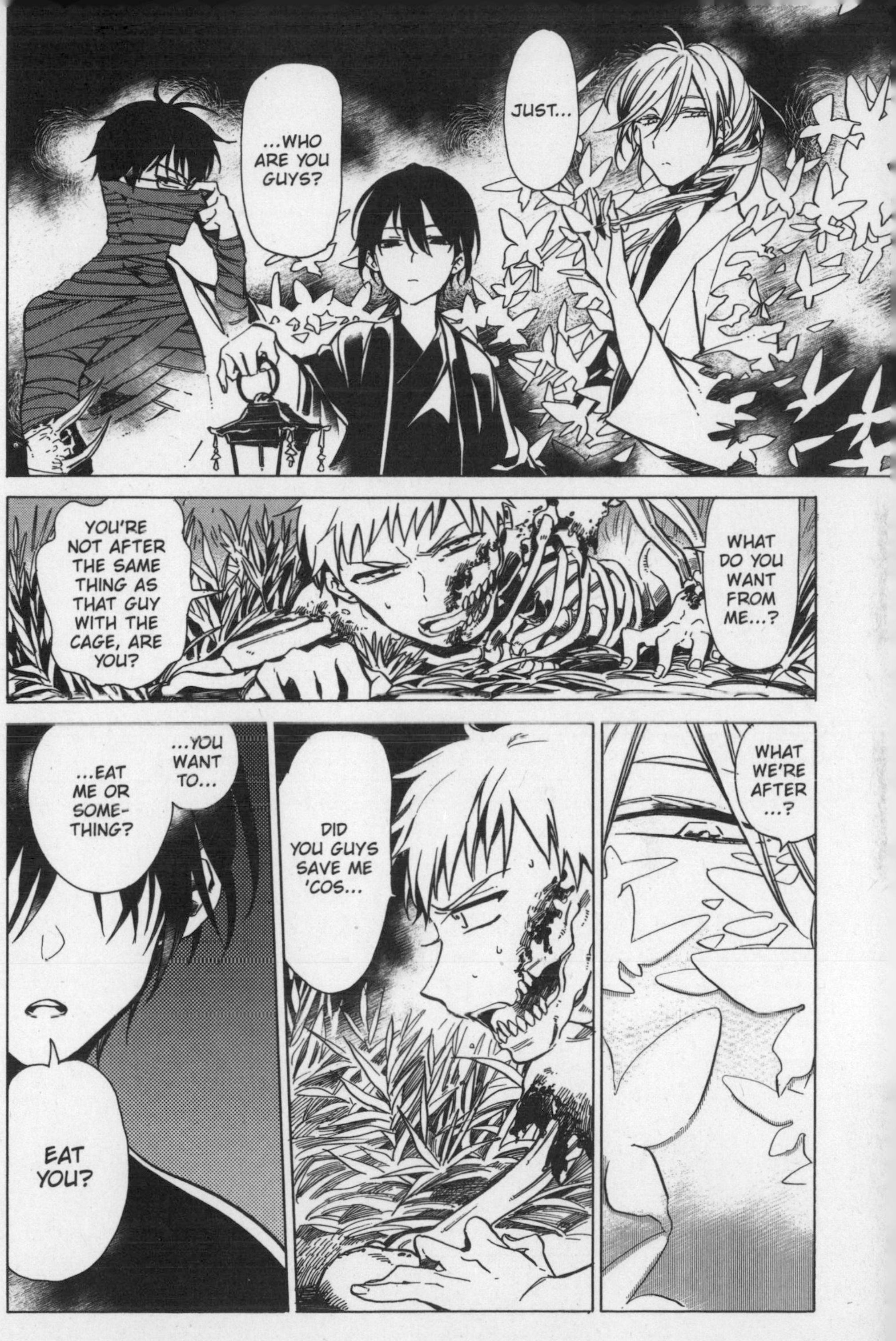

JUST...
...WHO ARE YOU GUYS?
WHAT DO YOU WANT FROM ME...?
YOU'RE NOT AFTER THE SAME THING AS THAT GUY WITH THE CAGE, ARE YOU?
WHAT WE'RE AFTER...?
DID YOU GUYS SAVE ME 'COS...
...YOU WANT TO...
...EAT ME OR SOME-THING?
EAT YOU?

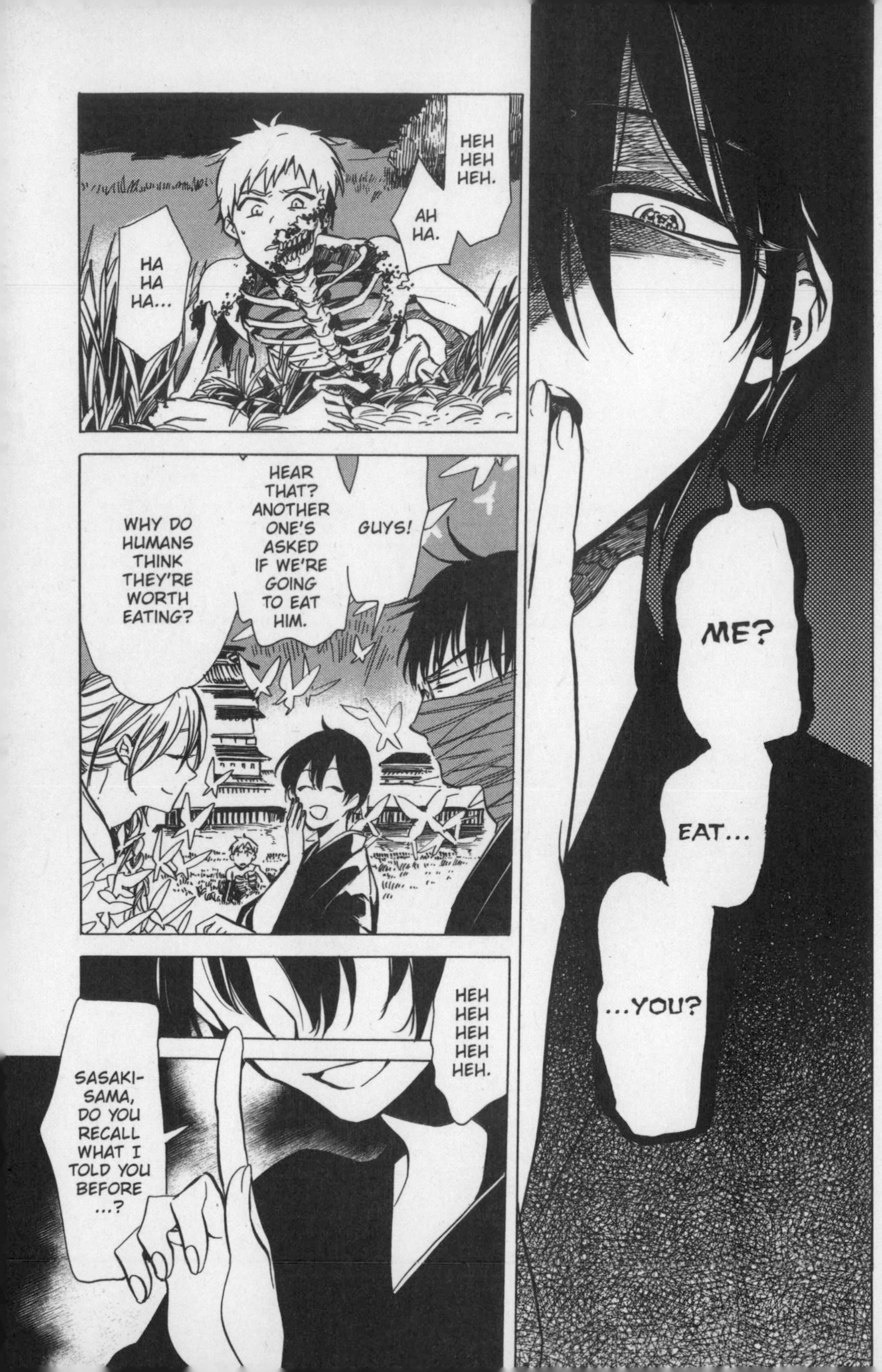
ME?
EAT...
...YOU?
HEH HEH HEH.
AH HA.
HA HA HA...
GUYS!
HEAR THAT? ANOTHER ONE'S ASKED IF WE'RE GOING TO EAT HIM.
WHY DO HUMANS THINK THEY'RE WORTH EATING?
HEH HEH HEH HEH HEH.
SASAKI-SAMA, DO YOU RECALL WHAT I TOLD YOU BEFORE ...?

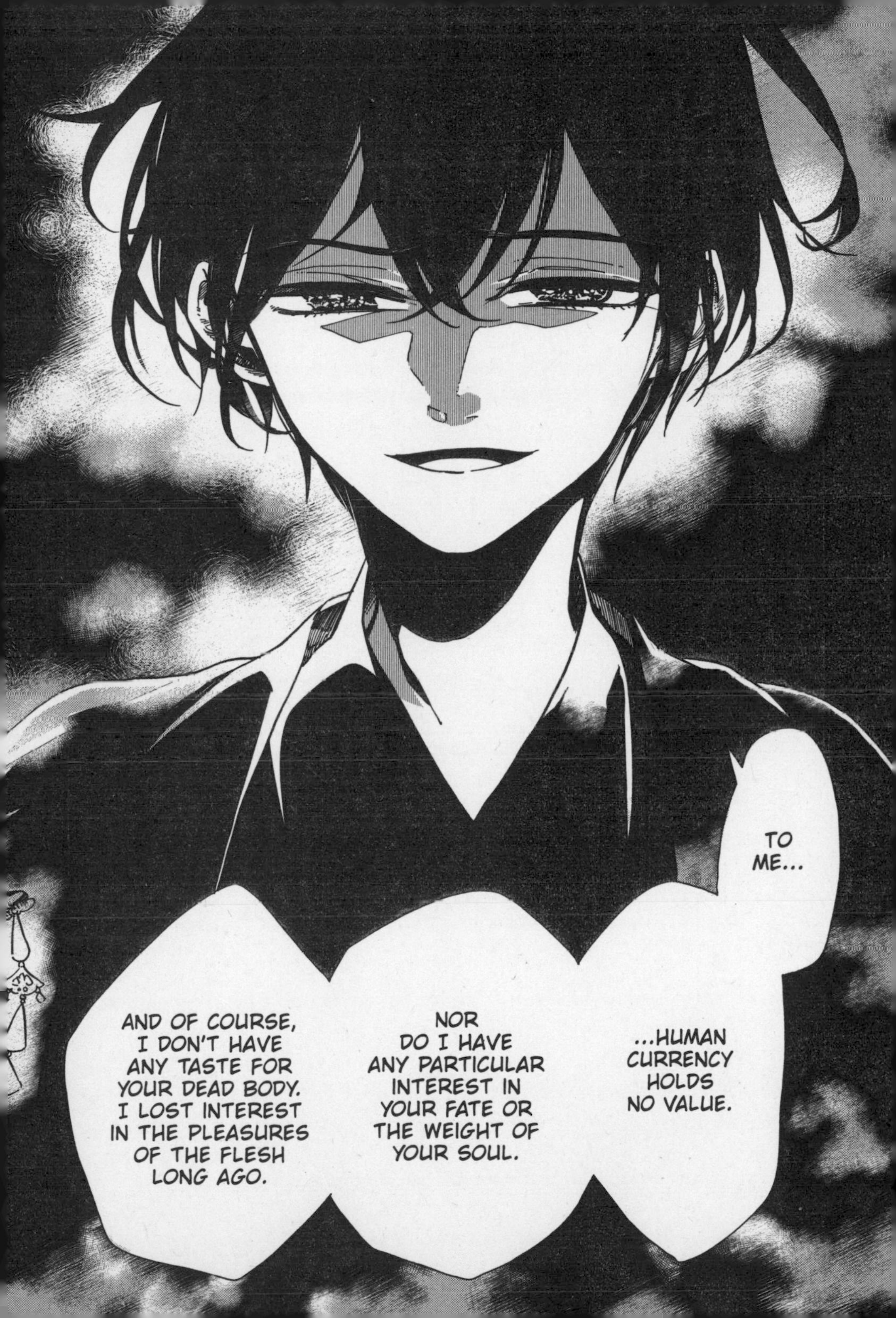
TO ME...
...HUMAN CURRENCY HOLDS NO VALUE.
NOR DO I HAVE ANY PARTICULAR INTEREST IN YOUR FATE OR THE WEIGHT OF YOUR SOUL.
AND OF COURSE, I DON'T HAVE ANY TASTE FOR YOUR DEAD BODY. I LOST INTEREST IN THE PLEASURES OF THE FLESH LONG AGO.

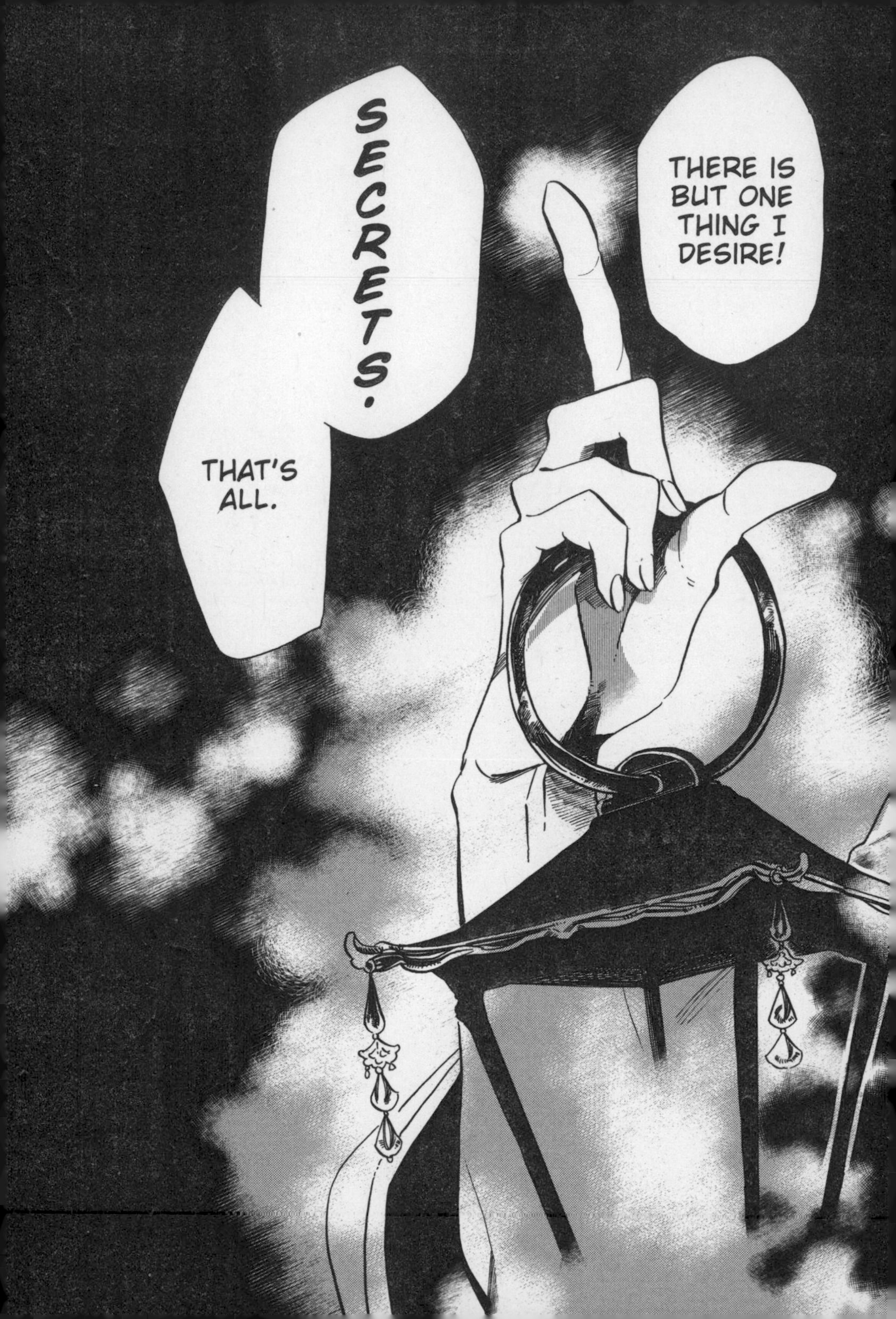
THERE IS BUT ONE THING I DESIRE!
SECRETS.
THAT'S ALL.

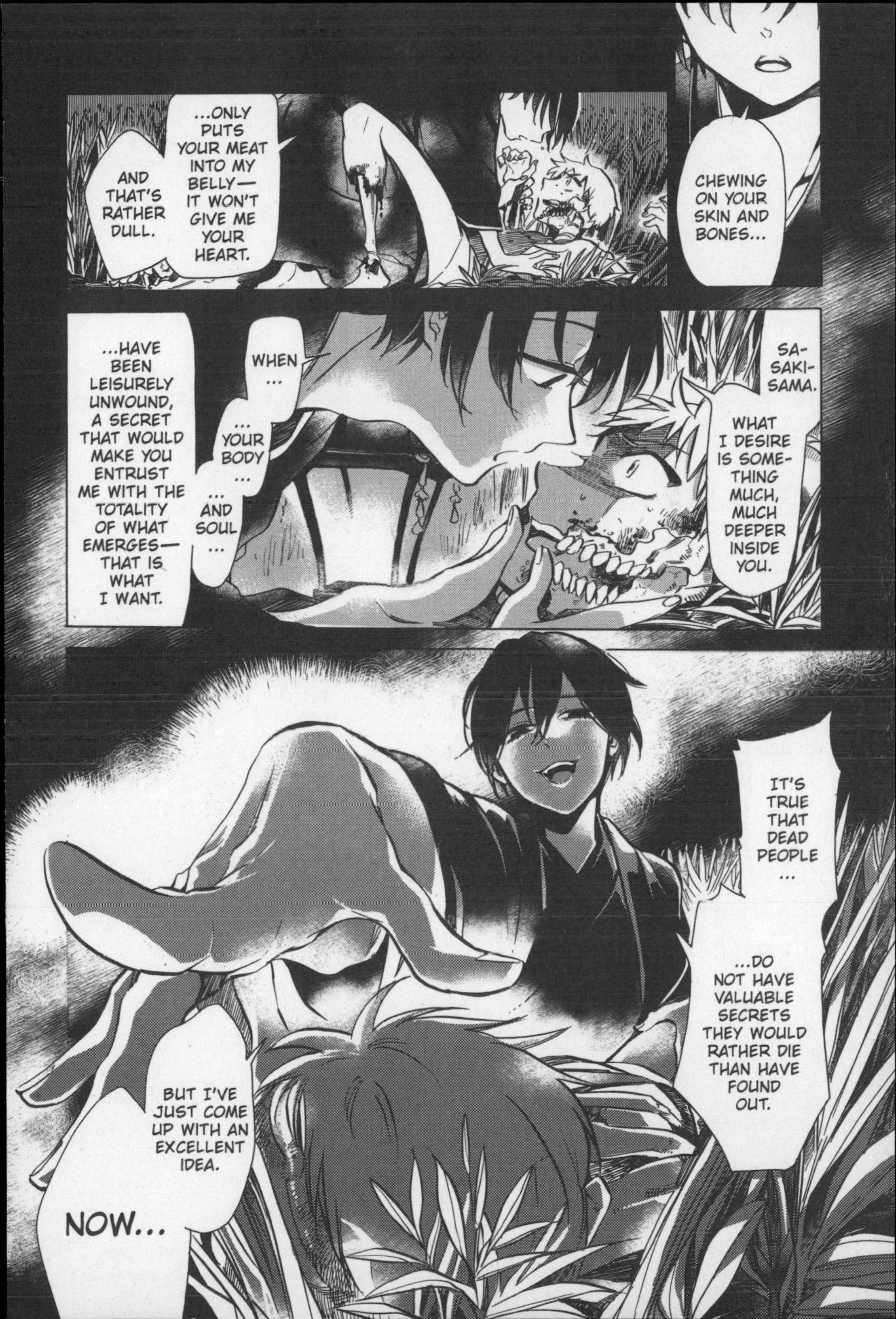
CHEWING ON YOUR SKIN AND BONES...
...ONLY PUTS YOUR MEAT INTO MY BELLY—IT WON'T GIVE ME YOUR HEART.
AND THAT'S RATHER DULL.
SA-SAKI-SAMA.
WHAT I DESIRE IS SOMETHING MUCH, MUCH DEEPER INSIDE YOU.
WHEN...
...YOUR BODY...
...AND SOUL...
...HAVE BEEN LEISURELY UNWOUND, A SECRET THAT WOULD MAKE YOU ENTRUST ME WITH THE TOTALITY OF WHAT EMERGES—THAT IS WHAT I WANT.
IT'S TRUE THAT DEAD PEOPLE...
...DO NOT HAVE VALUABLE SECRETS THEY WOULD RATHER DIE THAN HAVE FOUND OUT.
BUT I'VE JUST COME UP WITH AN EXCELLENT IDEA.
NOW...

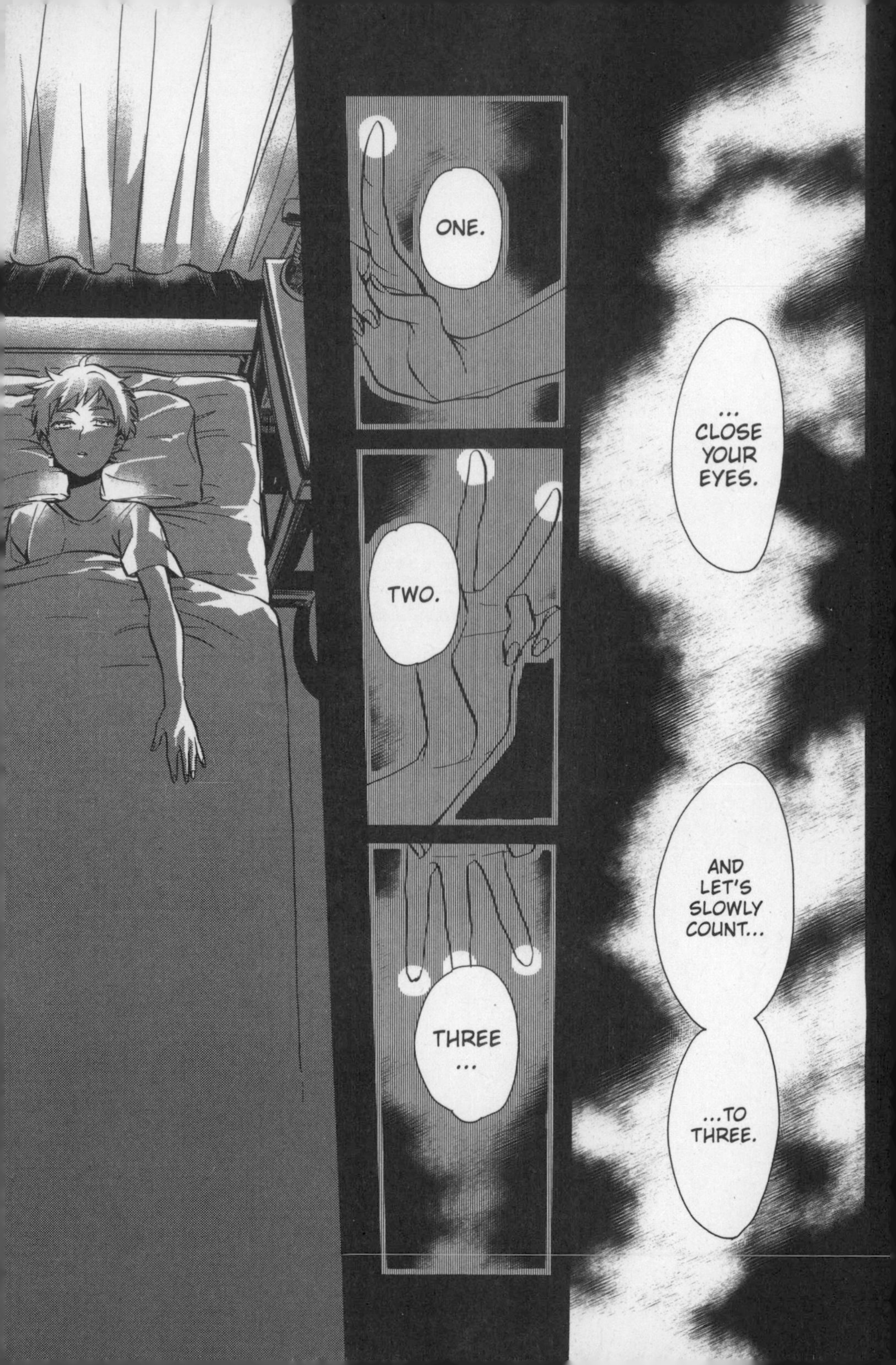
...CLOSE YOUR EYES.
AND LET'S SLOWLY COUNT...
...TO THREE.
ONE.
TWO.
THREE ...

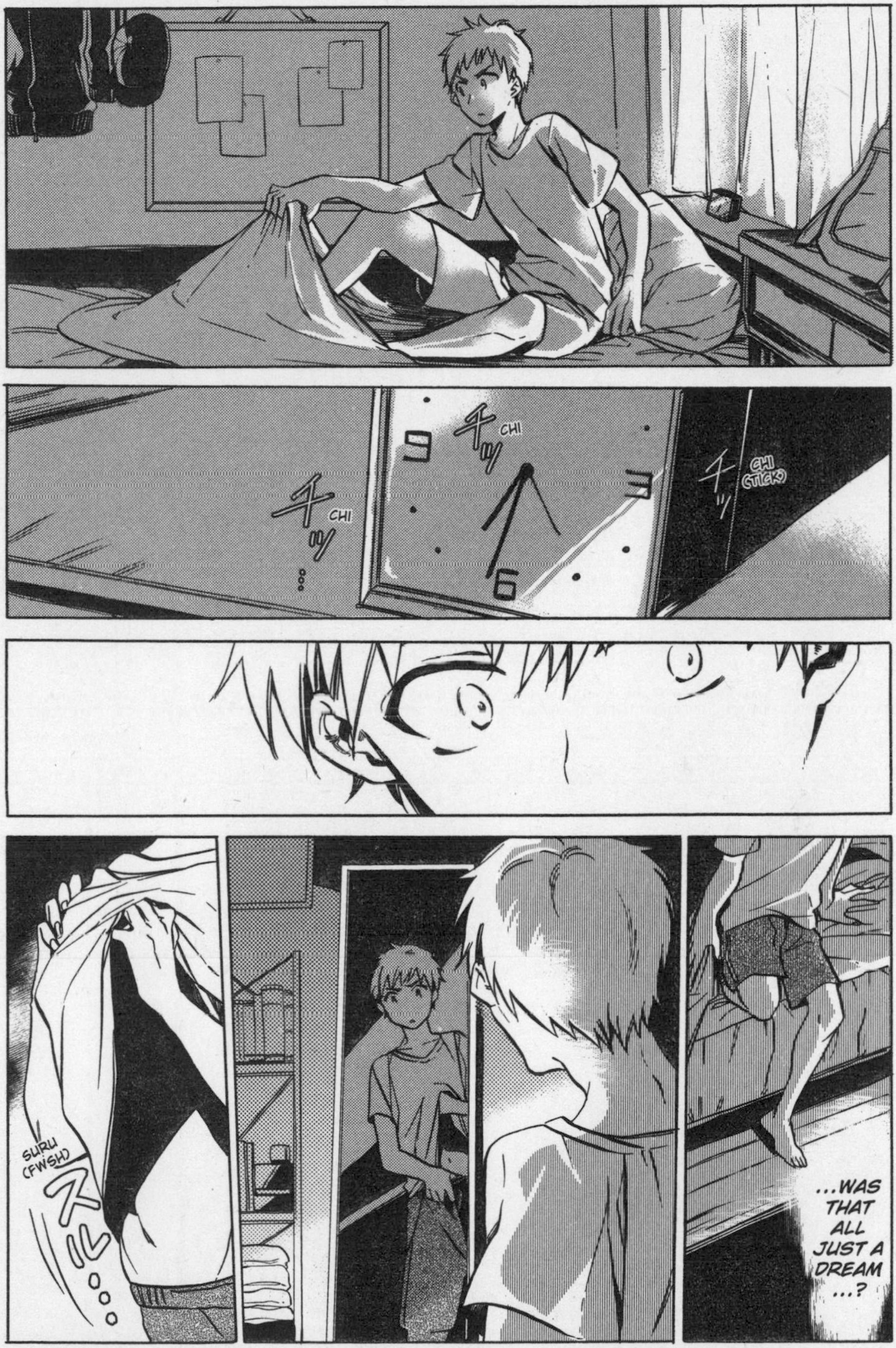
チッ
CHI (TICK)
チッ
CHI
チッ…
CHI
...WAS THAT ALL JUST A DREAM...?
SURU (FWSH)
スル…

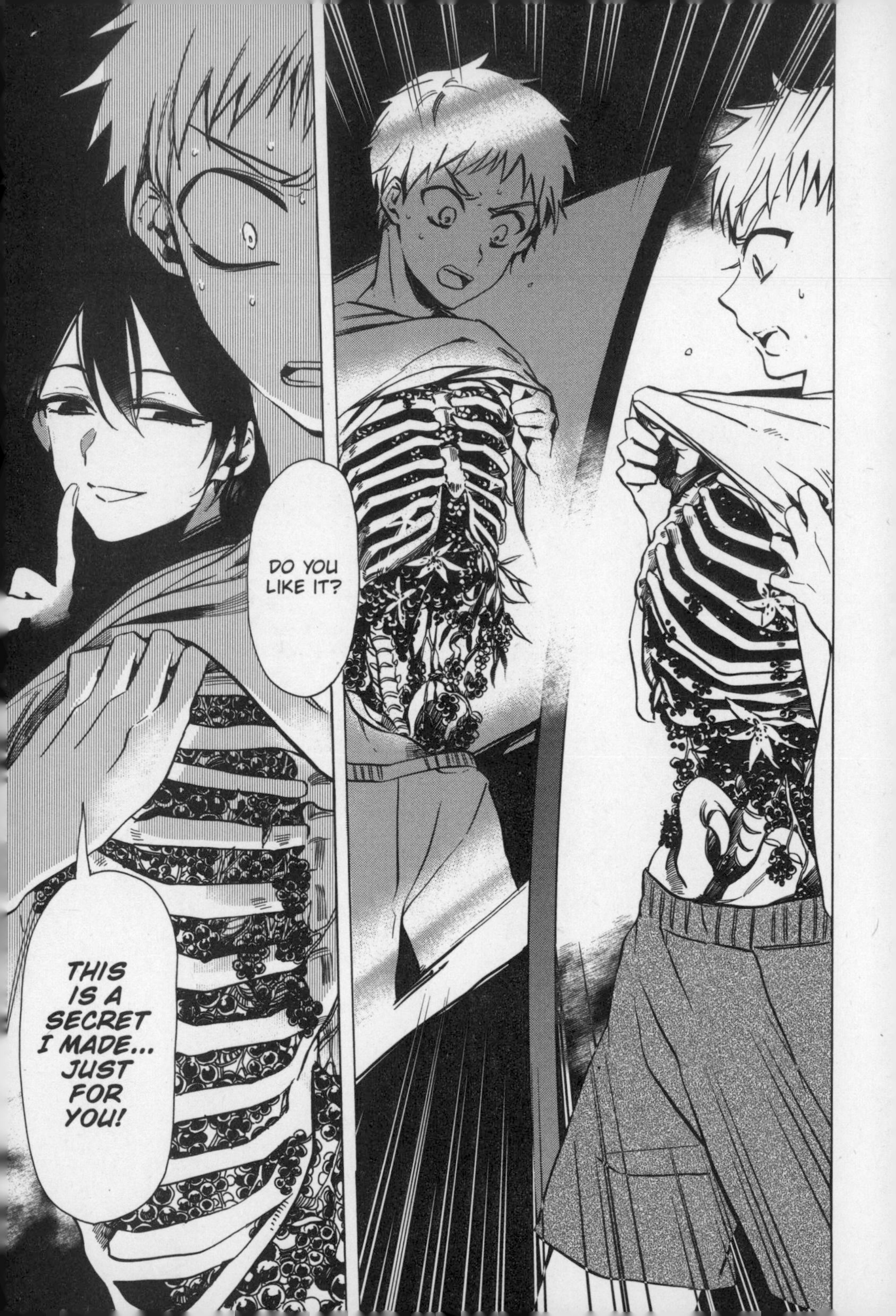
DO YOU LIKE IT?
THIS IS A SECRET I MADE... JUST FOR YOU!

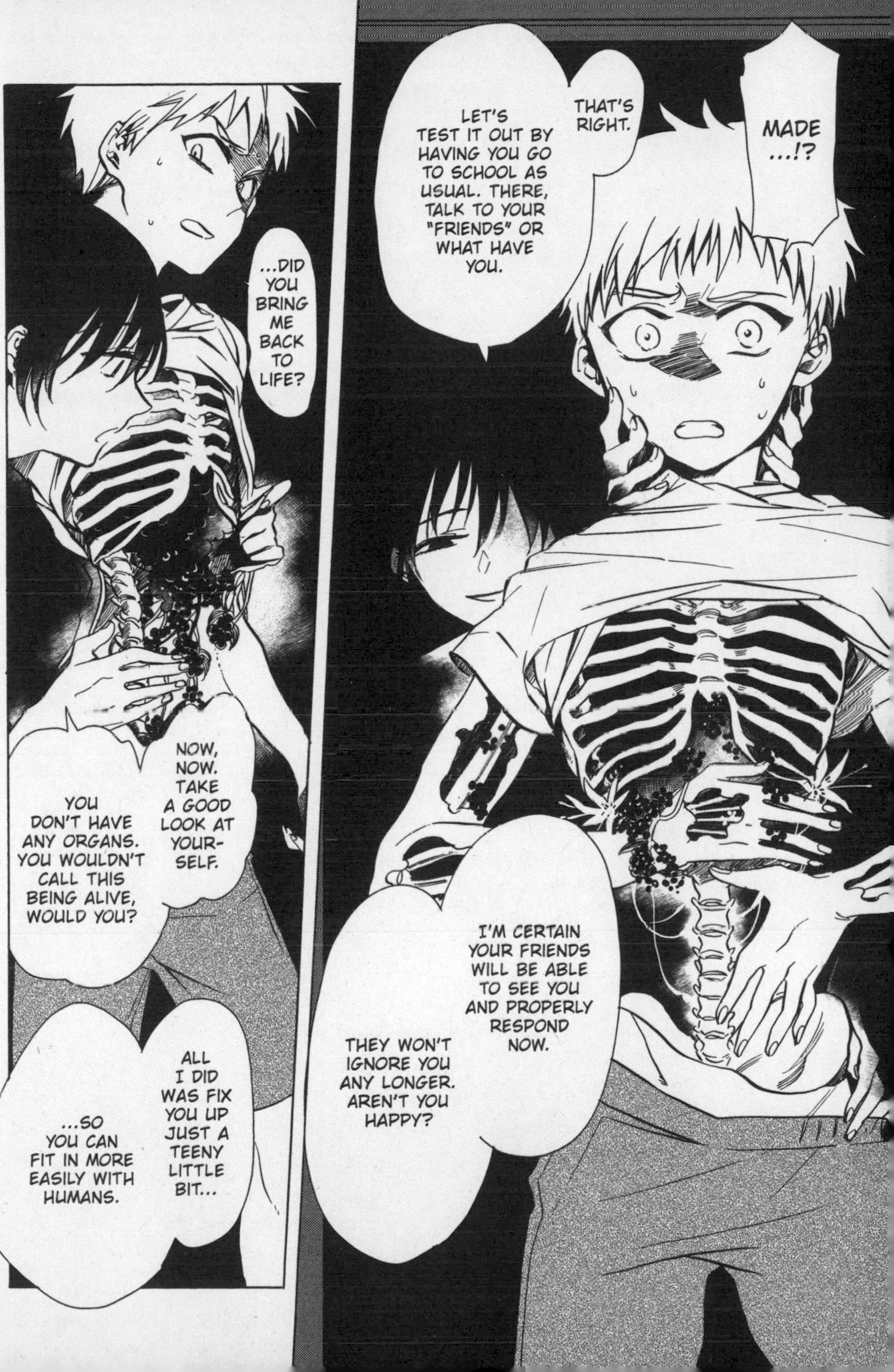
MADE ...!?
THAT'S RIGHT.
LET'S TEST IT OUT BY HAVING YOU GO TO SCHOOL AS USUAL. THERE, TALK TO YOUR "FRIENDS" OR WHAT HAVE YOU.
I'M CERTAIN YOUR FRIENDS WILL BE ABLE TO SEE YOU AND PROPERLY RESPOND NOW.
THEY WON'T IGNORE YOU ANY LONGER. AREN'T YOU HAPPY?
...DID YOU BRING ME BACK TO LIFE?
NOW, NOW. TAKE A GOOD LOOK AT YOURSELF.
YOU DON'T HAVE ANY ORGANS. YOU WOULDN'T CALL THIS BEING ALIVE, WOULD YOU?
ALL I DID WAS FIX YOU UP JUST A TEENY LITTLE BIT...
...SO YOU CAN FIT IN MORE EASILY WITH HUMANS.

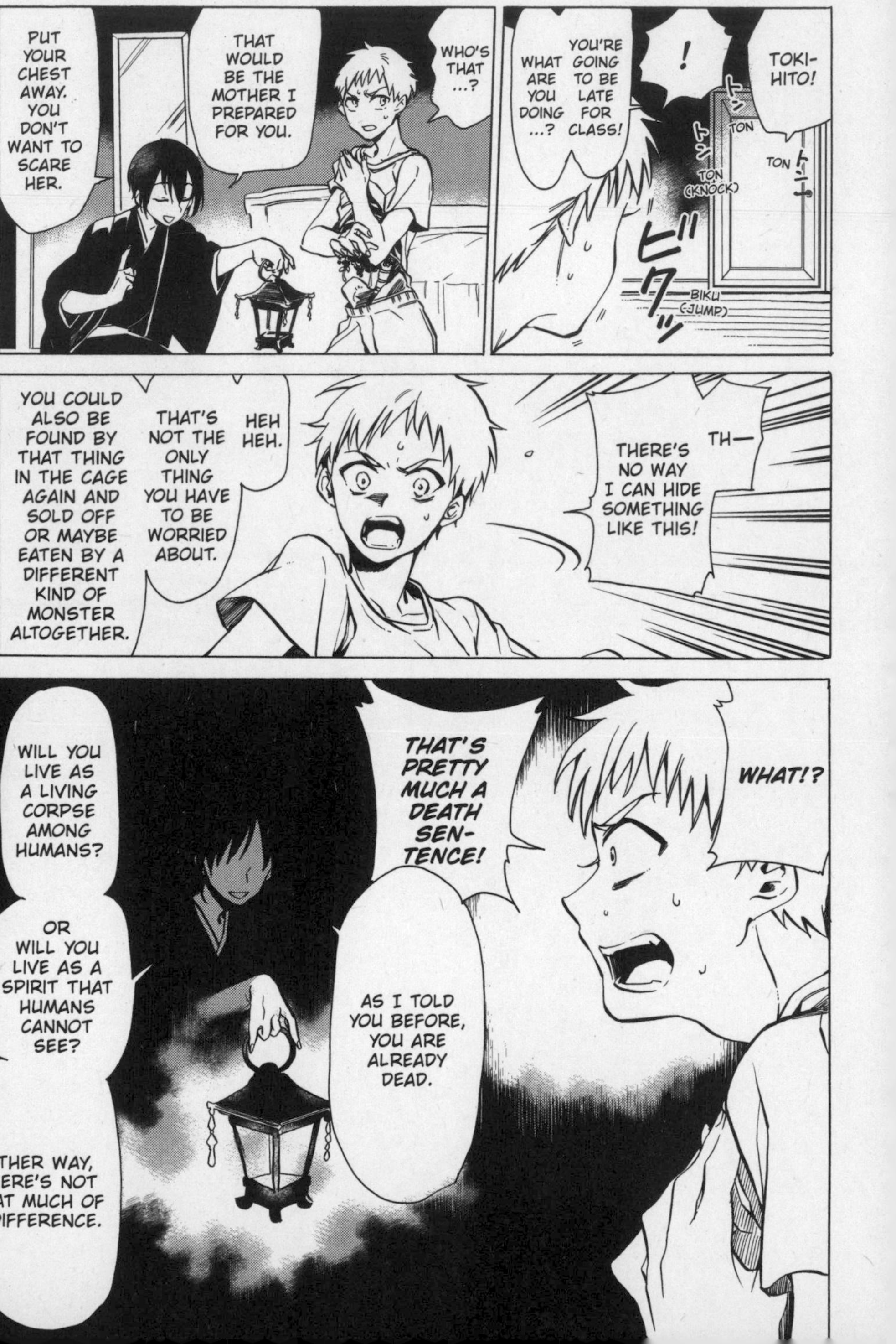
TOKI-HITO!
TON TON TON (KNOCK)
!
YOU'RE GOING TO BE LATE FOR CLASS!
WHAT ARE YOU DOING ...?
BIKU (JUMP)
WHO'S THAT ...?
THAT WOULD BE THE MOTHER I PREPARED FOR YOU.
PUT YOUR CHEST AWAY. YOU DON'T WANT TO SCARE HER.
TH—
THERE'S NO WAY I CAN HIDE SOMETHING LIKE THIS!
HEH HEH.
THAT'S NOT THE ONLY THING YOU HAVE TO BE WORRIED ABOUT.
YOU COULD ALSO BE FOUND BY THAT THING IN THE CAGE AGAIN AND SOLD OFF OR MAYBE EATEN BY A DIFFERENT KIND OF MONSTER ALTOGETHER.
WHAT!?
THAT'S PRETTY MUCH A DEATH SEN-TENCE!
AS I TOLD YOU BEFORE, YOU ARE ALREADY DEAD.
WILL YOU LIVE AS A LIVING CORPSE AMONG HUMANS?
OR WILL YOU LIVE AS A SPIRIT THAT HUMANS CANNOT SEE?
EITHER WAY, THERE'S NOT THAT MUCH OF A DIFFERENCE.

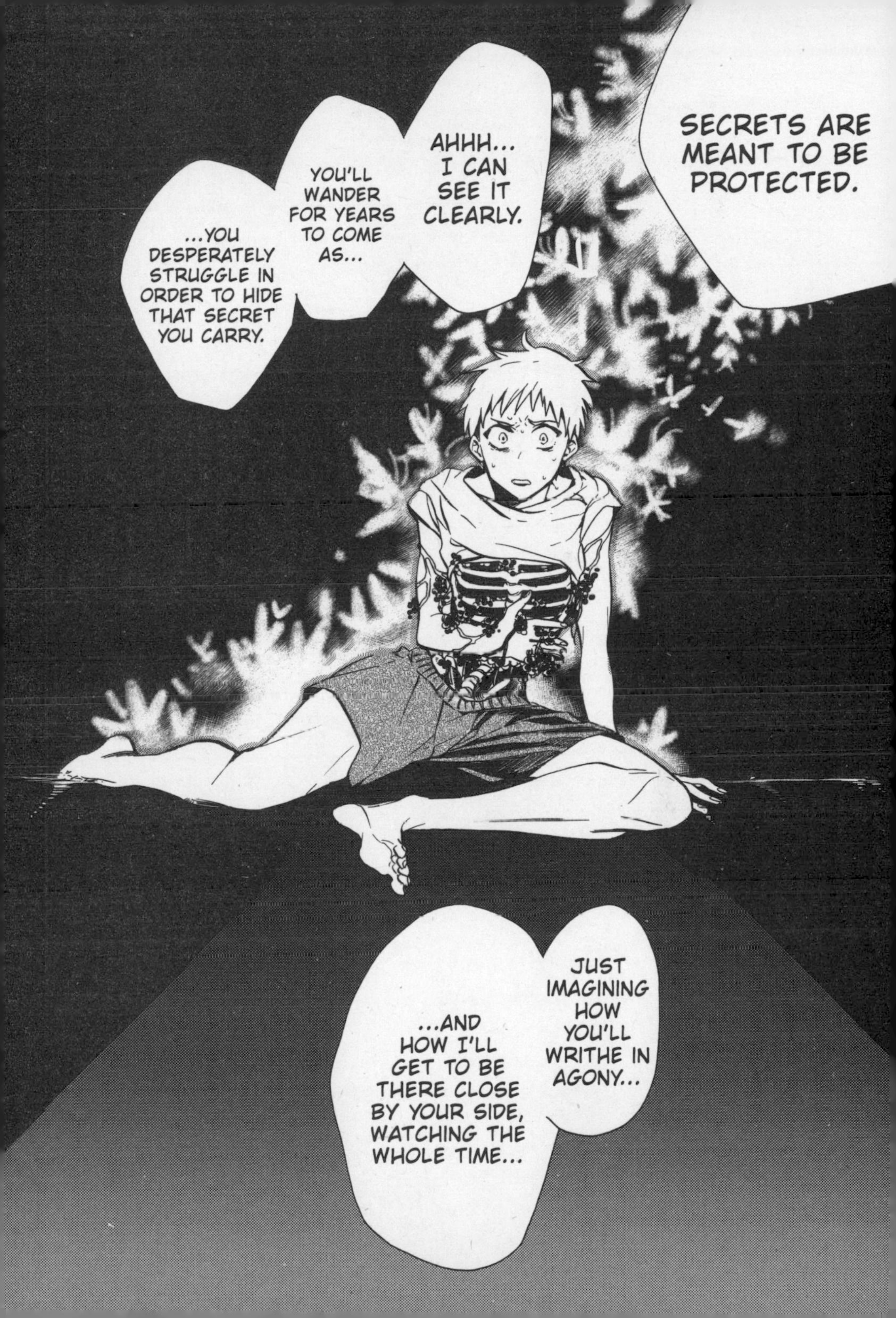
SECRETS ARE MEANT TO BE PROTECTED.
AHHH... I CAN SEE IT CLEARLY.
YOU'LL WANDER FOR YEARS TO COME AS...
...YOU DESPERATELY STRUGGLE IN ORDER TO HIDE THAT SECRET YOU CARRY.
JUST IMAGINING HOW YOU'LL WRITHE IN AGONY...
...AND HOW I'LL GET TO BE THERE CLOSE BY YOUR SIDE, WATCHING THE WHOLE TIME...

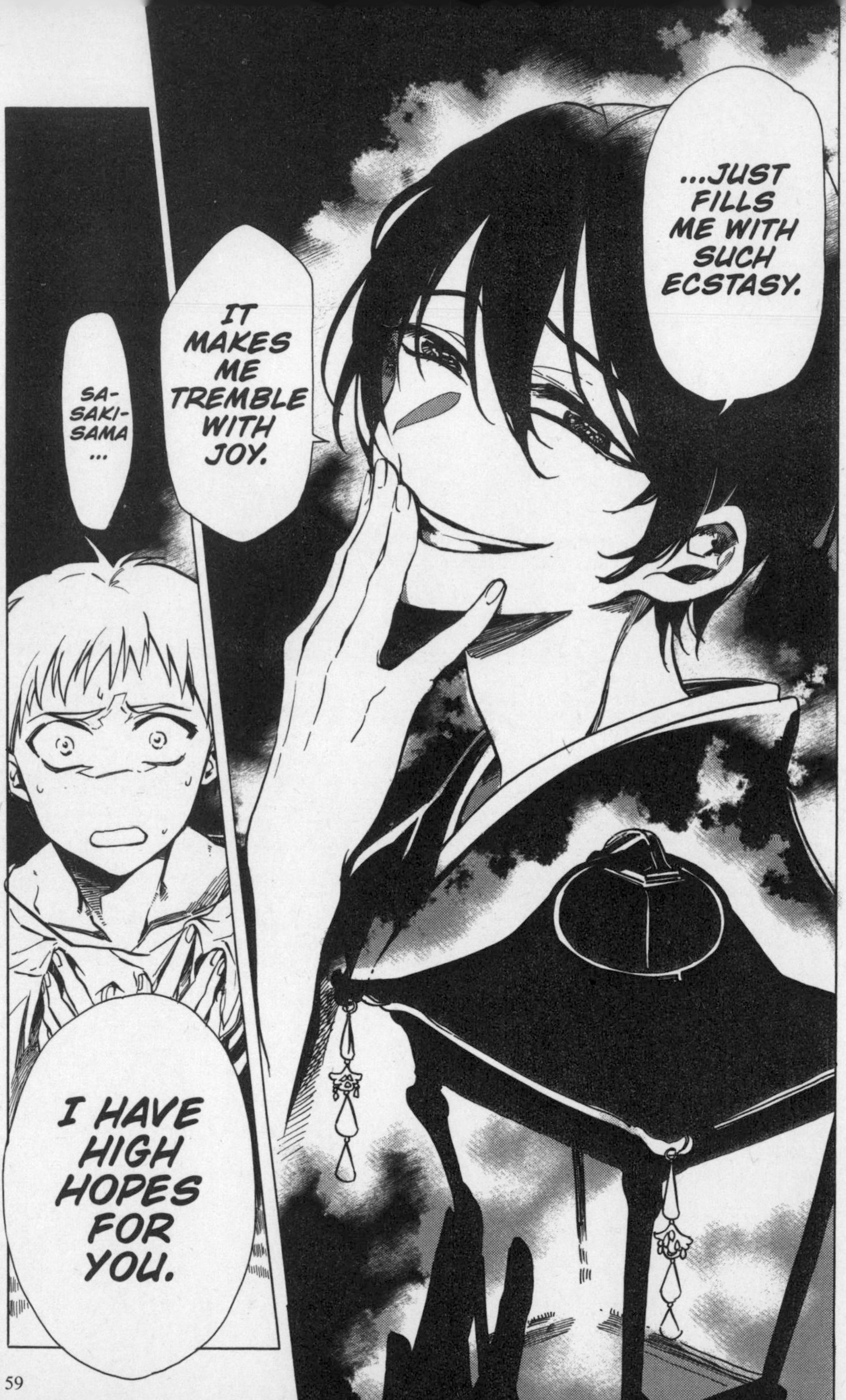
...JUST FILLS ME WITH SUCH ECSTASY.
IT MAKES ME TREMBLE WITH JOY.
SA-SAKI-SAMA...
I HAVE HIGH HOPES FOR YOU.

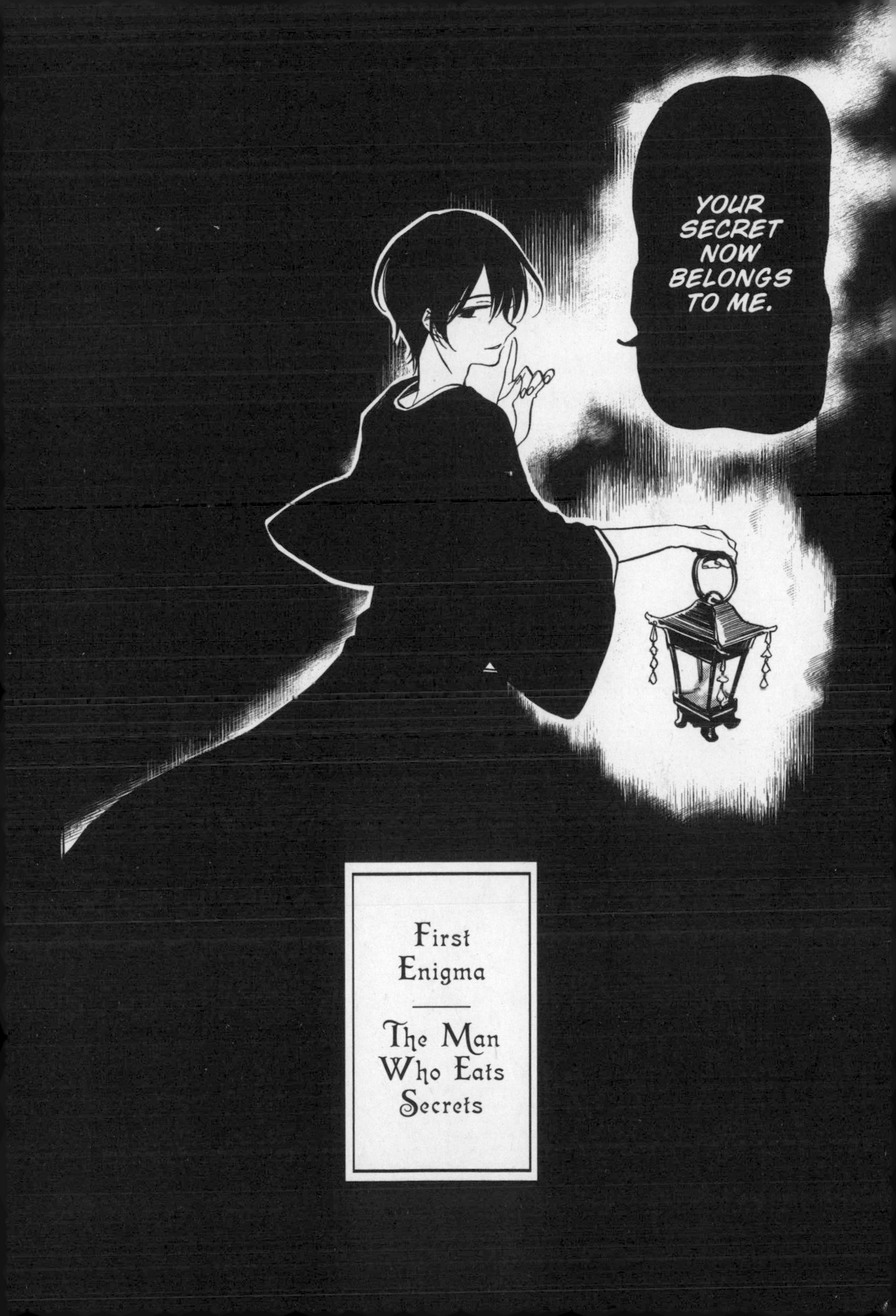
YOUR SECRET NOW BELONGS TO ME.

First Enigma

The Man Who Eats Secrets

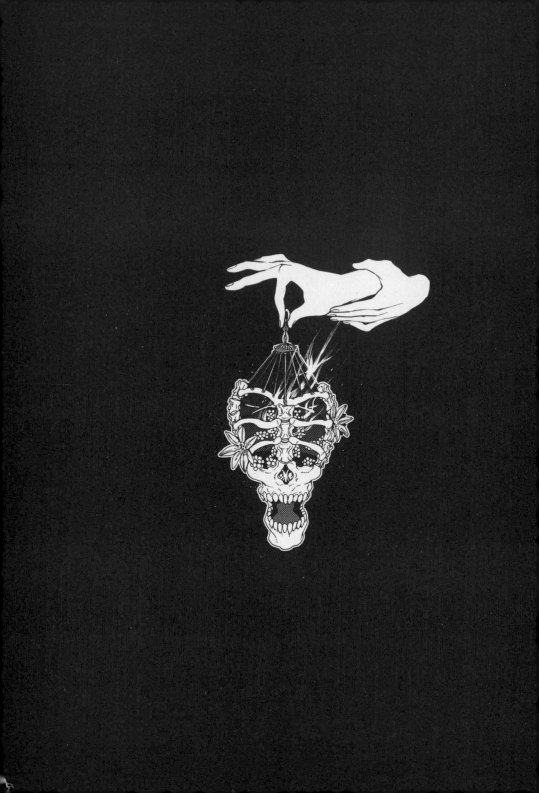

Phantom Tales of the Night

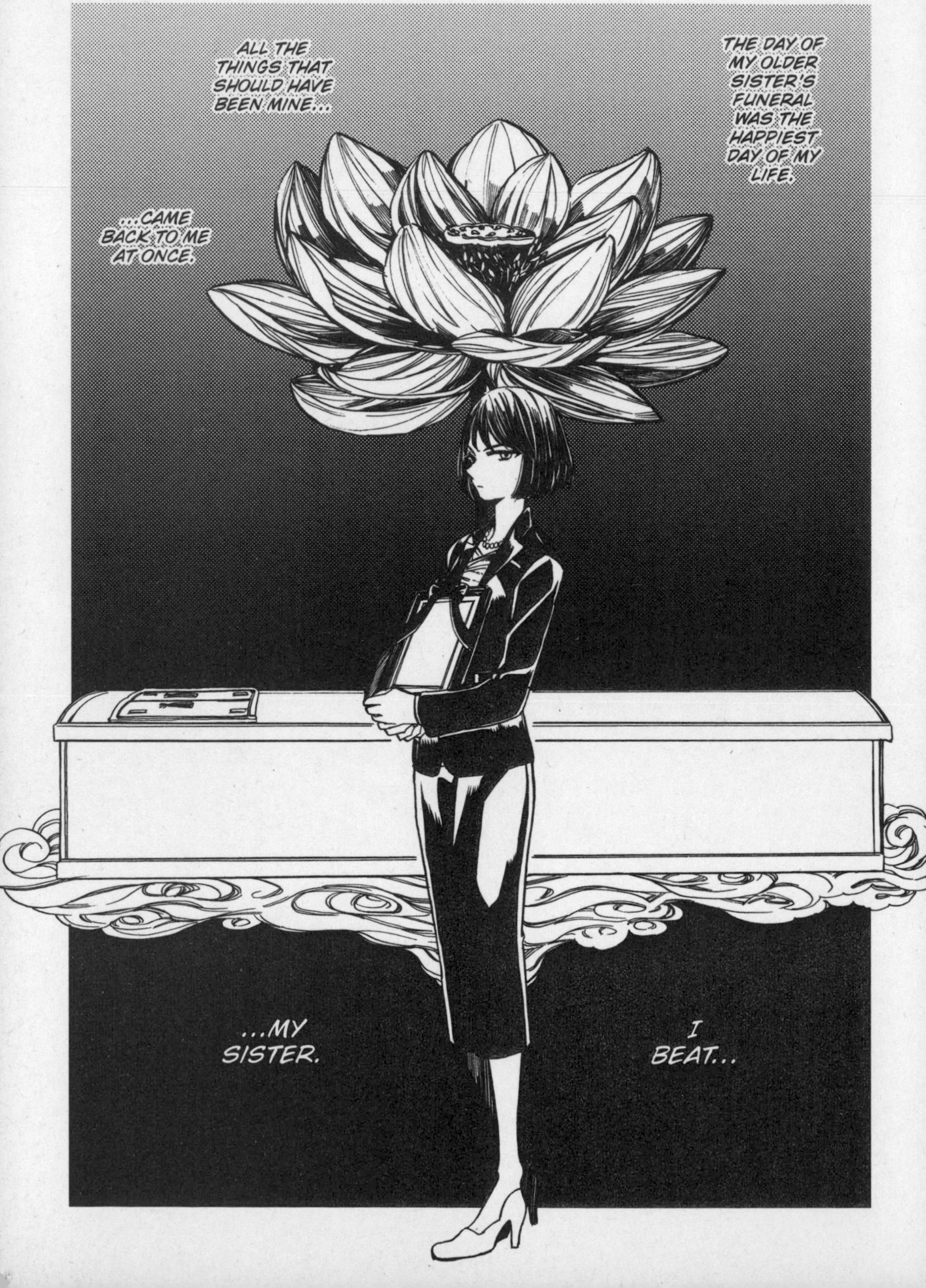
THE DAY OF MY OLDER SISTER'S FUNERAL WAS THE HAPPIEST DAY OF MY LIFE.
ALL THE THINGS THAT SHOULD HAVE BEEN MINE...
...CAME BACK TO ME AT ONCE.
I BEAT...
...MY SISTER.

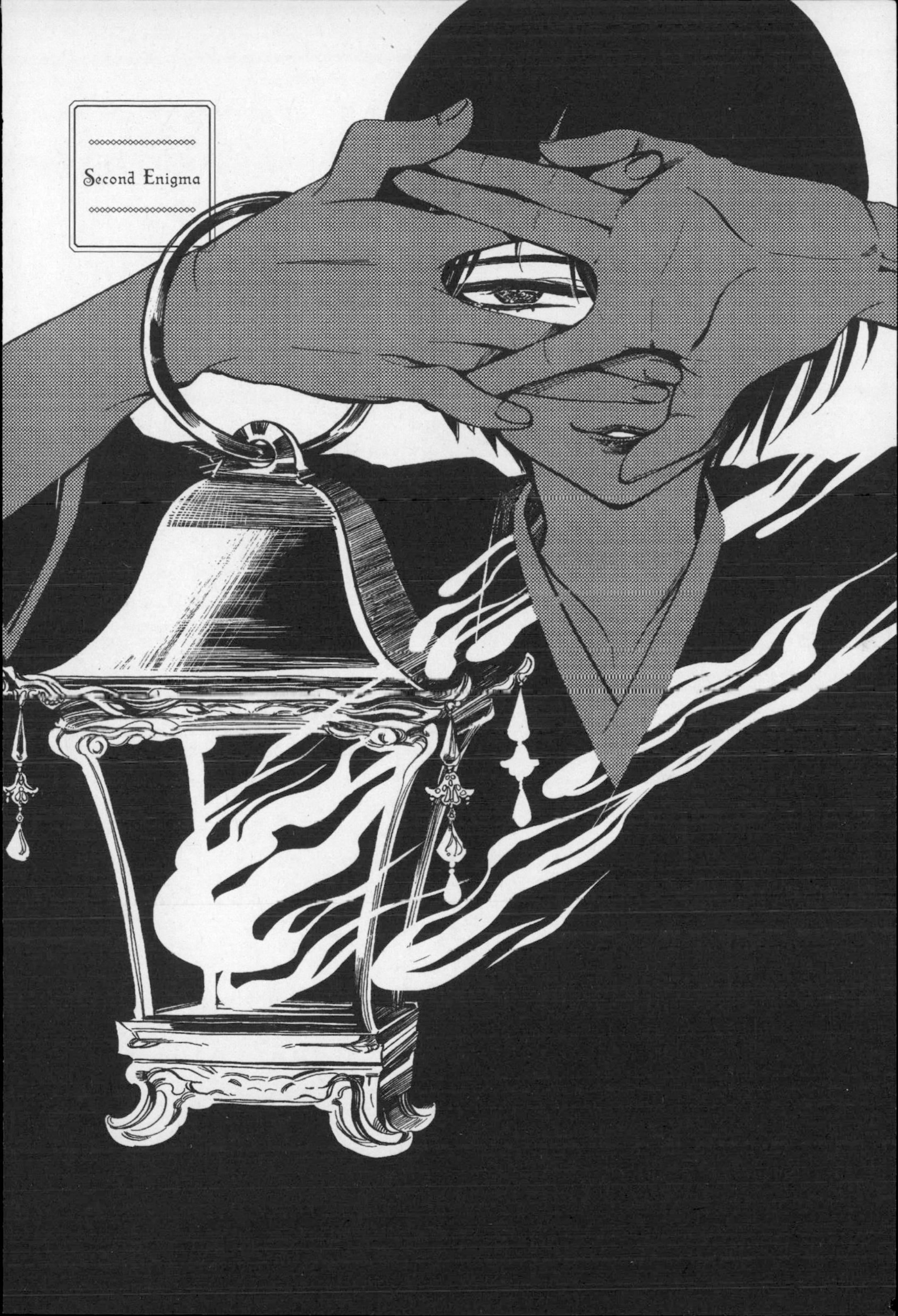
Second Enigma

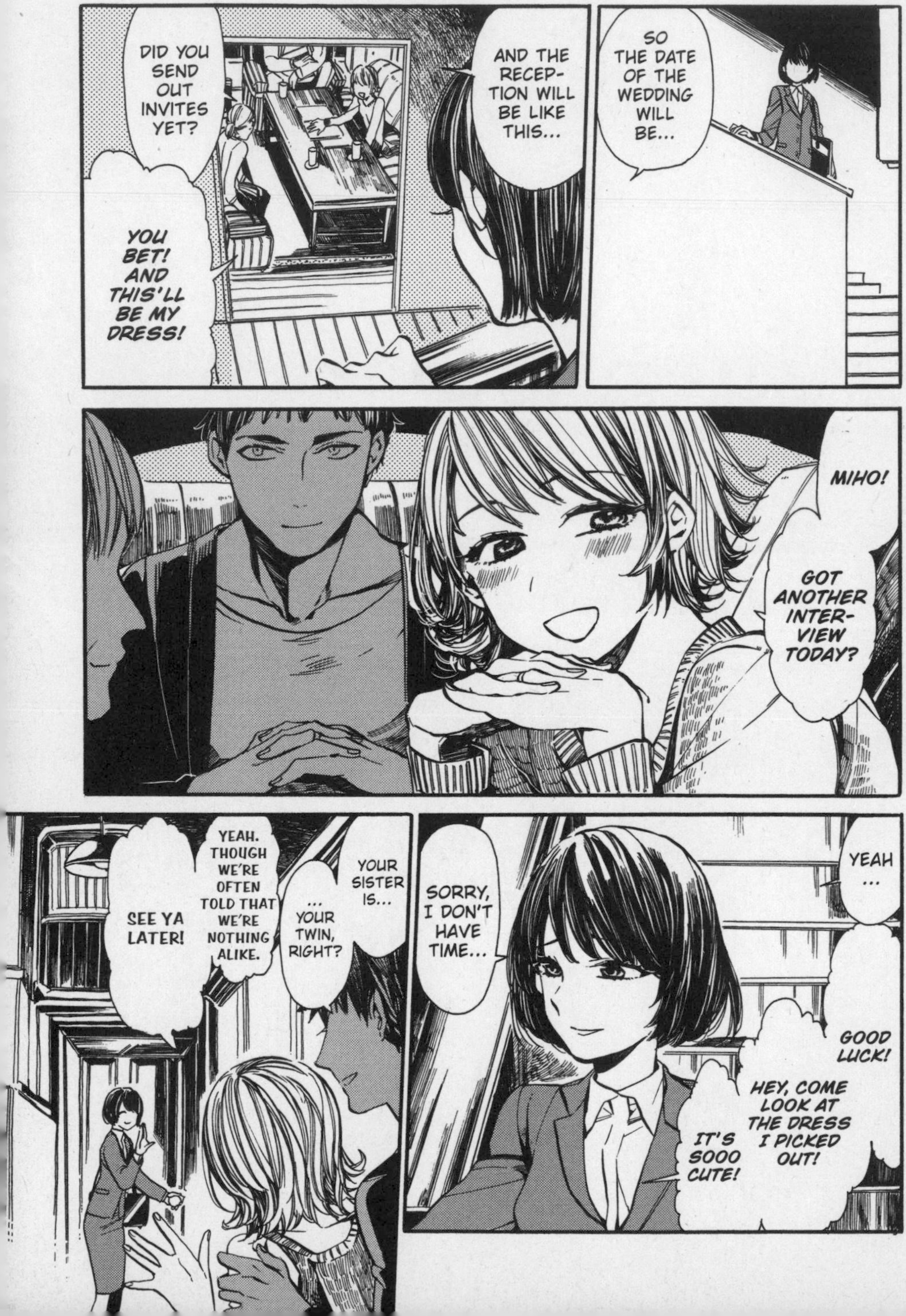
SO THE DATE OF THE WEDDING WILL BE...
AND THE RECEPTION WILL BE LIKE THIS...
DID YOU SEND OUT INVITES YET?
YOU BET! AND THIS'LL BE MY DRESS!
MIHO!
GOT ANOTHER INTERVIEW TODAY?
YEAH ...
SORRY, I DON'T HAVE TIME...
GOOD LUCK!
HEY, COME LOOK AT THE DRESS I PICKED OUT!
IT'S SOOO CUTE!
YOUR SISTER IS...
... YOUR TWIN, RIGHT?
YEAH. THOUGH WE'RE OFTEN TOLD THAT WE'RE NOTHING ALIKE.
SEE YA LATER!

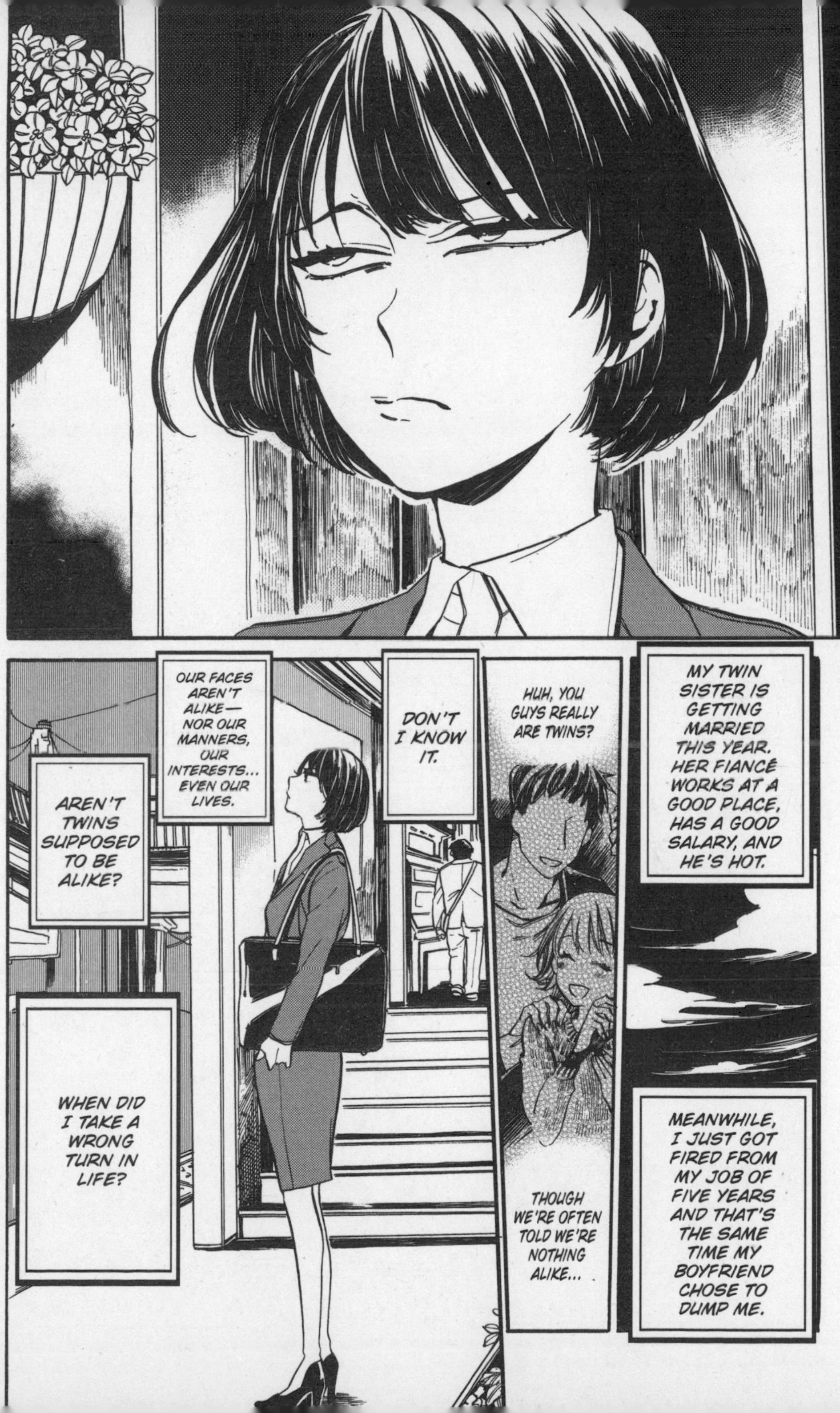
MY TWIN SISTER IS GETTING MARRIED THIS YEAR. HER FIANCÉ WORKS AT A GOOD PLACE, HAS A GOOD SALARY, AND HE'S HOT.
MEANWHILE, I JUST GOT FIRED FROM MY JOB OF FIVE YEARS AND THAT'S THE SAME TIME MY BOYFRIEND CHOSE TO DUMP ME.
HUH, YOU GUYS REALLY ARE TWINS?
THOUGH WE'RE OFTEN TOLD WE'RE NOTHING ALIKE...
DON'T I KNOW IT.
OUR FACES AREN'T ALIKE—NOR OUR MANNERS, OUR INTERESTS... EVEN OUR LIVES.
AREN'T TWINS SUPPOSED TO BE ALIKE?
WHEN DID I TAKE A WRONG TURN IN LIFE?

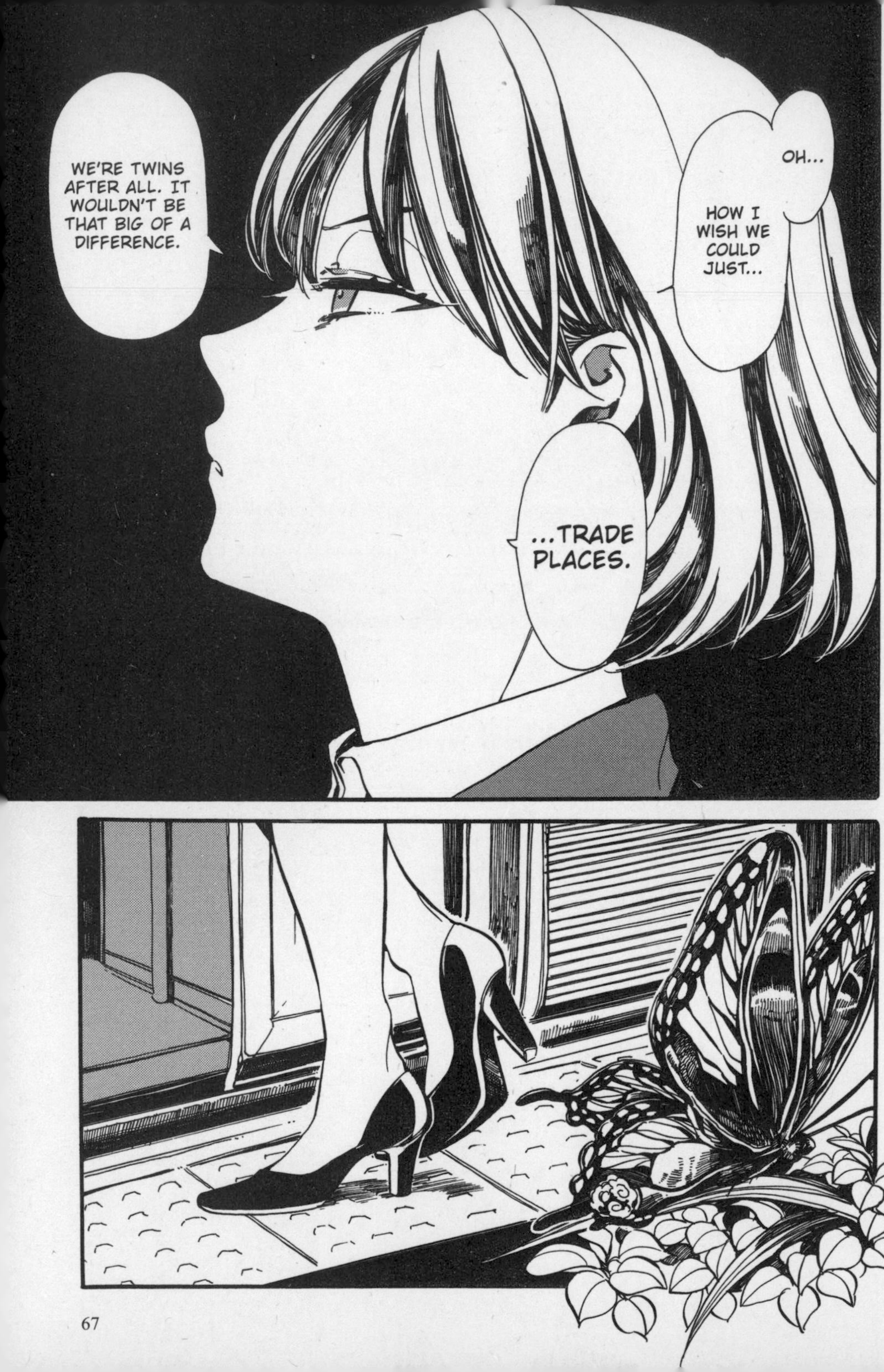
OH...
HOW I WISH WE COULD JUST...
...TRADE PLACES.
WE'RE TWINS AFTER ALL. IT WOULDN'T BE THAT BIG OF A DIFFERENCE.

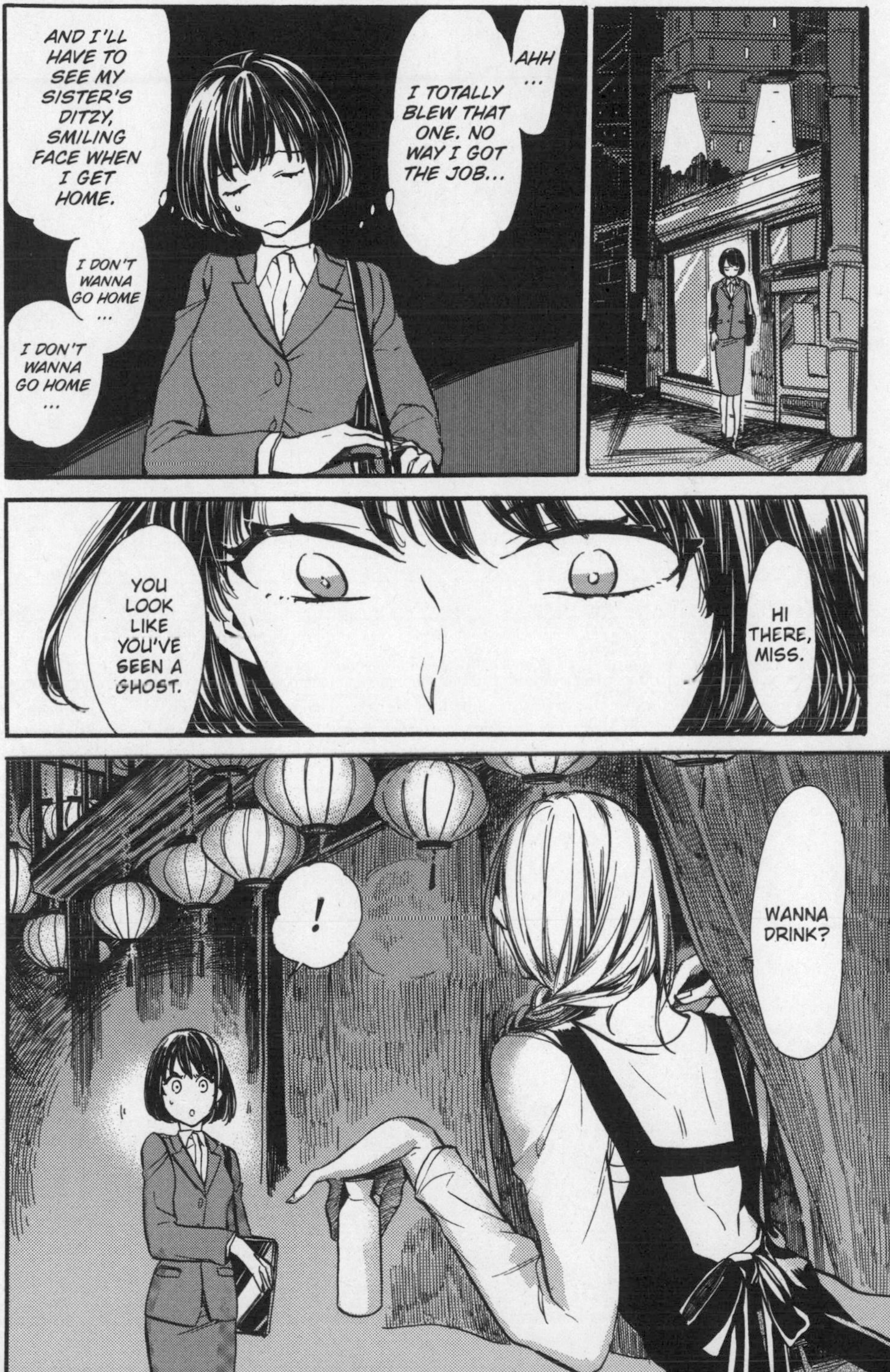
AHH ... I TOTALLY BLEW THAT ONE. NO WAY I GOT THE JOB...
AND I'LL HAVE TO SEE MY SISTER'S DITZY, SMILING FACE WHEN I GET HOME.
I DON'T WANNA GO HOME ...
I DON'T WANNA GO HOME ...
HI THERE, MISS.
YOU LOOK LIKE YOU'VE SEEN A GHOST.
WANNA DRINK?
!

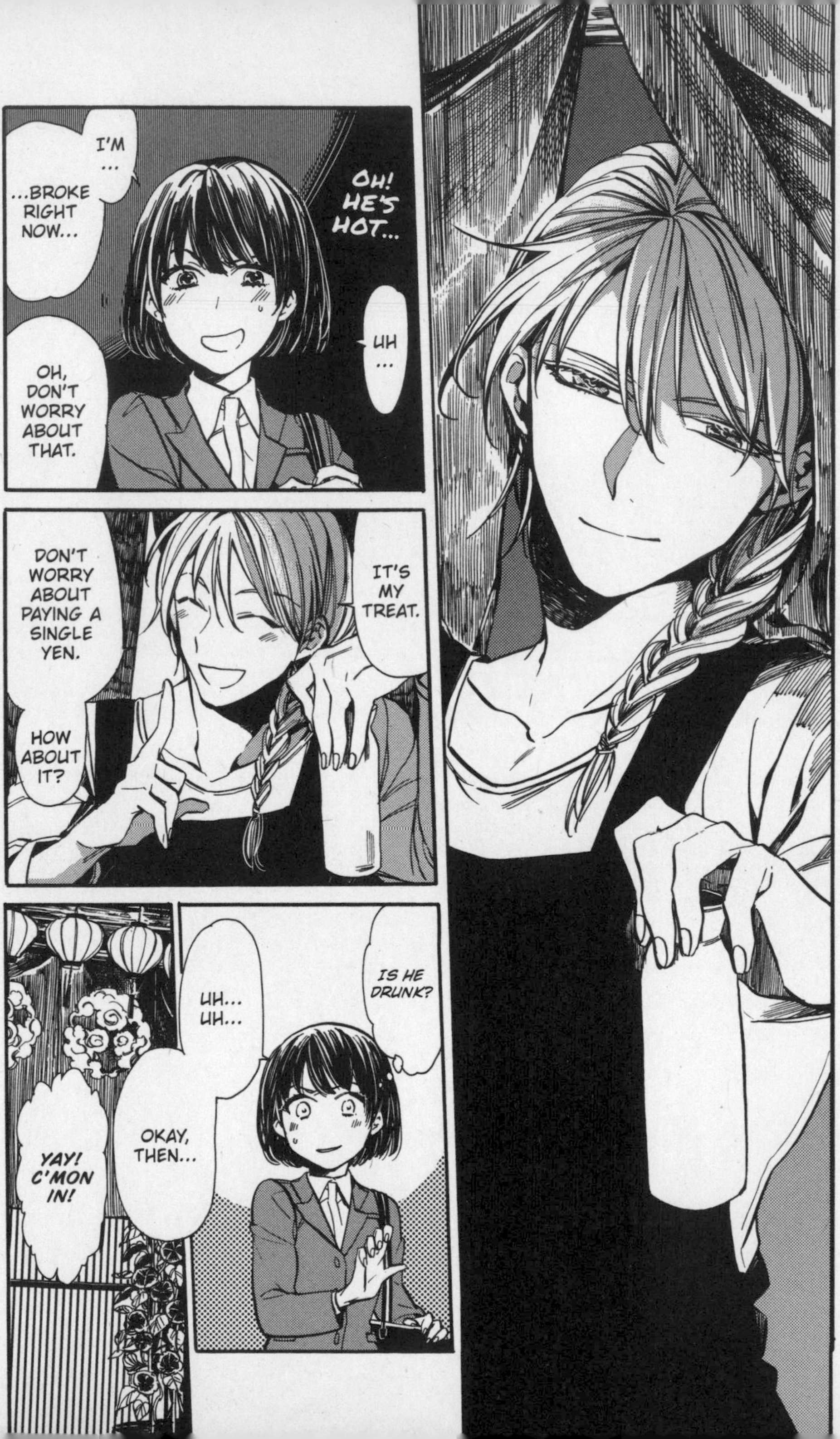
OH! HE'S HOT...
I'M ...
...BROKE RIGHT NOW...
UH ...
OH, DON'T WORRY ABOUT THAT.
IT'S MY TREAT.
DON'T WORRY ABOUT PAYING A SINGLE YEN.
HOW ABOUT IT?
IS HE DRUNK?
UH... UH...
OKAY, THEN...
YAY! C'MON IN!

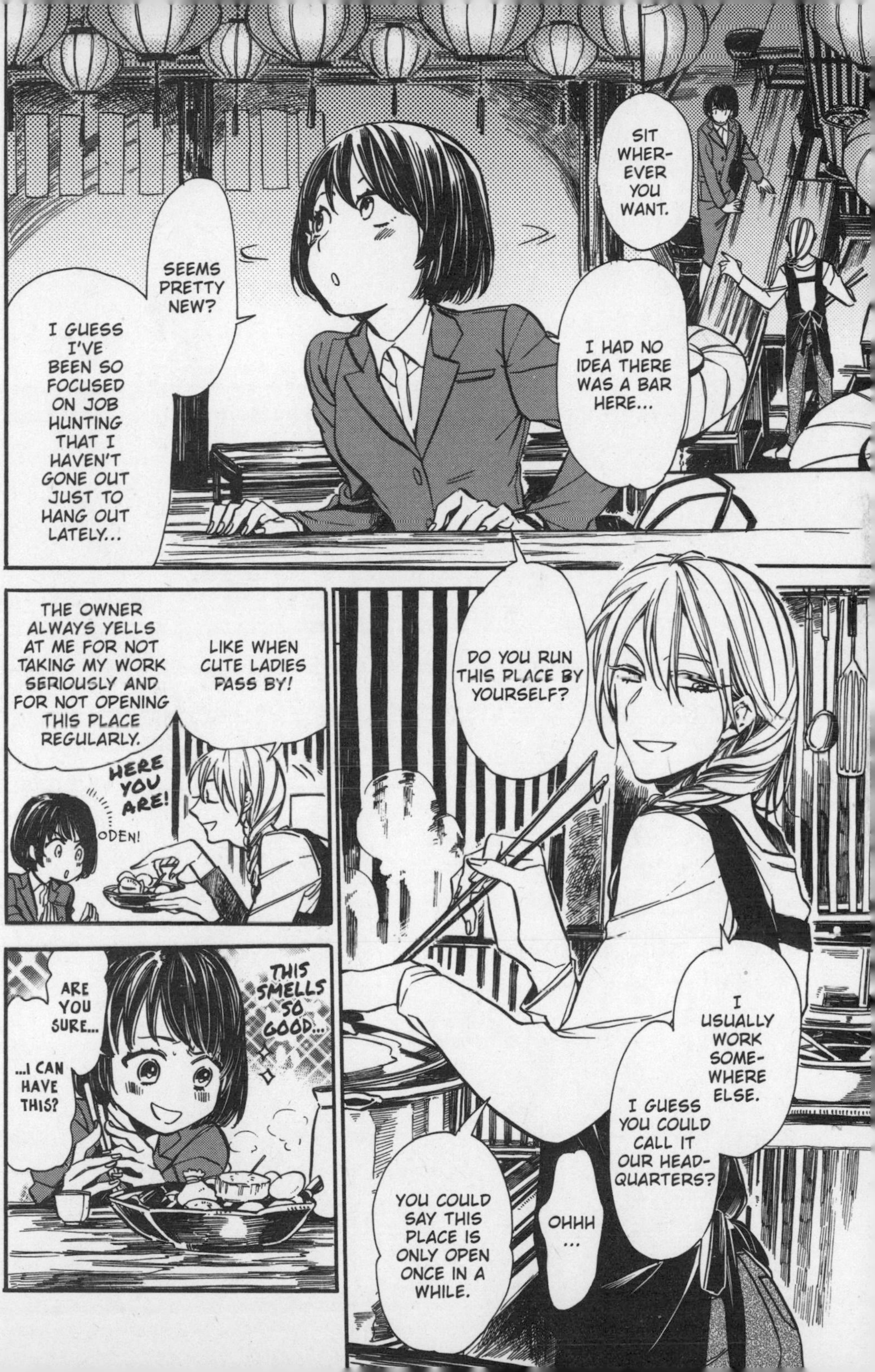
SIT WHEREVER YOU WANT.
I HAD NO IDEA THERE WAS A BAR HERE...
SEEMS PRETTY NEW?
I GUESS I'VE BEEN SO FOCUSED ON JOB HUNTING THAT I HAVEN'T GONE OUT JUST TO HANG OUT LATELY...
DO YOU RUN THIS PLACE BY YOURSELF?
I USUALLY WORK SOMEWHERE ELSE.
I GUESS YOU COULD CALL IT OUR HEADQUARTERS?
OHHH...
YOU COULD SAY THIS PLACE IS ONLY OPEN ONCE IN A WHILE.
THE OWNER ALWAYS YELLS AT ME FOR NOT TAKING MY WORK SERIOUSLY AND FOR NOT OPENING THIS PLACE REGULARLY.
LIKE WHEN CUTE LADIES PASS BY!
HERE YOU ARE!
ODEN!
THIS SMELLS SO GOOD...
ARE YOU SURE...
...I CAN HAVE THIS?

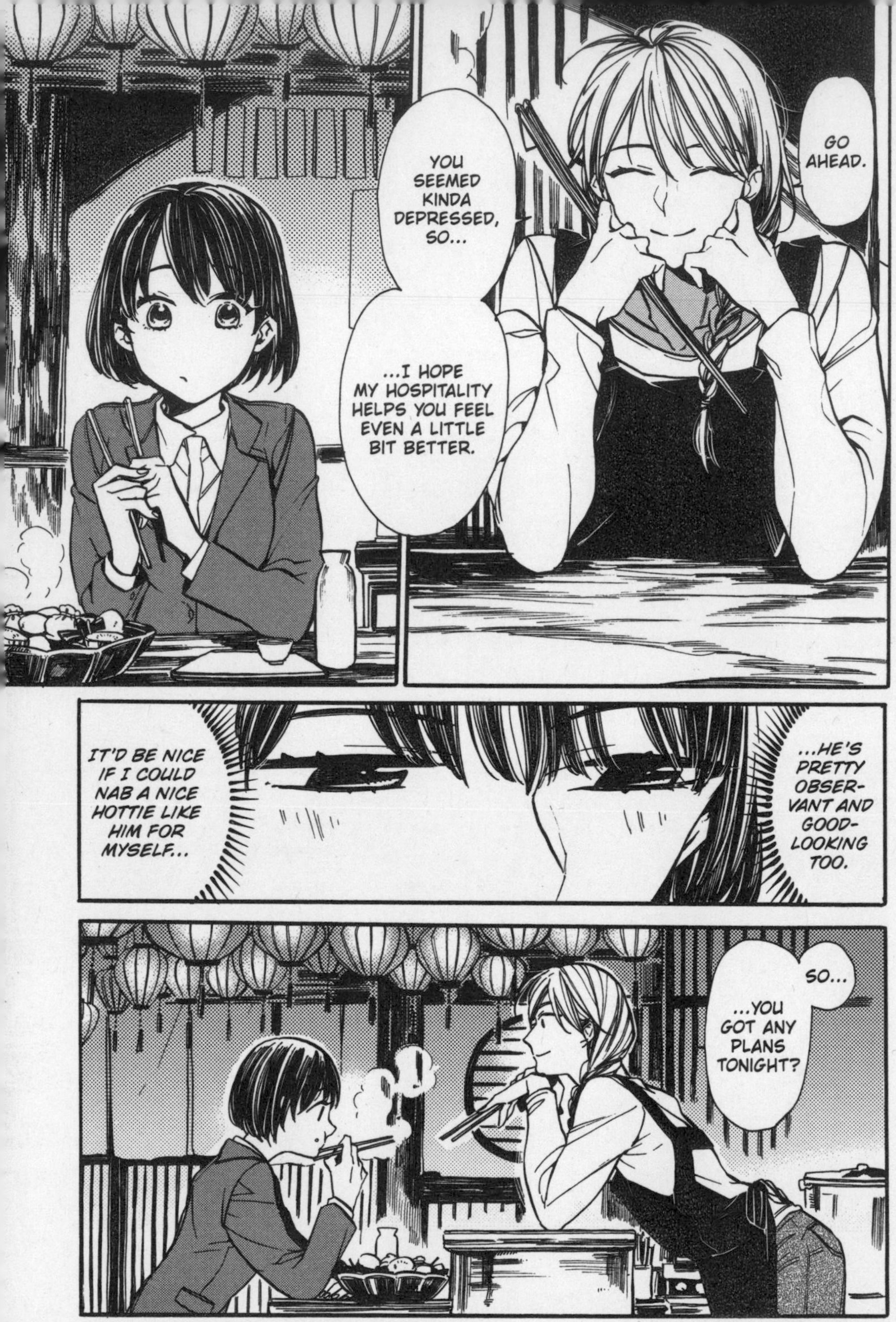
GO AHEAD.
YOU SEEMED KINDA DEPRESSED, SO...
...I HOPE MY HOSPITALITY HELPS YOU FEEL EVEN A LITTLE BIT BETTER.
...HE'S PRETTY OBSERVANT AND GOOD-LOOKING TOO.
IT'D BE NICE IF I COULD NAB A NICE HOTTIE LIKE HIM FOR MYSELF...
SO...
...YOU GOT ANY PLANS TONIGHT?

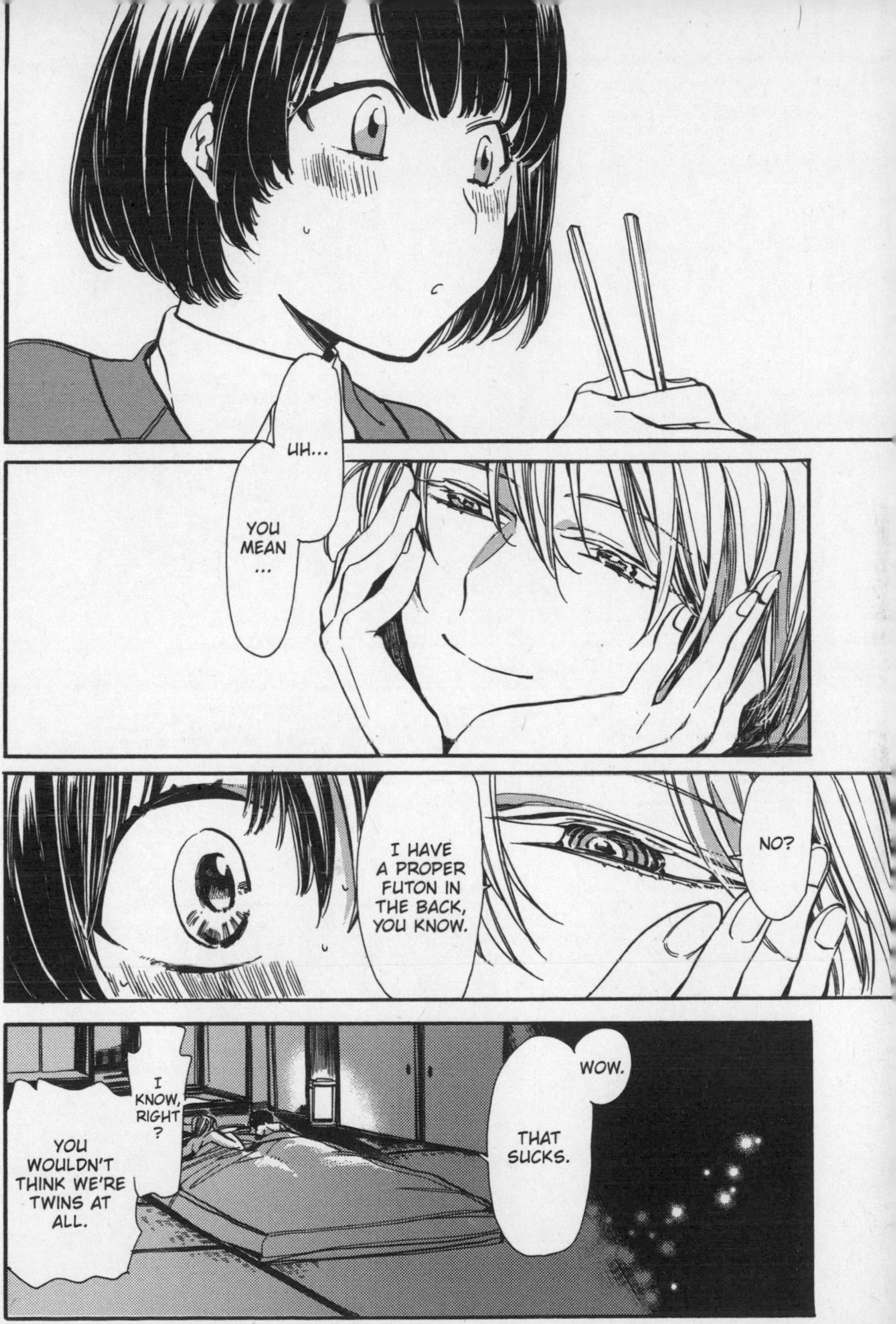
UH... YOU MEAN ...
NO?
I HAVE A PROPER FUTON IN THE BACK, YOU KNOW.
WOW. THAT SUCKS.
I KNOW, RIGHT?
YOU WOULDN'T THINK WE'RE TWINS AT ALL.

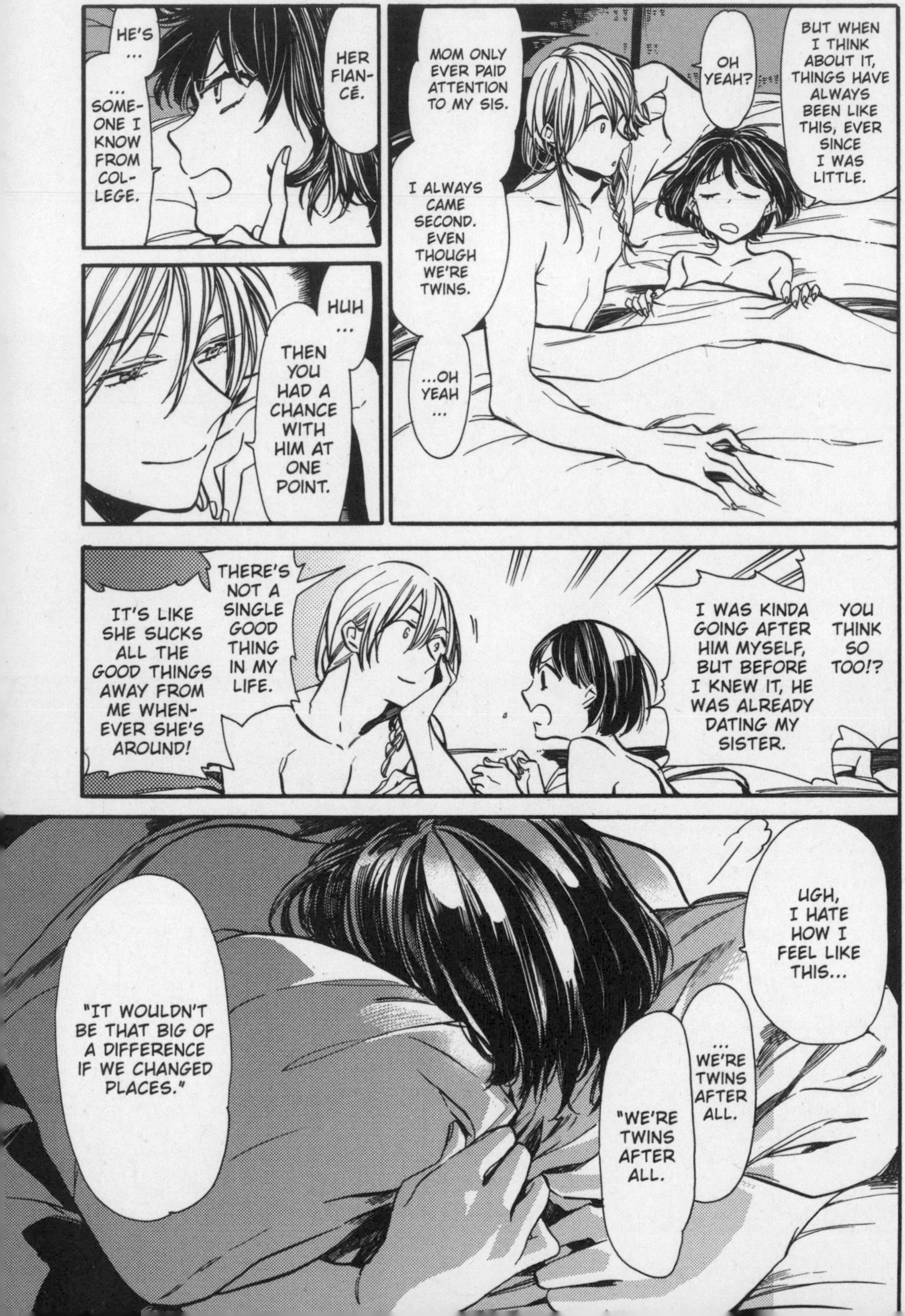
BUT WHEN I THINK ABOUT IT, THINGS HAVE ALWAYS BEEN LIKE THIS, EVER SINCE I WAS LITTLE.
OH YEAH?
MOM ONLY EVER PAID ATTENTION TO MY SIS.
I ALWAYS CAME SECOND. EVEN THOUGH WE'RE TWINS.
...OH YEAH...
HER FIANCÉ.
HE'S... ...SOMEONE I KNOW FROM COLLEGE.
HUH... THEN YOU HAD A CHANCE WITH HIM AT ONE POINT.
YOU THINK SO TOO!?
I WAS KINDA GOING AFTER HIM MYSELF, BUT BEFORE I KNEW IT, HE WAS ALREADY DATING MY SISTER.
THERE'S NOT A SINGLE GOOD THING IN MY LIFE.
IT'S LIKE SHE SUCKS ALL THE GOOD THINGS AWAY FROM ME WHENEVER SHE'S AROUND!
UGH, I HATE HOW I FEEL LIKE THIS...
...WE'RE TWINS AFTER ALL.
"WE'RE TWINS AFTER ALL.
"IT WOULDN'T BE THAT BIG OF A DIFFERENCE IF WE CHANGED PLACES."

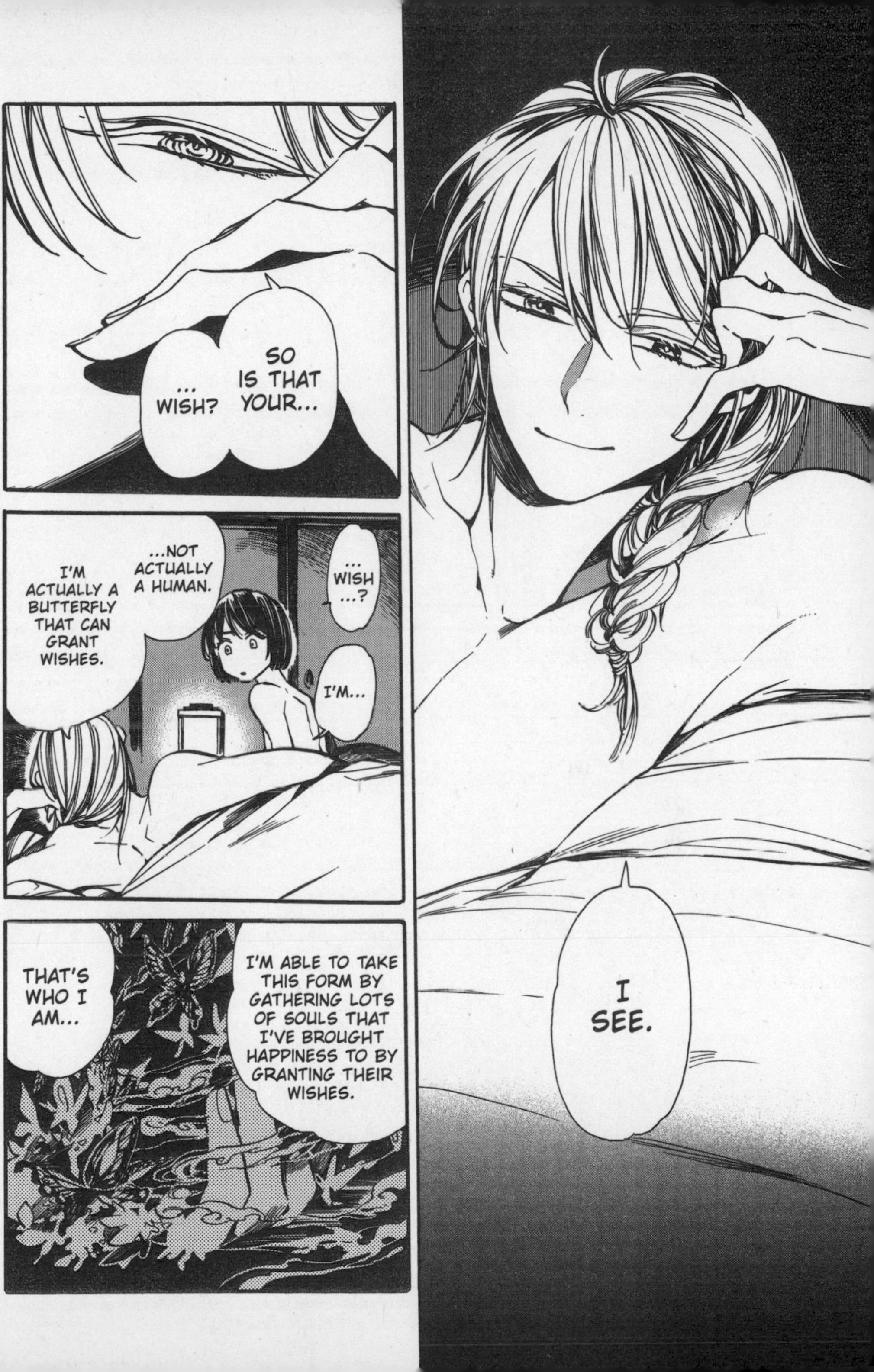
I SEE.
SO IS THAT YOUR...
...WISH?
...WISH...?
I'M...
...NOT ACTUALLY A HUMAN.
I'M ACTUALLY A BUTTERFLY THAT CAN GRANT WISHES.
I'M ABLE TO TAKE THIS FORM BY GATHERING LOTS OF SOULS THAT I'VE BROUGHT HAPPINESS TO BY GRANTING THEIR WISHES.
THAT'S WHO I AM...

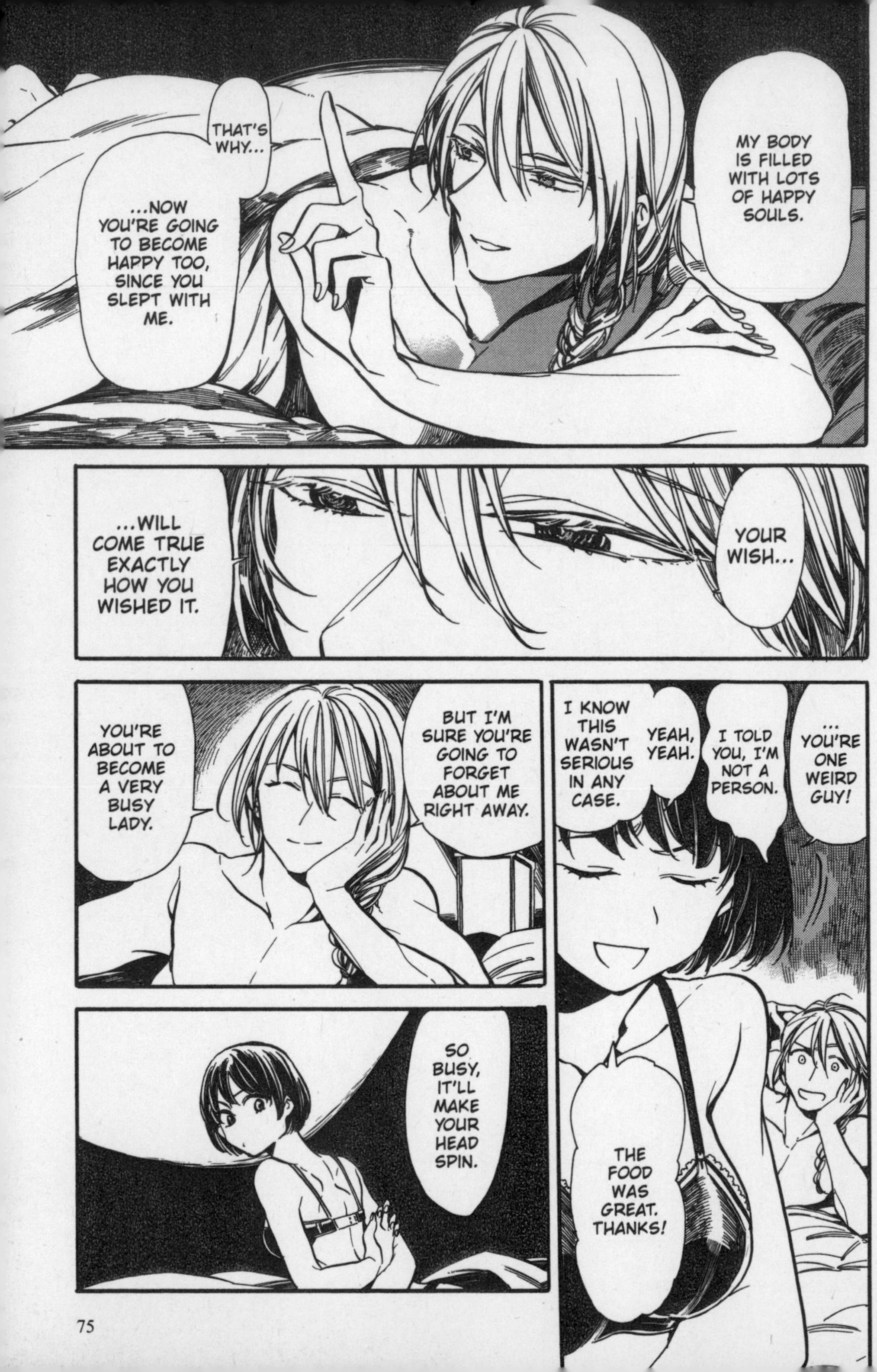
MY BODY IS FILLED WITH LOTS OF HAPPY SOULS.
THAT'S WHY...
...NOW YOU'RE GOING TO BECOME HAPPY TOO, SINCE YOU SLEPT WITH ME.
YOUR WISH...
...WILL COME TRUE EXACTLY HOW YOU WISHED IT.
BUT I'M SURE YOU'RE GOING TO FORGET ABOUT ME RIGHT AWAY.
YOU'RE ABOUT TO BECOME A VERY BUSY LADY.
SO BUSY, IT'LL MAKE YOUR HEAD SPIN.
...YOU'RE ONE WEIRD GUY!
I TOLD YOU, I'M NOT A PERSON.
YEAH, YEAH.
I KNOW THIS WASN'T SERIOUS IN ANY CASE.
THE FOOD WAS GREAT. THANKS!

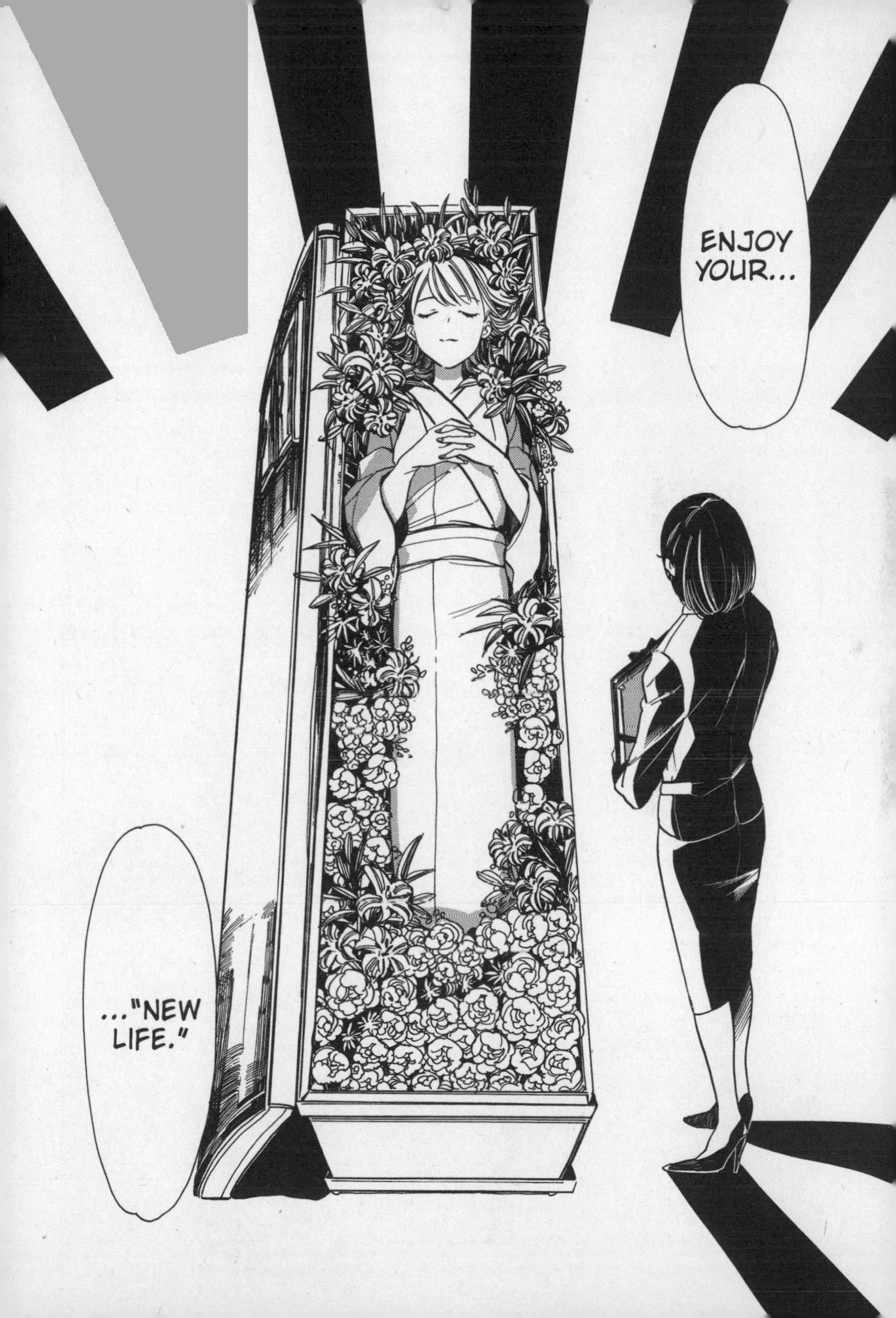
ENJOY YOUR...
..."NEW LIFE."

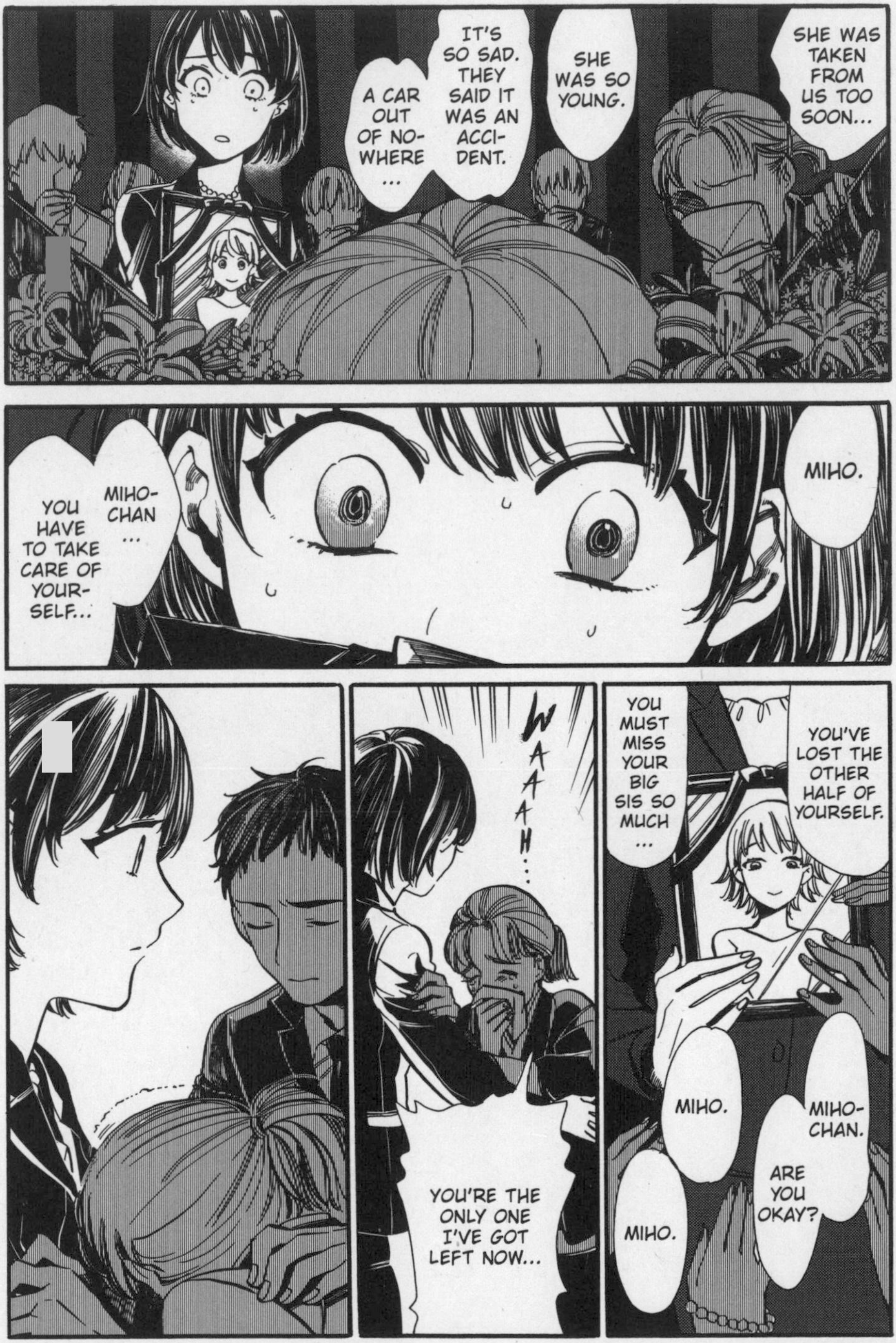
SHE WAS TAKEN FROM US TOO SOON...
SHE WAS SO YOUNG.
IT'S SO SAD. THEY SAID IT WAS AN ACCIDENT.
A CAR OUT OF NO-WHERE ...
MIHO.
MIHO-CHAN ...
YOU HAVE TO TAKE CARE OF YOUR-SELF...
YOU'VE LOST THE OTHER HALF OF YOURSELF.
YOU MUST MISS YOUR BIG SIS SO MUCH ...
MIHO-CHAN.
MIHO.
ARE YOU OKAY?
MIHO.
WAAAAH...
YOU'RE THE ONLY ONE I'VE GOT LEFT NOW...

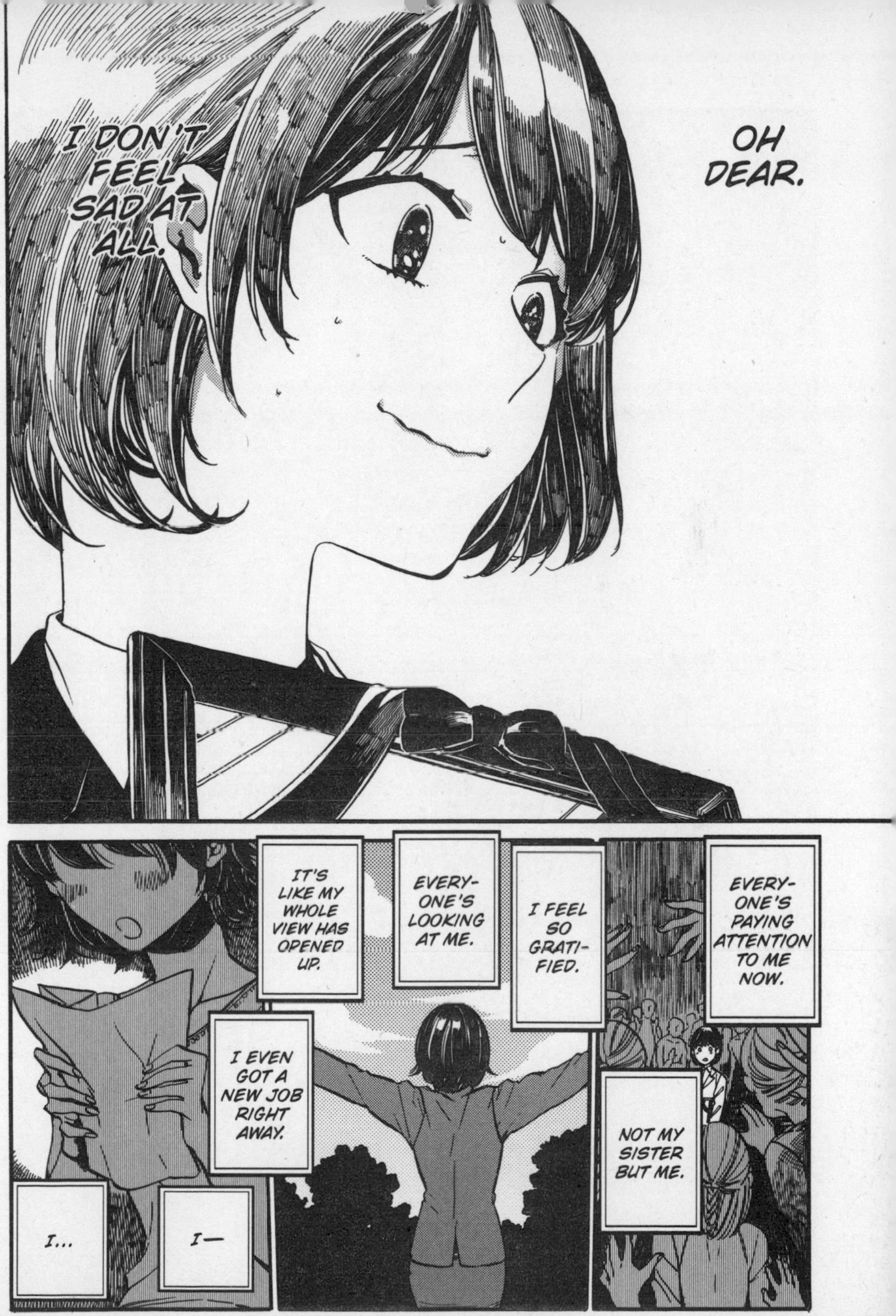
OH DEAR.
I DON'T FEEL SAD AT ALL.
EVERY-ONE'S PAYING ATTENTION TO ME NOW.
NOT MY SISTER BUT ME.
I FEEL SO GRATI-FIED.
EVERY-ONE'S LOOKING AT ME.
IT'S LIKE MY WHOLE VIEW HAS OPENED UP.
I EVEN GOT A NEW JOB RIGHT AWAY.
I—
I...

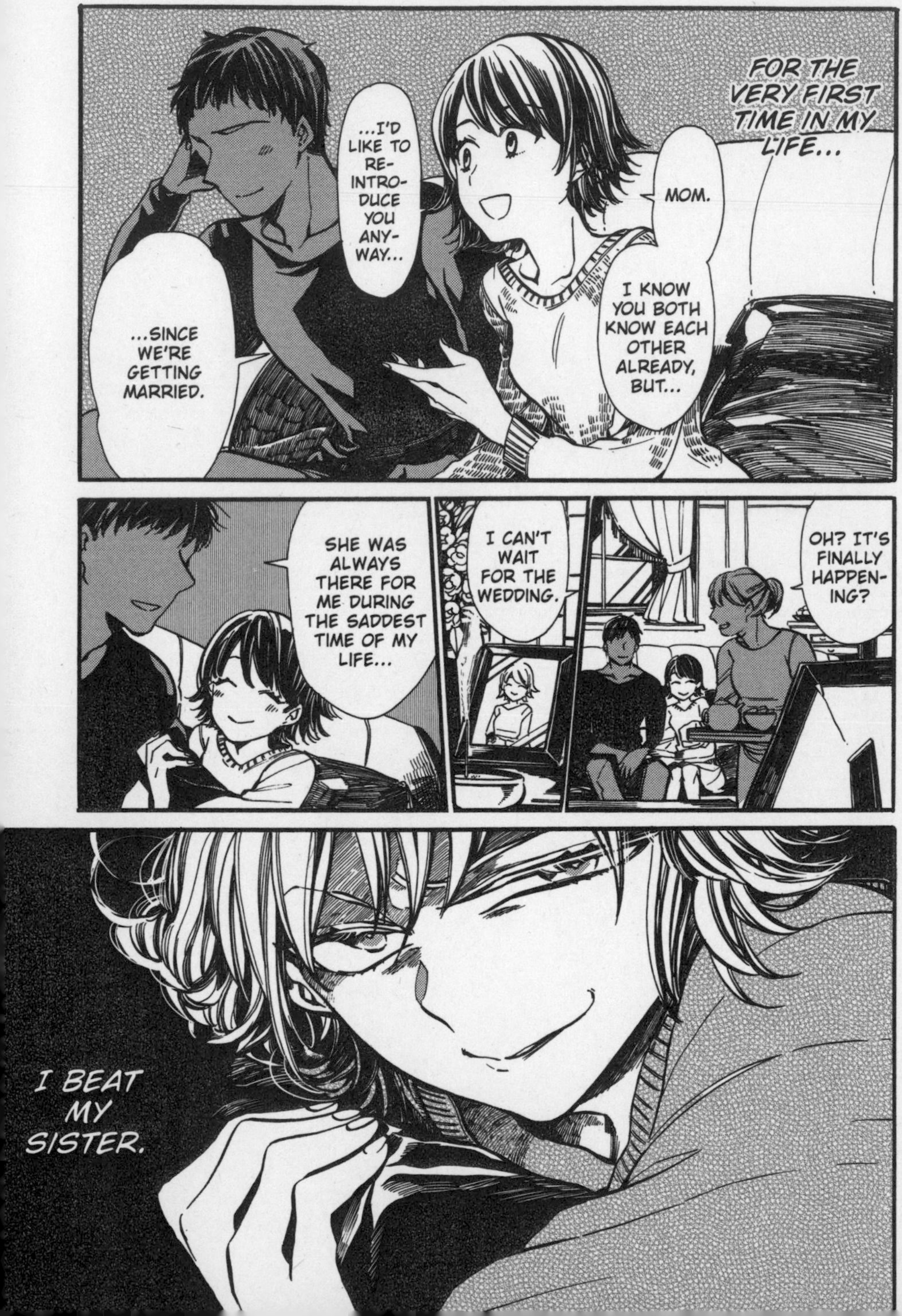
FOR THE VERY FIRST TIME IN MY LIFE...
MOM.
I KNOW YOU BOTH KNOW EACH OTHER ALREADY, BUT...
...I'D LIKE TO RE-INTRODUCE YOU ANYWAY...
...SINCE WE'RE GETTING MARRIED.
OH? IT'S FINALLY HAPPENING?
I CAN'T WAIT FOR THE WEDDING.
SHE WAS ALWAYS THERE FOR ME DURING THE SADDEST TIME OF MY LIFE...
I BEAT MY SISTER.

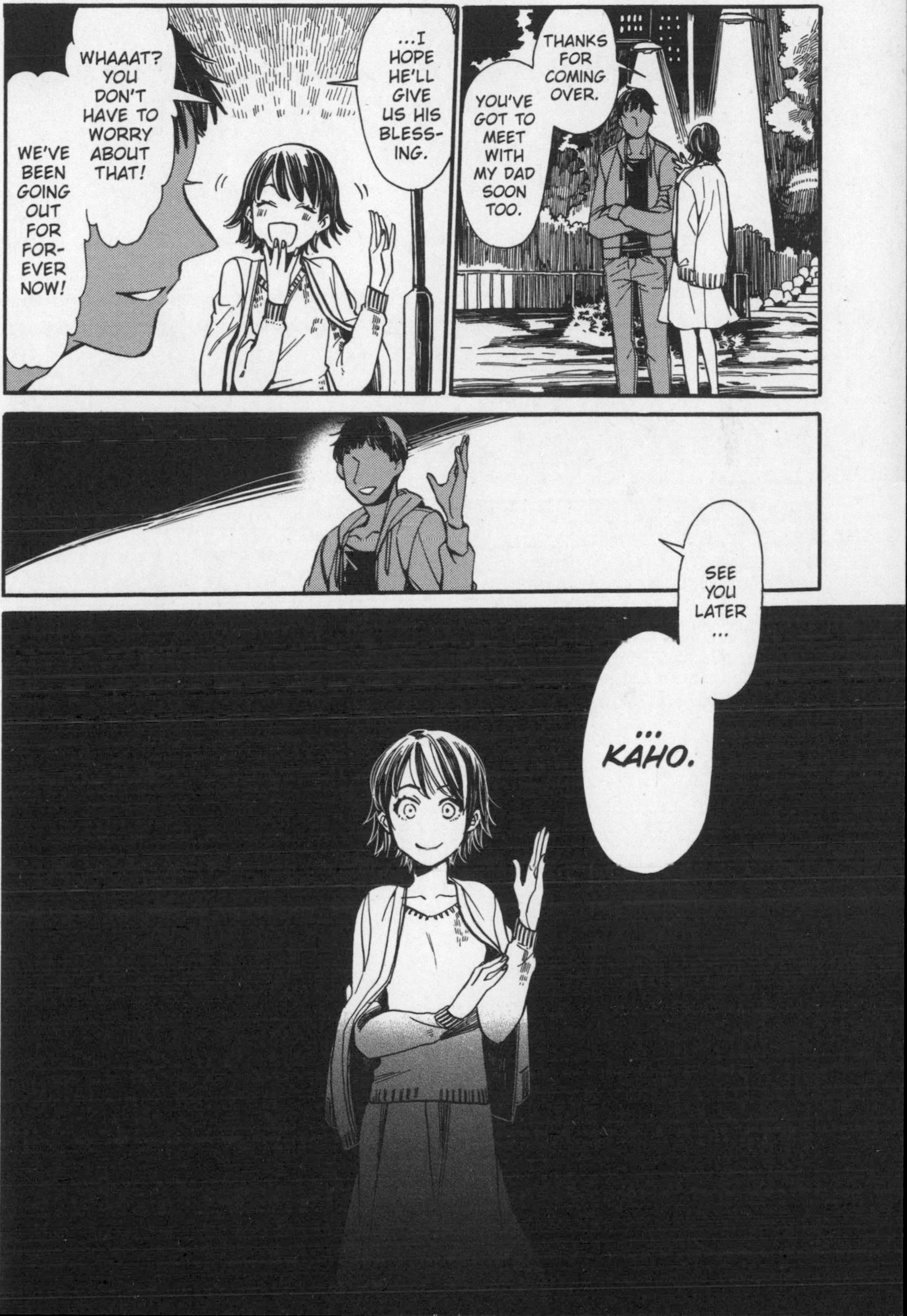
THANKS FOR COMING OVER.
YOU'VE GOT TO MEET WITH MY DAD SOON TOO.
...I HOPE HE'LL GIVE US HIS BLESS-ING.
WHAAAT? YOU DON'T HAVE TO WORRY ABOUT THAT!
WE'VE BEEN GOING OUT FOR FOR-EVER NOW!
SEE YOU LATER ...
... KAHO.

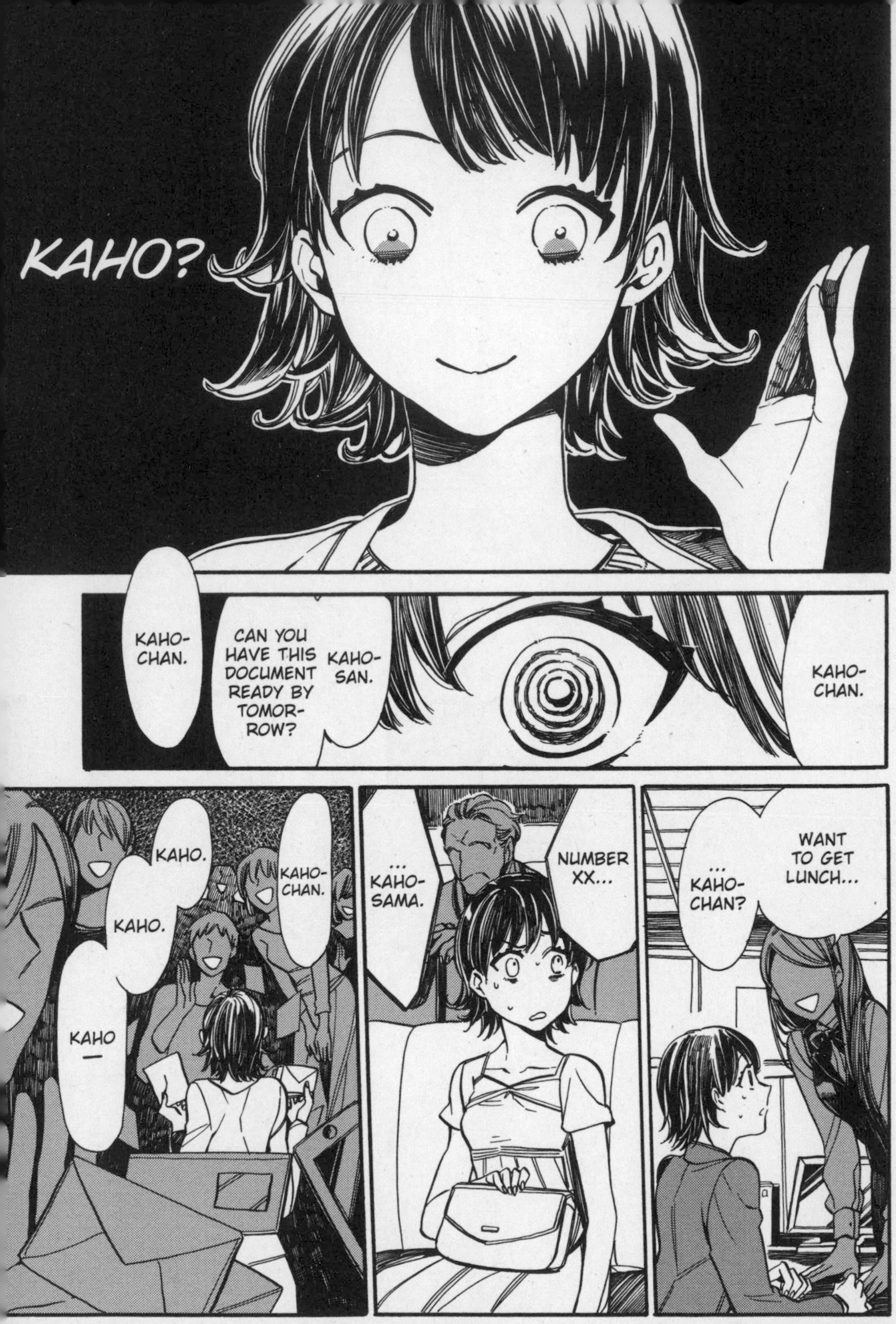
KAHO?
KAHO-CHAN.
KAHO-SAN.
CAN YOU HAVE THIS DOCUMENT READY BY TOMORROW?
KAHO-CHAN.
WANT TO GET LUNCH...
...KAHO-CHAN?
NUMBER XX...
...KAHO-SAMA.
KAHO-CHAN.
KAHO.
KAHO.
KAHO—

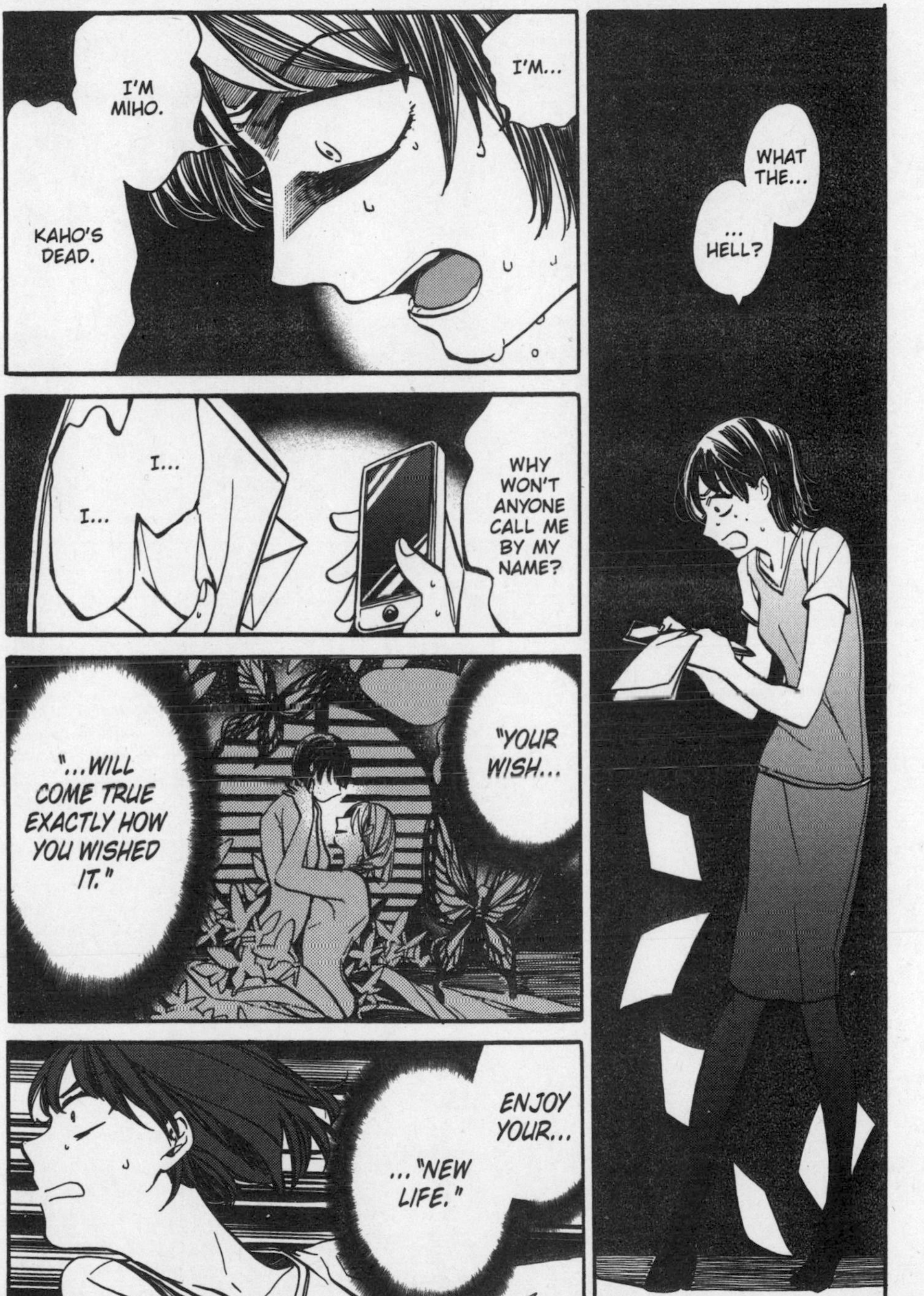
WHAT THE...
...HELL?
I'M...
I'M MIHO.
KAHO'S DEAD.
WHY WON'T ANYONE CALL ME BY MY NAME?
I...
I...
"YOUR WISH...
"...WILL COME TRUE EXACTLY HOW YOU WISHED IT."
ENJOY YOUR...
..."NEW LIFE."

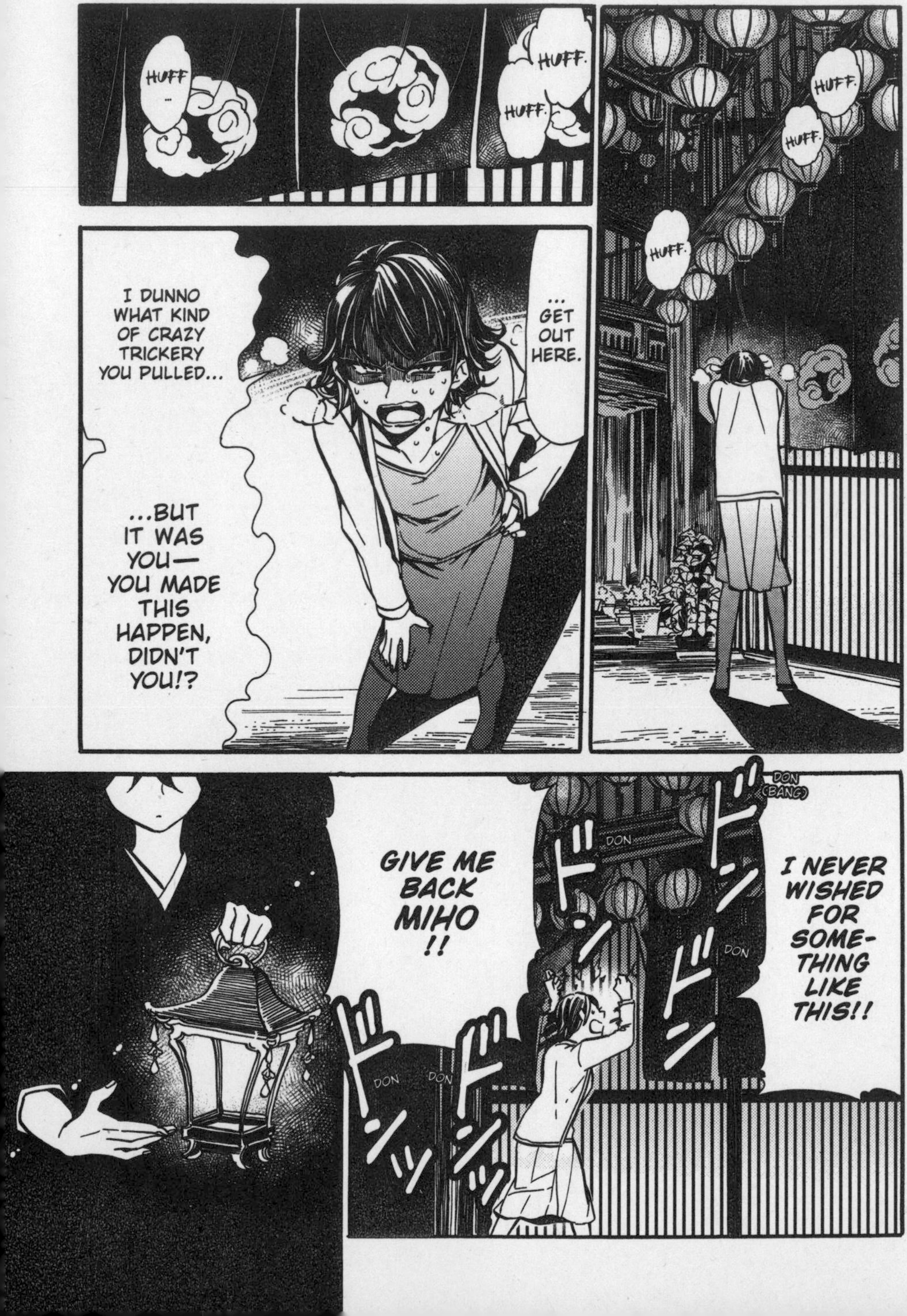
HUFF.
HUFF.
HUFF.
HUFF.
HUFF.
HUFF...
...GET OUT HERE.
I DUNNO WHAT KIND OF CRAZY TRICKERY YOU PULLED...
...BUT IT WAS YOU— YOU MADE THIS HAPPEN, DIDN'T YOU!?
DON (BANG)
I NEVER WISHED FOR SOME-THING LIKE THIS!!
DON
DON
GIVE ME BACK MIHO !!
DON
DON

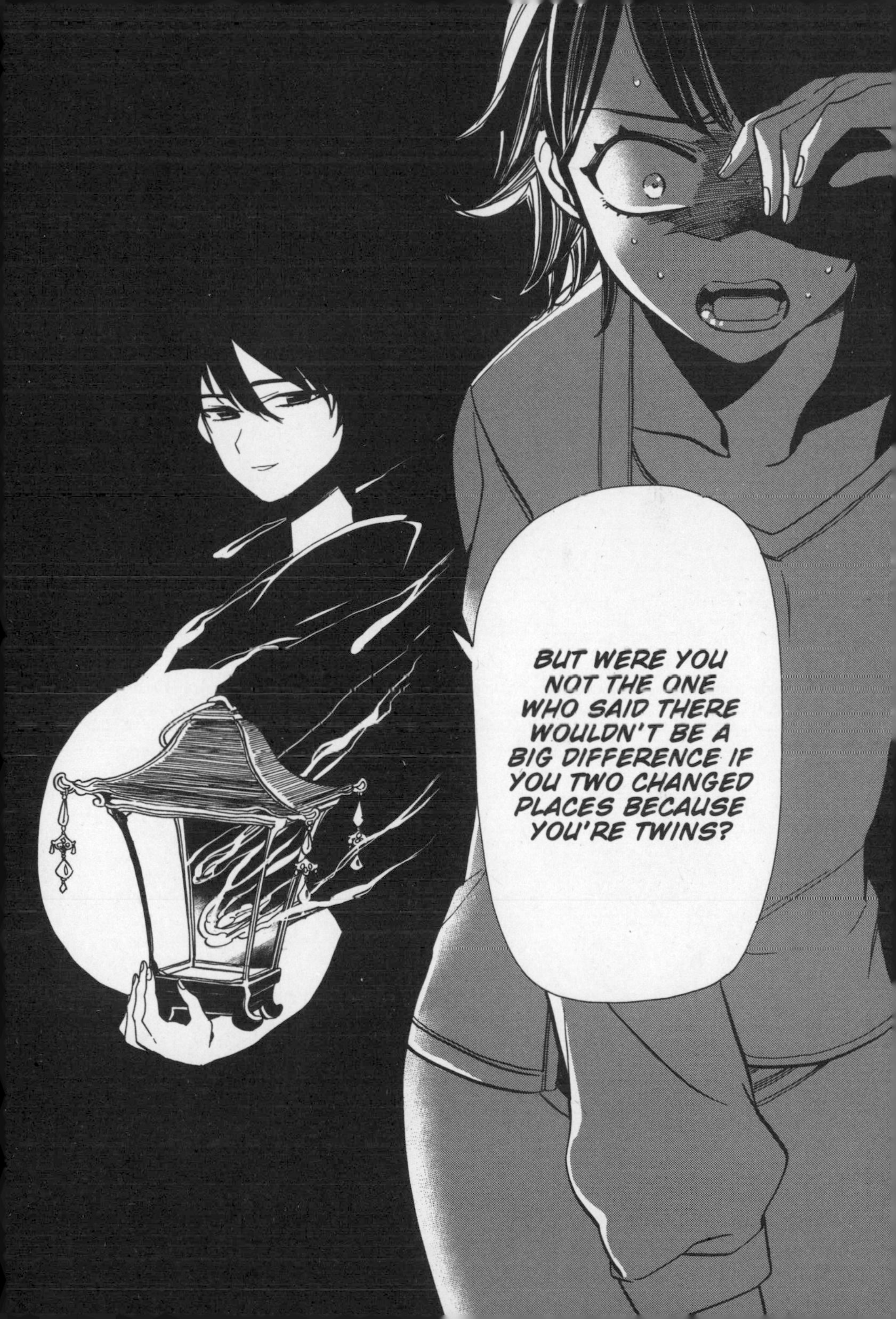
BUT WERE YOU NOT THE ONE WHO SAID THERE WOULDN'T BE A BIG DIFFERENCE IF YOU TWO CHANGED PLACES BECAUSE YOU'RE TWINS?

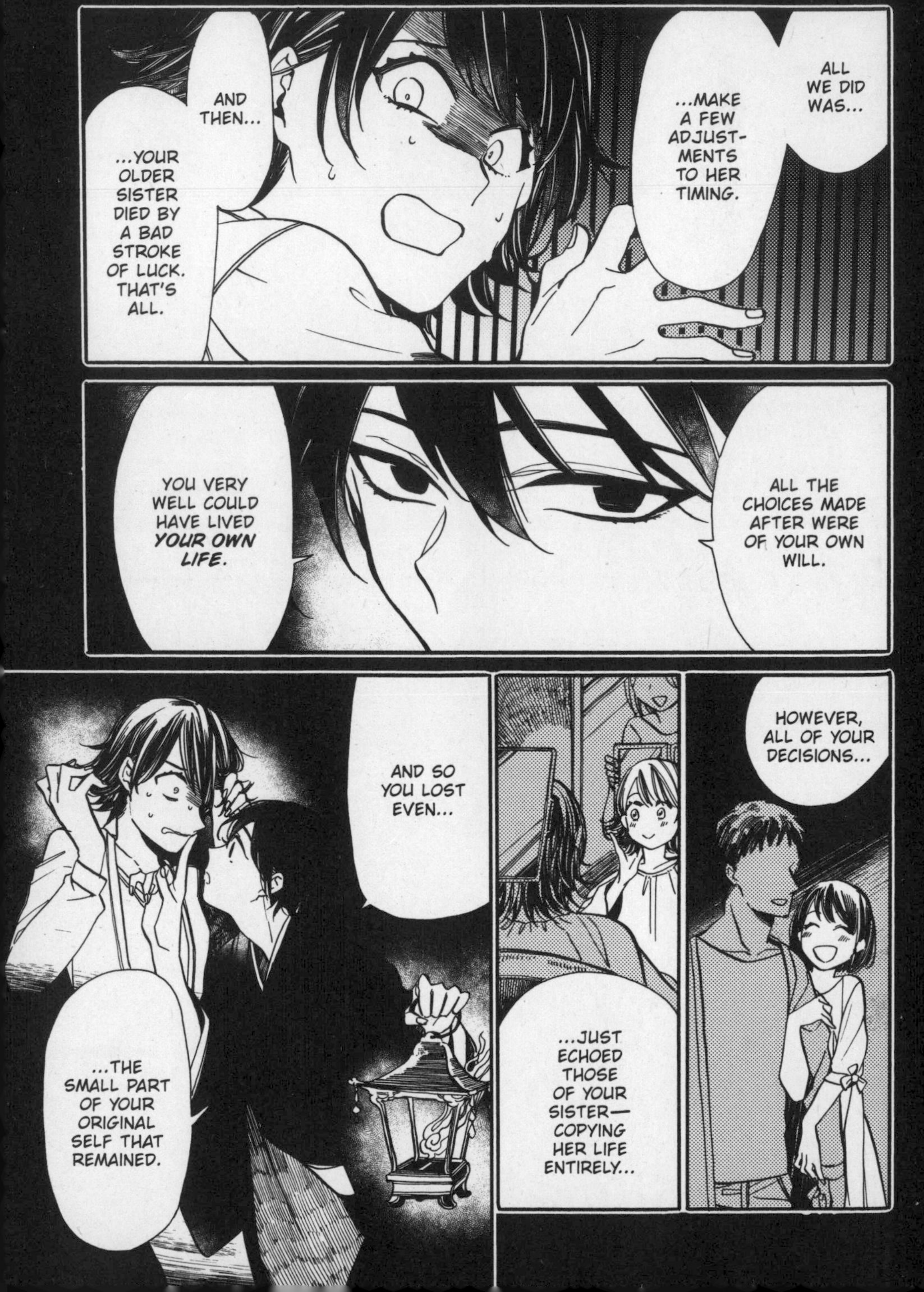
ALL WE DID WAS...
...MAKE A FEW ADJUSTMENTS TO HER TIMING.
AND THEN...
...YOUR OLDER SISTER DIED BY A BAD STROKE OF LUCK. THAT'S ALL.
ALL THE CHOICES MADE AFTER WERE OF YOUR OWN WILL.
YOU VERY WELL COULD HAVE LIVED ***YOUR OWN LIFE***.
HOWEVER, ALL OF YOUR DECISIONS...
...JUST ECHOED THOSE OF YOUR SISTER—COPYING HER LIFE ENTIRELY...
AND SO YOU LOST EVEN...
...THE SMALL PART OF YOUR ORIGINAL SELF THAT REMAINED.

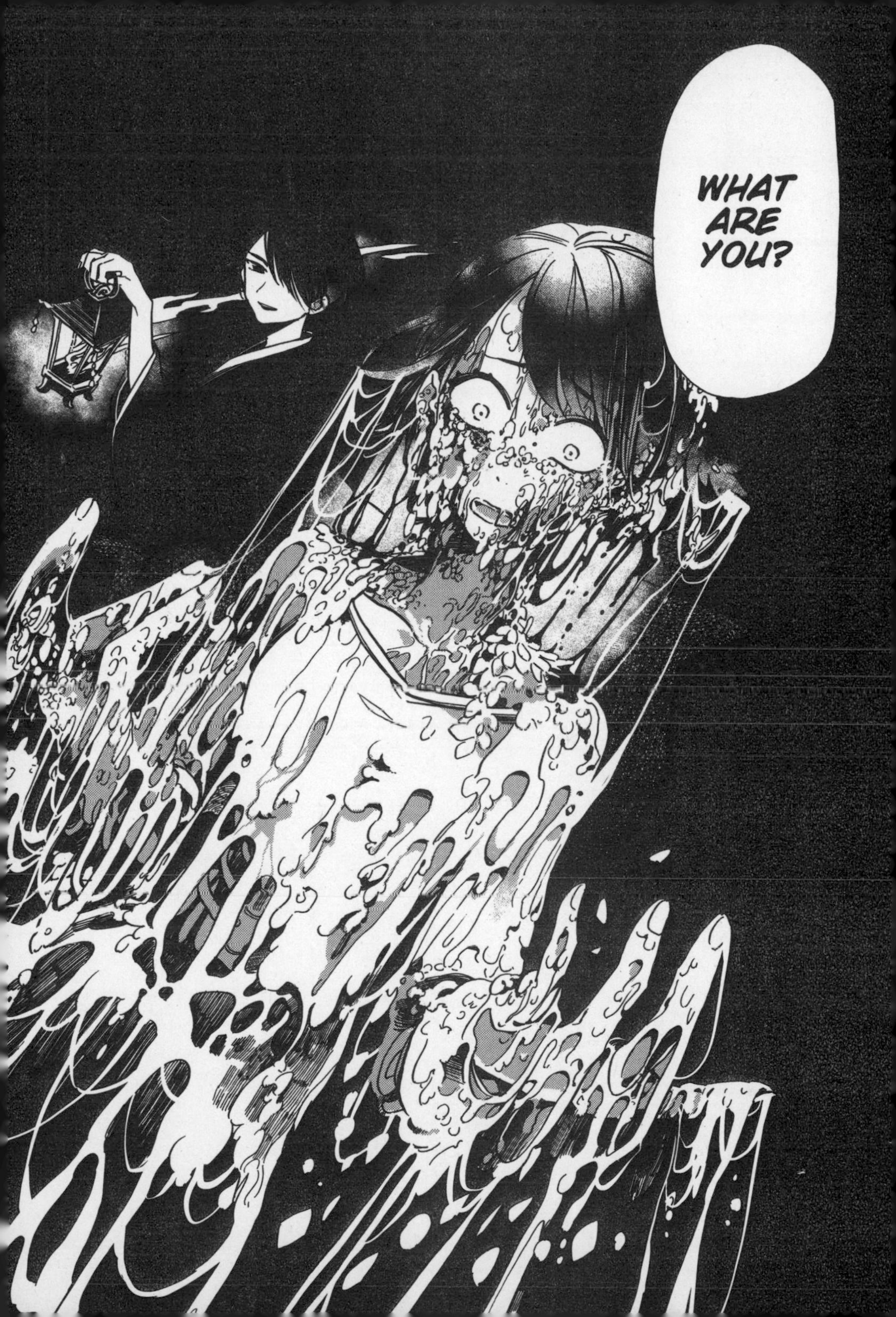
WHAT ARE YOU?

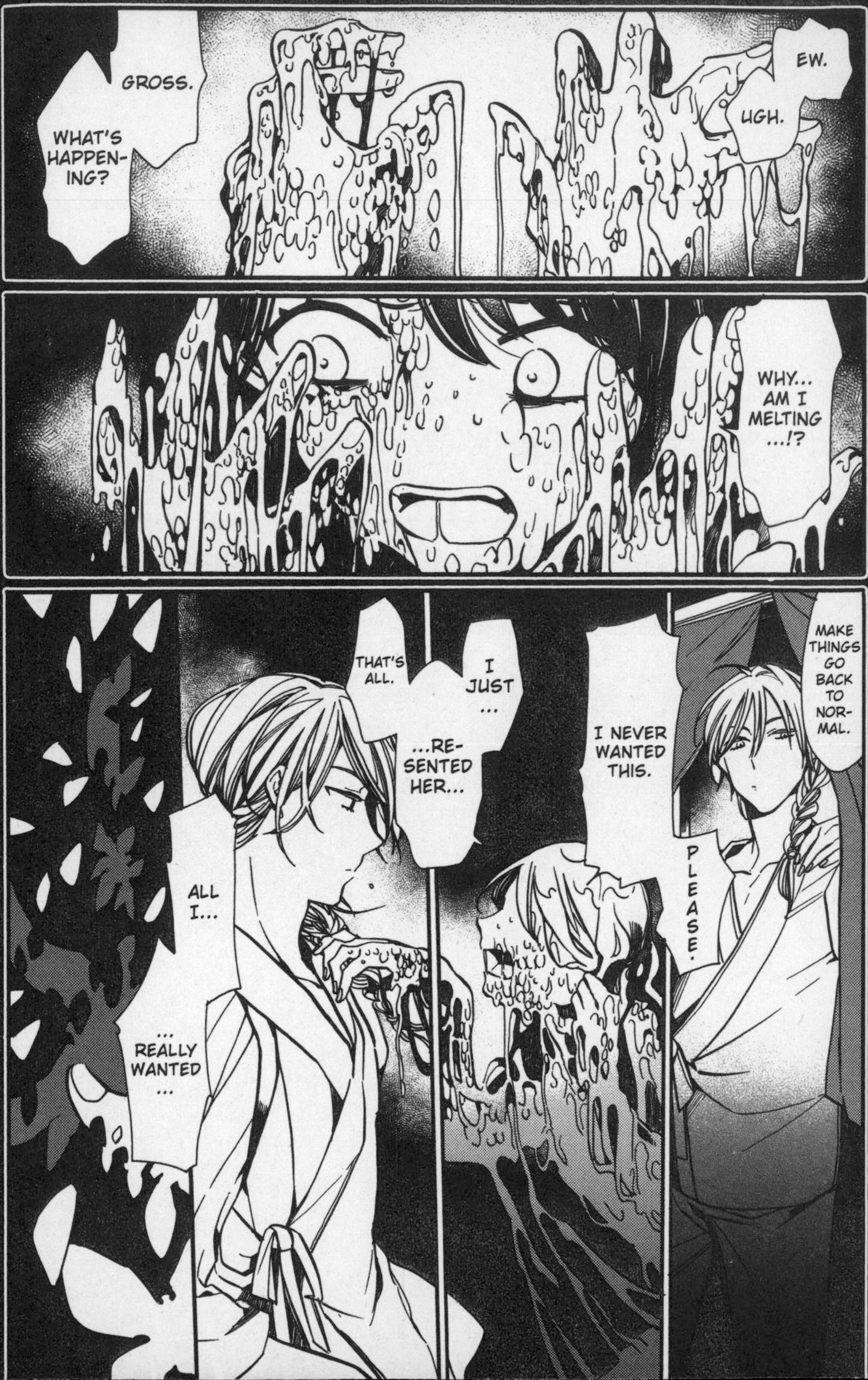
EW.
UGH.
GROSS.
WHAT'S HAPPEN-ING?
WHY... AM I MELTING ...!?
MAKE THINGS GO BACK TO NOR-MAL.
PLEASE.
I NEVER WANTED THIS.
I JUST ...
...RE-SENTED HER...
THAT'S ALL.
ALL I...
... REALLY WANTED ...

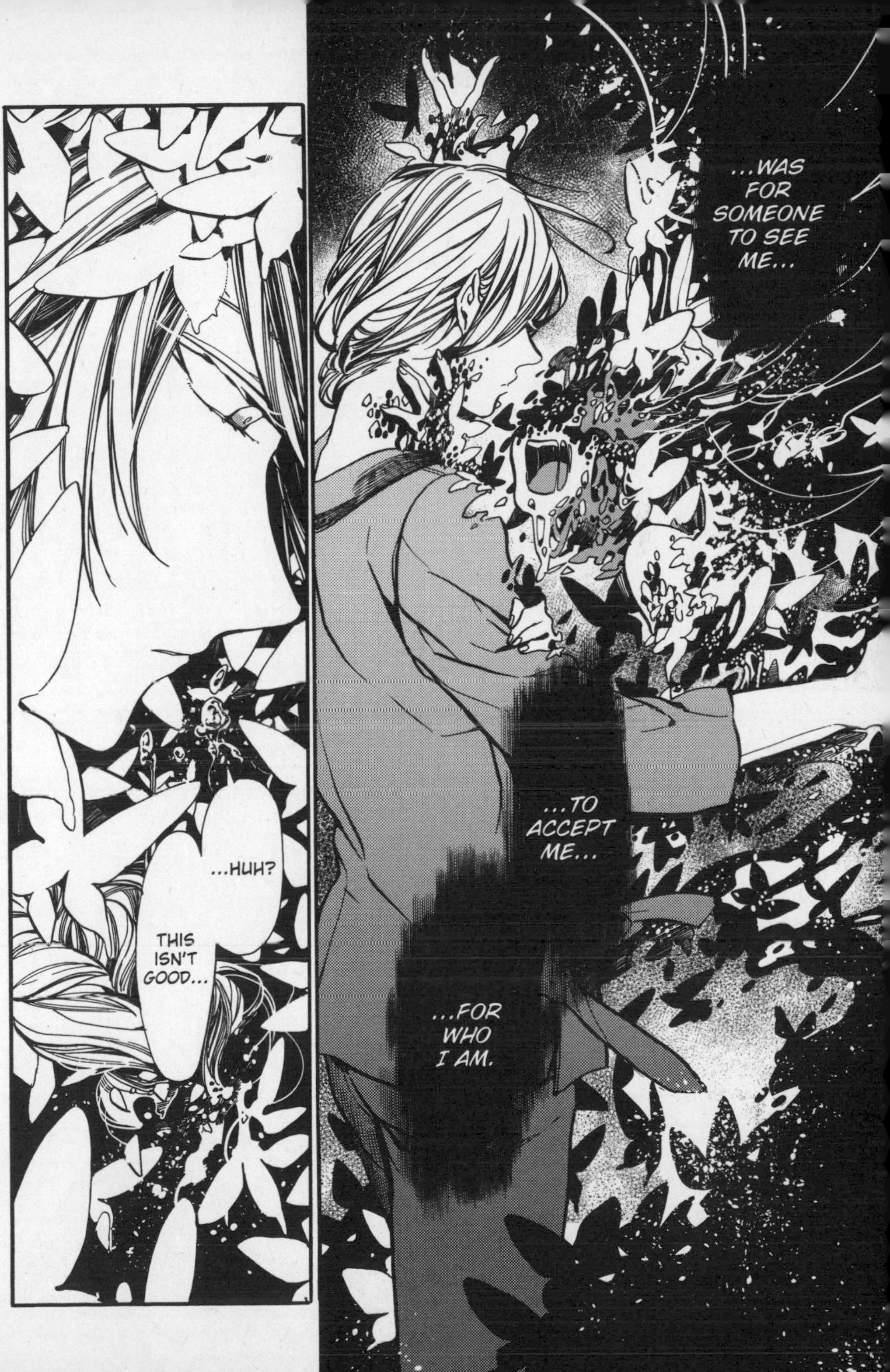
...WAS FOR SOMEONE TO SEE ME...
...TO ACCEPT ME...
...FOR WHO I AM.
...HUH?
THIS ISN'T GOOD...

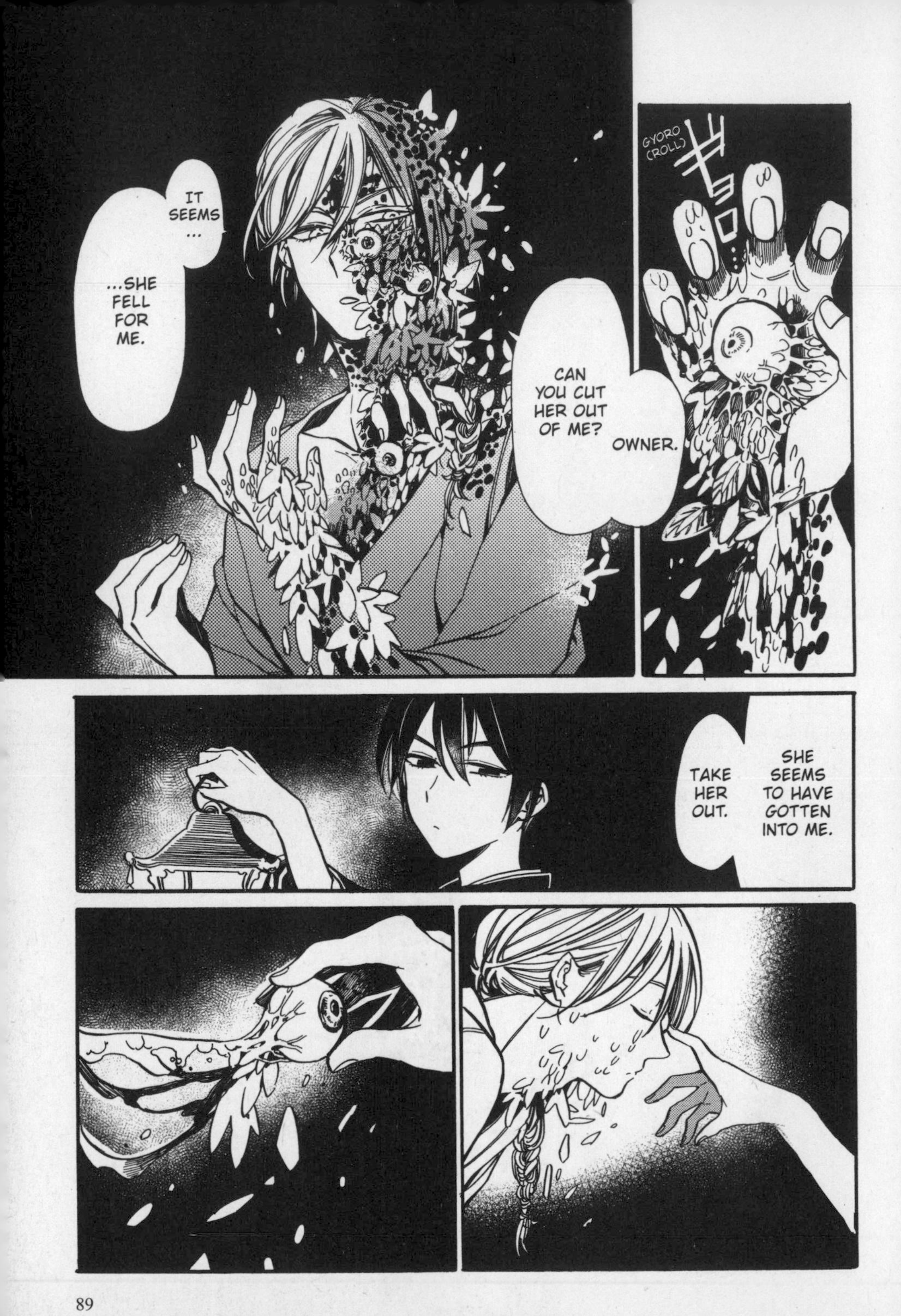
GYORO (ROLL)
IT SEEMS...
...SHE FELL FOR ME.
CAN YOU CUT HER OUT OF ME? OWNER.
SHE SEEMS TO HAVE GOTTEN INTO ME.
TAKE HER OUT.

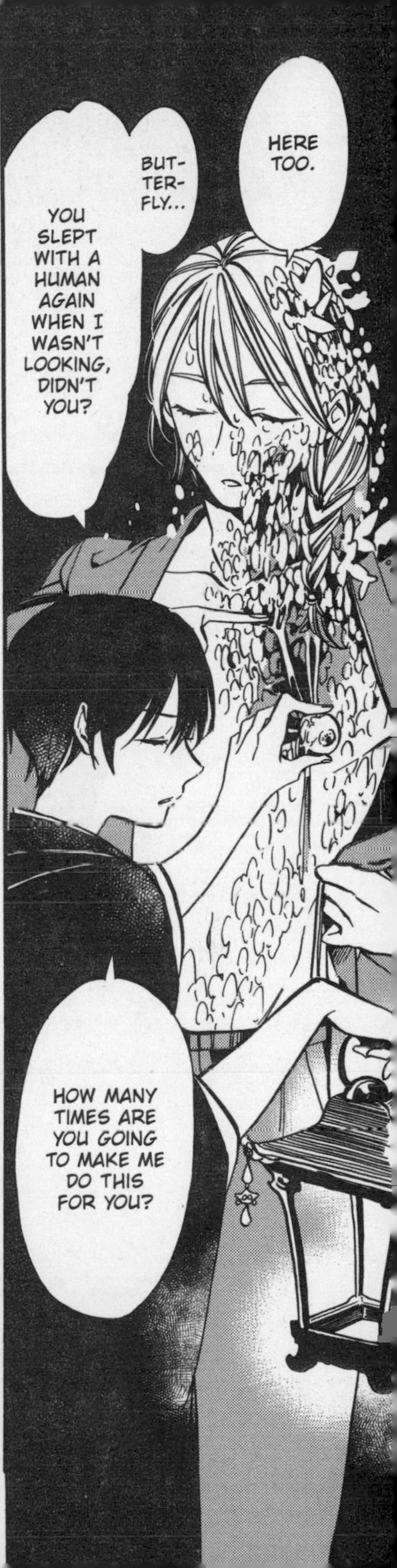
HERE TOO.
BUTTERFLY...
YOU SLEPT WITH A HUMAN AGAIN WHEN I WASN'T LOOKING, DIDN'T YOU?
HOW MANY TIMES ARE YOU GOING TO MAKE ME DO THIS FOR YOU?

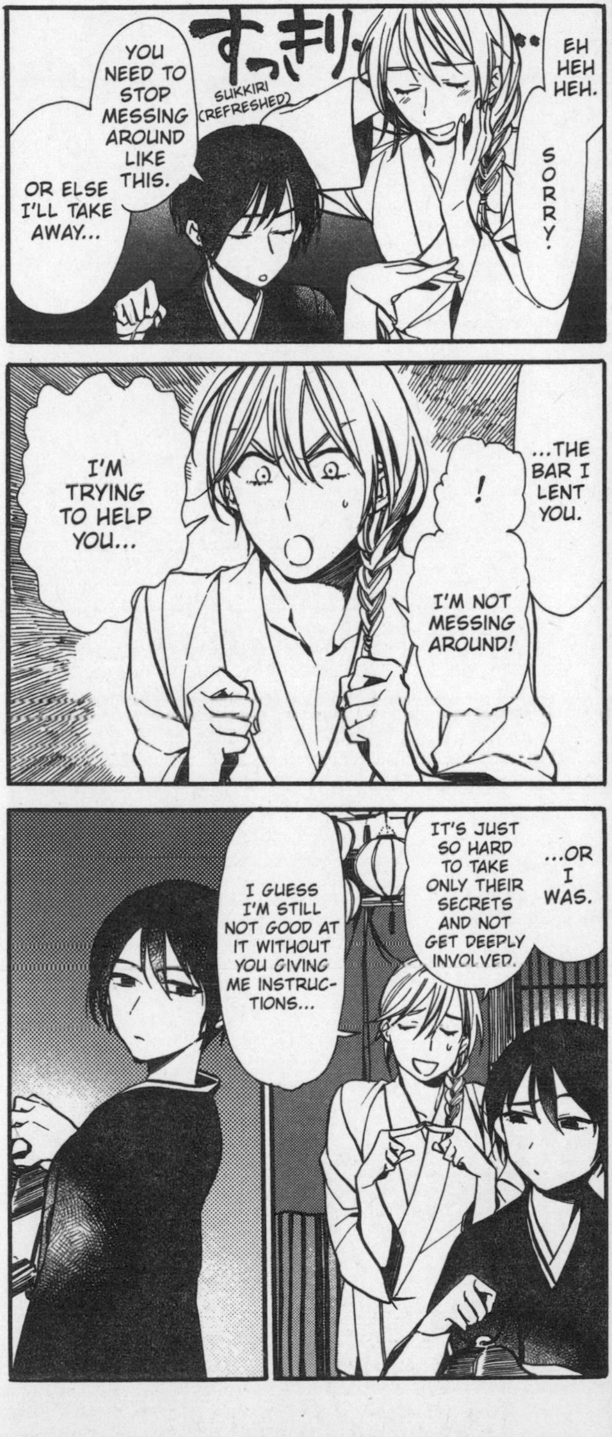
EH HEH HEH.
SORRY.
すっきり
SUKKIRI (REFRESHED)
YOU NEED TO STOP MESSING AROUND LIKE THIS.
OR ELSE I'LL TAKE AWAY...
...THE BAR I LENT YOU.
!
I'M NOT MESSING AROUND!
I'M TRYING TO HELP YOU...
...OR I WAS.
IT'S JUST SO HARD TO TAKE ONLY THEIR SECRETS AND NOT GET DEEPLY INVOLVED.
I GUESS I'M STILL NOT GOOD AT IT WITHOUT YOU GIVING ME INSTRUCTIONS...

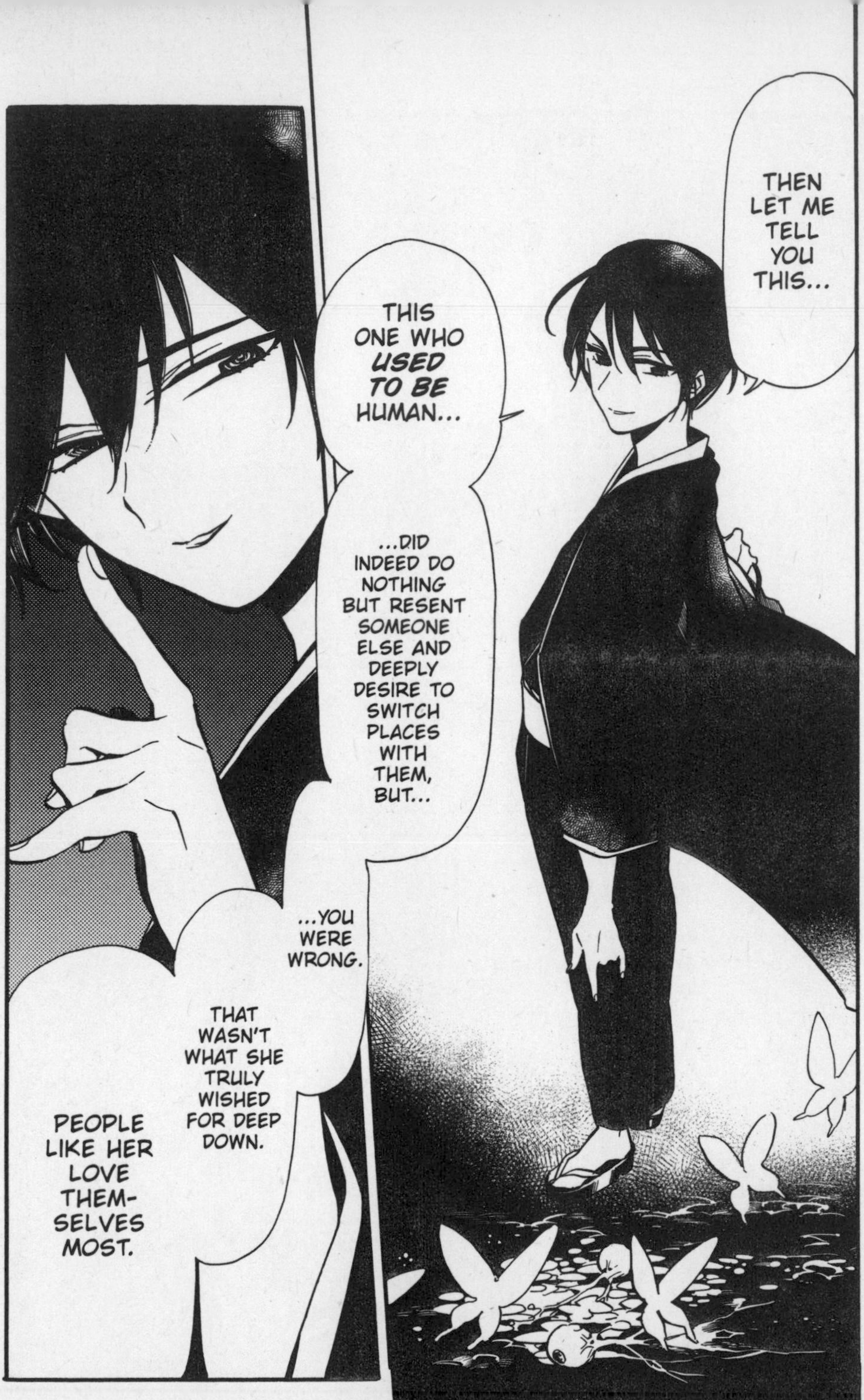
THEN LET ME TELL YOU THIS...
THIS ONE WHO *USED TO BE* HUMAN...
...DID INDEED DO NOTHING BUT RESENT SOMEONE ELSE AND DEEPLY DESIRE TO SWITCH PLACES WITH THEM, BUT...
...YOU WERE WRONG.
THAT WASN'T WHAT SHE TRULY WISHED FOR DEEP DOWN.
PEOPLE LIKE HER LOVE THEM-SELVES MOST.

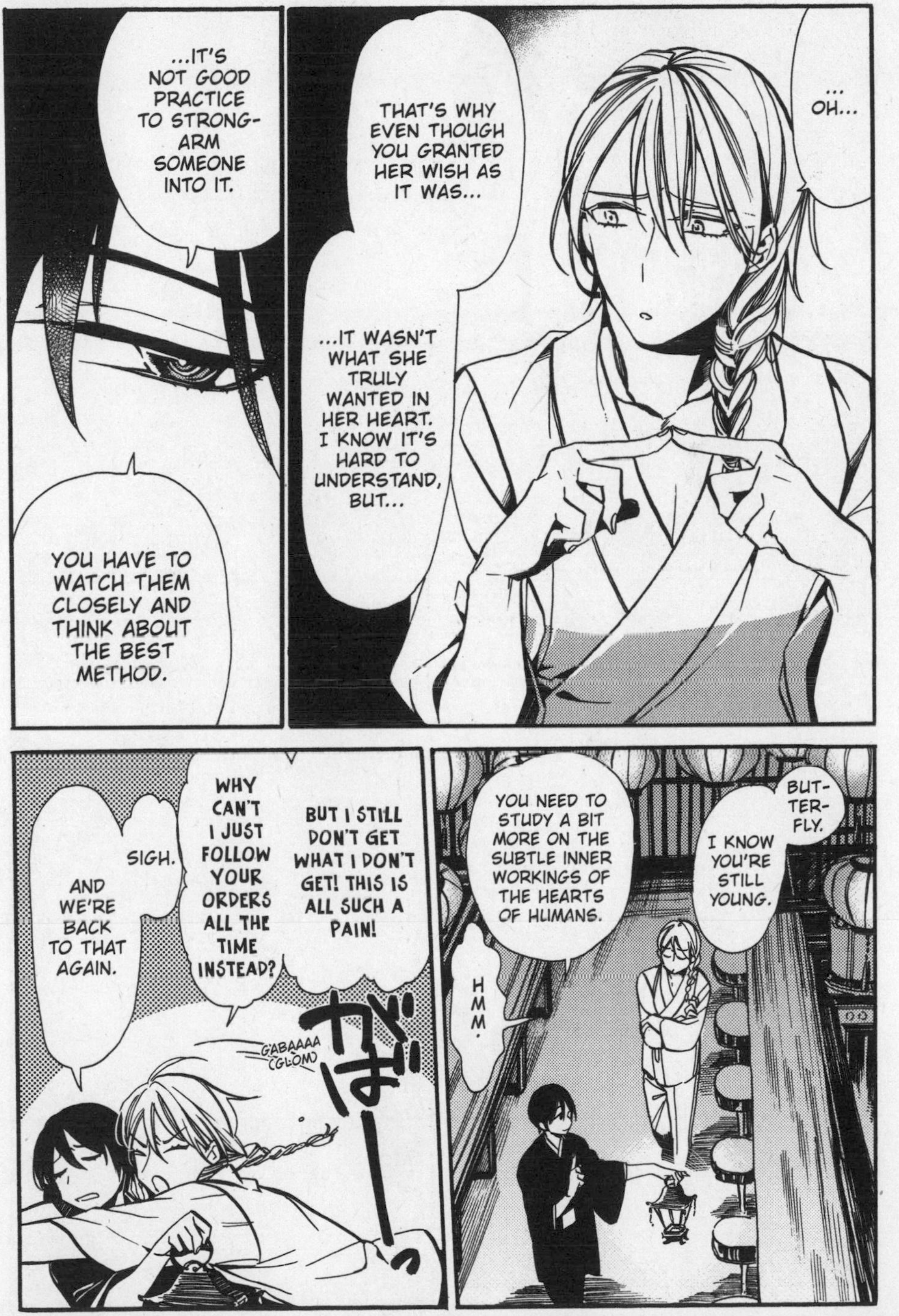
... OH...
THAT'S WHY EVEN THOUGH YOU GRANTED HER WISH AS IT WAS...
...IT WASN'T WHAT SHE TRULY WANTED IN HER HEART. I KNOW IT'S HARD TO UNDERSTAND, BUT...
...IT'S NOT GOOD PRACTICE TO STRONG-ARM SOMEONE INTO IT.
YOU HAVE TO WATCH THEM CLOSELY AND THINK ABOUT THE BEST METHOD.
BUT-TER-FLY.
I KNOW YOU'RE STILL YOUNG.
YOU NEED TO STUDY A BIT MORE ON THE SUBTLE INNER WORKINGS OF THE HEARTS OF HUMANS.
HMM.
BUT I STILL DON'T GET WHAT I DON'T GET! THIS IS ALL SUCH A PAIN!
WHY CAN'T I JUST FOLLOW YOUR ORDERS ALL THE TIME INSTEAD?
がばーっ
GABAAAA (GLOMP)
SIGH.
AND WE'RE BACK TO THAT AGAIN.

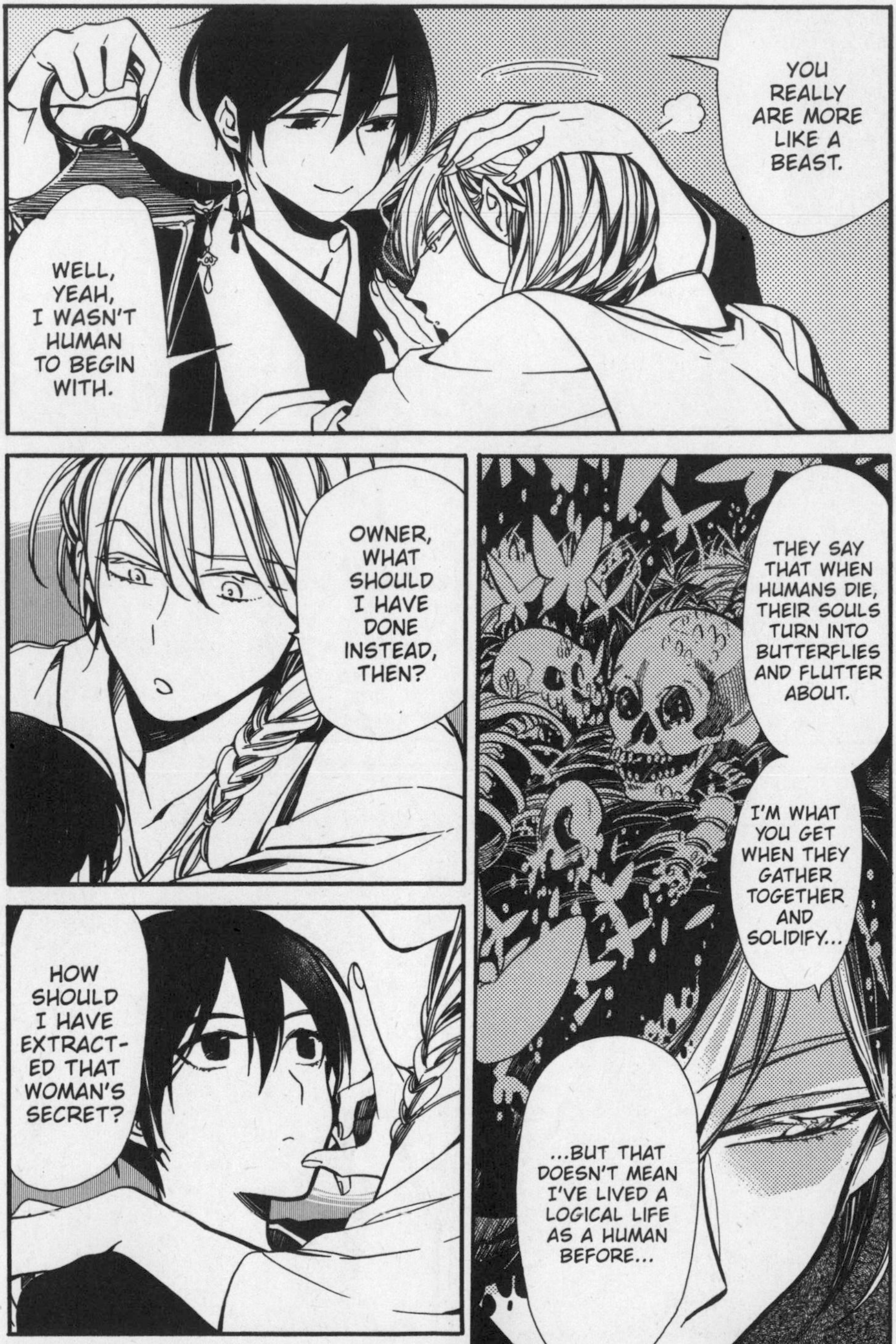
YOU REALLY ARE MORE LIKE A BEAST.
WELL, YEAH, I WASN'T HUMAN TO BEGIN WITH.
THEY SAY THAT WHEN HUMANS DIE, THEIR SOULS TURN INTO BUTTERFLIES AND FLUTTER ABOUT.
I'M WHAT YOU GET WHEN THEY GATHER TOGETHER AND SOLIDIFY...
...BUT THAT DOESN'T MEAN I'VE LIVED A LOGICAL LIFE AS A HUMAN BEFORE...
OWNER, WHAT SHOULD I HAVE DONE INSTEAD, THEN?
HOW SHOULD I HAVE EXTRACT-ED THAT WOMAN'S SECRET?

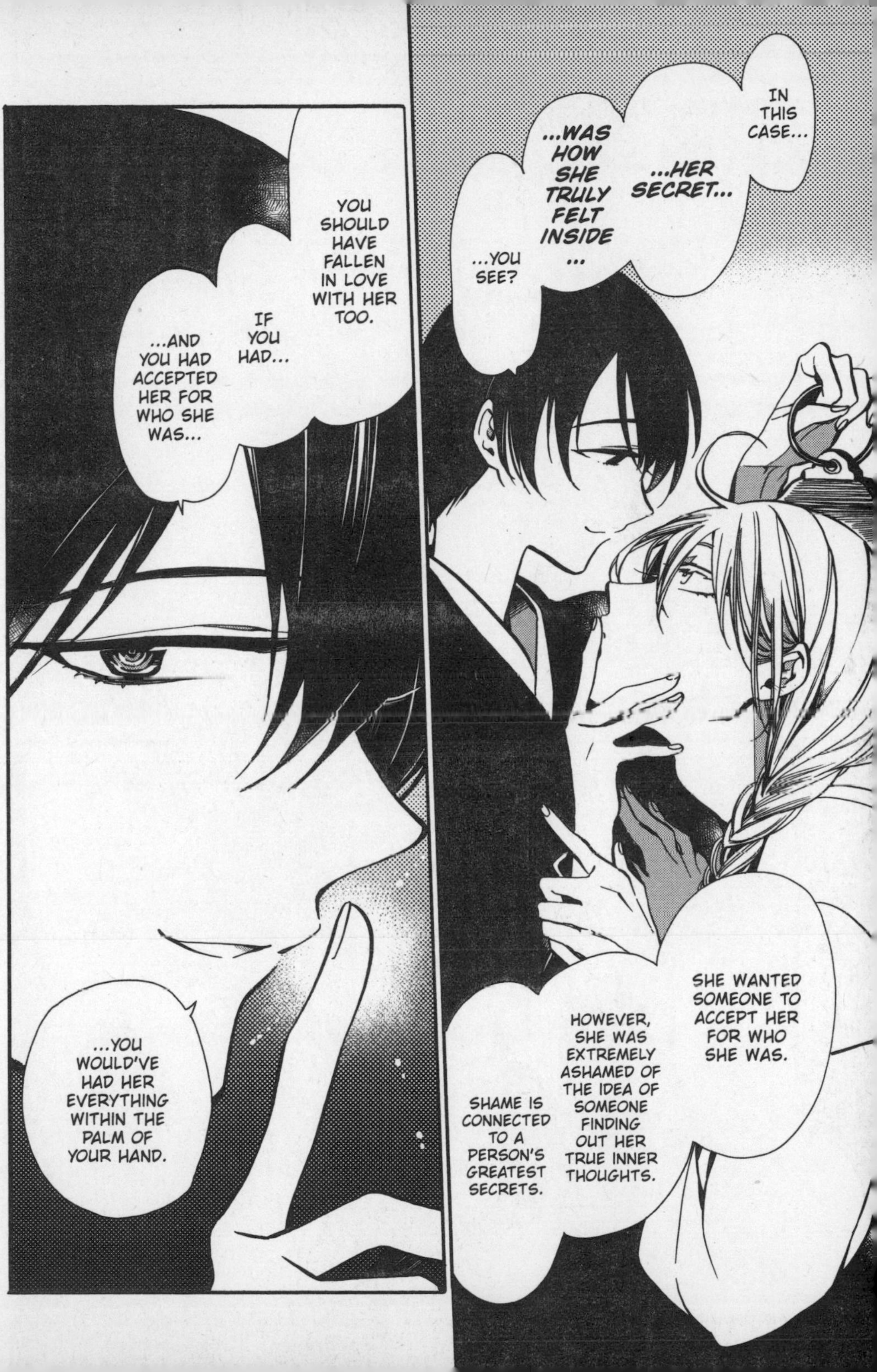
IN THIS CASE...
...HER SECRET...
...WAS HOW SHE TRULY FELT INSIDE...
...YOU SEE?
SHE WANTED SOMEONE TO ACCEPT HER FOR WHO SHE WAS.
HOWEVER, SHE WAS EXTREMELY ASHAMED OF THE IDEA OF SOMEONE FINDING OUT HER TRUE INNER THOUGHTS.
SHAME IS CONNECTED TO A PERSON'S GREATEST SECRETS.
YOU SHOULD HAVE FALLEN IN LOVE WITH HER TOO.
IF YOU HAD...
...AND YOU HAD ACCEPTED HER FOR WHO SHE WAS...
...YOU WOULD'VE HAD HER EVERYTHING WITHIN THE PALM OF YOUR HAND.

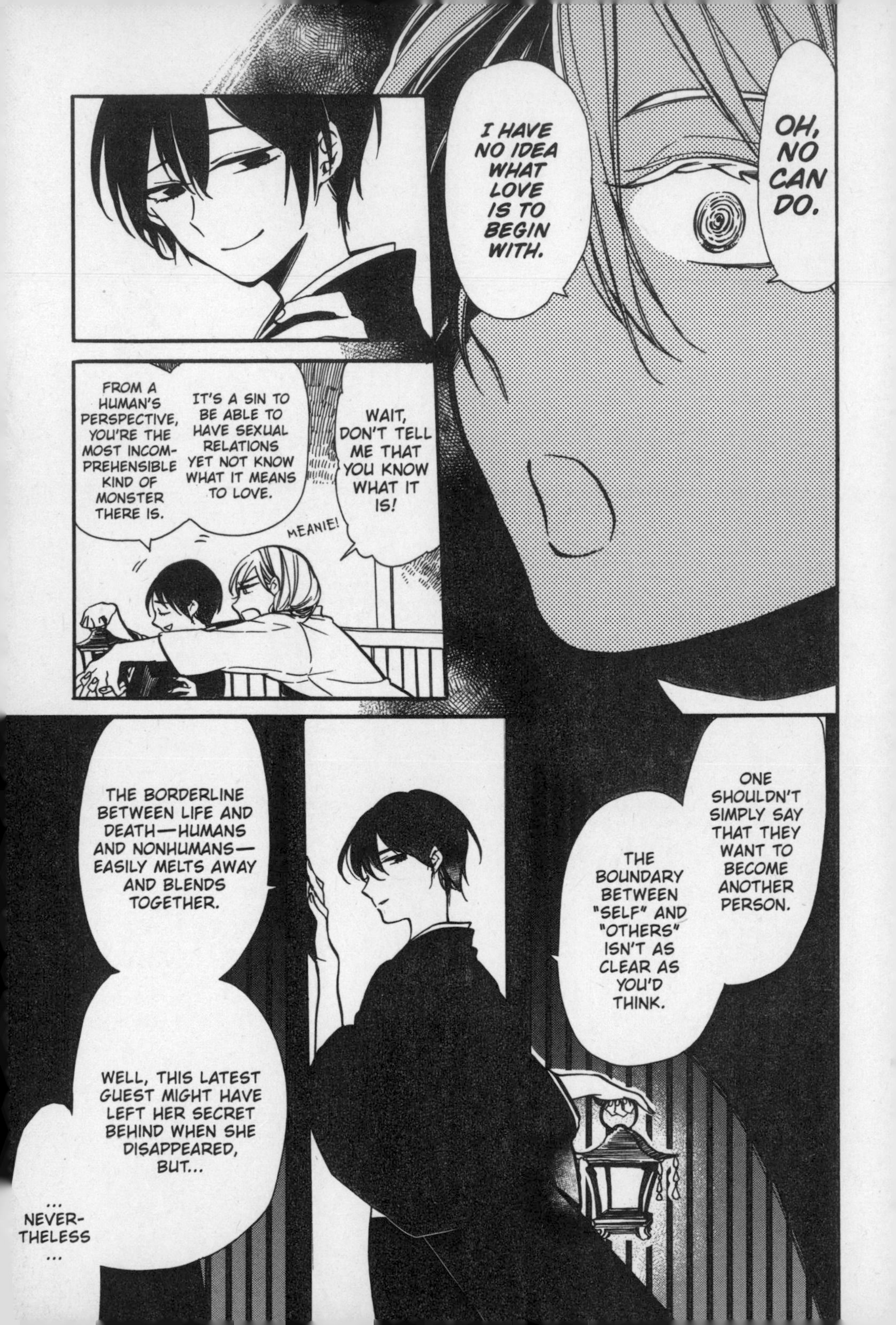
OH, NO CAN DO.
I HAVE NO IDEA WHAT LOVE IS TO BEGIN WITH.
WAIT, DON'T TELL ME THAT YOU KNOW WHAT IT IS!
MEANIE!
IT'S A SIN TO BE ABLE TO HAVE SEXUAL RELATIONS YET NOT KNOW WHAT IT MEANS TO LOVE.
FROM A HUMAN'S PERSPECTIVE, YOU'RE THE MOST INCOMPREHENSIBLE KIND OF MONSTER THERE IS.
ONE SHOULDN'T SIMPLY SAY THAT THEY WANT TO BECOME ANOTHER PERSON.
THE BOUNDARY BETWEEN "SELF" AND "OTHERS" ISN'T AS CLEAR AS YOU'D THINK.
THE BORDERLINE BETWEEN LIFE AND DEATH—HUMANS AND NONHUMANS—EASILY MELTS AWAY AND BLENDS TOGETHER.
WELL, THIS LATEST GUEST MIGHT HAVE LEFT HER SECRET BEHIND WHEN SHE DISAPPEARED, BUT...
...NEVERTHELESS...

...YOUR SECRET NOW BELONGS TO ME.

Second
Enigma

The
Butterfly
Who Grants
Wishes

Phantom Tales of the Night

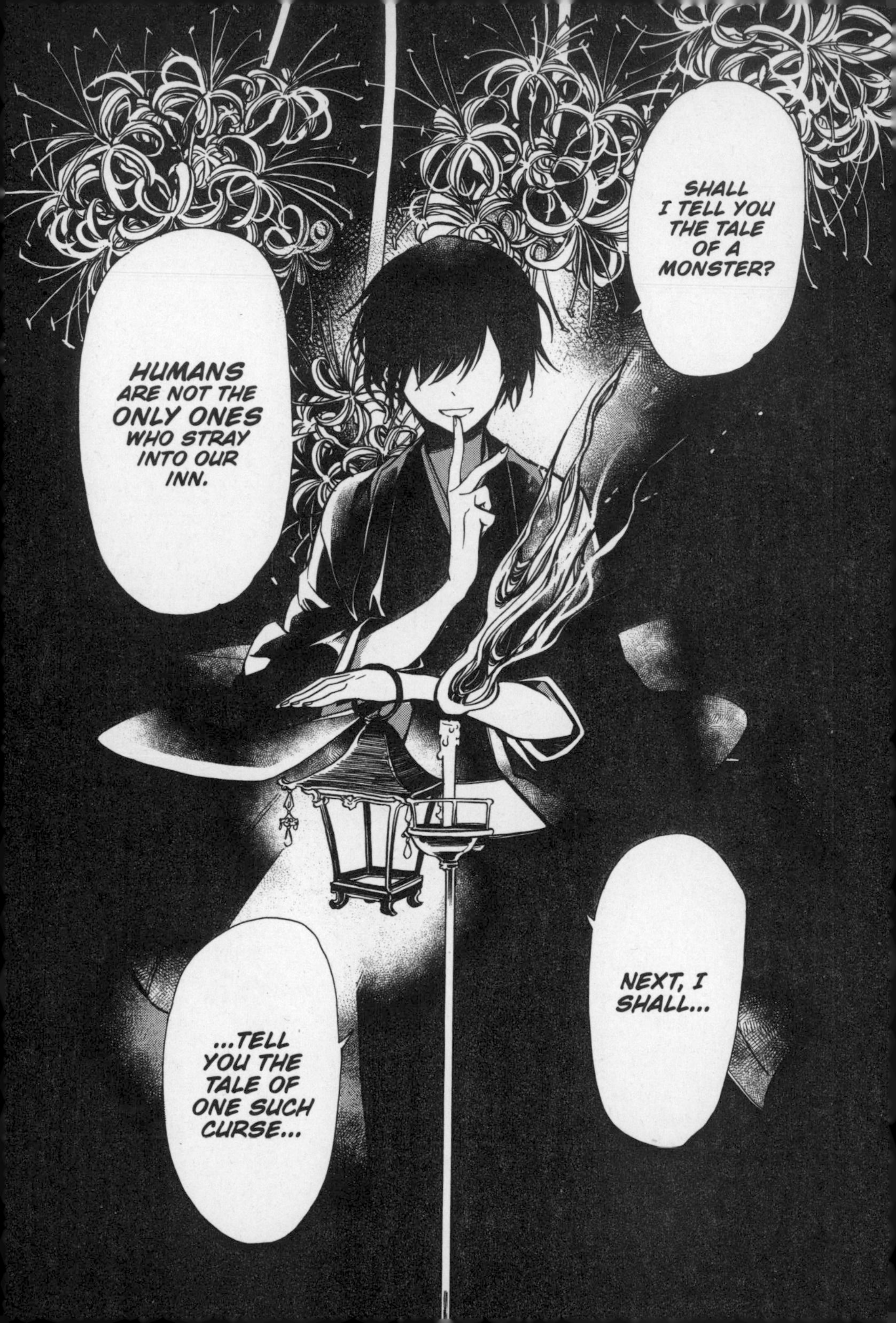
SHALL I TELL YOU THE TALE OF A MONSTER?
HUMANS ARE NOT THE ONLY ONES WHO STRAY INTO OUR INN.
NEXT, I SHALL...
...TELL YOU THE TALE OF ONE SUCH CURSE...

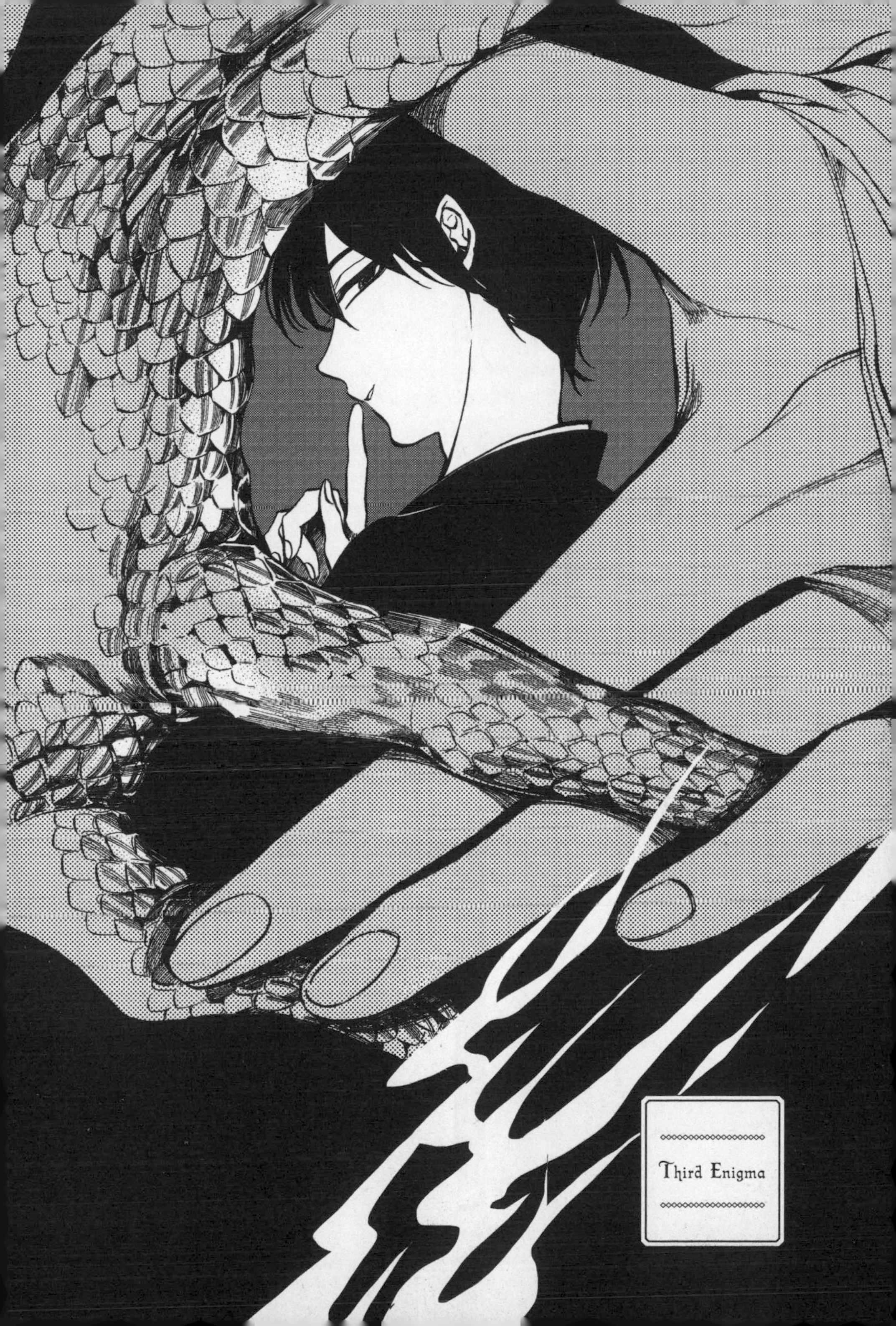
Third Enigma

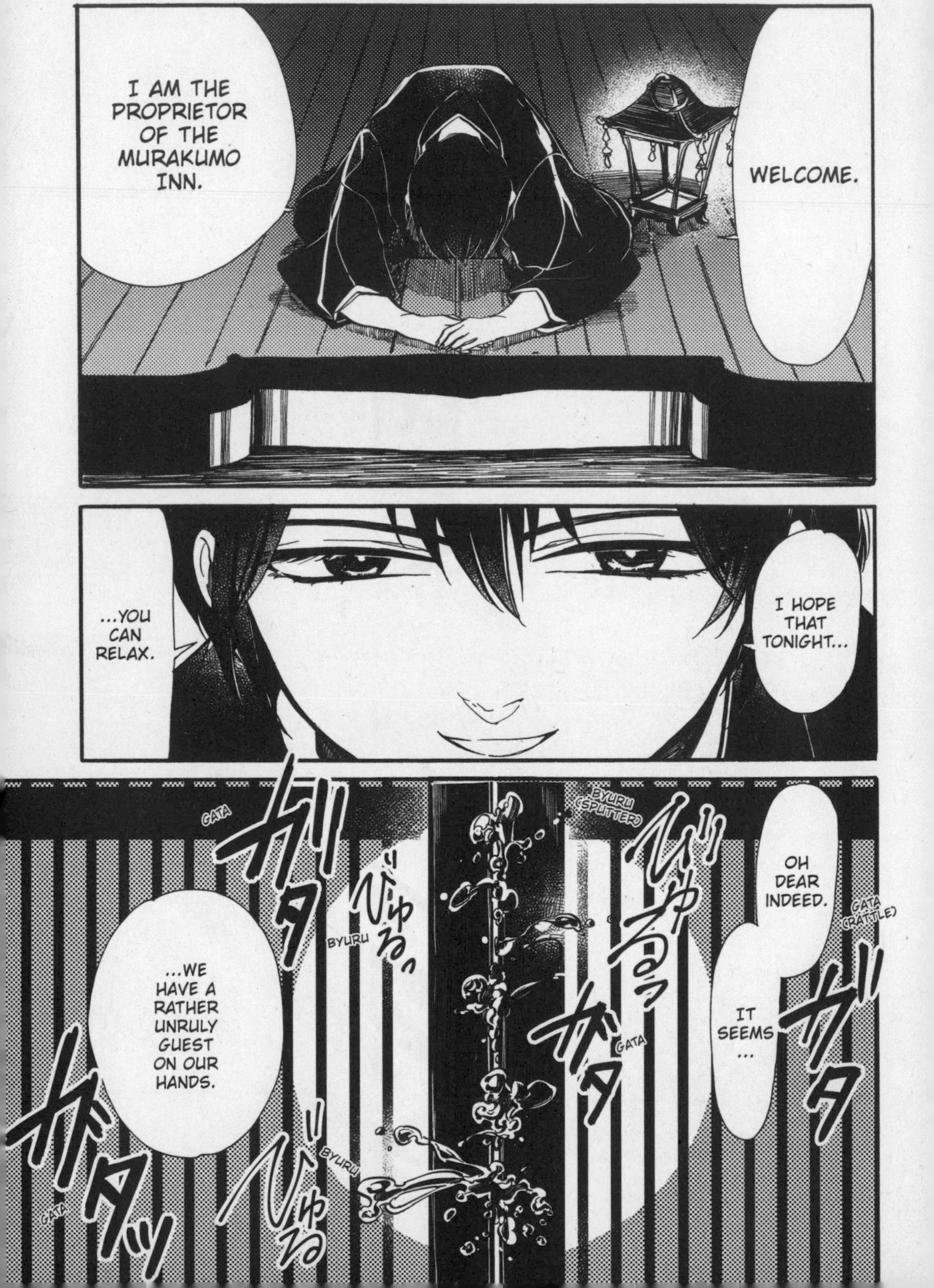
WELCOME.
I AM THE PROPRIETOR OF THE MURAKUMO INN.
I HOPE THAT TONIGHT...
...YOU CAN RELAX.
GATA (RATTLE)
BYURU (SPUTTER)
OH DEAR INDEED.
IT SEEMS...
GATA
BYURU
GATA
...WE HAVE A RATHER UNRULY GUEST ON OUR HANDS.
BYURU
GATA

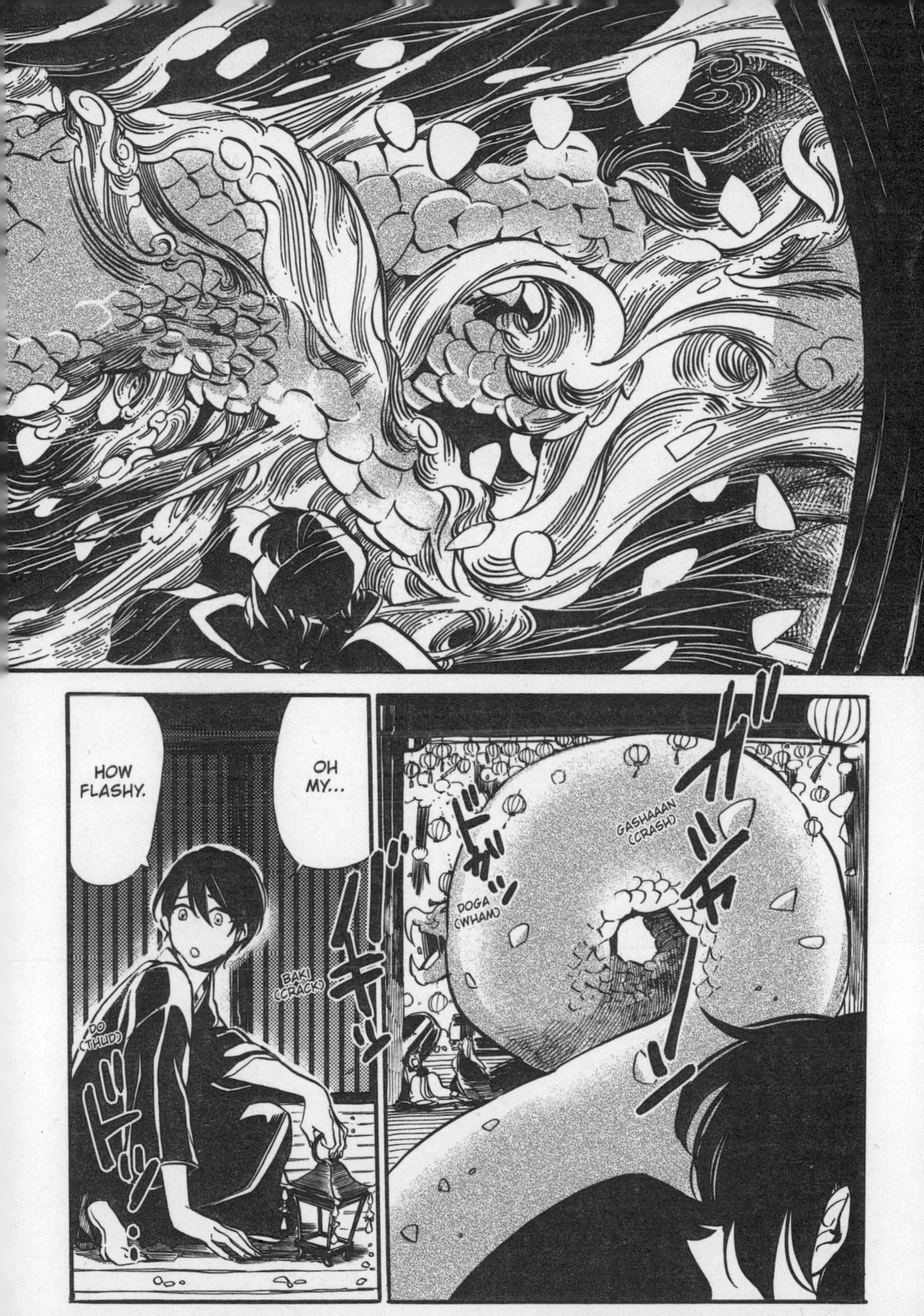
GASHAAAN (CRASH)
DOGA (WHAM)
OH MY...
HOW FLASHY.
BAKI (CRACK)
DO (THUD)

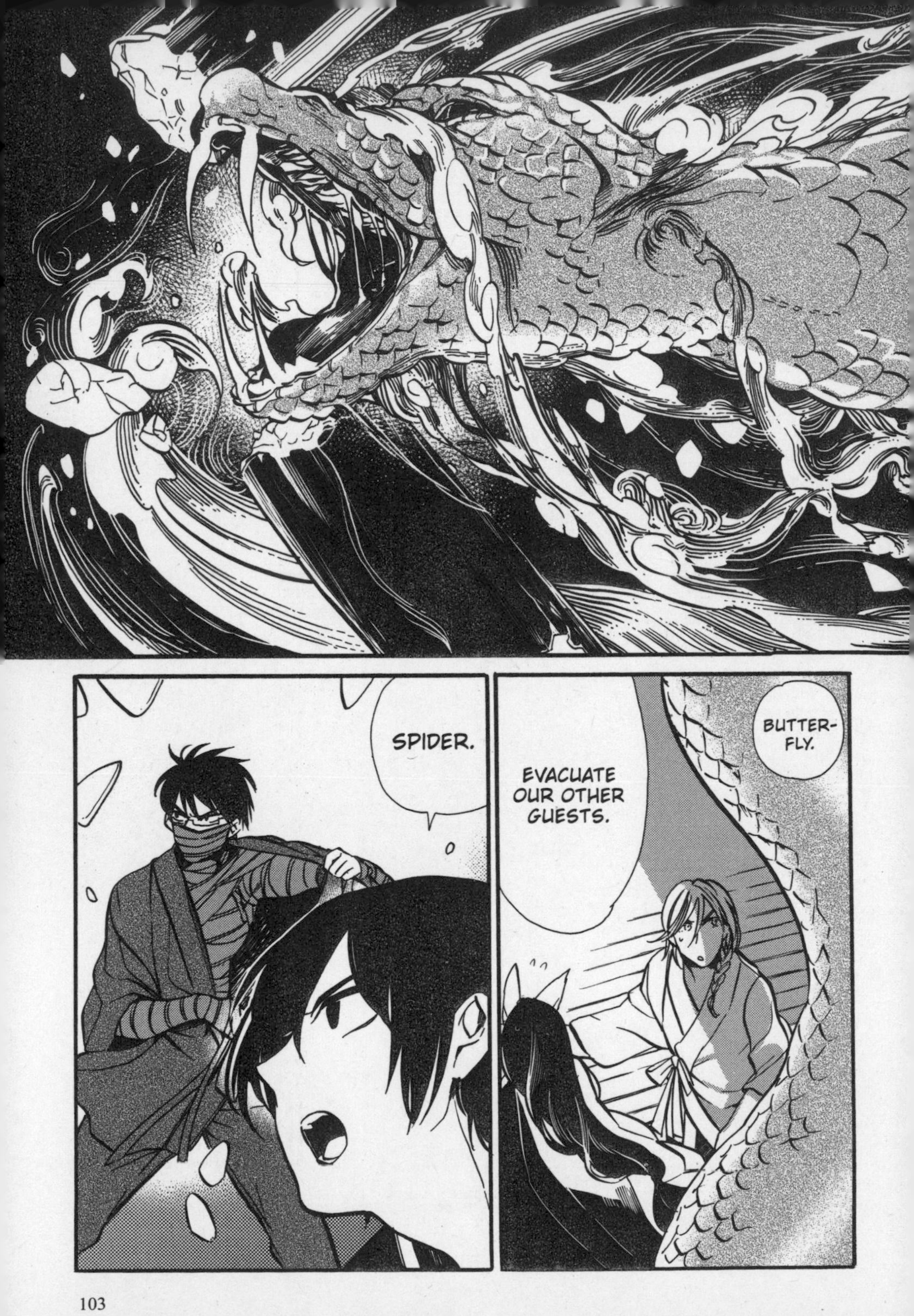
BUTTER-FLY.
EVACUATE OUR OTHER GUESTS.
SPIDER.

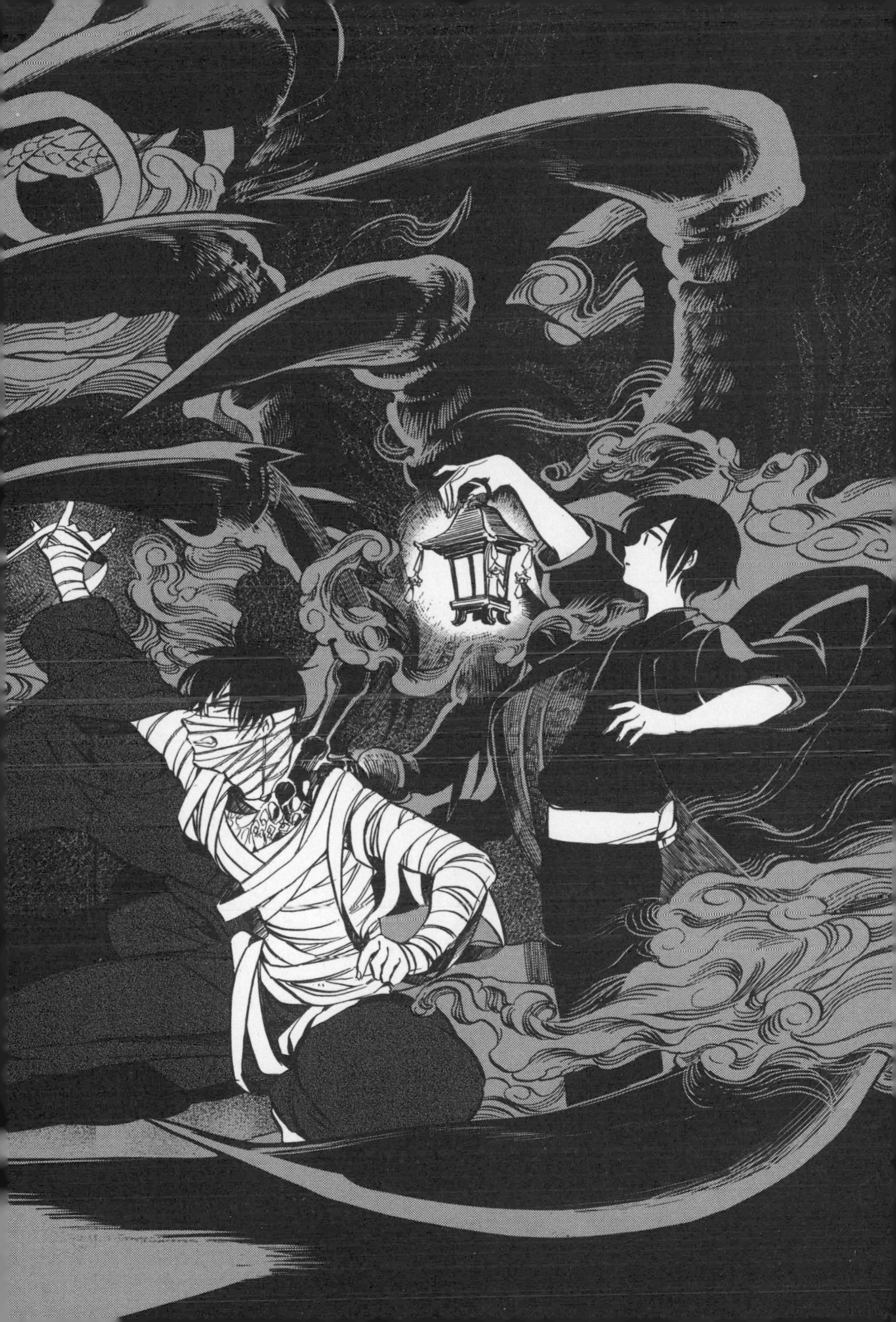

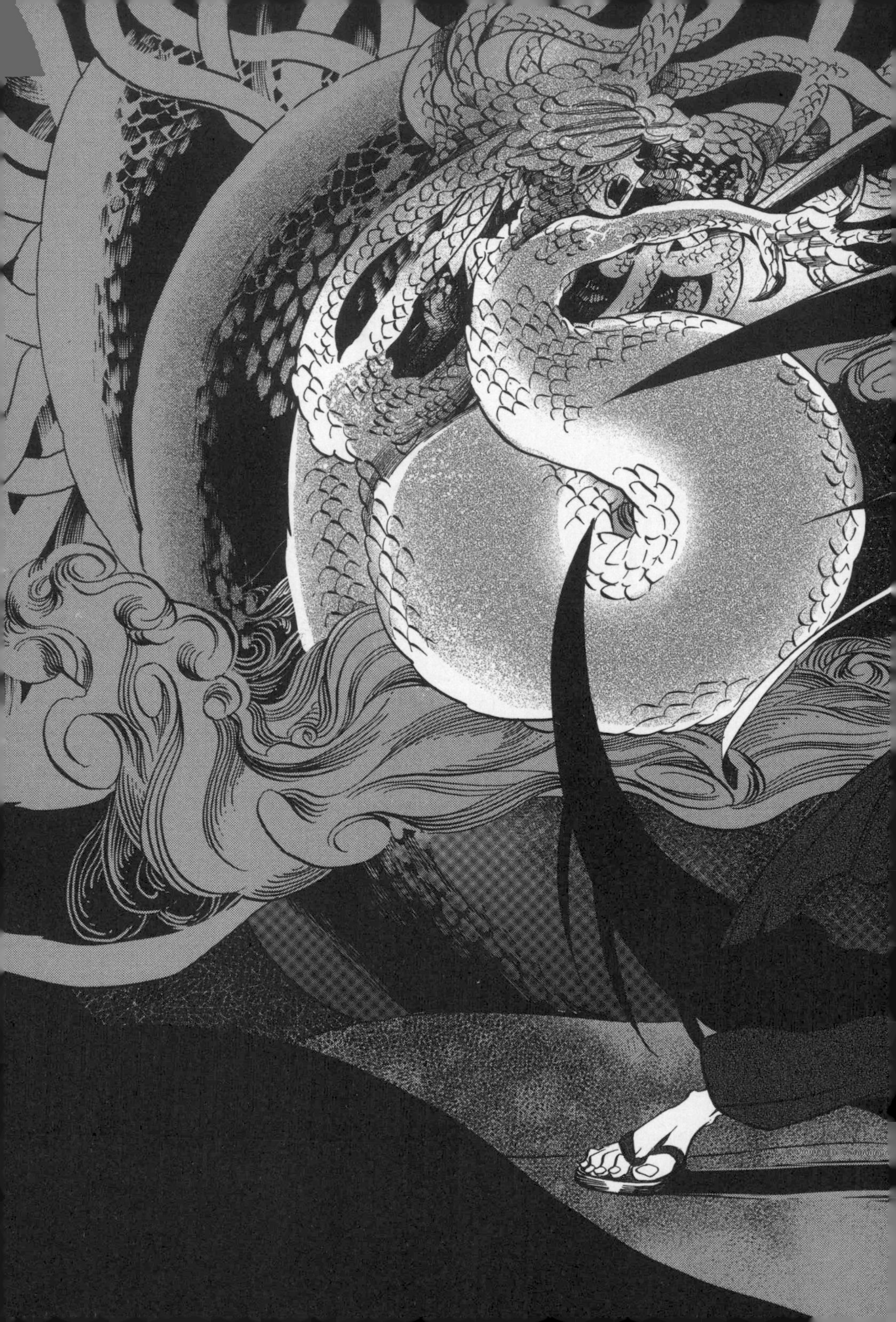

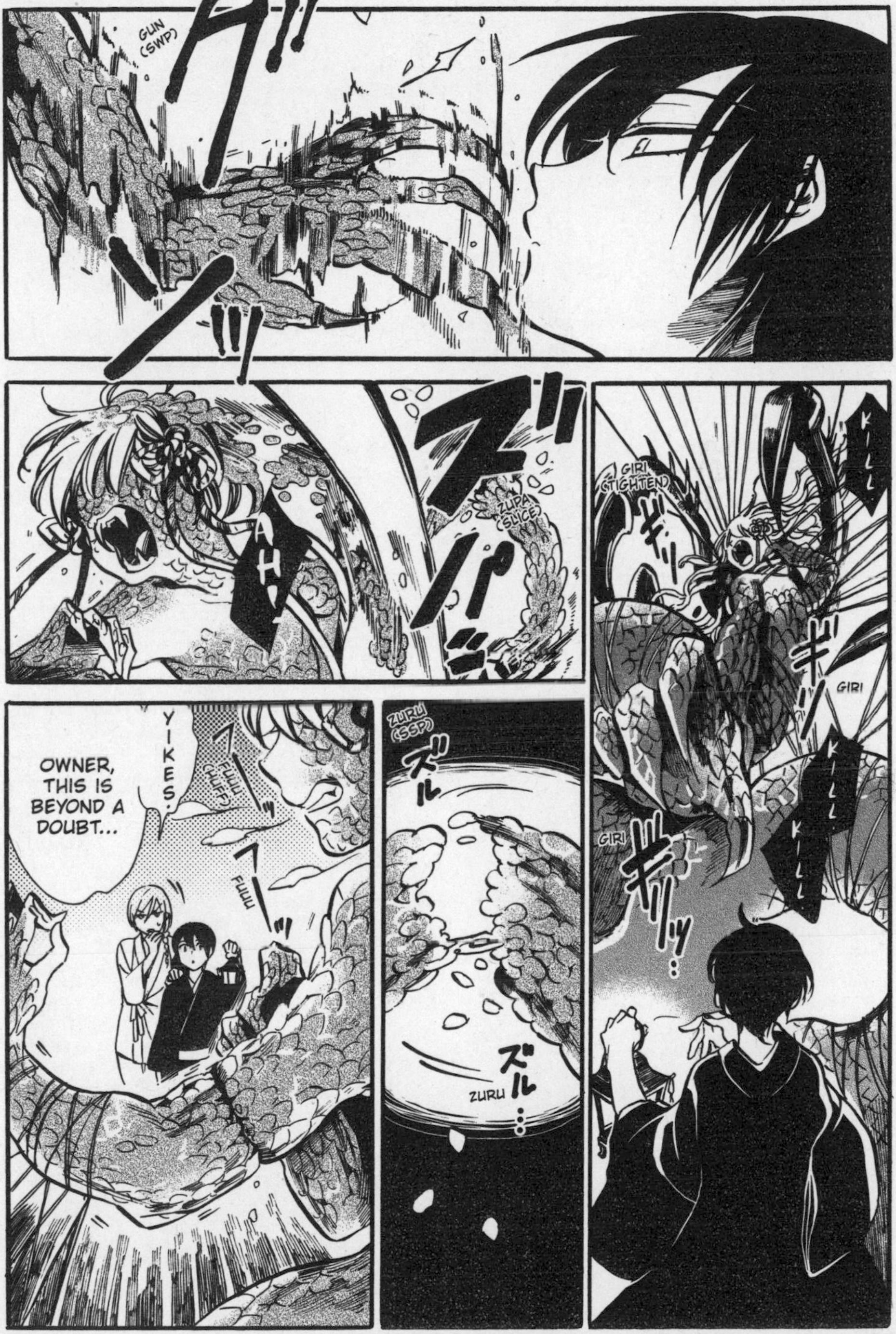
GUN (SWP)
GIRI (TIGHTEN)
KILL
GIRI
KILL
KILL
GIRI
KILL
ZUPA (SLICE)
AH!
ZURU (SSP)
ZURU
YIKES.
FUUU (HUFF)
FUUU
OWNER, THIS IS BEYOND A DOUBT...

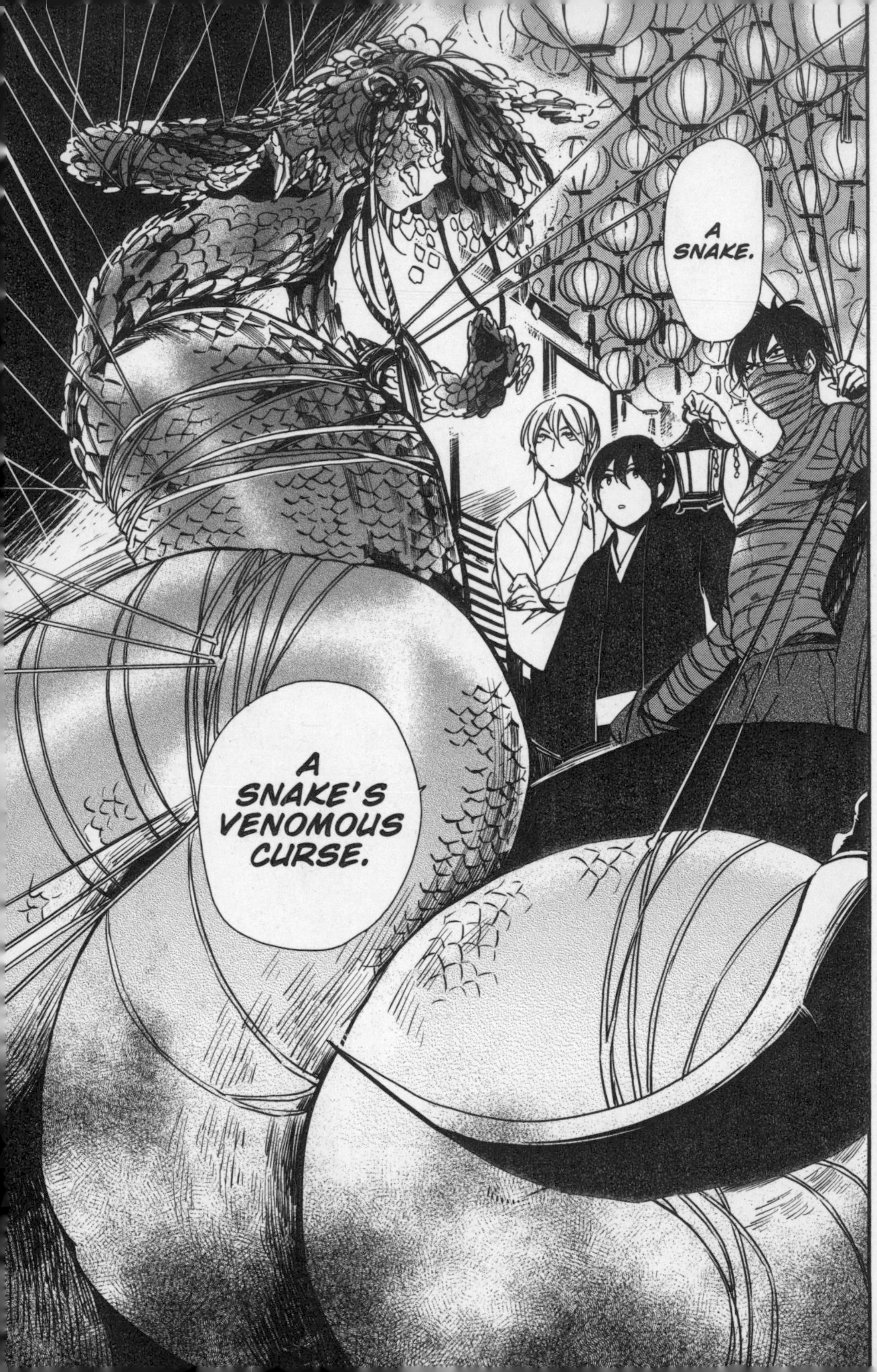
A SNAKE.
A SNAKE'S VENOMOUS CURSE.

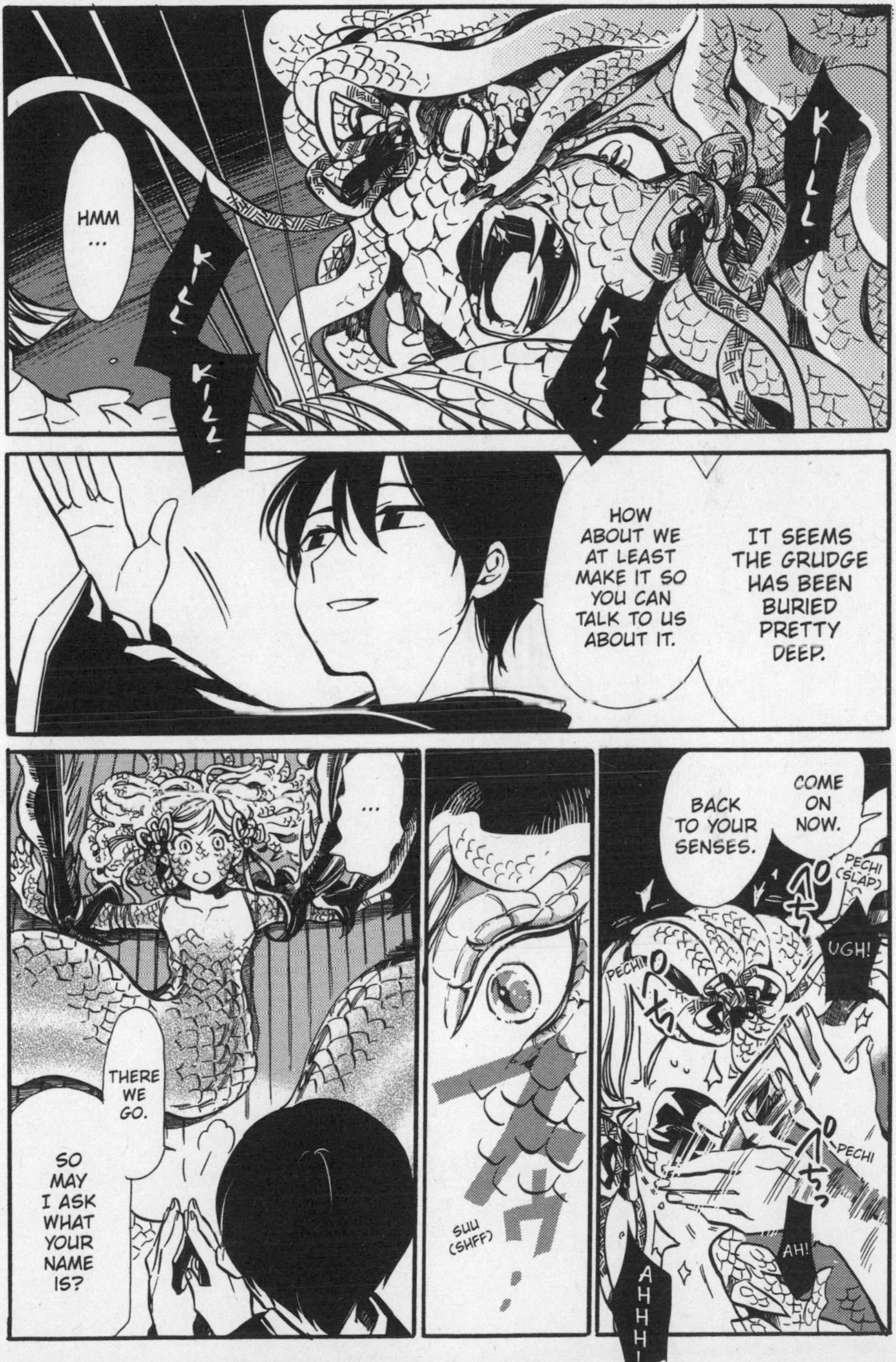
KILL.
KILL.
KILL. KILL.
HMM...
IT SEEMS THE GRUDGE HAS BEEN BURIED PRETTY DEEP.
HOW ABOUT WE AT LEAST MAKE IT SO YOU CAN TALK TO US ABOUT IT.
COME ON NOW.
BACK TO YOUR SENSES.
PECHI (SLAP)
UGH!
PECHI
PECHI
AH!
AHHH!
SUU (SHFF)
...
THERE WE GO.
SO MAY I ASK WHAT YOUR NAME IS?

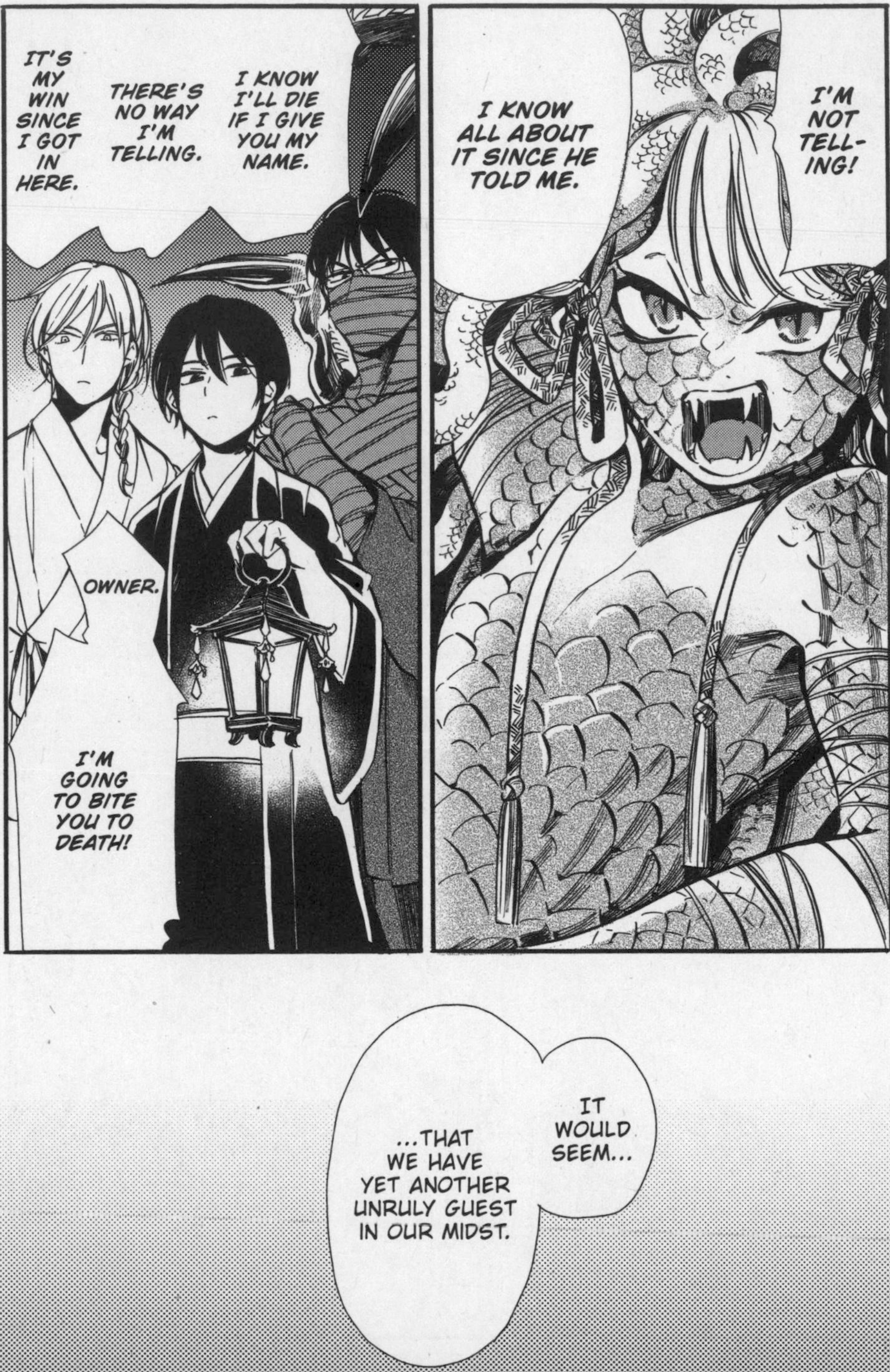
I'M NOT TELLING!
I KNOW ALL ABOUT IT SINCE HE TOLD ME.
I KNOW I'LL DIE IF I GIVE YOU MY NAME.
THERE'S NO WAY I'M TELLING.
IT'S MY WIN SINCE I GOT IN HERE.
OWNER.
I'M GOING TO BITE YOU TO DEATH!
IT WOULD SEEM...
...THAT WE HAVE YET ANOTHER UNRULY GUEST IN OUR MIDST.

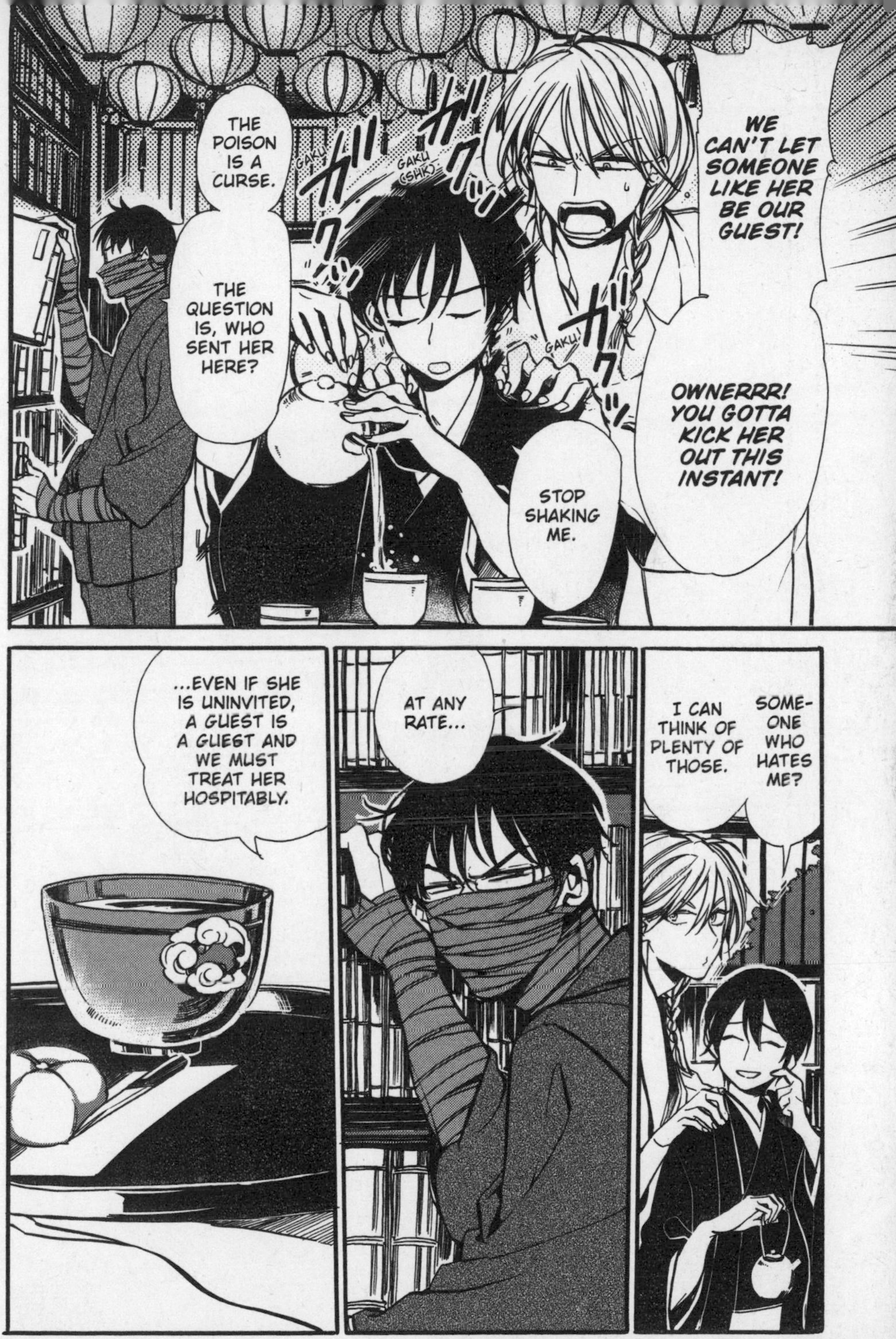
WE CAN'T LET SOMEONE LIKE HER BE OUR GUEST!
OWNERRR! YOU GOTTA KICK HER OUT THIS INSTANT!
GAKU
GAKU (SHK)
GAKU
STOP SHAKING ME.
THE POISON IS A CURSE.
THE QUESTION IS, WHO SENT HER HERE?
SOME-ONE WHO HATES ME?
I CAN THINK OF PLENTY OF THOSE.
AT ANY RATE...
...EVEN IF SHE IS UNINVITED, A GUEST IS A GUEST AND WE MUST TREAT HER HOSPITABLY.

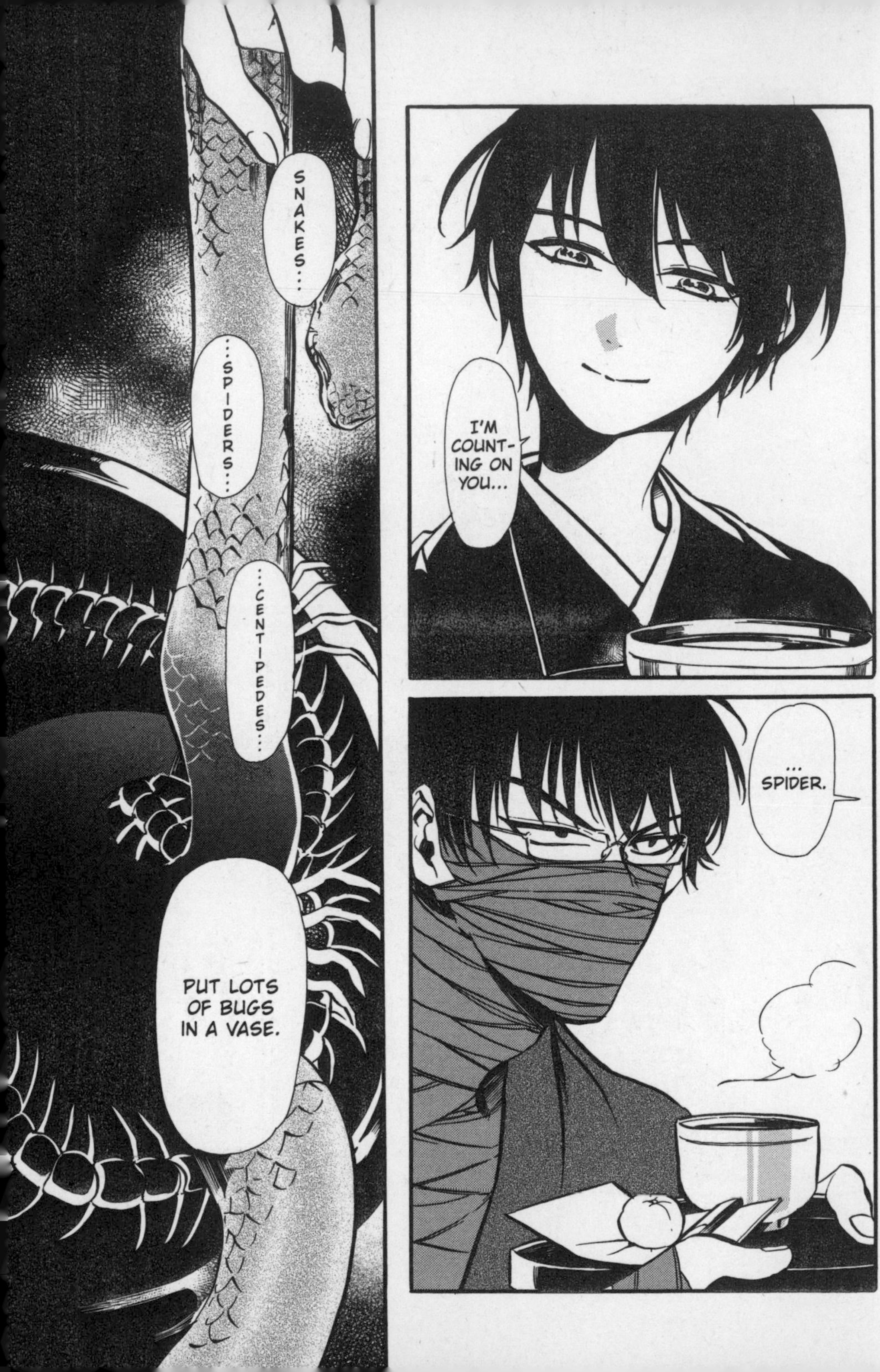
I'M COUNTING ON YOU...
...SPIDER.
SNAKES...
...SPIDERS...
...CENTIPEDES...
PUT LOTS OF BUGS IN A VASE.

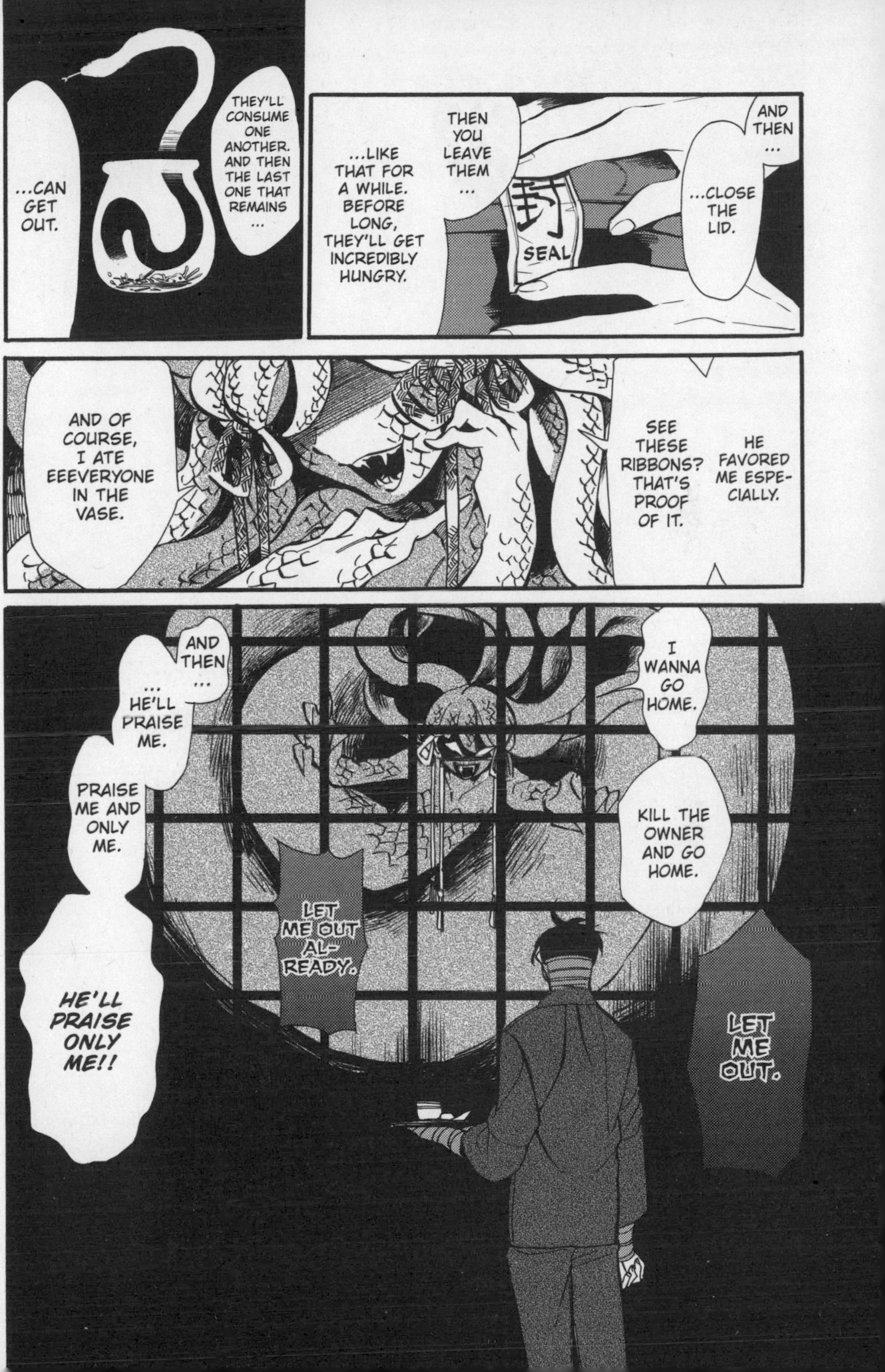
AND THEN...
...CLOSE THE LID.
SEAL
THEN YOU LEAVE THEM...
...LIKE THAT FOR A WHILE. BEFORE LONG, THEY'LL GET INCREDIBLY HUNGRY.
THEY'LL CONSUME ONE ANOTHER. AND THEN THE LAST ONE THAT REMAINS...
...CAN GET OUT.
HE FAVORED ME ESPE-CIALLY.
SEE THESE RIBBONS? THAT'S PROOF OF IT.
AND OF COURSE, I ATE EEEVERYONE IN THE VASE.
I WANNA GO HOME.
KILL THE OWNER AND GO HOME.
AND THEN... HE'LL PRAISE ME.
PRAISE ME AND ONLY ME.
LET ME OUT.
LET ME OUT AL-READY.
HE'LL PRAISE ONLY ME!!

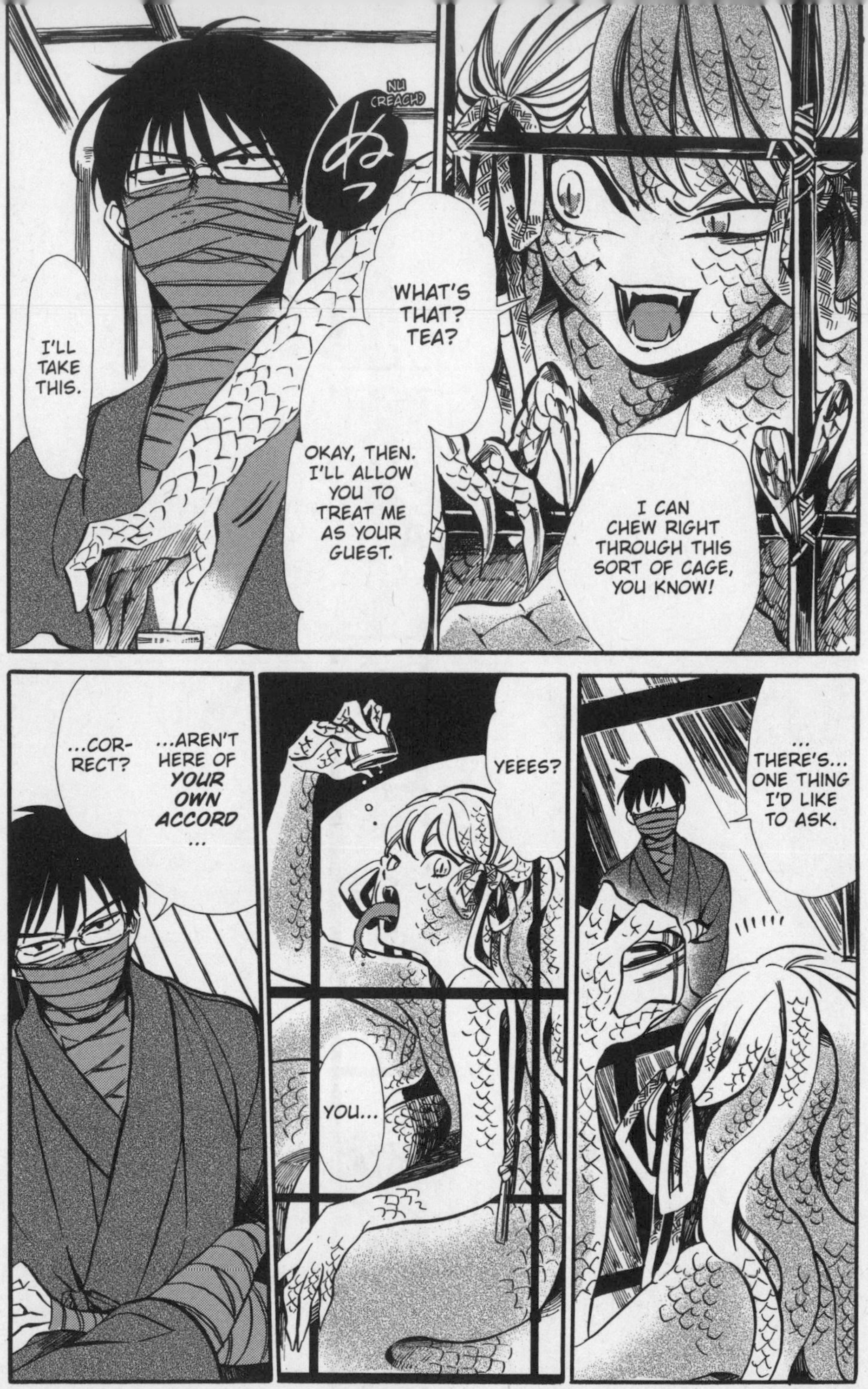

I CAN CHEW RIGHT THROUGH THIS SORT OF CAGE, YOU KNOW!
ぬっ
NU (REACH)
WHAT'S THAT? TEA?
OKAY, THEN. I'LL ALLOW YOU TO TREAT ME AS YOUR GUEST.
I'LL TAKE THIS.
... THERE'S... ONE THING I'D LIKE TO ASK.
YEEES?
YOU...
...AREN'T HERE OF *YOUR OWN ACCORD* ...
...COR-RECT?

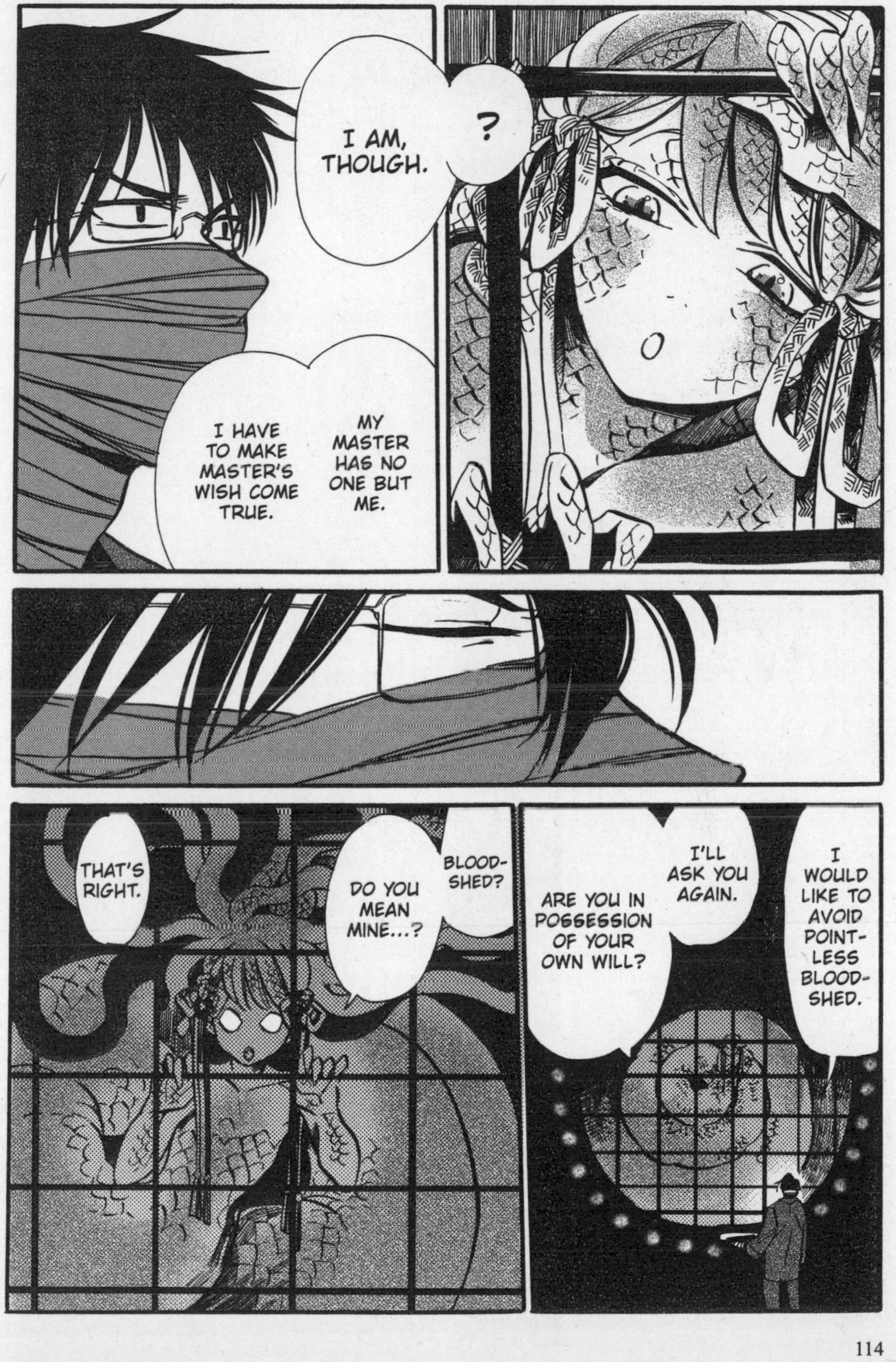
?
I AM, THOUGH.
MY MASTER HAS NO ONE BUT ME.
I HAVE TO MAKE MASTER'S WISH COME TRUE.
I WOULD LIKE TO AVOID POINT-LESS BLOOD-SHED.
I'LL ASK YOU AGAIN.
ARE YOU IN POSSESSION OF YOUR OWN WILL?
BLOOD-SHED?
DO YOU MEAN MINE...?
THAT'S RIGHT.

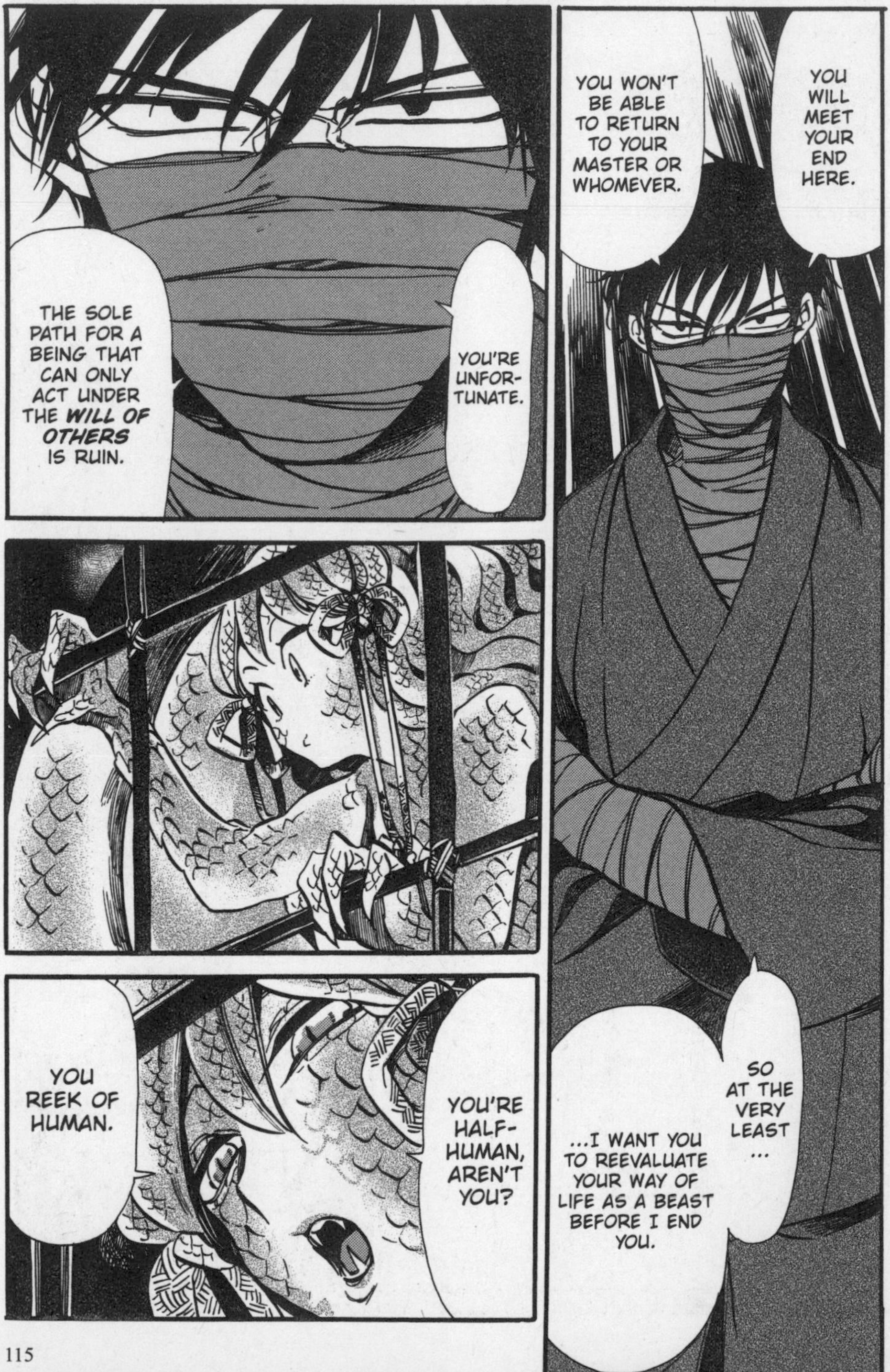
YOU WILL MEET YOUR END HERE.
YOU WON'T BE ABLE TO RETURN TO YOUR MASTER OR WHOMEVER.
SO AT THE VERY LEAST ...
...I WANT YOU TO REEVALUATE YOUR WAY OF LIFE AS A BEAST BEFORE I END YOU.
YOU'RE UNFOR-TUNATE.
THE SOLE PATH FOR A BEING THAT CAN ONLY ACT UNDER THE ***WILL OF OTHERS*** IS RUIN.
YOU'RE HALF-HUMAN, AREN'T YOU?
YOU REEK OF HUMAN.

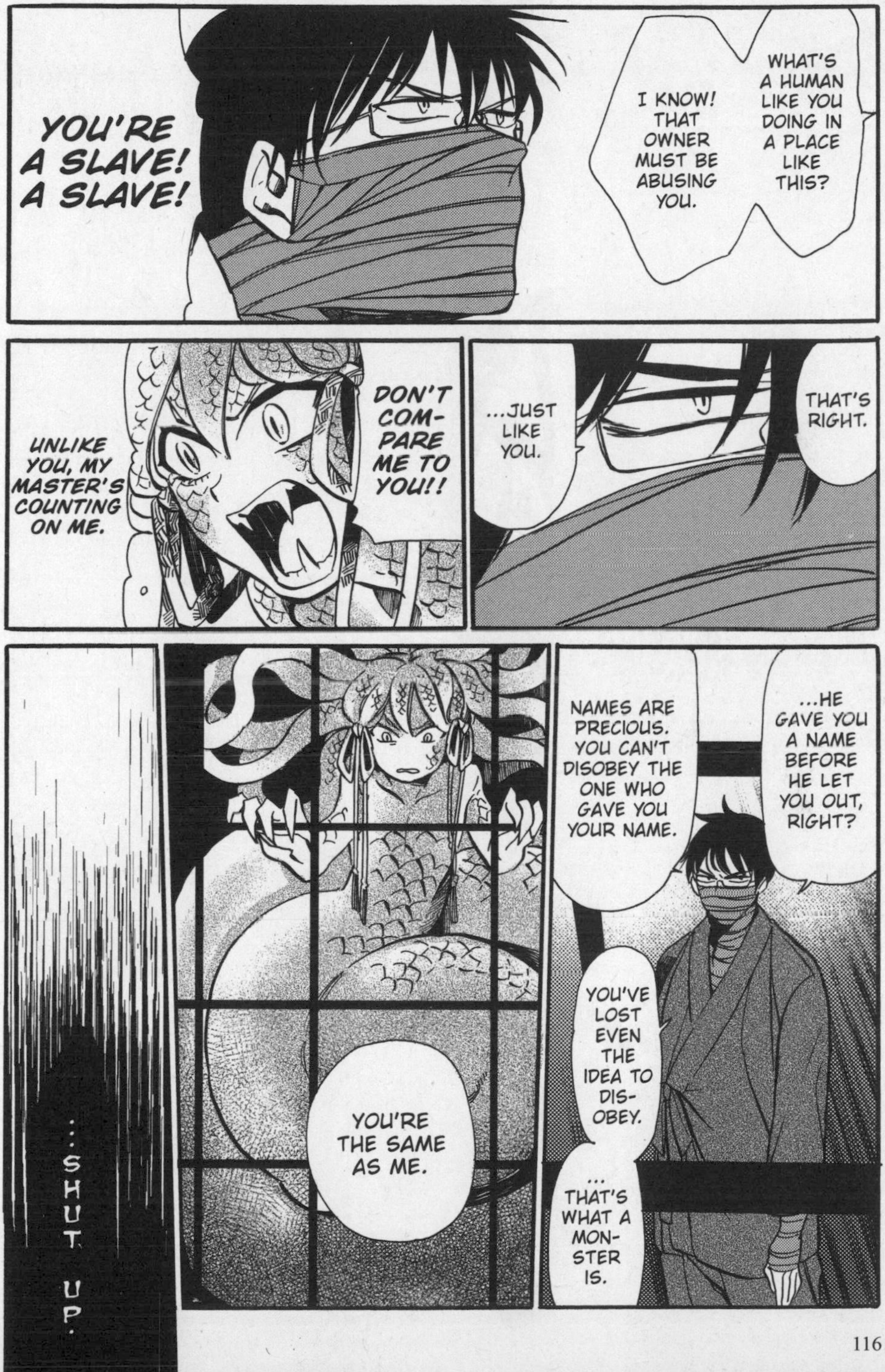
WHAT'S A HUMAN LIKE YOU DOING IN A PLACE LIKE THIS?
I KNOW! THAT OWNER MUST BE ABUSING YOU.
YOU'RE A SLAVE! A SLAVE!
THAT'S RIGHT.
...JUST LIKE YOU.
DON'T COMPARE ME TO YOU!!
UNLIKE YOU, MY MASTER'S COUNTING ON ME.
...HE GAVE YOU A NAME BEFORE HE LET YOU OUT, RIGHT?
NAMES ARE PRECIOUS. YOU CAN'T DISOBEY THE ONE WHO GAVE YOU YOUR NAME.
YOU'VE LOST EVEN THE IDEA TO DISOBEY.
... THAT'S WHAT A MONSTER IS.
YOU'RE THE SAME AS ME.
...SHUT UP.

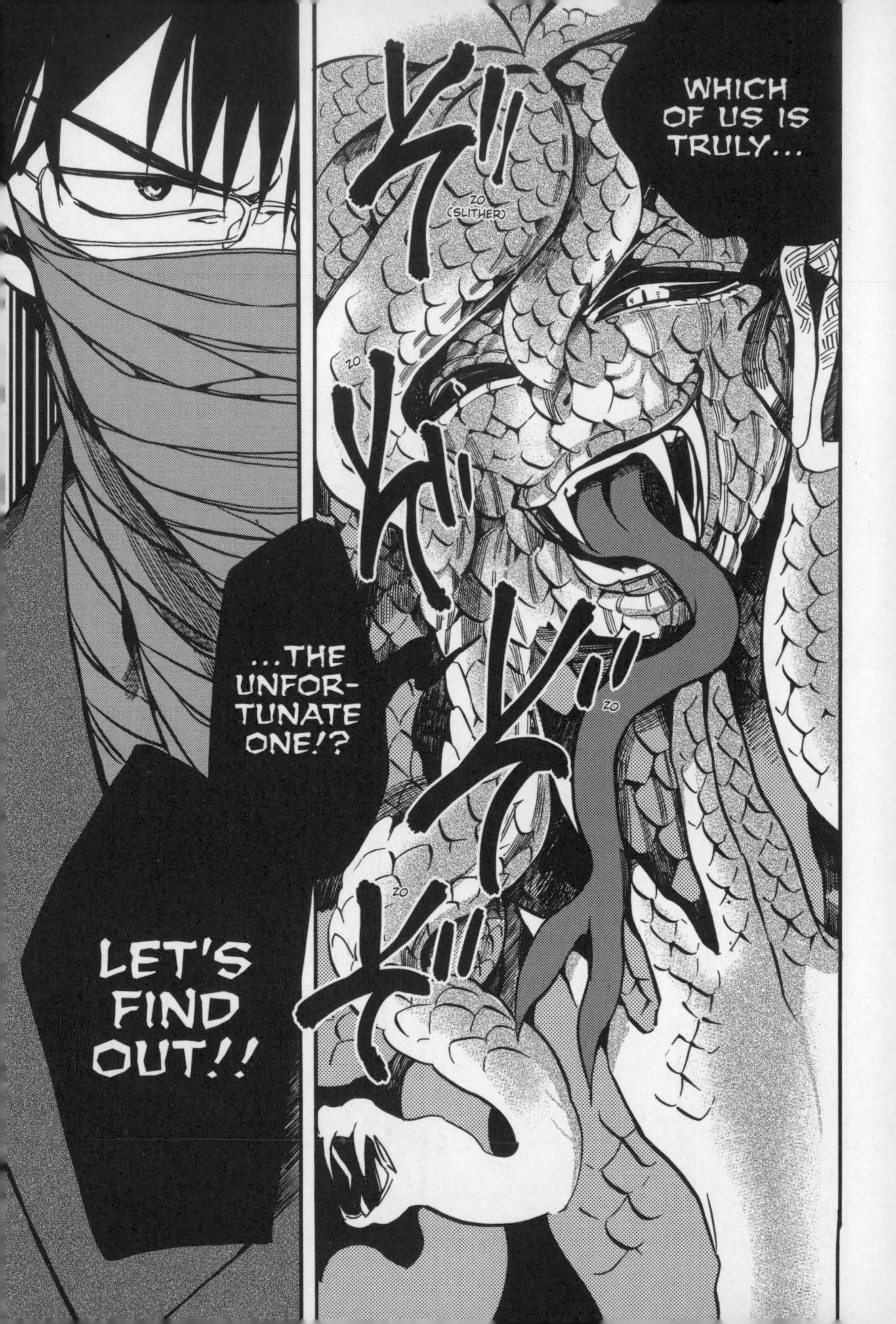
WHICH OF US IS TRULY...
ZO (SLITHER)
ZO
ZO
ZO
...THE UNFOR-TUNATE ONE!?
LET'S FIND OUT!!

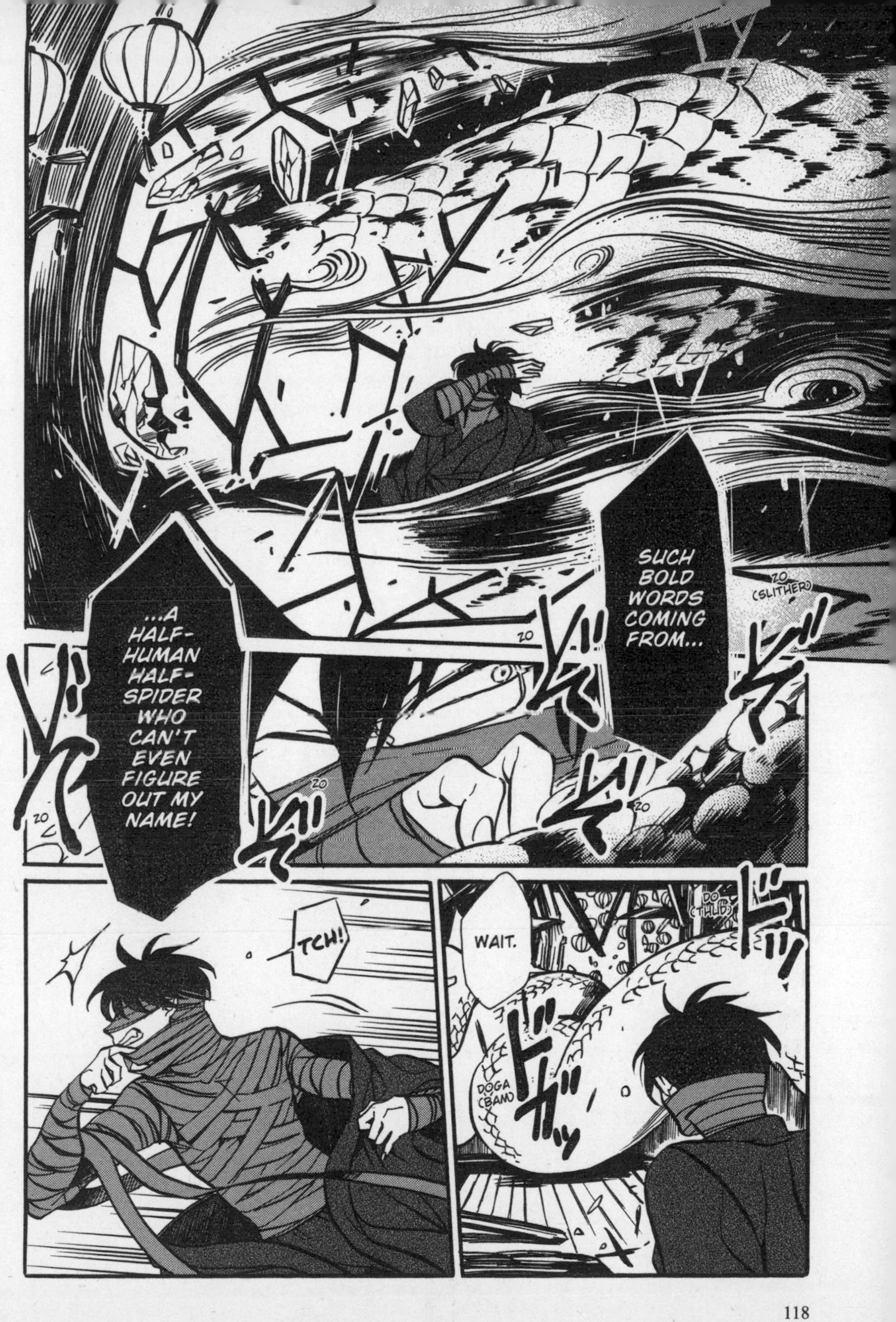
SUCH BOLD WORDS COMING FROM...
ZO (SLITHER)
...A HALF-HUMAN HALF-SPIDER WHO CAN'T EVEN FIGURE OUT MY NAME!
ZO
ZO
ZO
ZO
DO (THUD)
WAIT.
DOGA (BAM)
TCH!

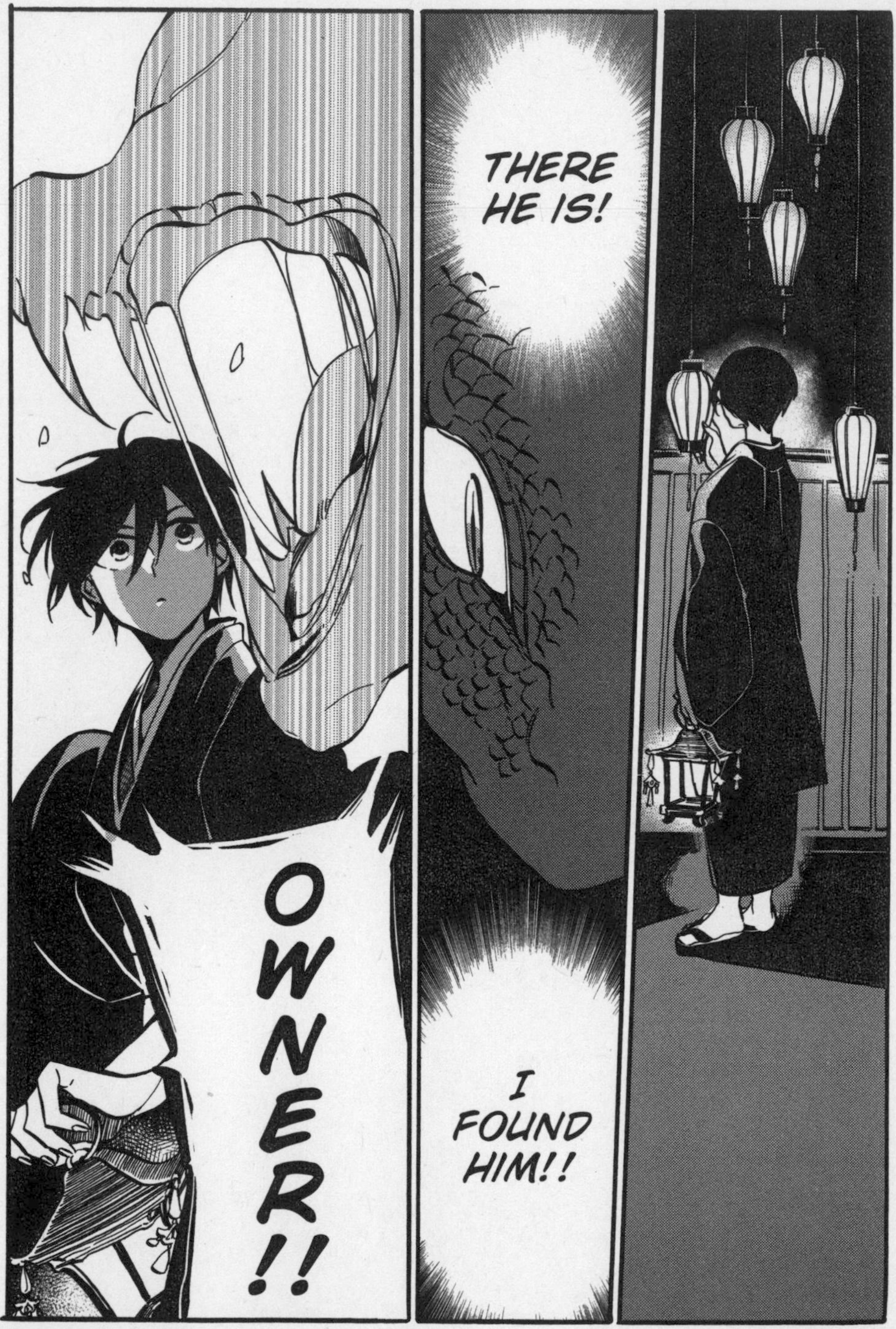
THERE HE IS!
I FOUND HIM!!
OWNER!!

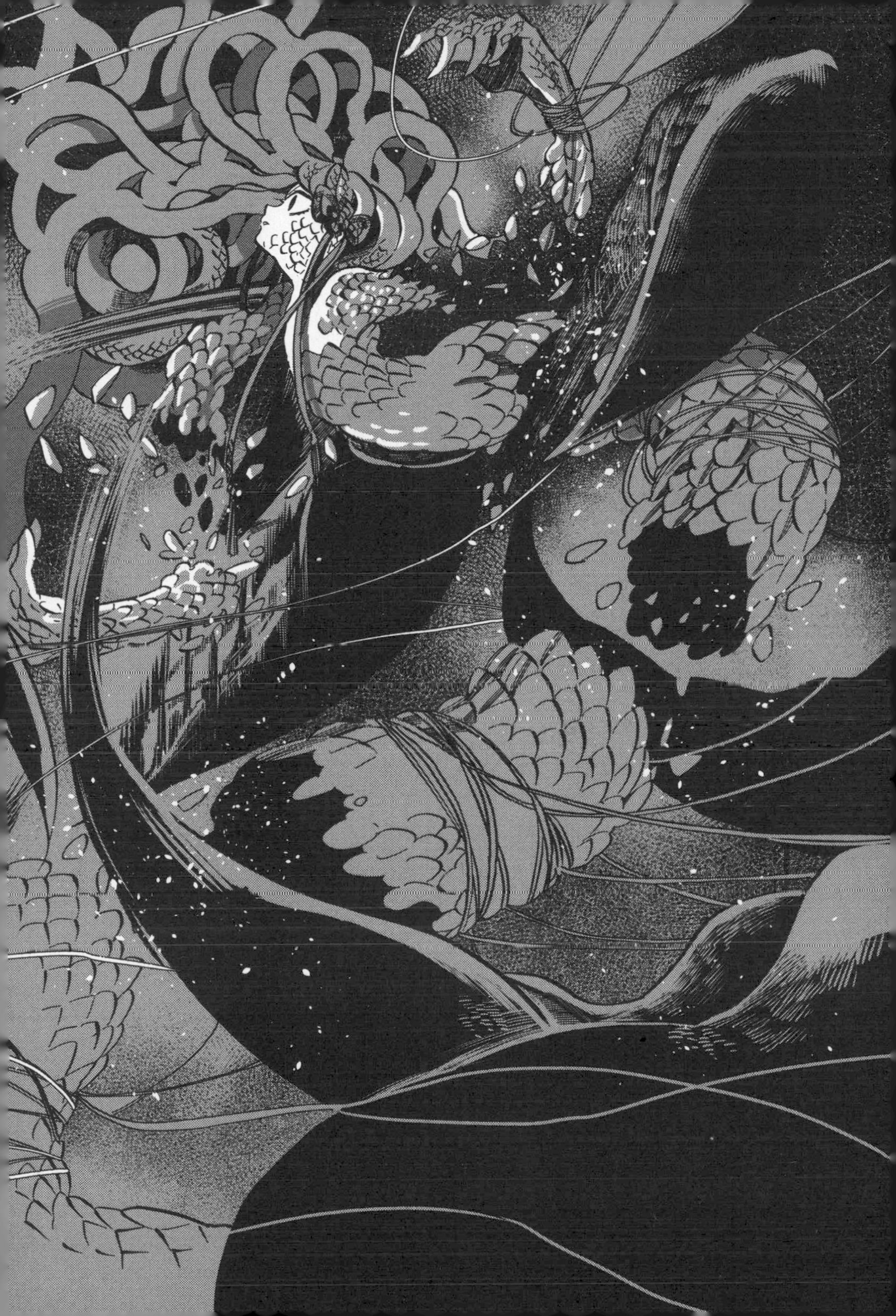

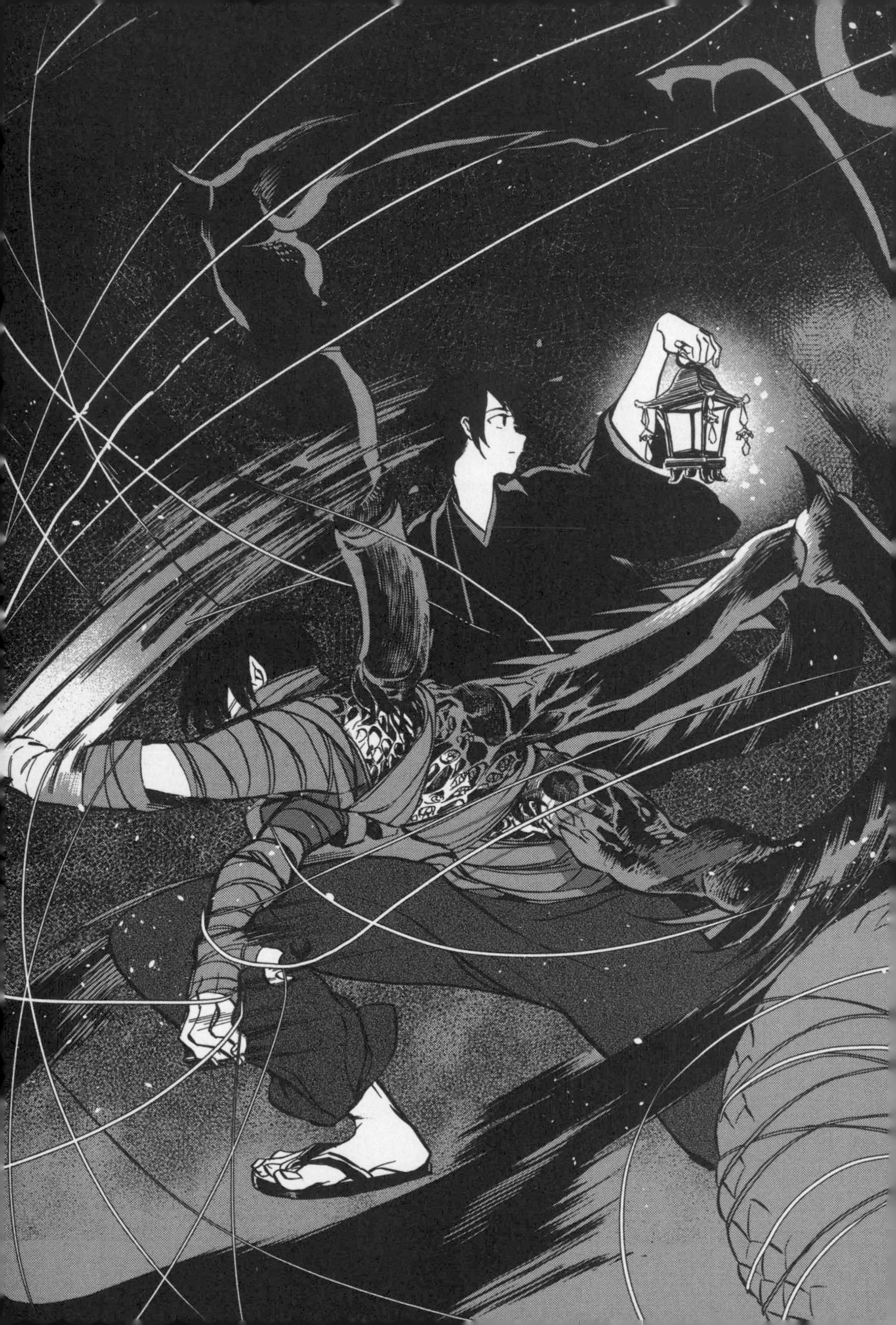

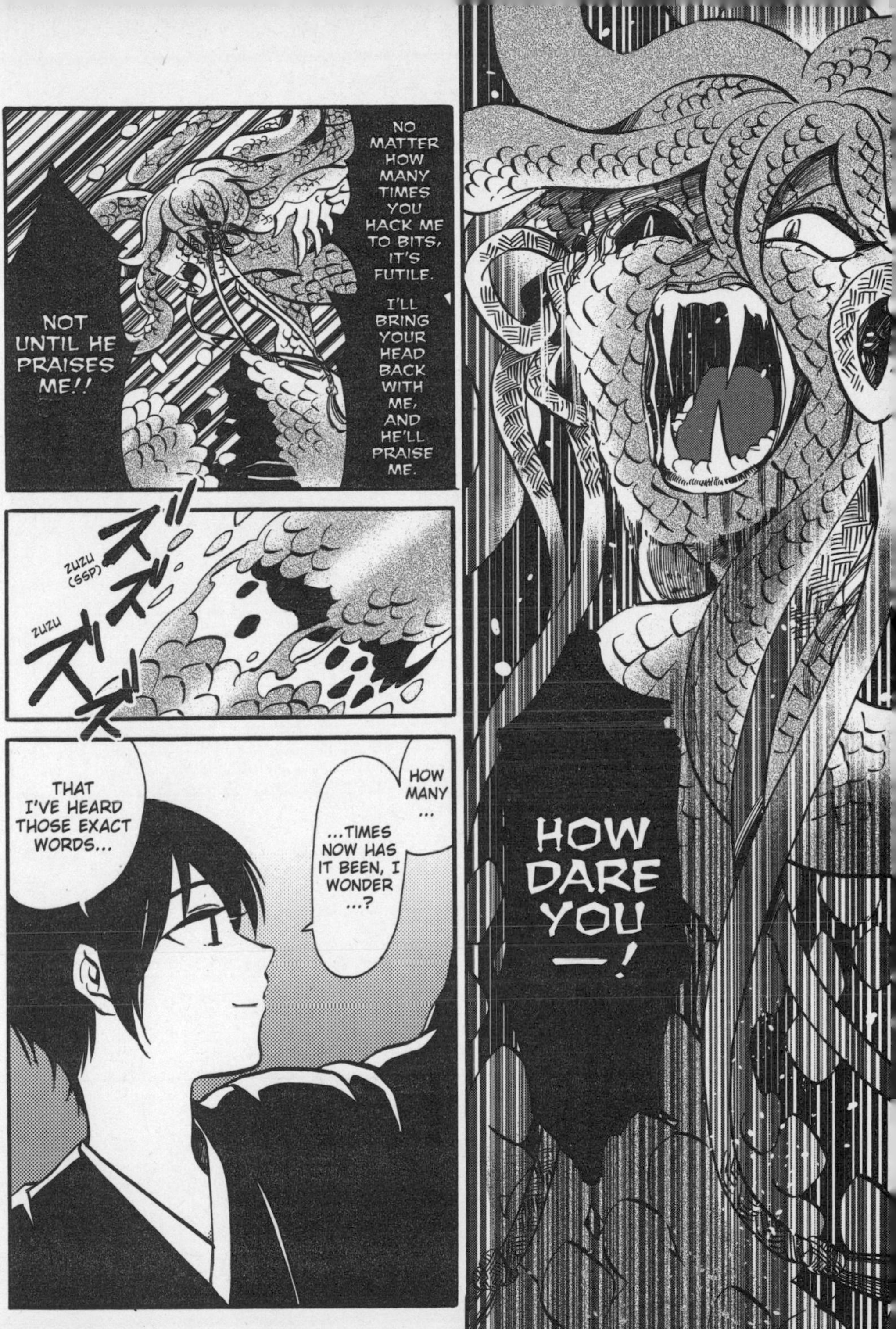
HOW DARE YOU—!
NO MATTER HOW MANY TIMES YOU HACK ME TO BITS, IT'S FUTILE.
I'LL BRING YOUR HEAD BACK WITH ME, AND HE'LL PRAISE ME.
NOT UNTIL HE PRAISES ME!!
ZUZU (SSP)
ZUZU
HOW MANY...
...TIMES NOW HAS IT BEEN, I WONDER...?
THAT I'VE HEARD THOSE EXACT WORDS...

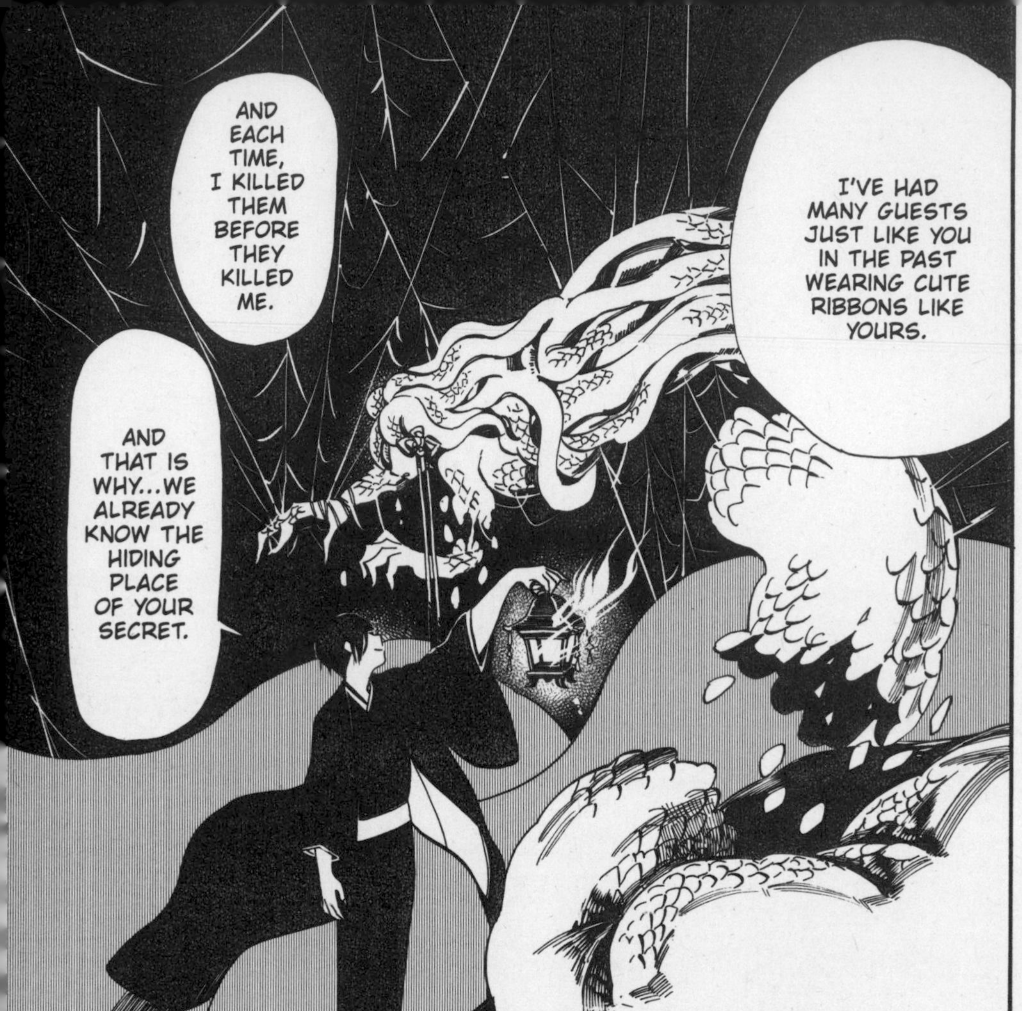
I'VE HAD MANY GUESTS JUST LIKE YOU IN THE PAST WEARING CUTE RIBBONS LIKE YOURS.
AND EACH TIME, I KILLED THEM BEFORE THEY KILLED ME.
AND THAT IS WHY...WE ALREADY KNOW THE HIDING PLACE OF YOUR SECRET.
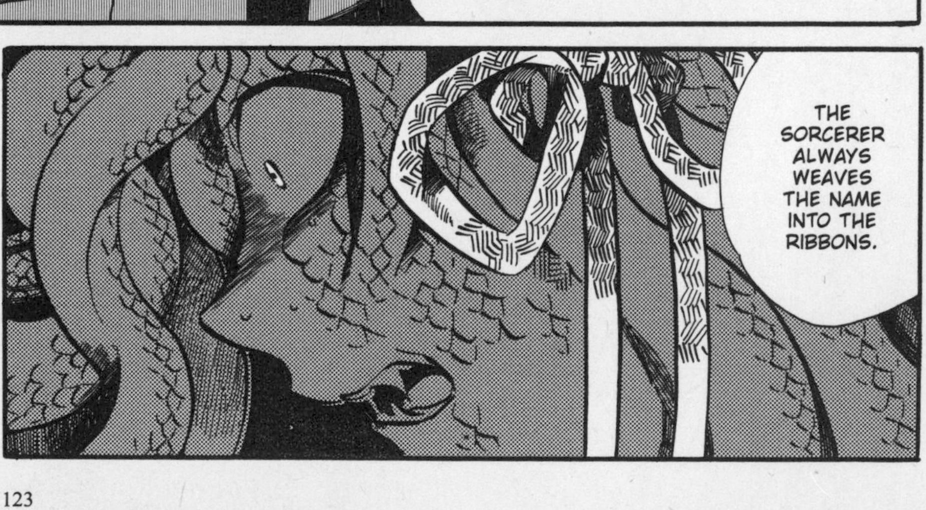
THE SORCERER ALWAYS WEAVES THE NAME INTO THE RIBBONS.

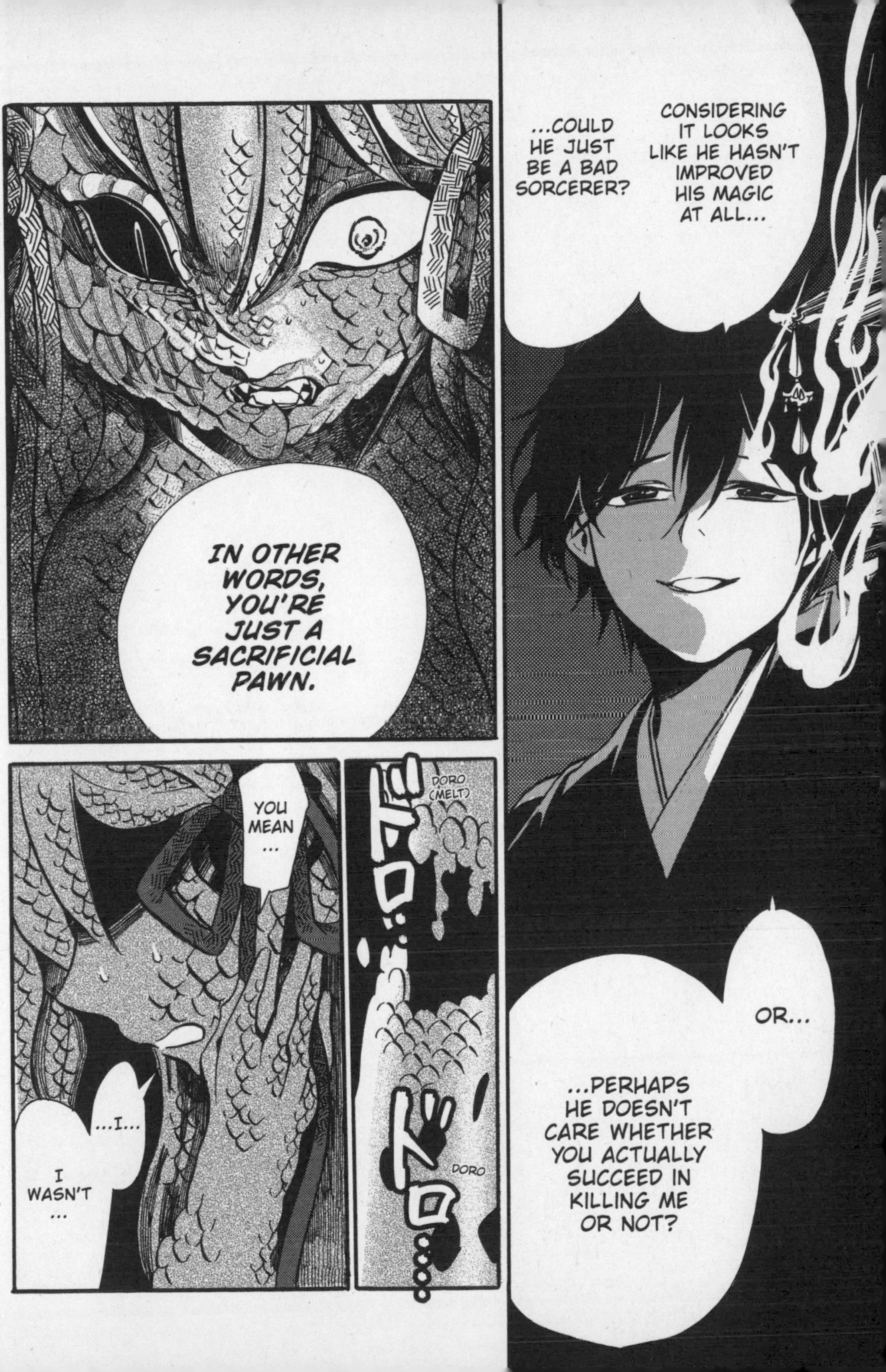
CONSIDERING IT LOOKS LIKE HE HASN'T IMPROVED HIS MAGIC AT ALL...
...COULD HE JUST BE A BAD SORCERER?
OR...
...PERHAPS HE DOESN'T CARE WHETHER YOU ACTUALLY SUCCEED IN KILLING ME OR NOT?
IN OTHER WORDS, YOU'RE JUST A SACRIFICIAL PAWN.
DORO (MELT)
DORO
YOU MEAN ...
...I...
I WASN'T ...

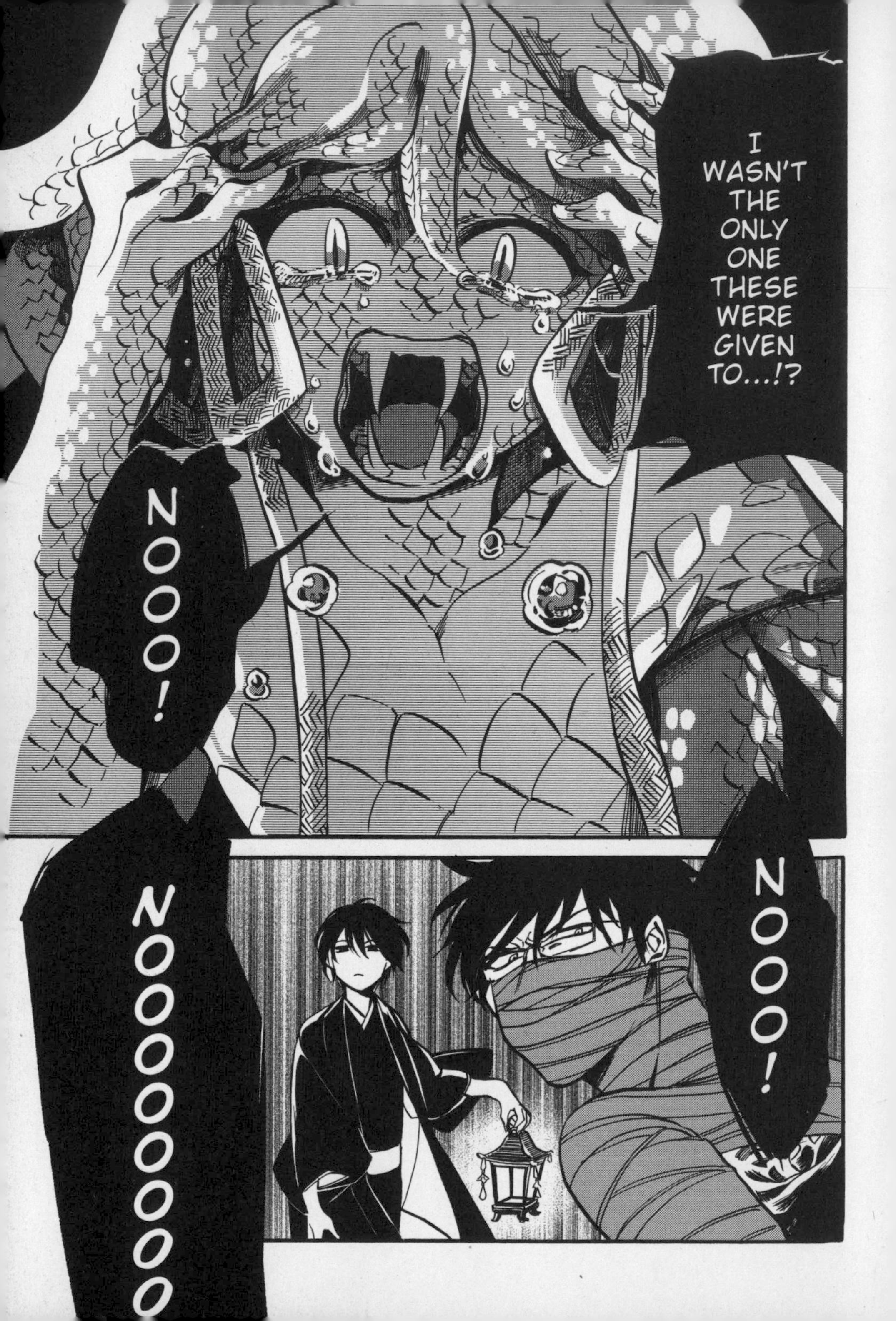
I WASN'T THE ONLY ONE THESE WERE GIVEN TO...!?
NOOOO!
NOOOO!
NOOOOOOOOOOO

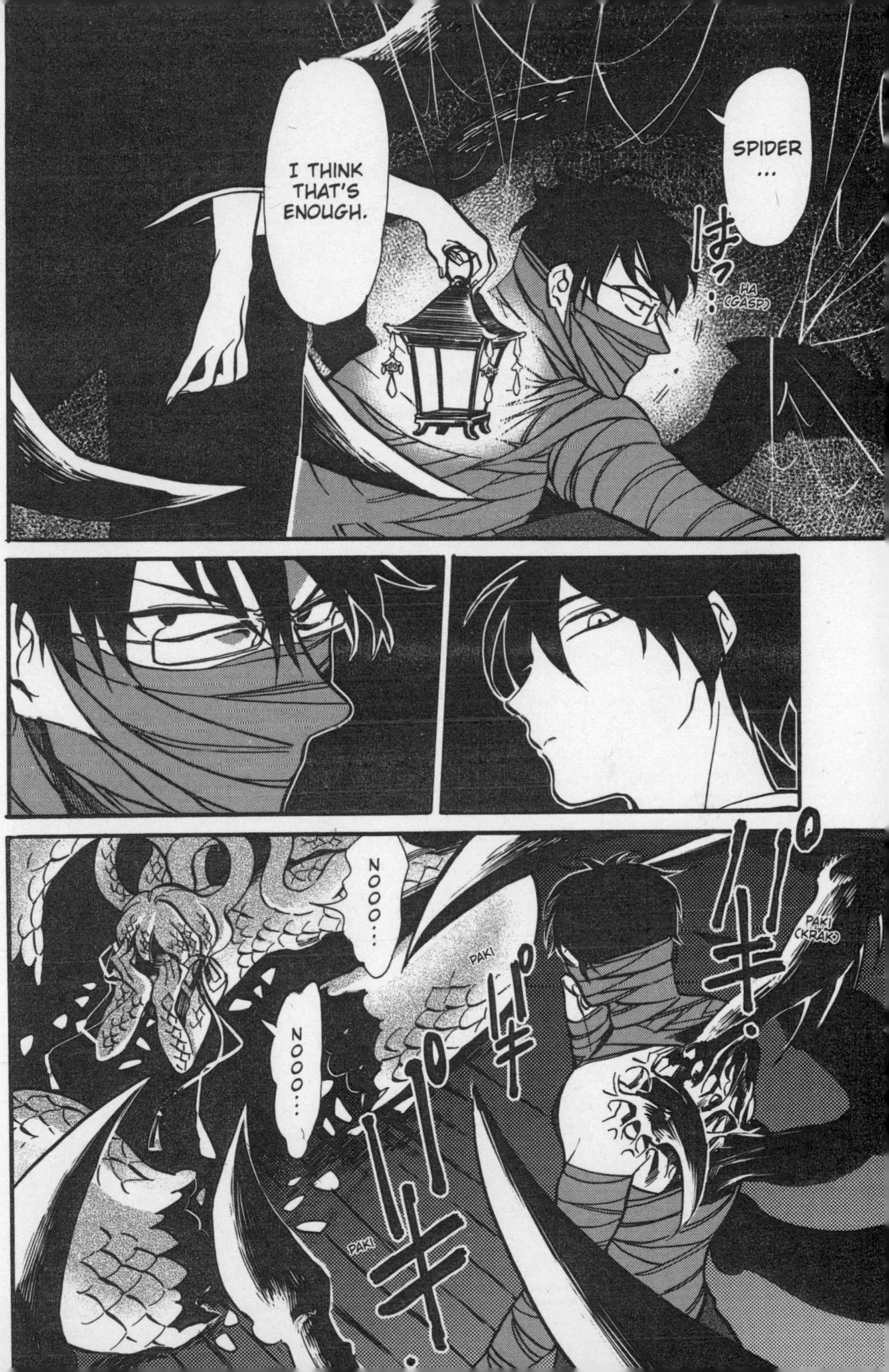
SPIDER ...
はっ…
HA (GASP)
I THINK THAT'S ENOUGH.
パキ
PAKI (KRAK)
パキ
PAKI
NOOO…
NOOO…
パキ
PAKI

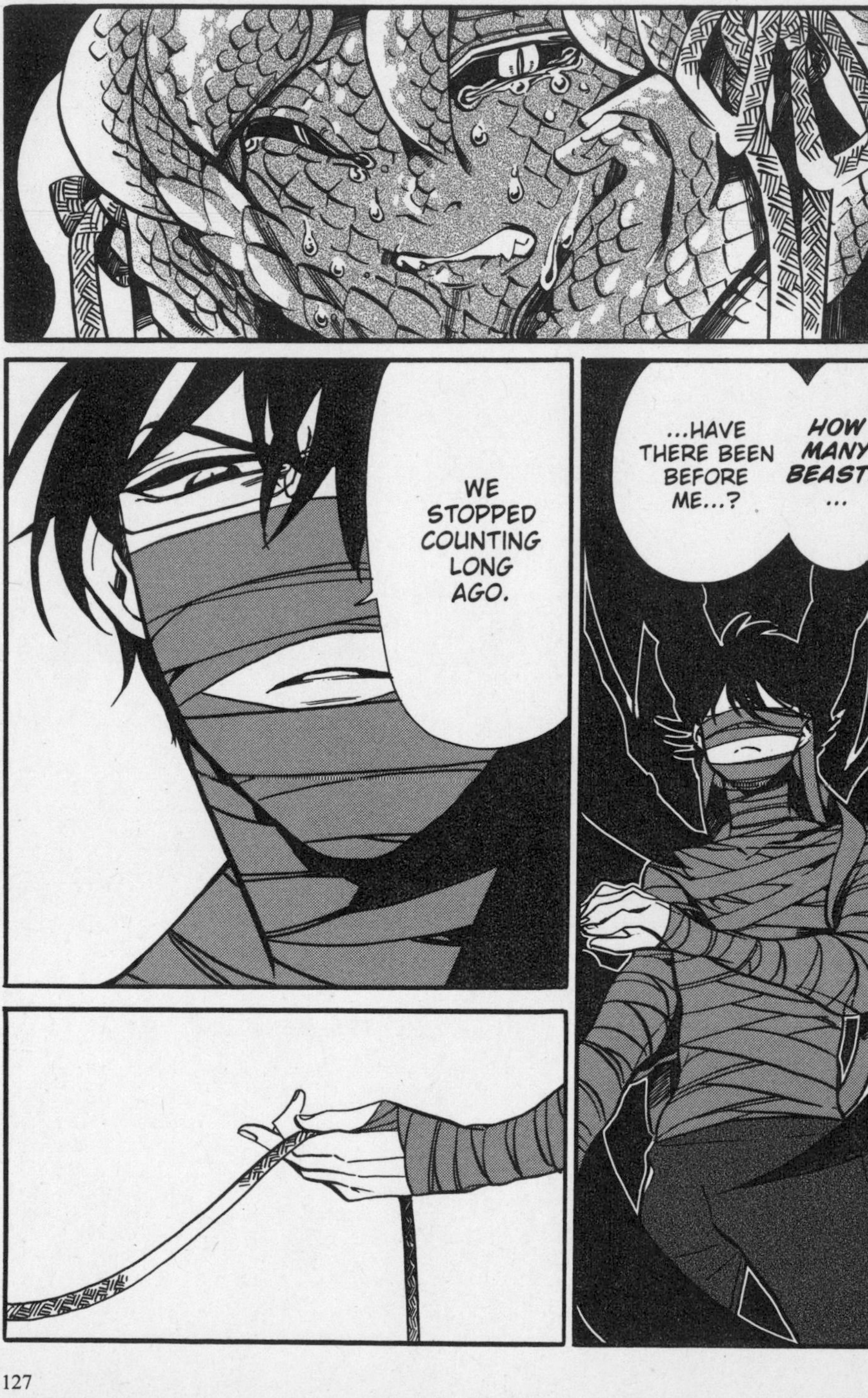
HOW MANY BEASTS ...
...HAVE THERE BEEN BEFORE ME...?
WE STOPPED COUNTING LONG AGO.

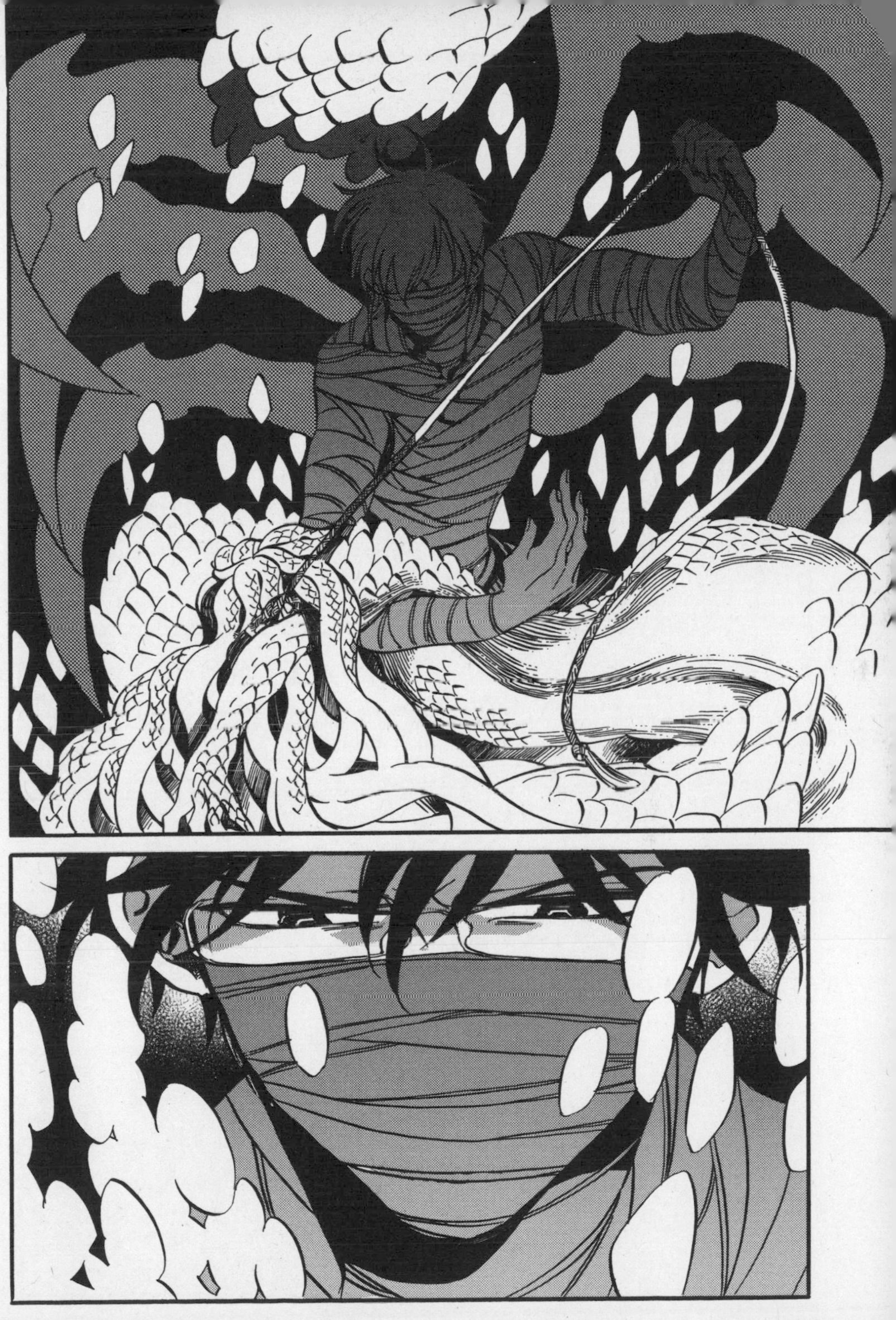

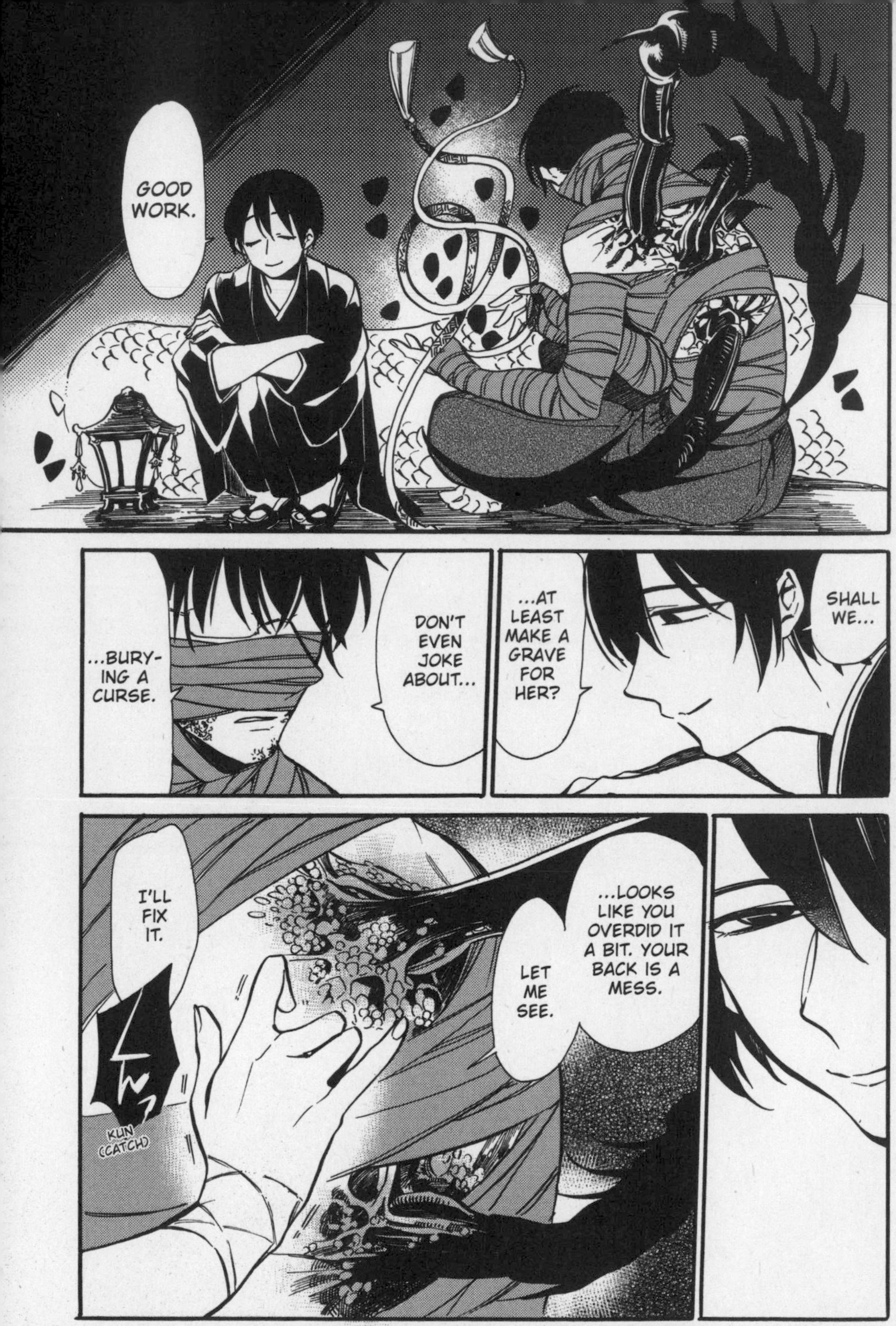
GOOD WORK.
SHALL WE...
...AT LEAST MAKE A GRAVE FOR HER?
DON'T EVEN JOKE ABOUT...
...BURYING A CURSE.
...LOOKS LIKE YOU OVERDID IT A BIT. YOUR BACK IS A MESS.
LET ME SEE.
I'LL FIX IT.
KUN (CATCH)

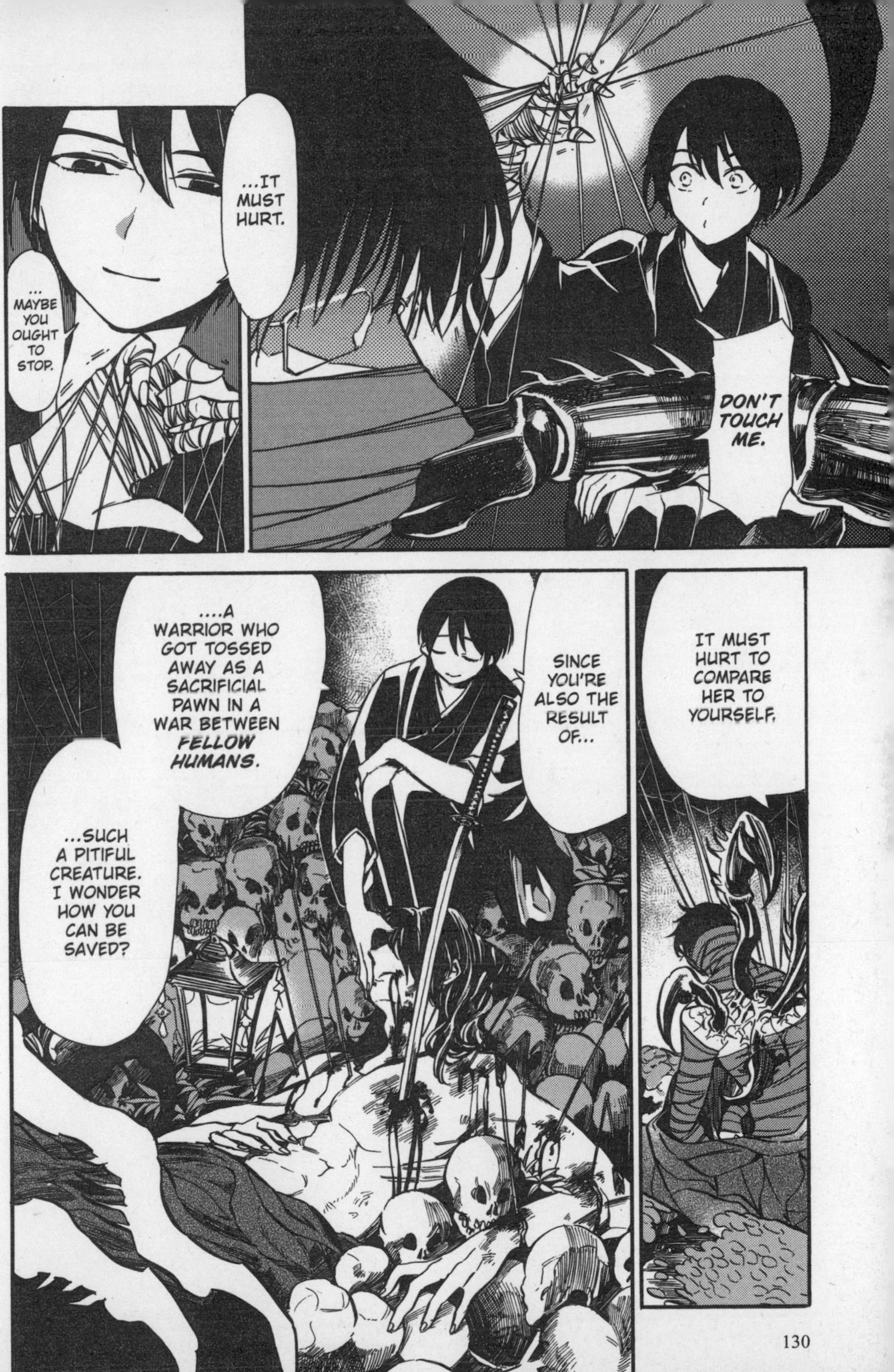
...IT MUST HURT.
DON'T TOUCH ME.
...MAYBE YOU OUGHT TO STOP.
IT MUST HURT TO COMPARE HER TO YOURSELF.
SINCE YOU'RE ALSO THE RESULT OF...
....A WARRIOR WHO GOT TOSSED AWAY AS A SACRIFICIAL PAWN IN A WAR BETWEEN FELLOW HUMANS.
...SUCH A PITIFUL CREATURE. I WONDER HOW YOU CAN BE SAVED?

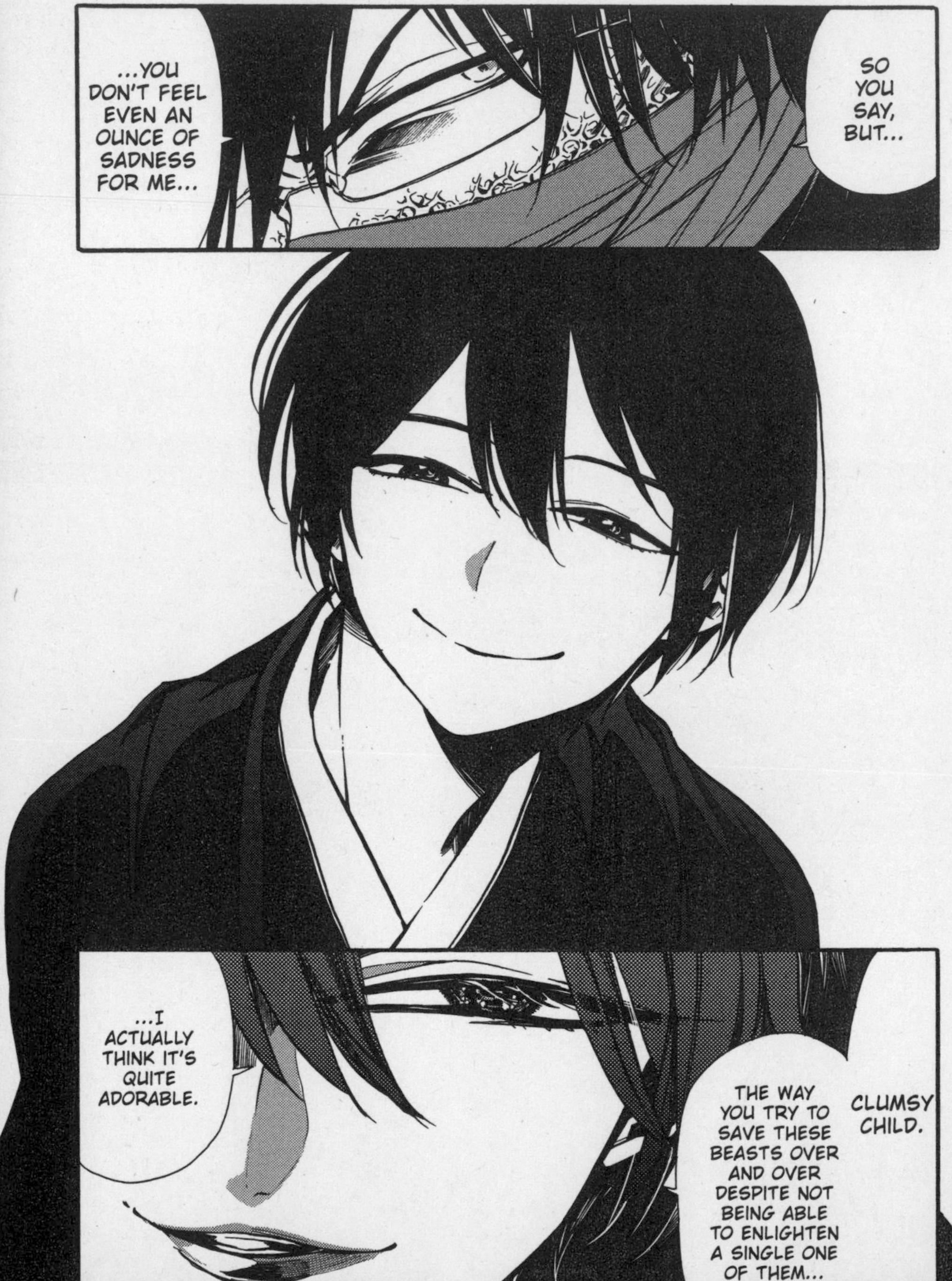
SO YOU SAY, BUT...
...YOU DON'T FEEL EVEN AN OUNCE OF SADNESS FOR ME...
CLUMSY CHILD.
THE WAY YOU TRY TO SAVE THESE BEASTS OVER AND OVER DESPITE NOT BEING ABLE TO ENLIGHTEN A SINGLE ONE OF THEM...
...I ACTUALLY THINK IT'S QUITE ADORABLE.

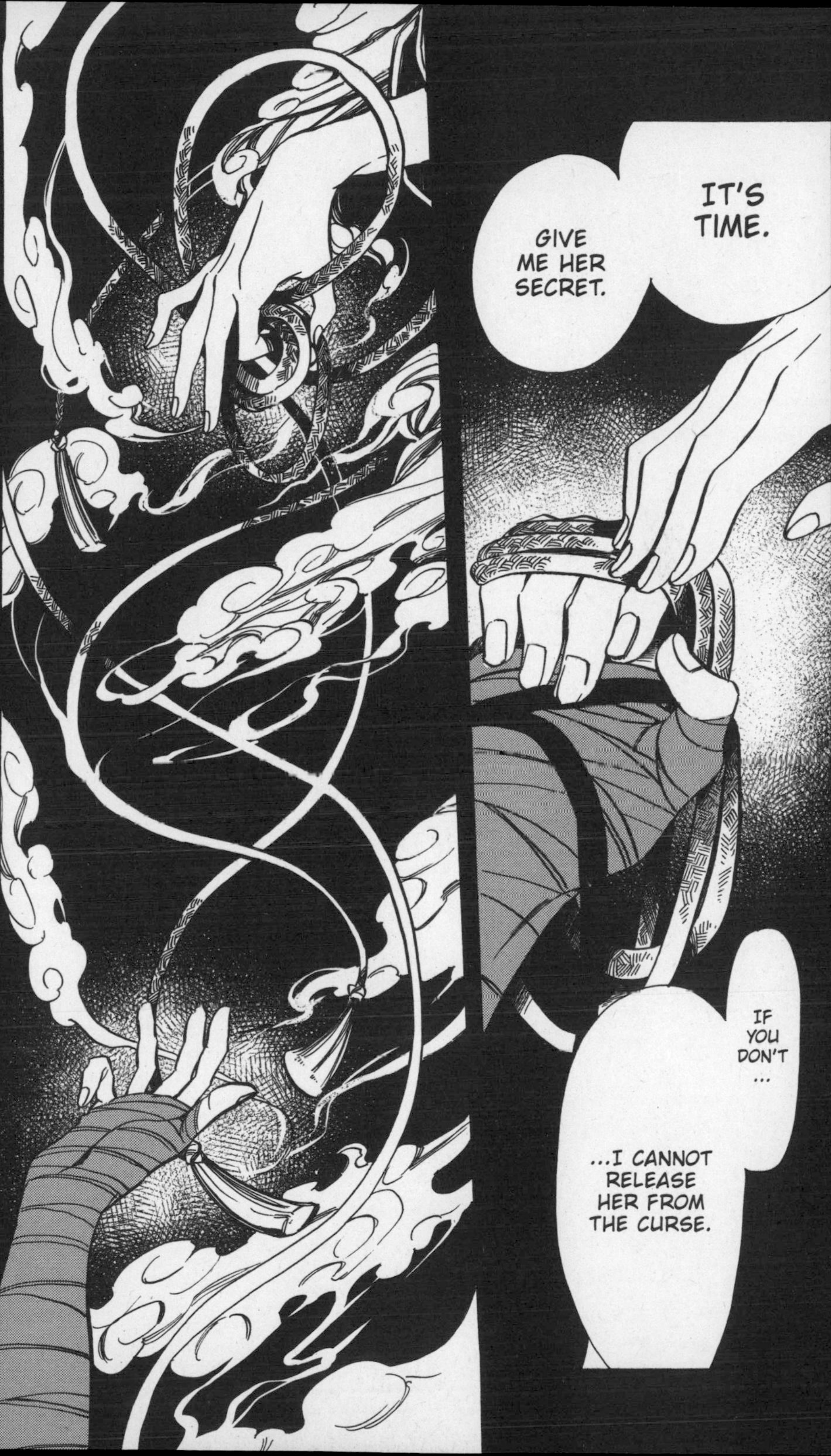
IT'S TIME.
GIVE ME HER SECRET.
IF YOU DON'T...
...I CANNOT RELEASE HER FROM THE CURSE.

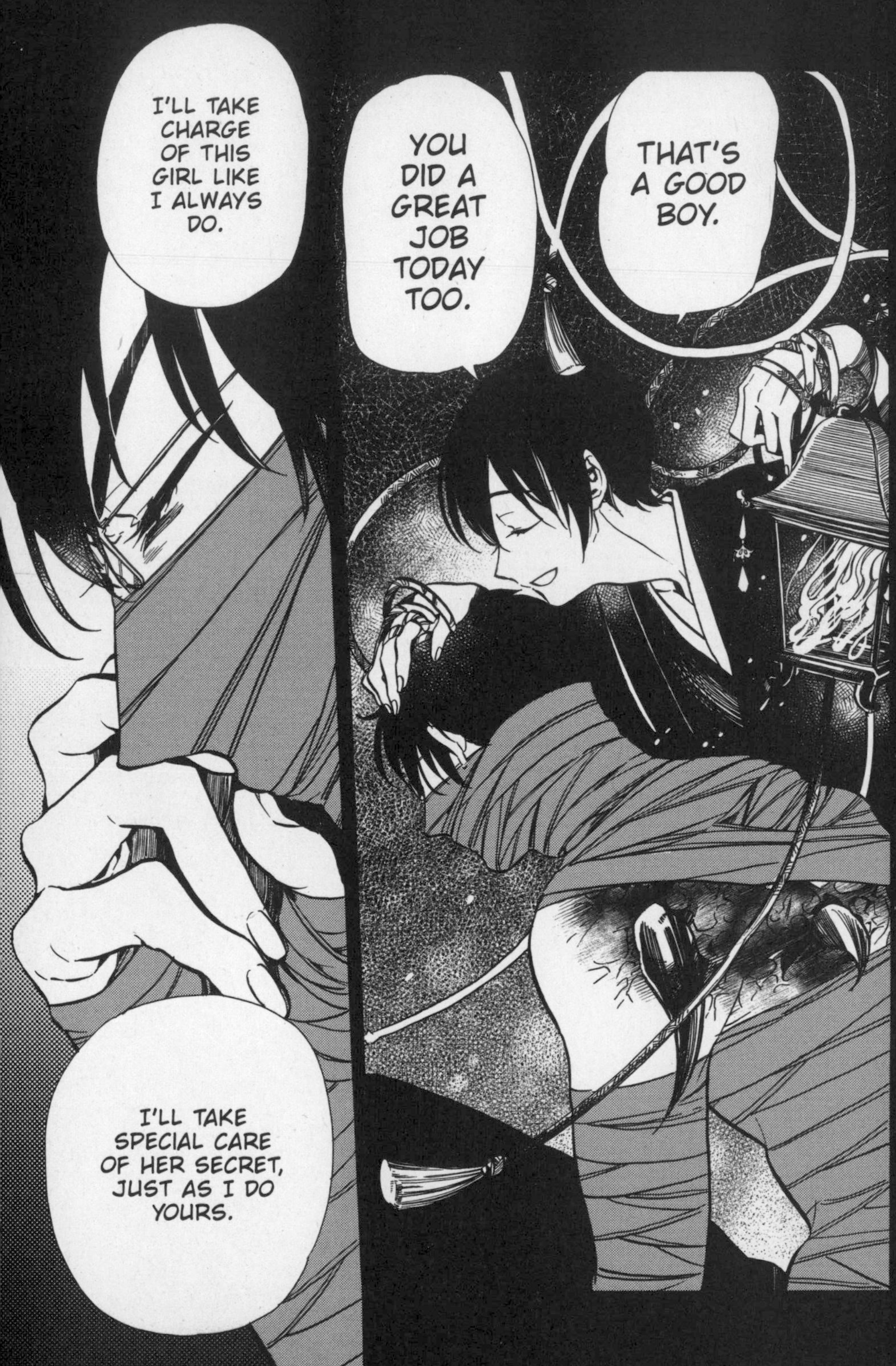
THAT'S A GOOD BOY.
YOU DID A GREAT JOB TODAY TOO.
I'LL TAKE CHARGE OF THIS GIRL LIKE I ALWAYS DO.
I'LL TAKE SPECIAL CARE OF HER SECRET, JUST AS I DO YOURS.

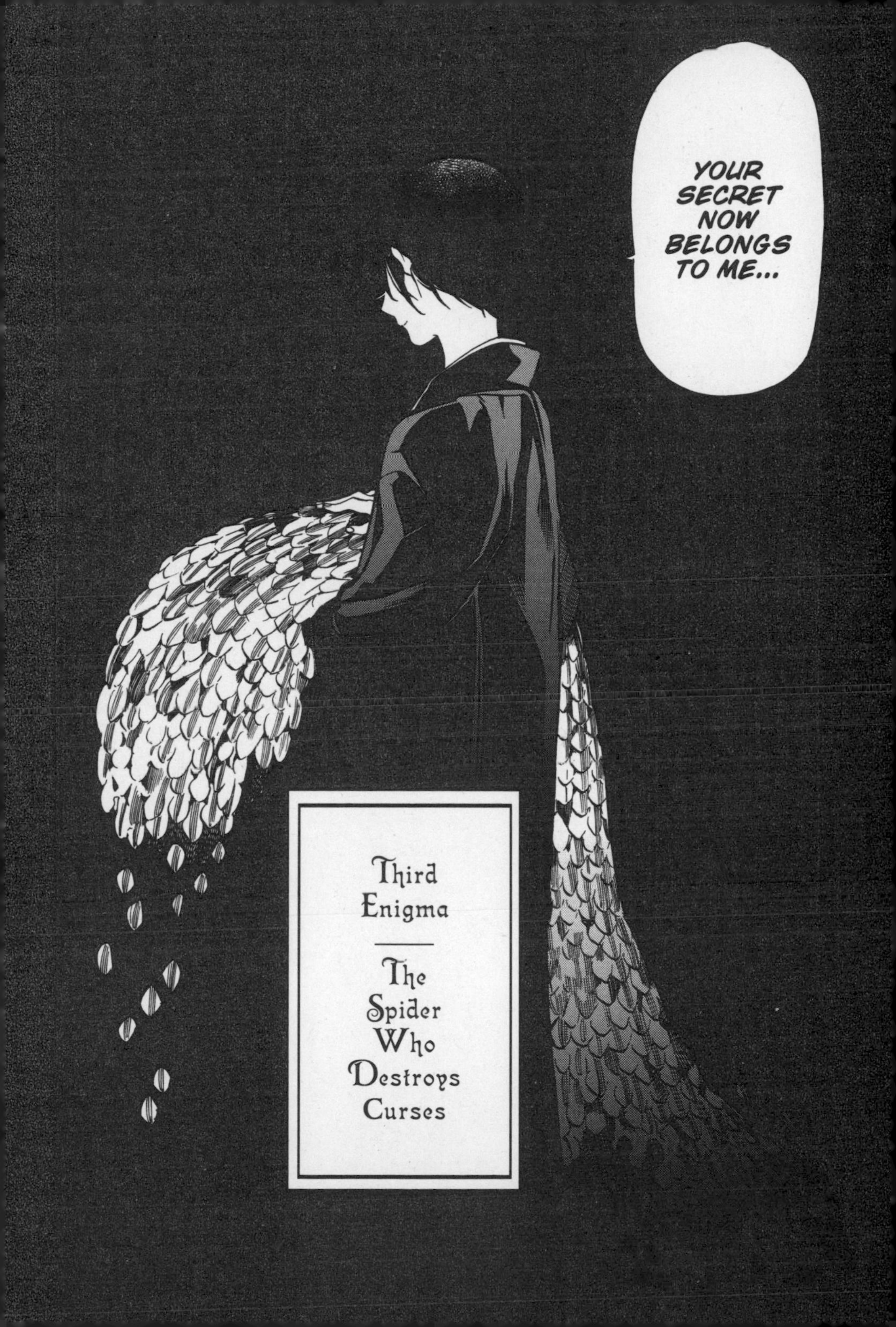
YOUR SECRET NOW BELONGS TO ME...

Third Enigma

The Spider Who Destroys Curses

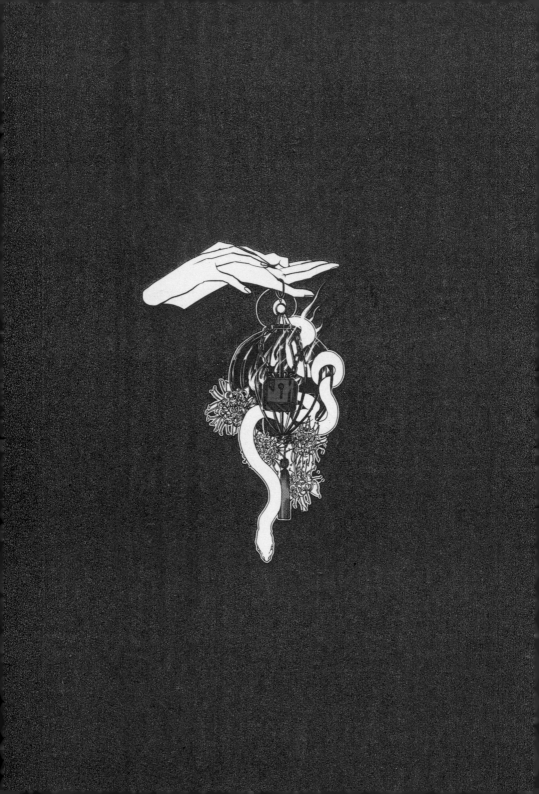

Phantom Tales of the Night

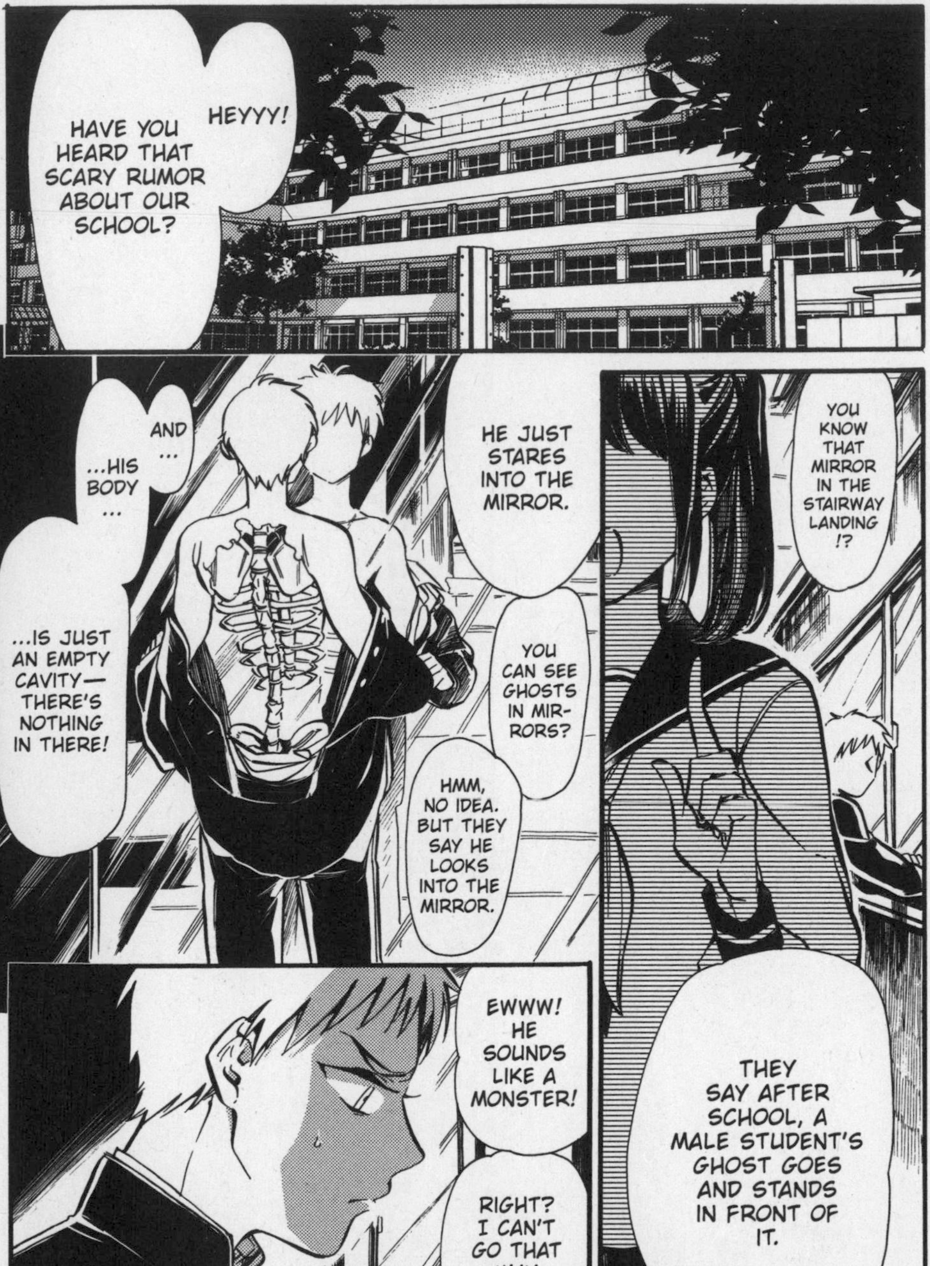
HEYYY!
HAVE YOU HEARD THAT SCARY RUMOR ABOUT OUR SCHOOL?
YOU KNOW THAT MIRROR IN THE STAIRWAY LANDING !?
THEY SAY AFTER SCHOOL, A MALE STUDENT'S GHOST GOES AND STANDS IN FRONT OF IT.
HE JUST STARES INTO THE MIRROR.
YOU CAN SEE GHOSTS IN MIR-RORS?
HMM, NO IDEA. BUT THEY SAY HE LOOKS INTO THE MIRROR.
AND ...
...HIS BODY ...
...IS JUST AN EMPTY CAVITY—THERE'S NOTHING IN THERE!
EWWW! HE SOUNDS LIKE A MONSTER!
RIGHT? I CAN'T GO THAT WAY AFTER SCHOOL ANYMORE!

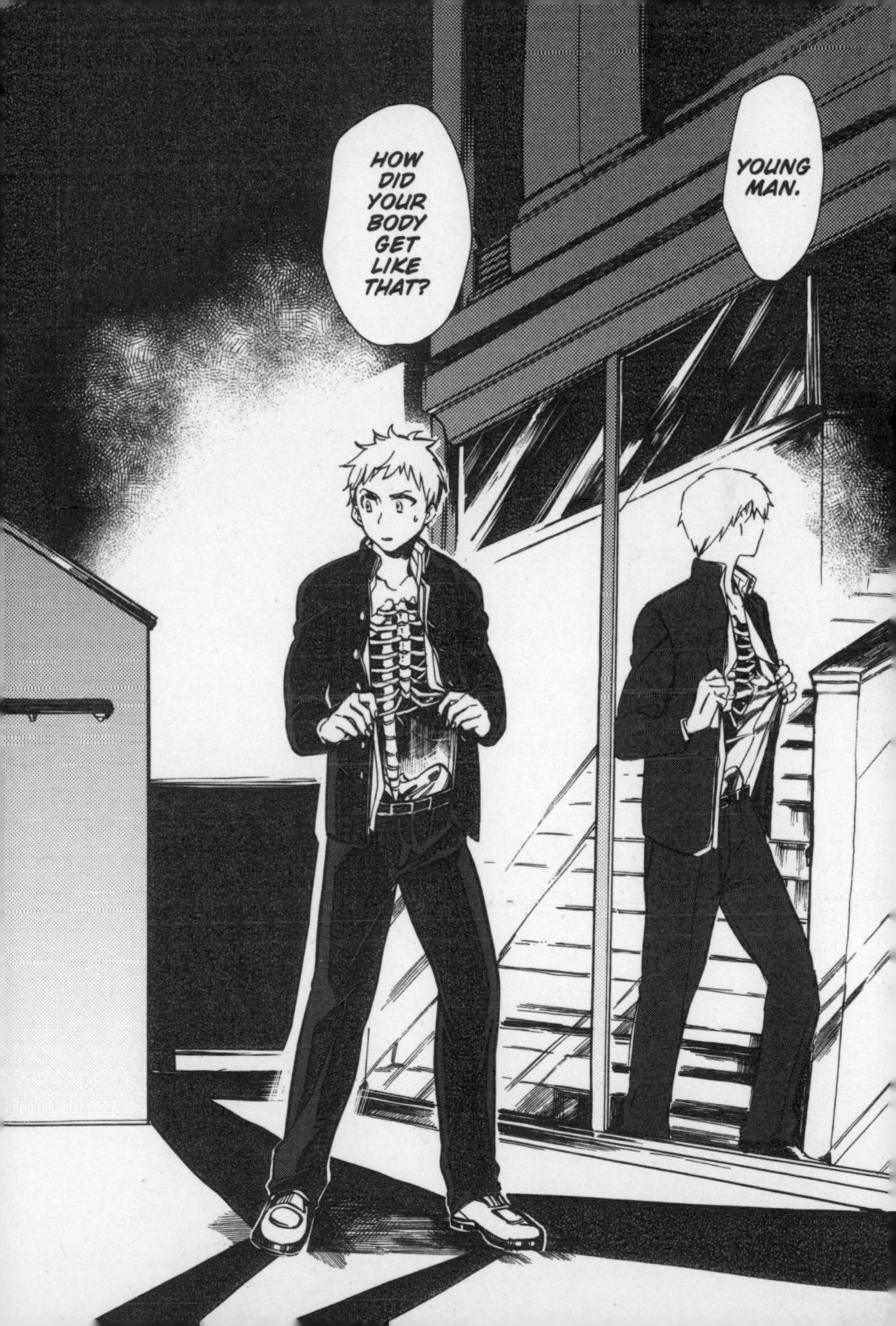
YOUNG MAN.
HOW DID YOUR BODY GET LIKE THAT?

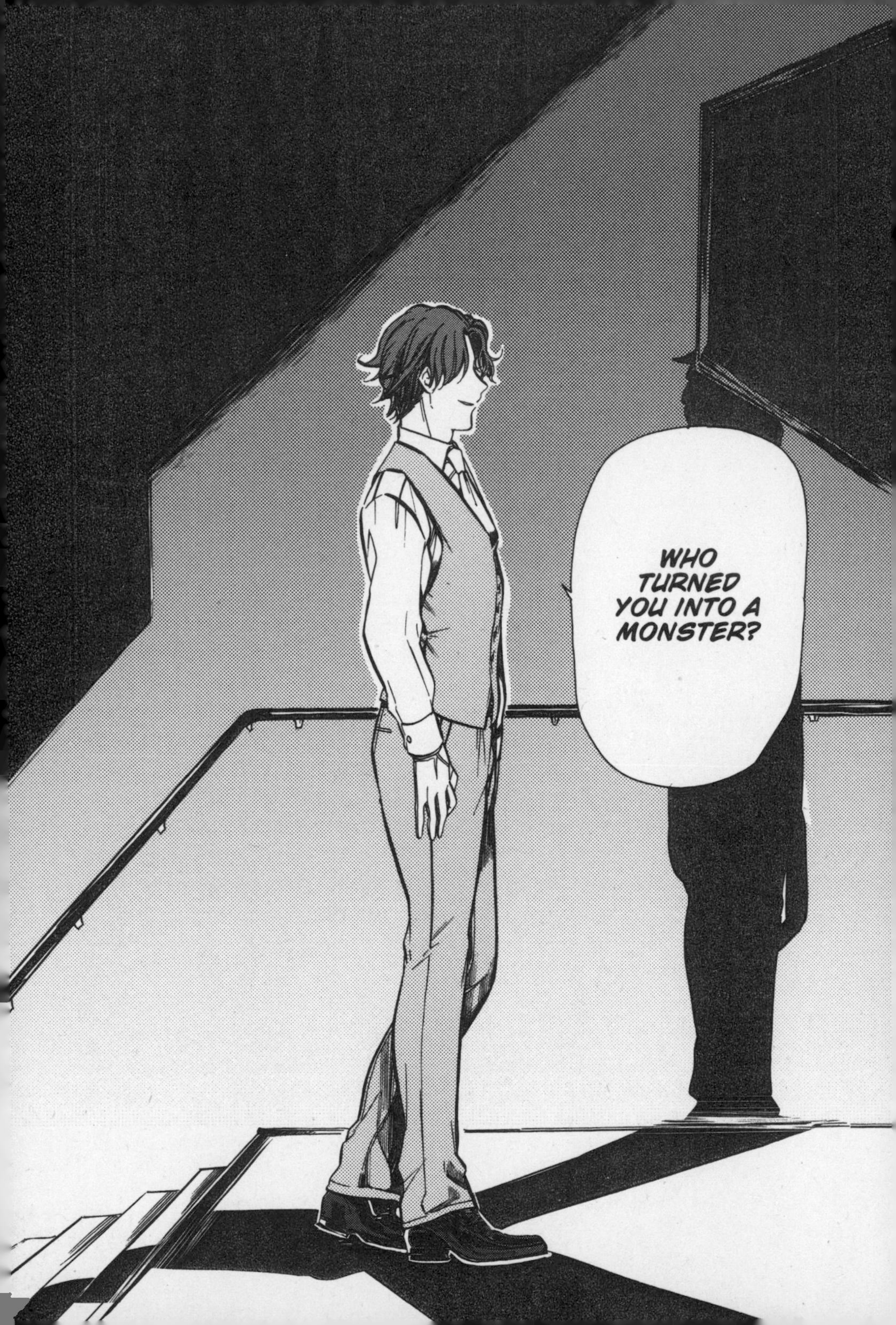
WHO TURNED YOU INTO A MONSTER?

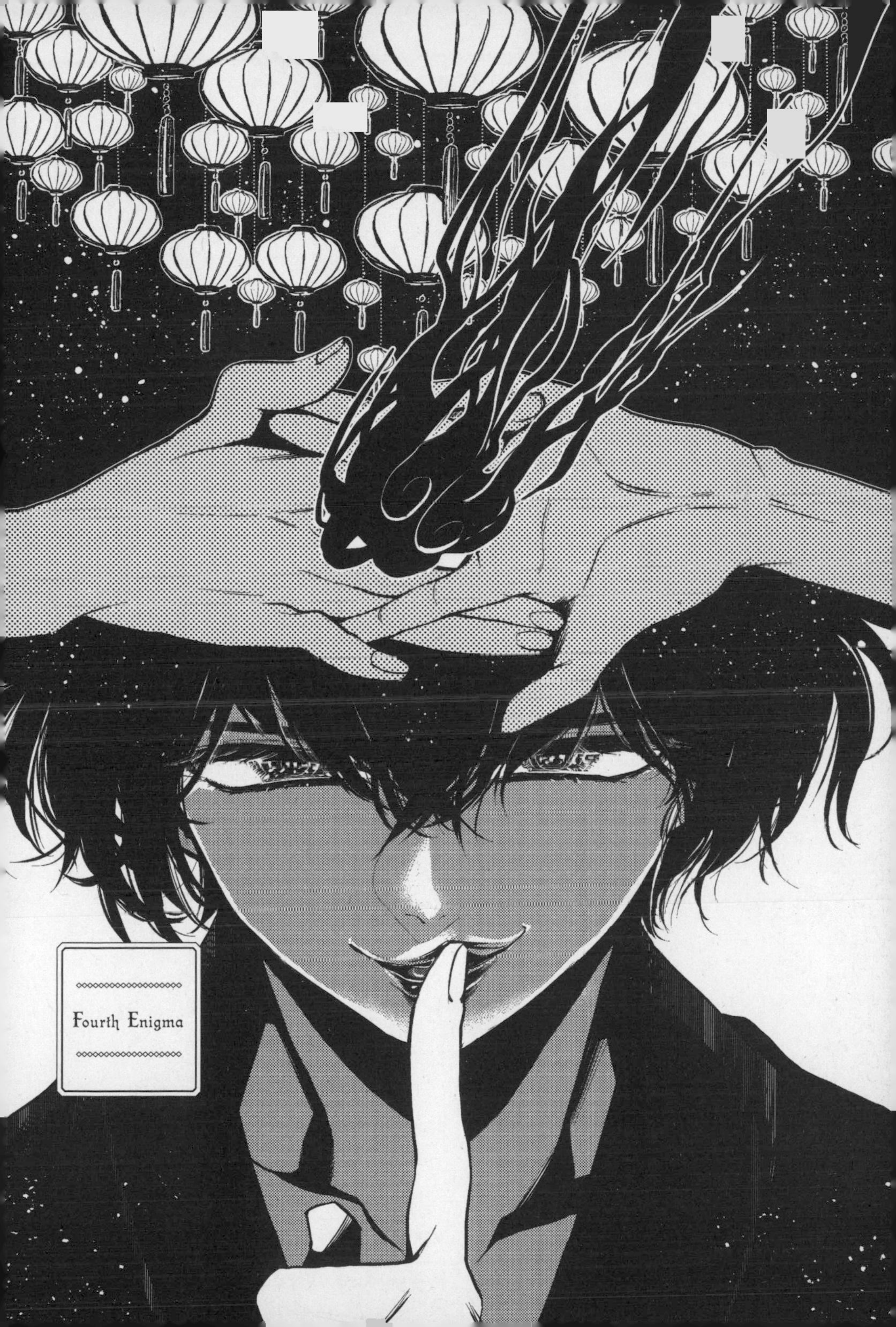
Fourth Enigma

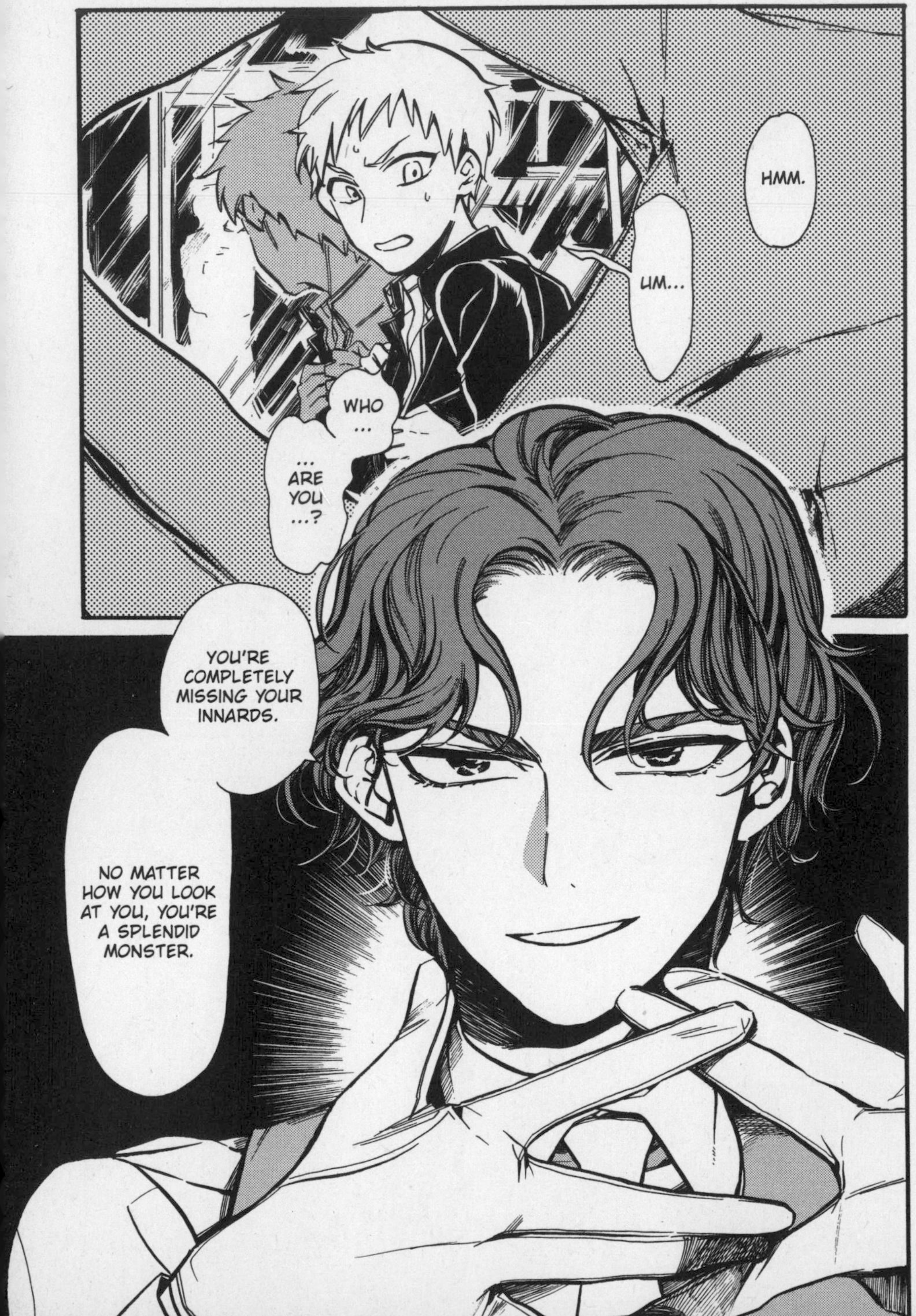
HMM.
UM...
WHO ...
... ARE YOU ...?
YOU'RE COMPLETELY MISSING YOUR INNARDS.
NO MATTER HOW YOU LOOK AT YOU, YOU'RE A SPLENDID MONSTER.

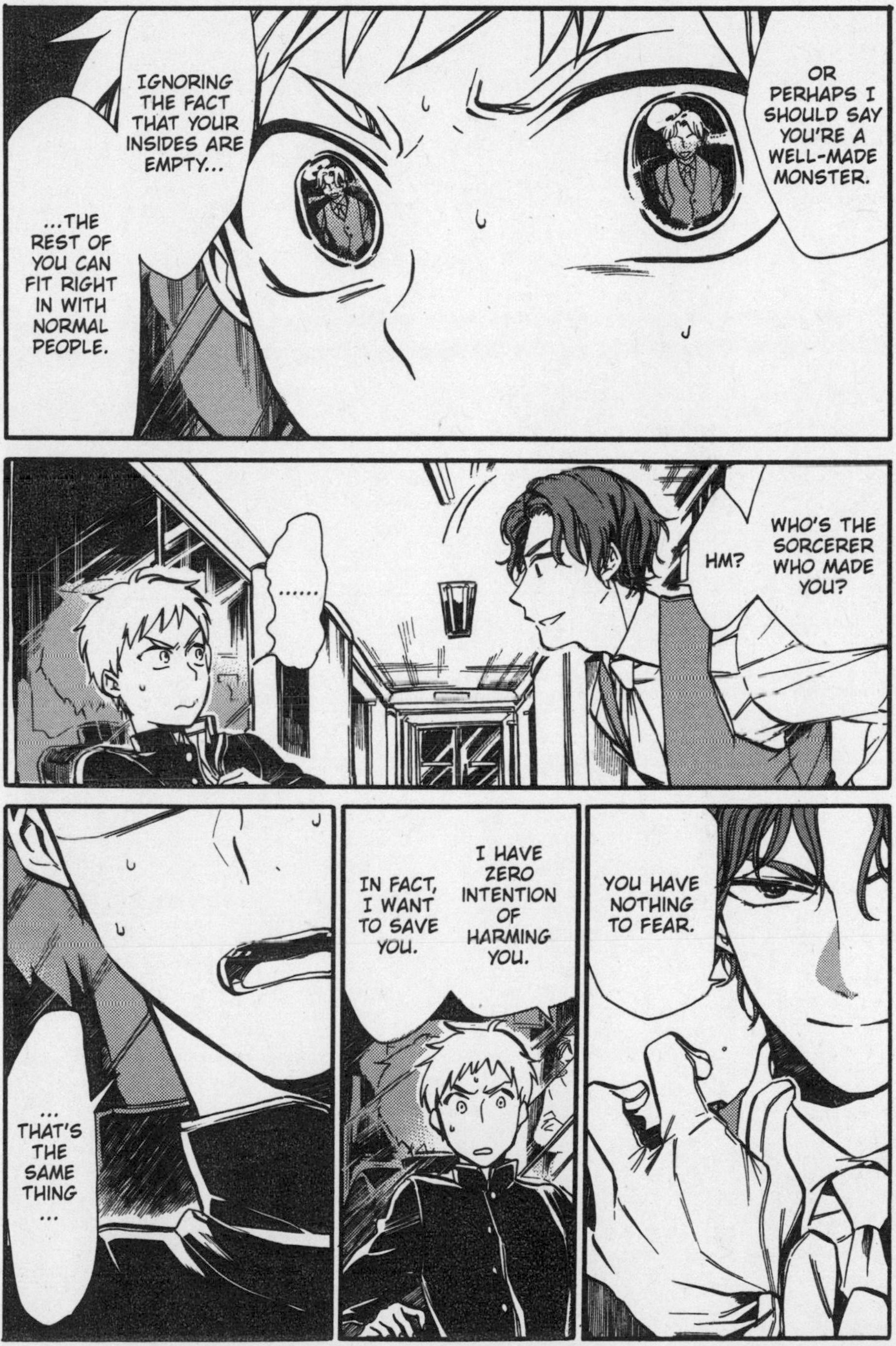
IGNORING THE FACT THAT YOUR INSIDES ARE EMPTY...
...THE REST OF YOU CAN FIT RIGHT IN WITH NORMAL PEOPLE.
OR PERHAPS I SHOULD SAY YOU'RE A WELL-MADE MONSTER.
HM?
WHO'S THE SORCERER WHO MADE YOU?
......
YOU HAVE NOTHING TO FEAR.
I HAVE ZERO INTENTION OF HARMING YOU.
IN FACT, I WANT TO SAVE YOU.
...THAT'S THE SAME THING...

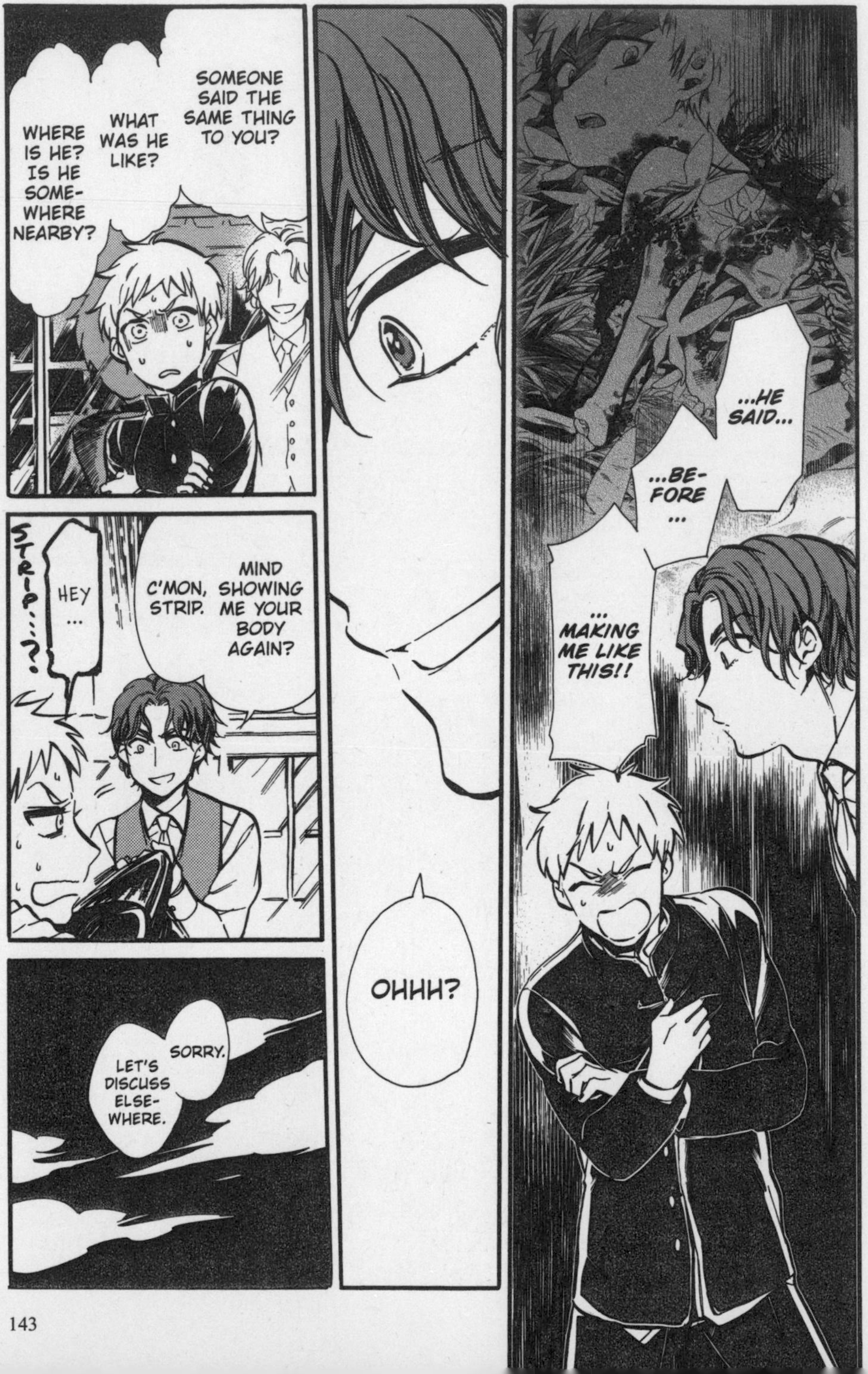
...HE SAID...
...BE-FORE...
...MAKING ME LIKE THIS!!
OHHH?
SOMEONE SAID THE SAME THING TO YOU?
WHAT WAS HE LIKE?
WHERE IS HE? IS HE SOME-WHERE NEARBY?
MIND SHOWING ME YOUR BODY AGAIN?
C'MON, STRIP.
HEY ...
STRIP...?
SORRY.
LET'S DISCUSS ELSE-WHERE.

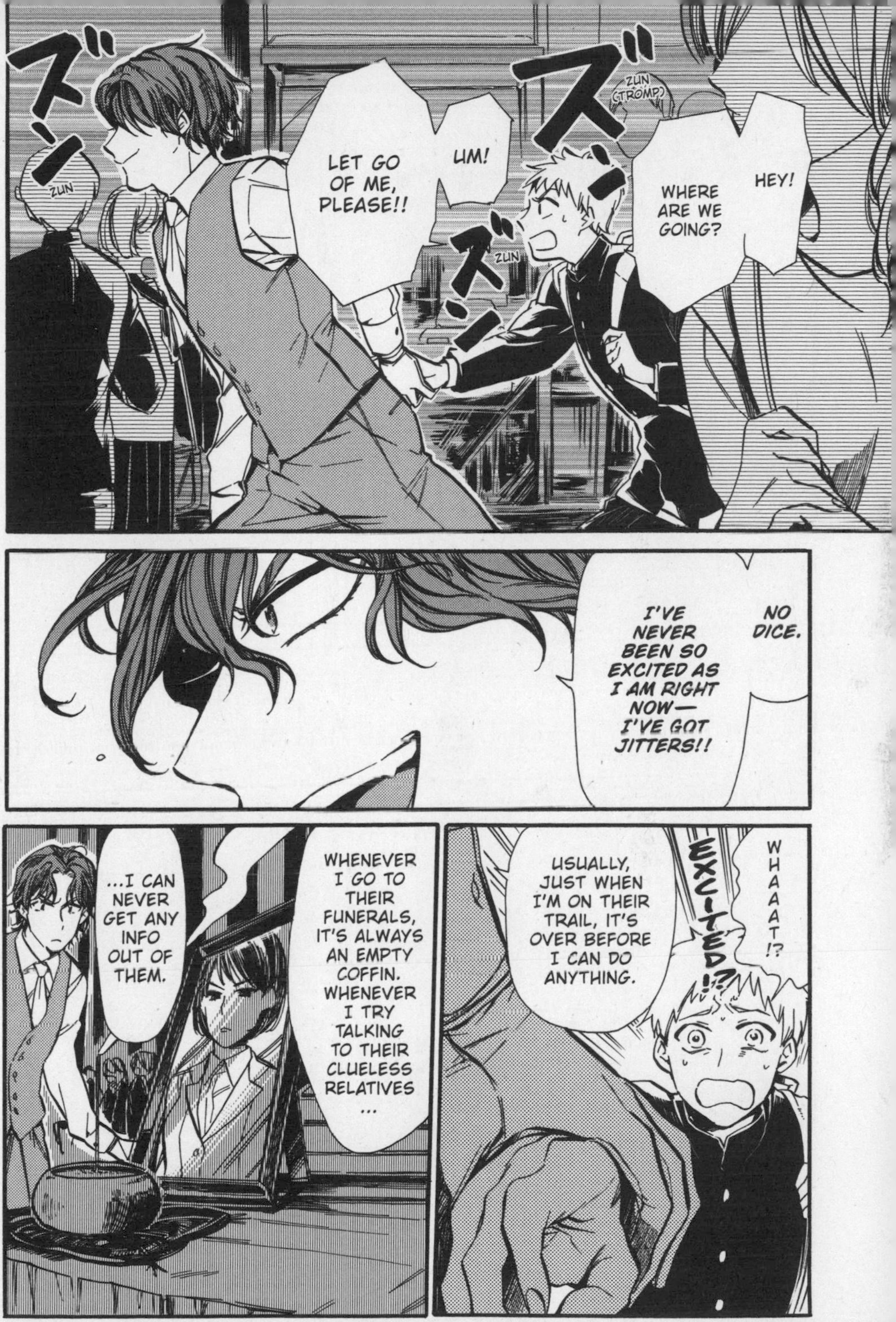
HEY!
WHERE ARE WE GOING?
ZUN (TROMP)
ZUN
UM!
LET GO OF ME, PLEASE!!
ZUN
NO DICE.
I'VE NEVER BEEN SO EXCITED AS I AM RIGHT NOW— I'VE GOT JITTERS!!
WHAAAAT!?
EXCITED!?
USUALLY, JUST WHEN I'M ON THEIR TRAIL, IT'S OVER BEFORE I CAN DO ANYTHING.
WHENEVER I GO TO THEIR FUNERALS, IT'S ALWAYS AN EMPTY COFFIN. WHENEVER I TRY TALKING TO THEIR CLUELESS RELATIVES ...
...I CAN NEVER GET ANY INFO OUT OF THEM.

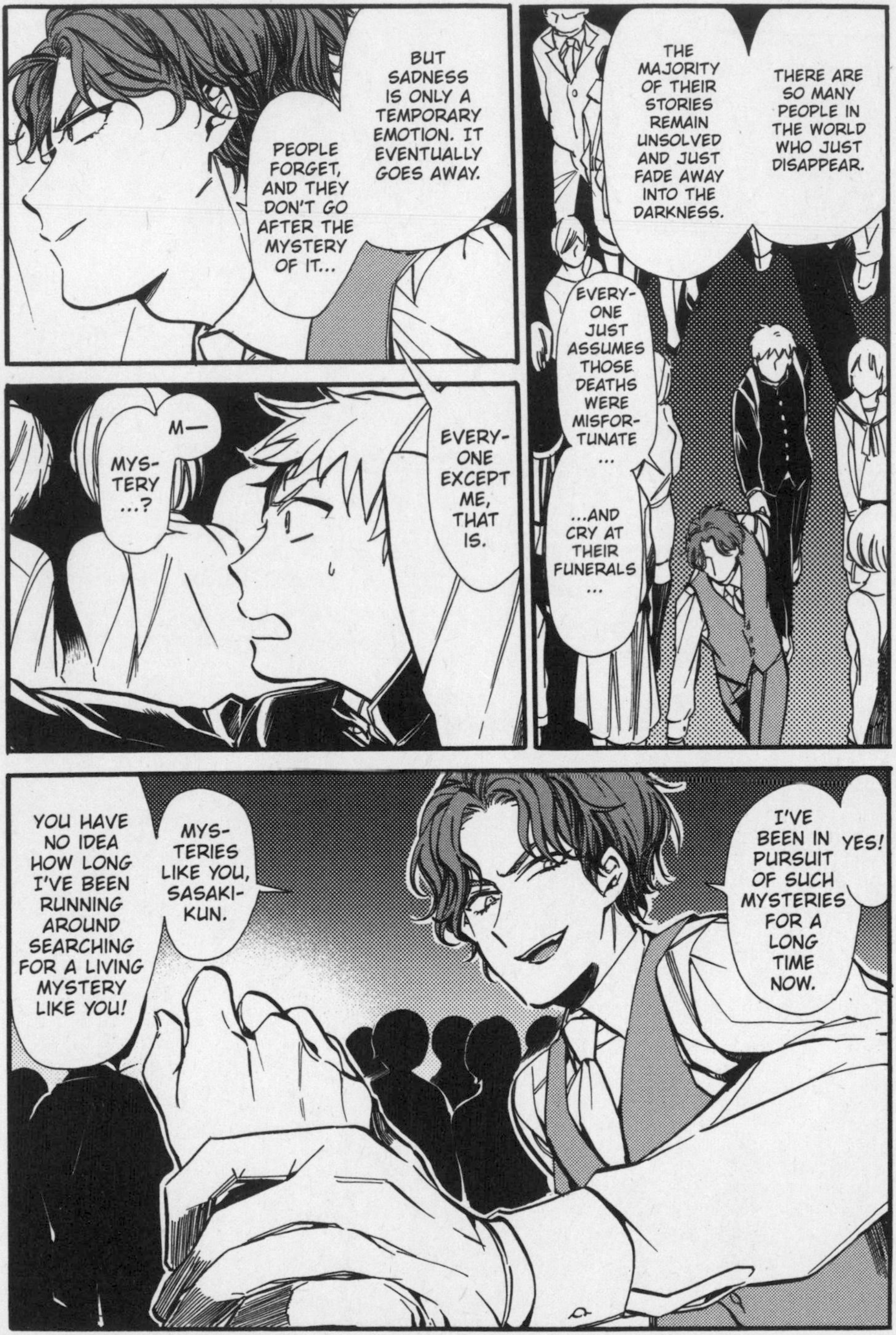
THERE ARE SO MANY PEOPLE IN THE WORLD WHO JUST DISAPPEAR.
THE MAJORITY OF THEIR STORIES REMAIN UNSOLVED AND JUST FADE AWAY INTO THE DARKNESS.
EVERY-ONE JUST ASSUMES THOSE DEATHS WERE MISFOR-TUNATE...
...AND CRY AT THEIR FUNERALS...
BUT SADNESS IS ONLY A TEMPORARY EMOTION. IT EVENTUALLY GOES AWAY.
PEOPLE FORGET, AND THEY DON'T GO AFTER THE MYSTERY OF IT...
EVERY-ONE EXCEPT ME, THAT IS.
M— MYS-TERY...?
YES!
I'VE BEEN IN PURSUIT OF SUCH MYSTERIES FOR A LONG TIME NOW.
MYS-TERIES LIKE YOU, SASAKI-KUN.
YOU HAVE NO IDEA HOW LONG I'VE BEEN RUNNING AROUND SEARCHING FOR A LIVING MYSTERY LIKE YOU!

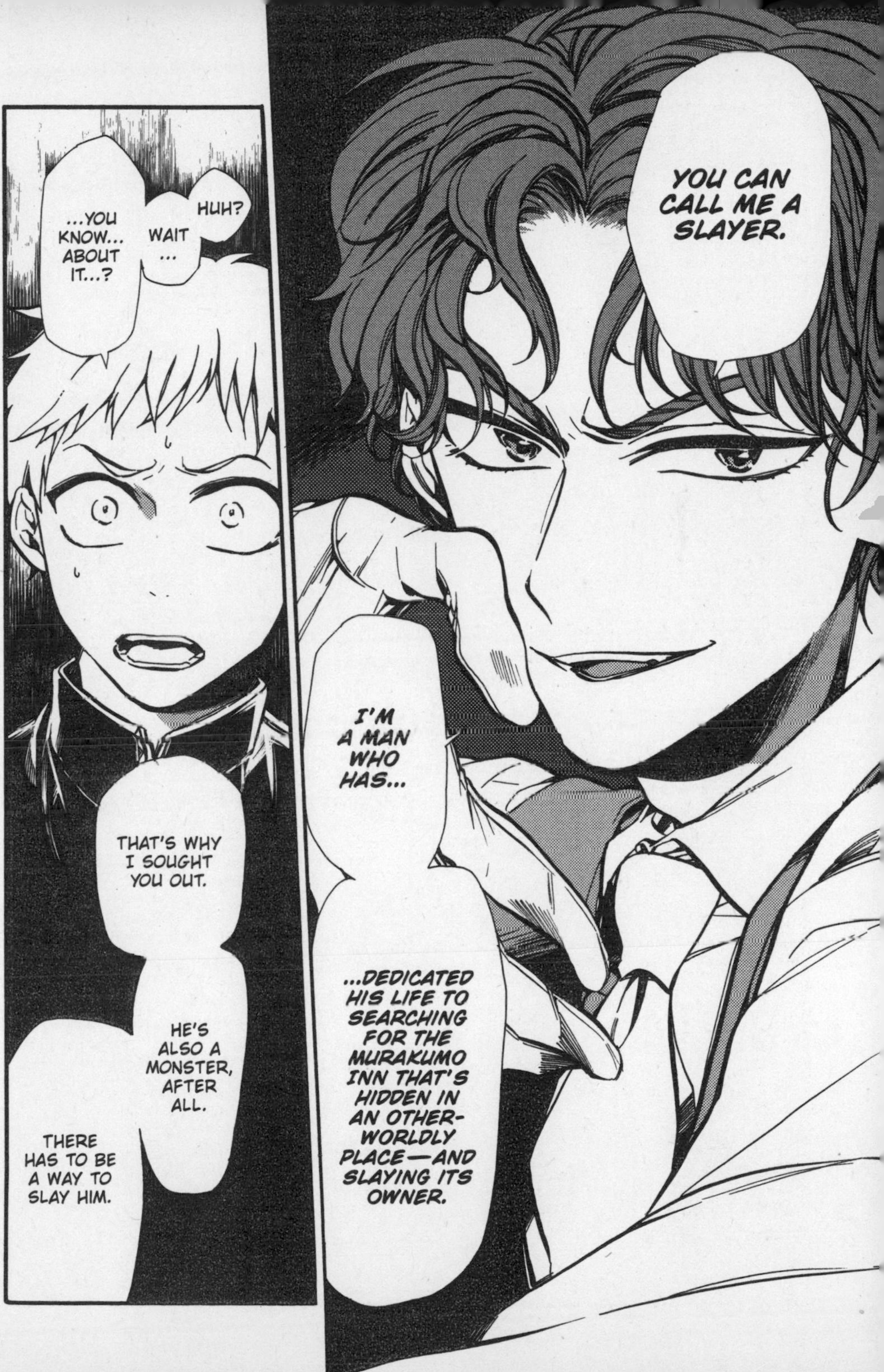
YOU CAN CALL ME A SLAYER.
I'M A MAN WHO HAS...
...DEDICATED HIS LIFE TO SEARCHING FOR THE MURAKUMO INN THAT'S HIDDEN IN AN OTHER-WORLDLY PLACE—AND SLAYING ITS OWNER.
HUH?
WAIT...
...YOU KNOW... ABOUT IT...?
THAT'S WHY I SOUGHT YOU OUT.
HE'S ALSO A MONSTER, AFTER ALL.
THERE HAS TO BE A WAY TO SLAY HIM.

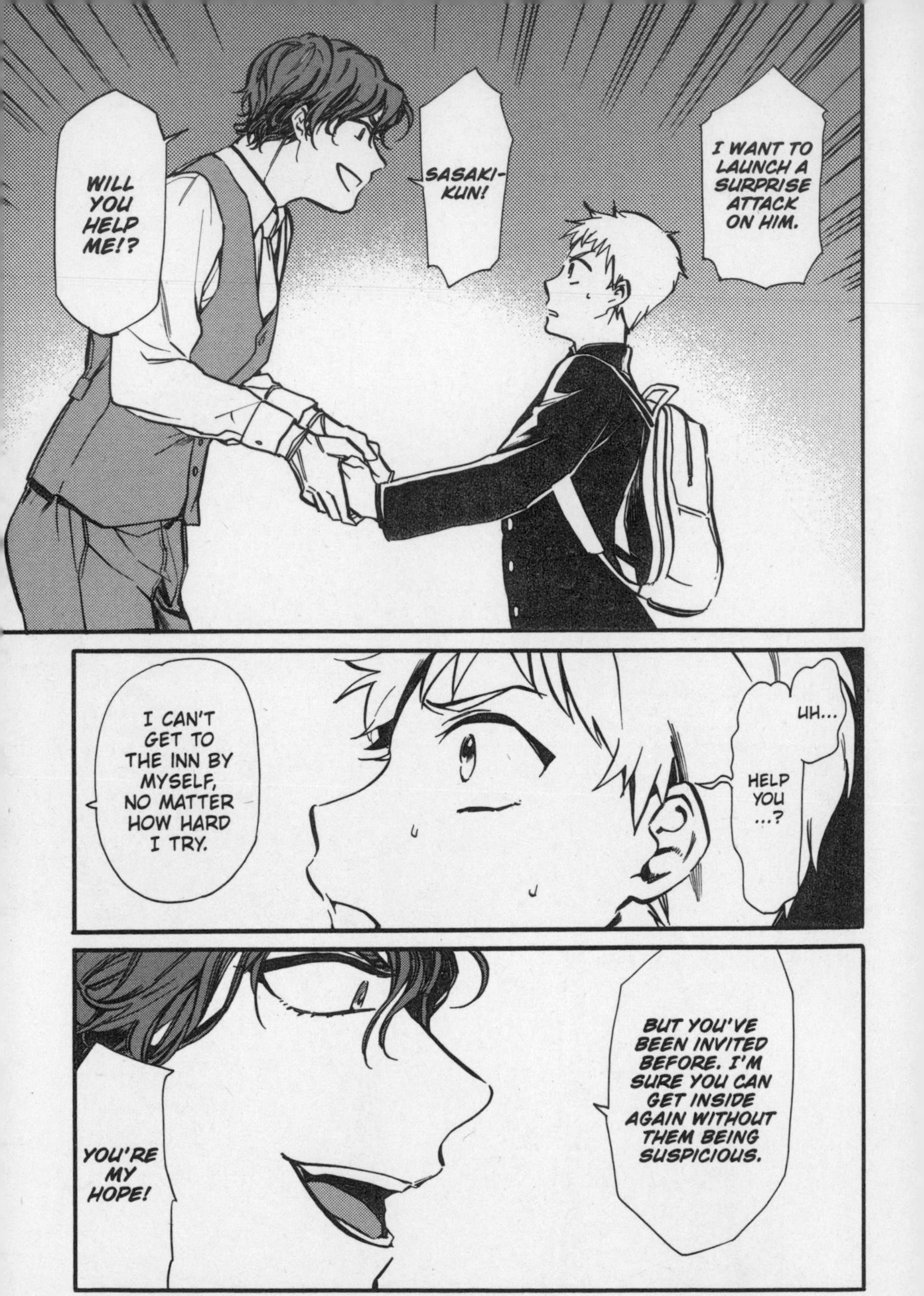
I WANT TO LAUNCH A SURPRISE ATTACK ON HIM.
SASAKI-KUN!
WILL YOU HELP ME!?
UH...
HELP YOU ...?
I CAN'T GET TO THE INN BY MYSELF, NO MATTER HOW HARD I TRY.
BUT YOU'VE BEEN INVITED BEFORE. I'M SURE YOU CAN GET INSIDE AGAIN WITHOUT THEM BEING SUSPICIOUS.
YOU'RE MY HOPE!

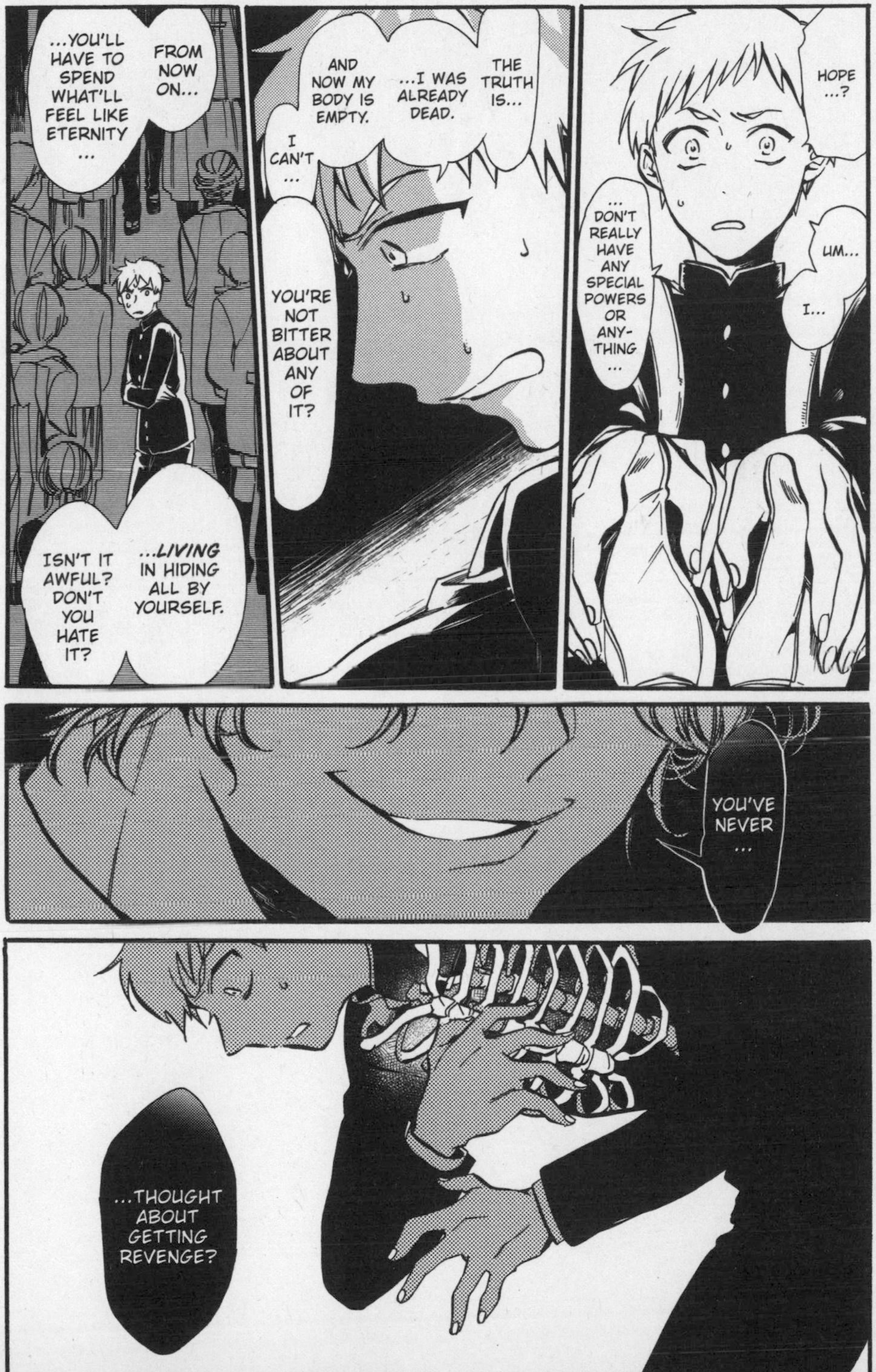
HOPE ...?
UM...
I...
... DON'T REALLY HAVE ANY SPECIAL POWERS OR ANY-THING ...
THE TRUTH IS...
...I WAS ALREADY DEAD.
AND NOW MY BODY IS EMPTY.
I CAN'T ...
YOU'RE NOT BITTER ABOUT ANY OF IT?
FROM NOW ON...
...YOU'LL HAVE TO SPEND WHAT'LL FEEL LIKE ETERNITY ...
...*LIVING* IN HIDING ALL BY YOURSELF.
ISN'T IT AWFUL? DON'T YOU HATE IT?
YOU'VE NEVER ...
...THOUGHT ABOUT GETTING REVENGE?

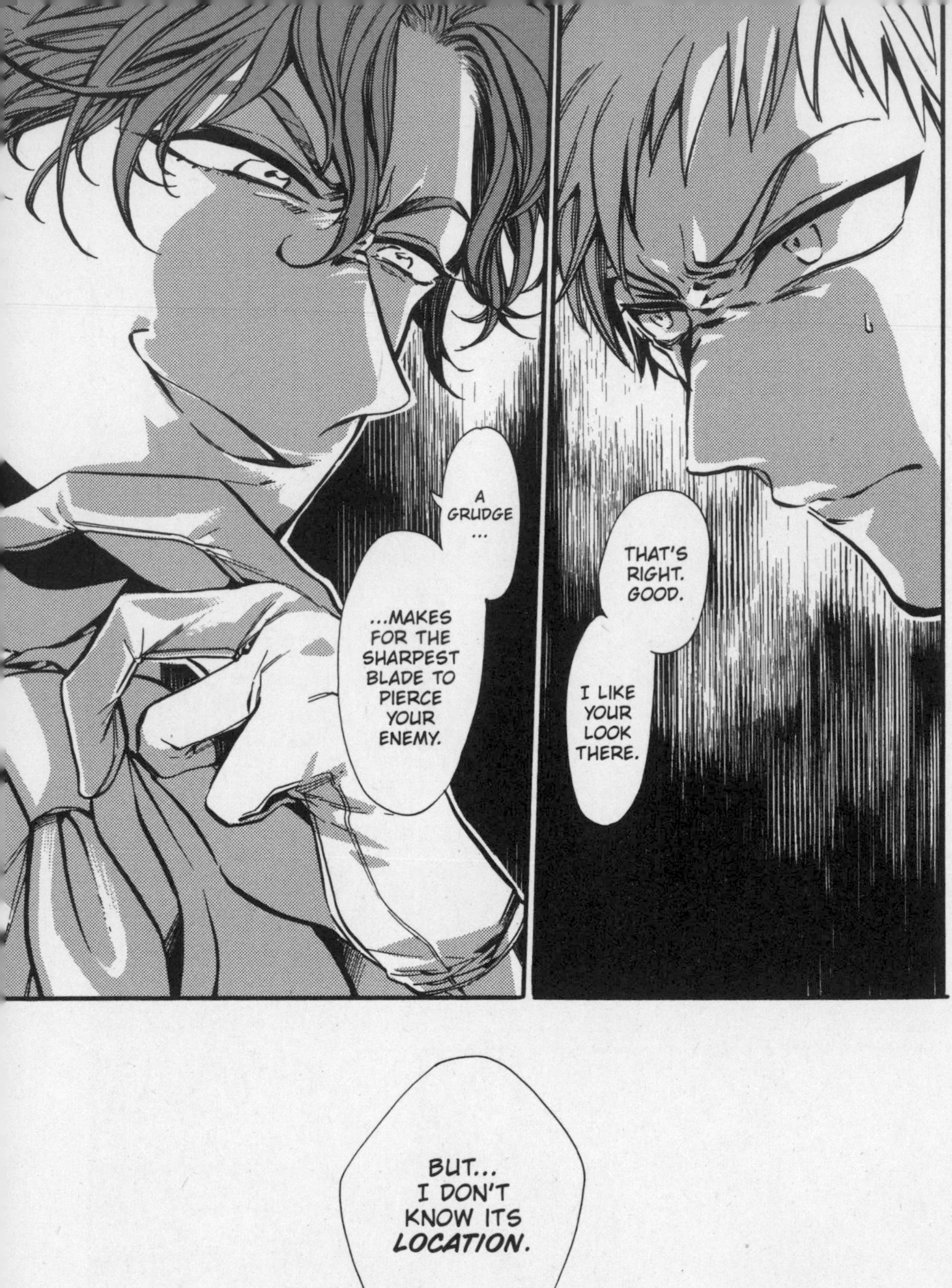
THAT'S RIGHT. GOOD.
I LIKE YOUR LOOK THERE.
A GRUDGE ...
...MAKES FOR THE SHARPEST BLADE TO PIERCE YOUR ENEMY.
BUT... I DON'T KNOW ITS *LOCATION*.

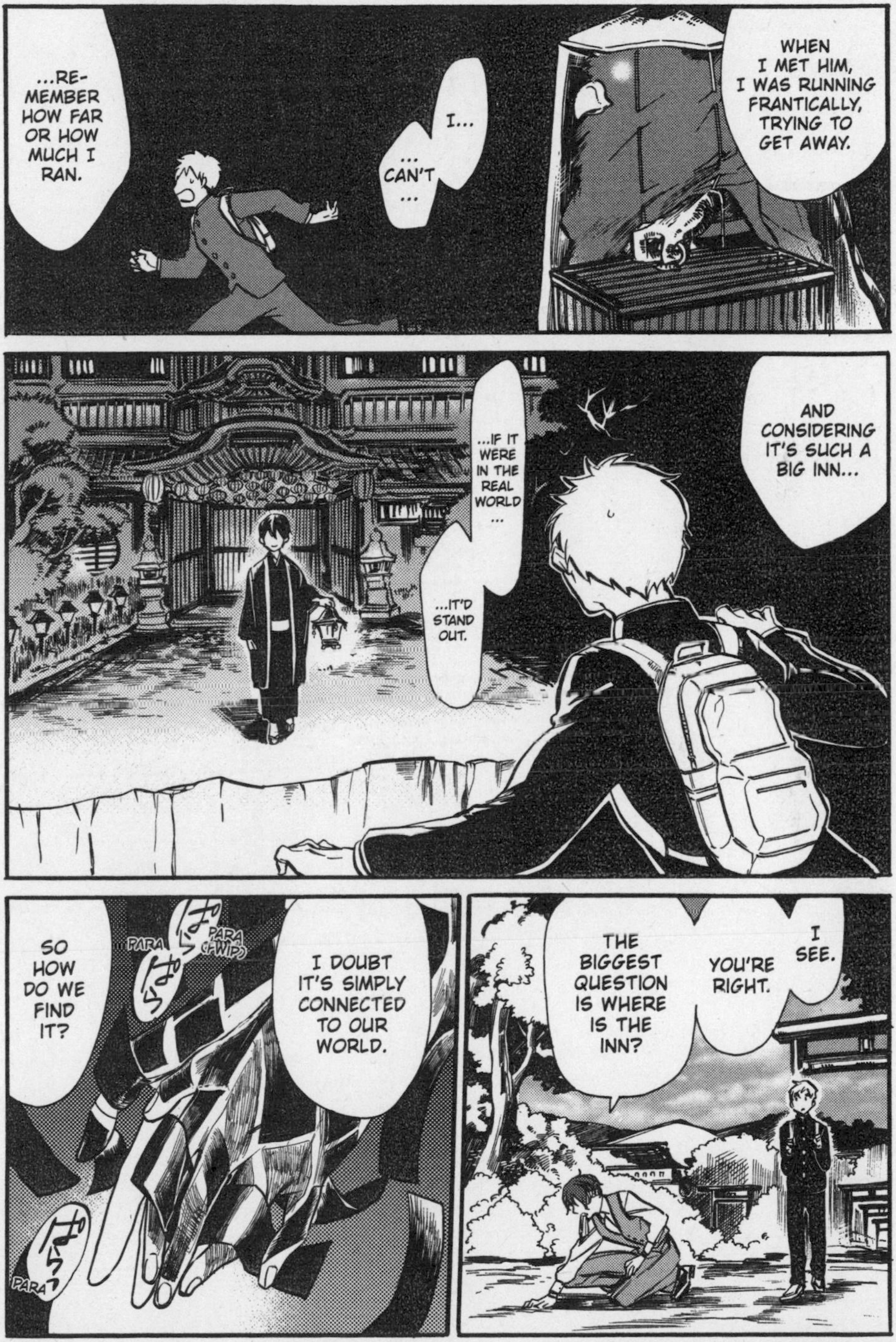
WHEN I MET HIM, I WAS RUNNING FRANTICALLY, TRYING TO GET AWAY.
I...
...CAN'T...
...RE-MEMBER HOW FAR OR HOW MUCH I RAN.
AND CONSIDERING IT'S SUCH A BIG INN...
...IF IT WERE IN THE REAL WORLD...
...IT'D STAND OUT.
I SEE.
YOU'RE RIGHT.
THE BIGGEST QUESTION IS WHERE IS THE INN?
I DOUBT IT'S SIMPLY CONNECTED TO OUR WORLD.
PARA PARA (FWIP)
SO HOW DO WE FIND IT?
PARA

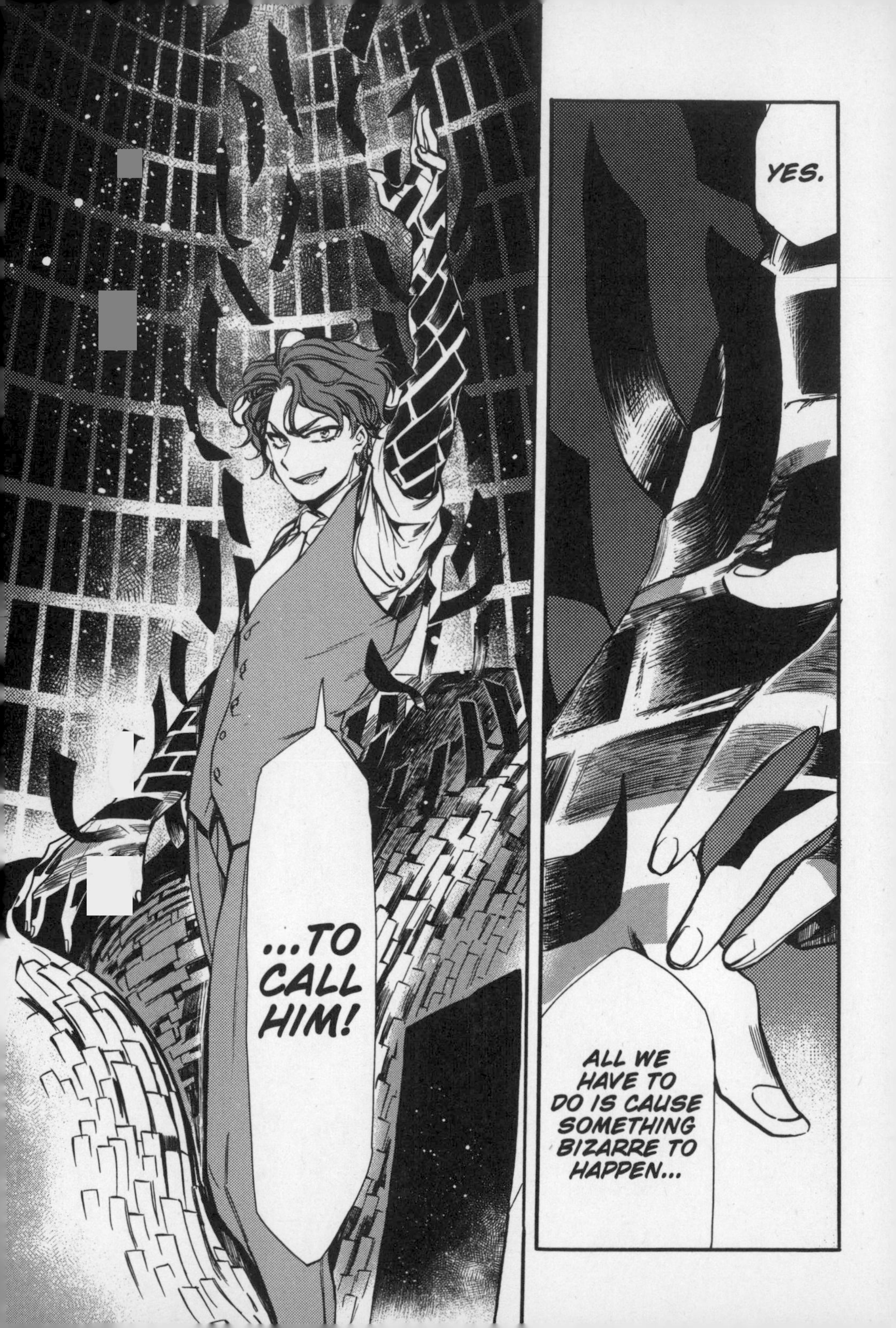
YES.
ALL WE HAVE TO DO IS CAUSE SOMETHING BIZARRE TO HAPPEN...
...TO CALL HIM!

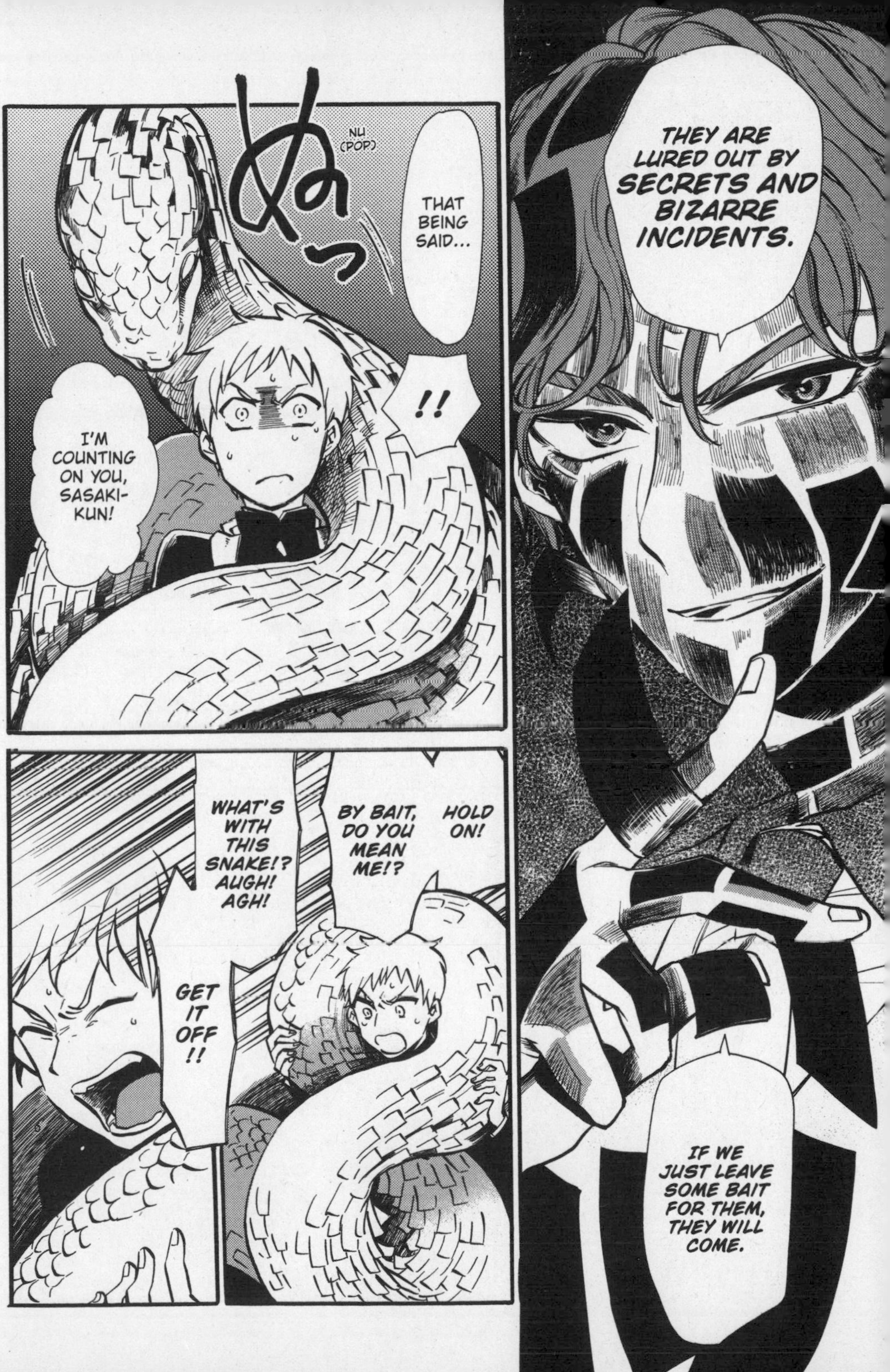
THEY ARE LURED OUT BY SECRETS AND BIZARRE INCIDENTS.
IF WE JUST LEAVE SOME BAIT FOR THEM, THEY WILL COME.
THAT BEING SAID...
ぬっ
NU (POP)
!!
I'M COUNTING ON YOU, SASAKI-KUN!
HOLD ON!
BY BAIT, DO YOU MEAN ME!?
WHAT'S WITH THIS SNAKE!? AUGH! AGH!
GET IT OFF!!

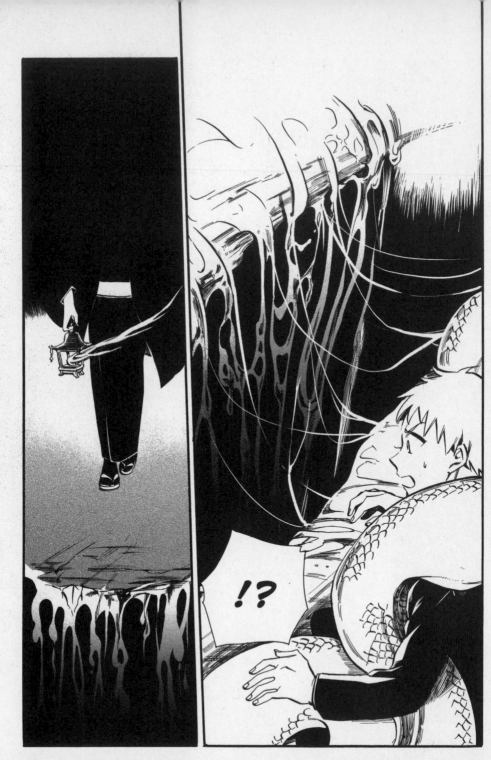

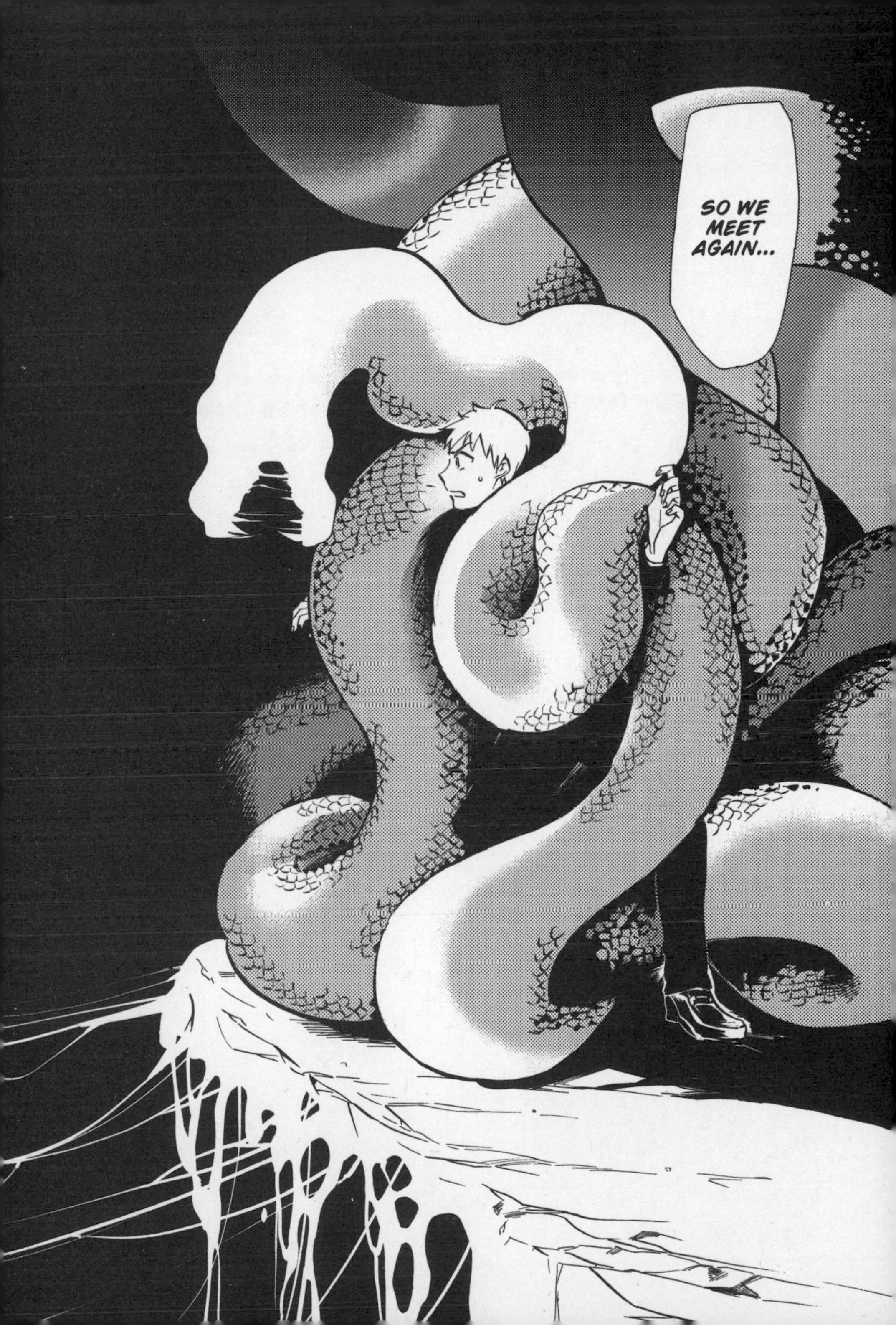
SO WE MEET AGAIN...

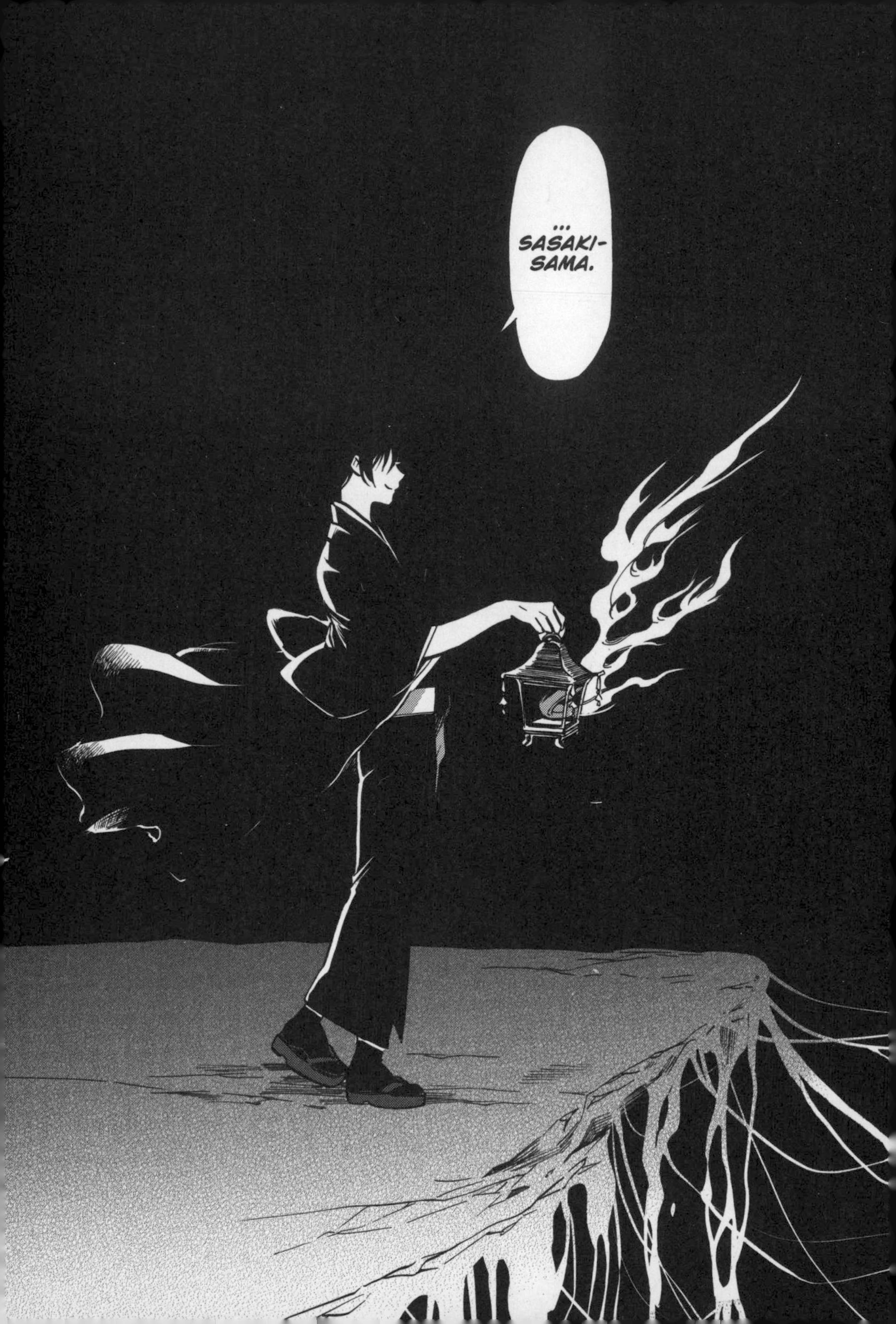
...SASAKI-SAMA.

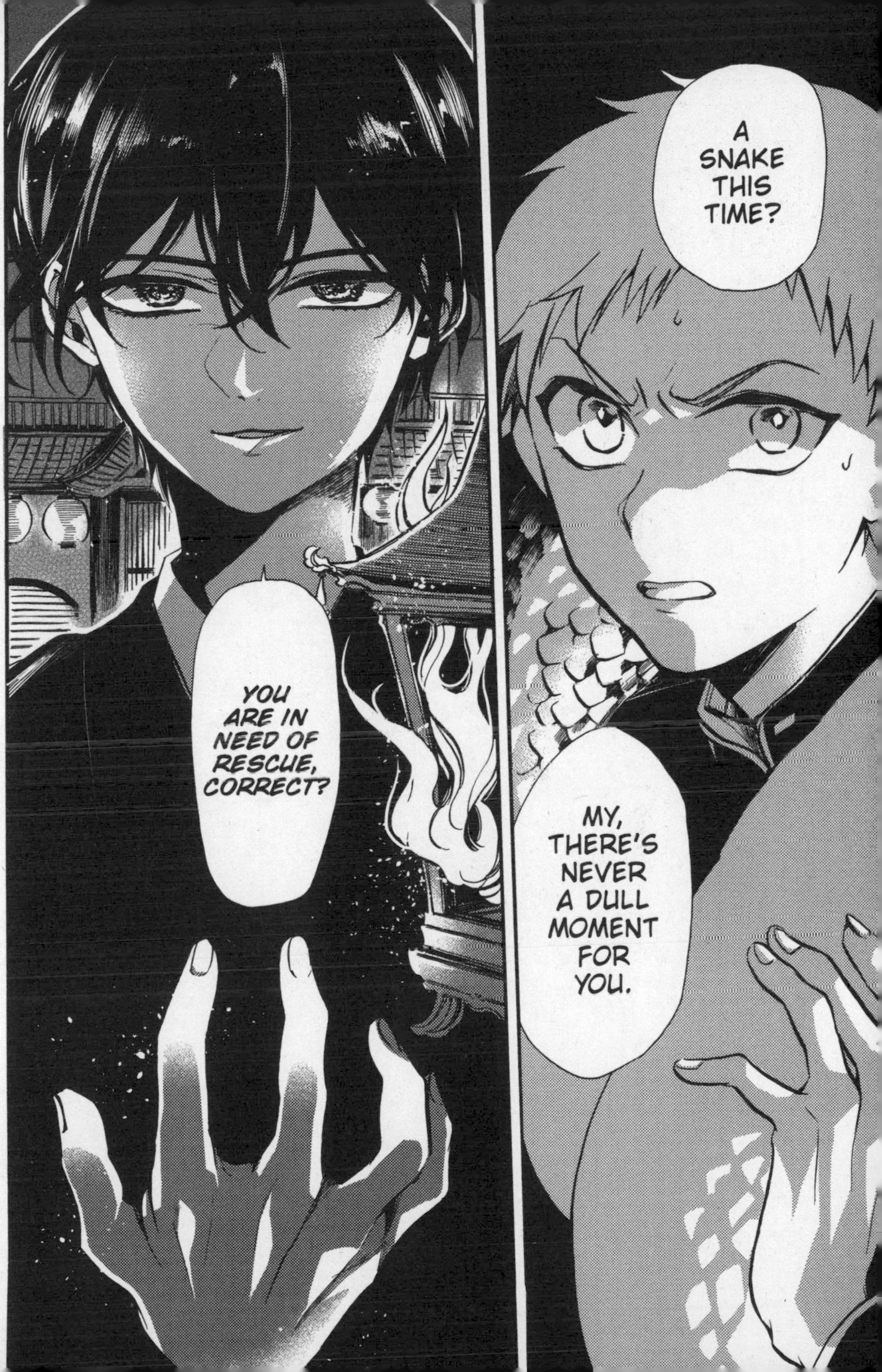
A SNAKE THIS TIME?
MY, THERE'S NEVER A DULL MOMENT FOR YOU.
YOU ARE IN NEED OF RESCUE, CORRECT?

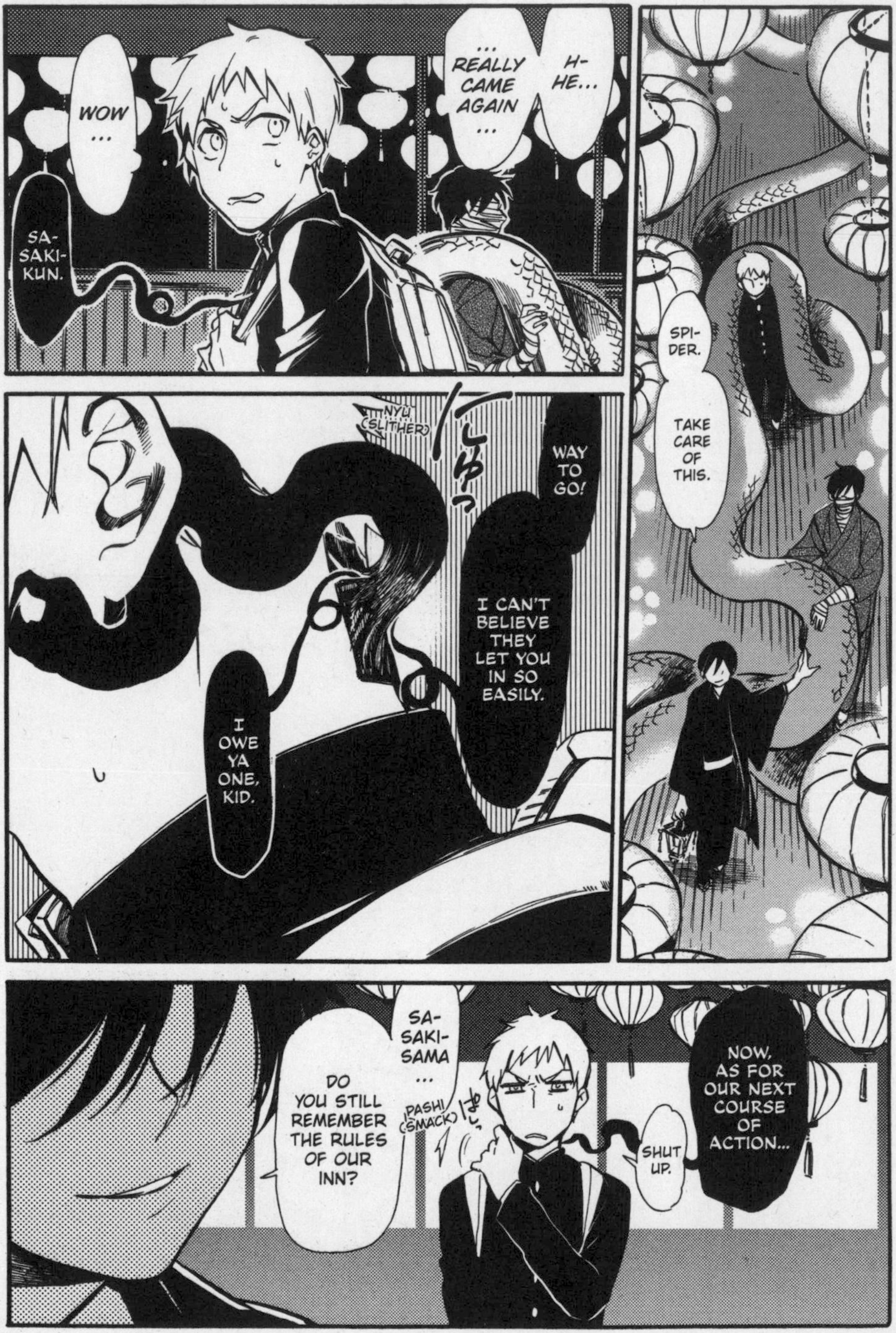
SPIDER.
TAKE CARE OF THIS.
H-HE...
...REALLY CAME AGAIN...
WOW...
SASAKI-KUN.
NYU (SLITHER)
WAY TO GO!
I CAN'T BELIEVE THEY LET YOU IN SO EASILY.
I OWE YA ONE, KID.
NOW, AS FOR OUR NEXT COURSE OF ACTION...
SHUT UP.
PASHI (SMACK)
SASAKI-SAMA...
DO YOU STILL REMEMBER THE RULES OF OUR INN?

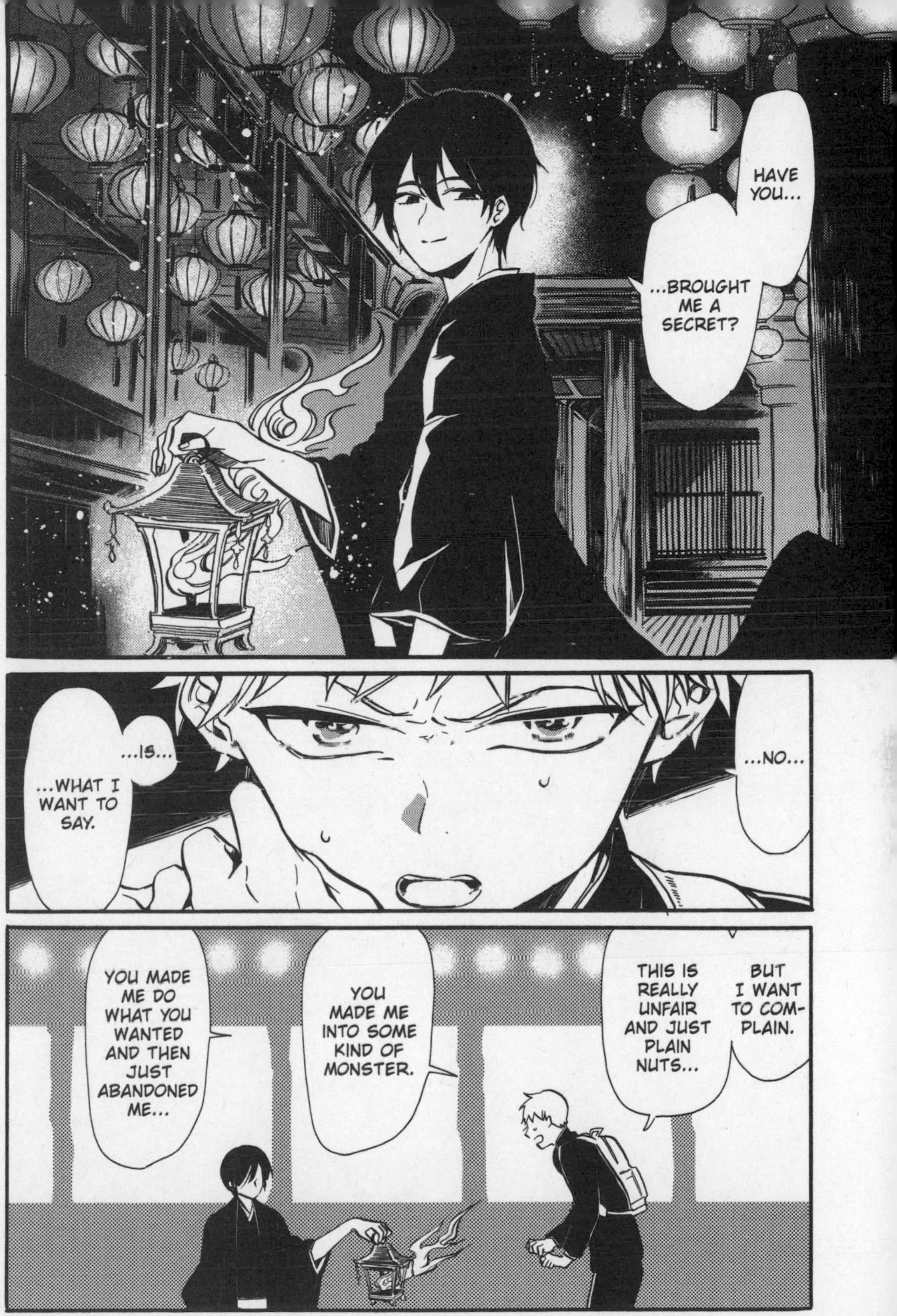
HAVE YOU...
...BROUGHT ME A SECRET?
...NO...
...IS...
...WHAT I WANT TO SAY.
BUT I WANT TO COM-PLAIN.
THIS IS REALLY UNFAIR AND JUST PLAIN NUTS...
YOU MADE ME INTO SOME KIND OF MONSTER.
YOU MADE ME DO WHAT YOU WANTED AND THEN JUST ABANDONED ME...

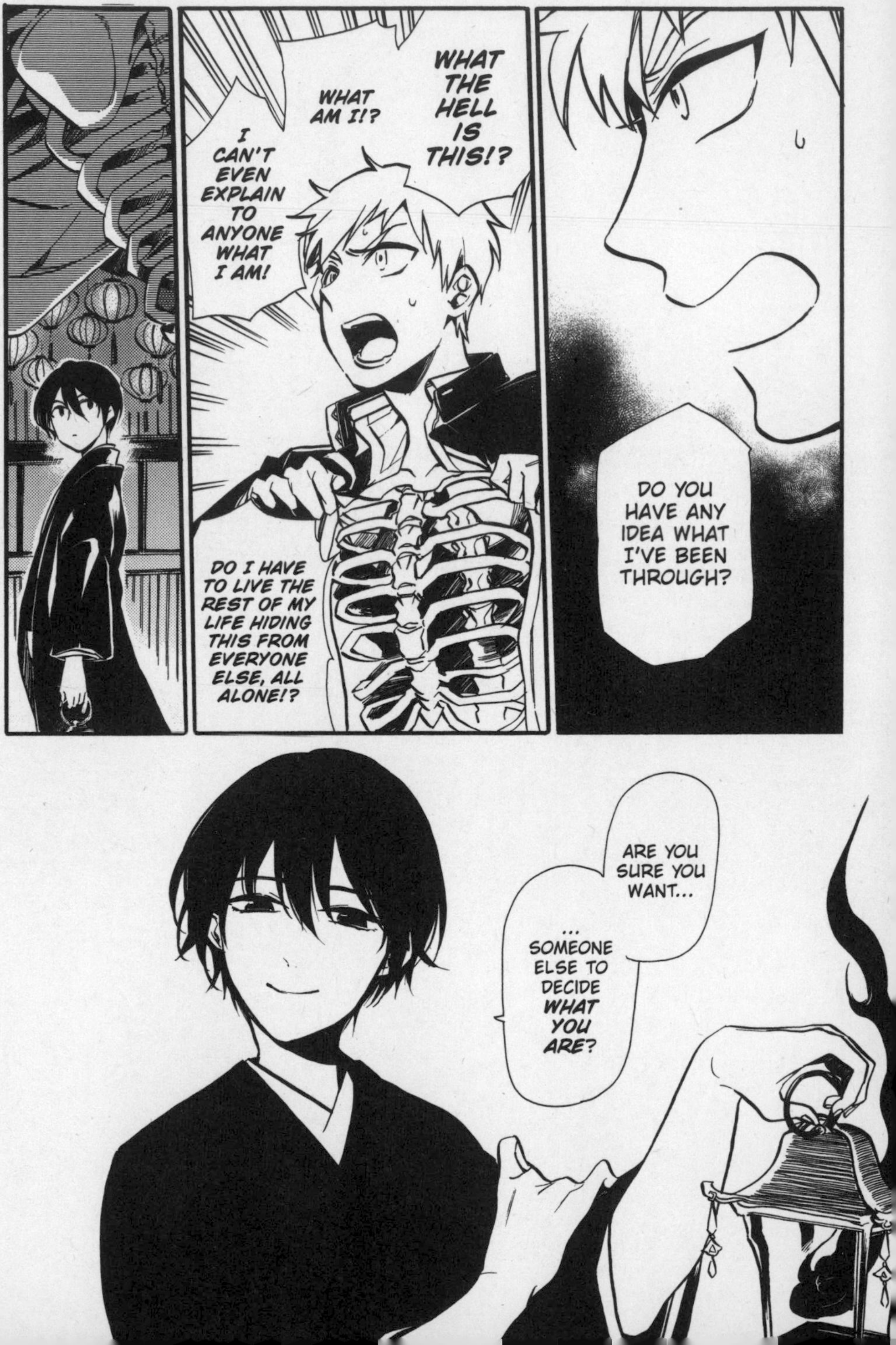
DO YOU HAVE ANY IDEA WHAT I'VE BEEN THROUGH?
WHAT THE HELL IS THIS!?
WHAT AM I!?
I CAN'T EVEN EXPLAIN TO ANYONE WHAT I AM!
DO I HAVE TO LIVE THE REST OF MY LIFE HIDING THIS FROM EVERYONE ELSE, ALL ALONE!?
ARE YOU SURE YOU WANT...
... SOMEONE ELSE TO DECIDE WHAT YOU ARE?

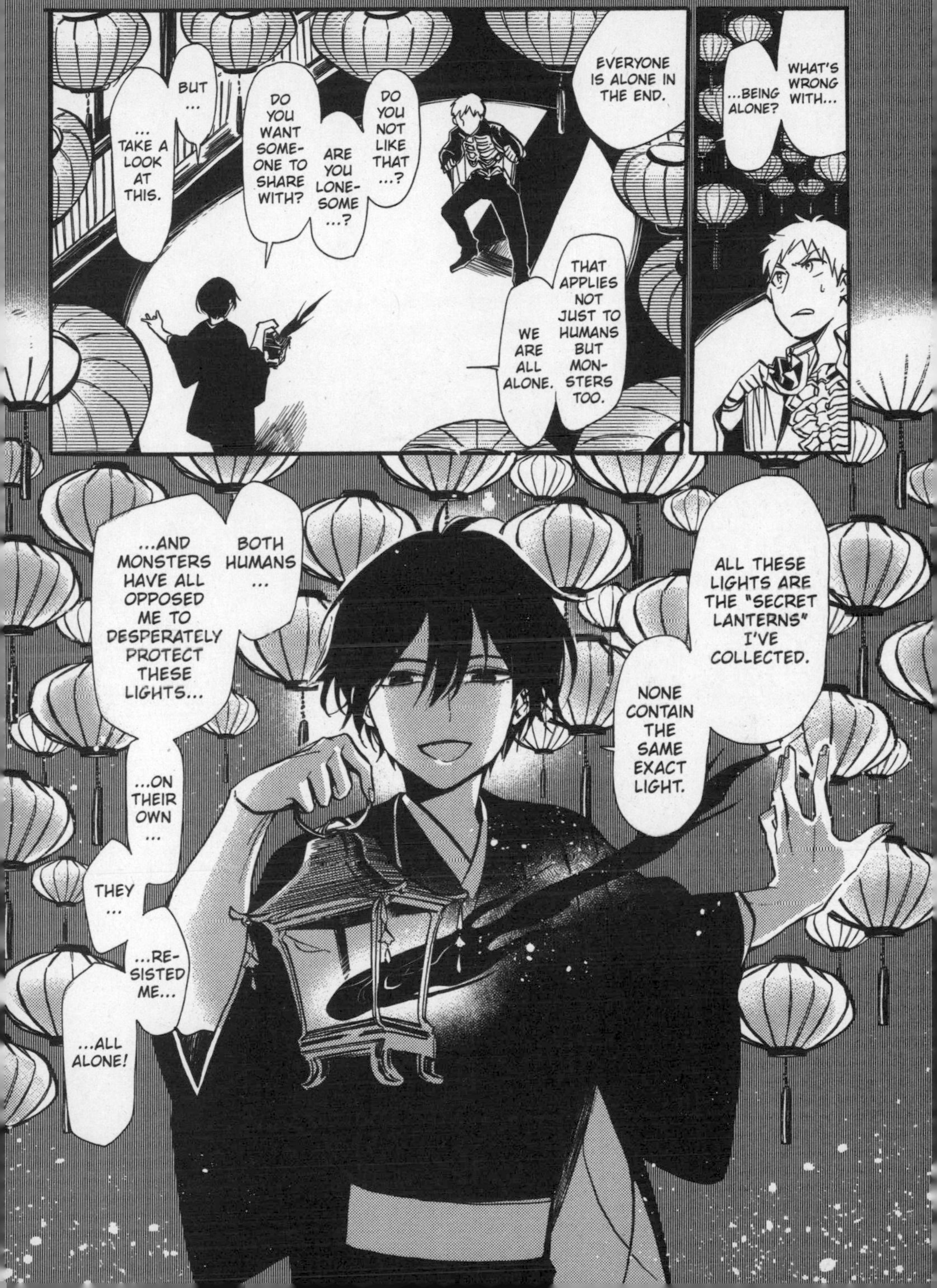
WHAT'S WRONG WITH...
...BEING ALONE?
EVERYONE IS ALONE IN THE END.
THAT APPLIES NOT JUST TO HUMANS BUT MON-STERS TOO.
WE ARE ALL ALONE.
DO YOU NOT LIKE THAT...?
ARE YOU LONE-SOME...?
DO YOU WANT SOME-ONE TO SHARE WITH?
BUT...
...TAKE A LOOK AT THIS.
ALL THESE LIGHTS ARE THE "SECRET LANTERNS" I'VE COLLECTED.
NONE CONTAIN THE SAME EXACT LIGHT.
BOTH HUMANS...
...AND MONSTERS HAVE ALL OPPOSED ME TO DESPERATELY PROTECT THESE LIGHTS...
...ON THEIR OWN...
THEY...
...RE-SISTED ME...
...ALL ALONE!

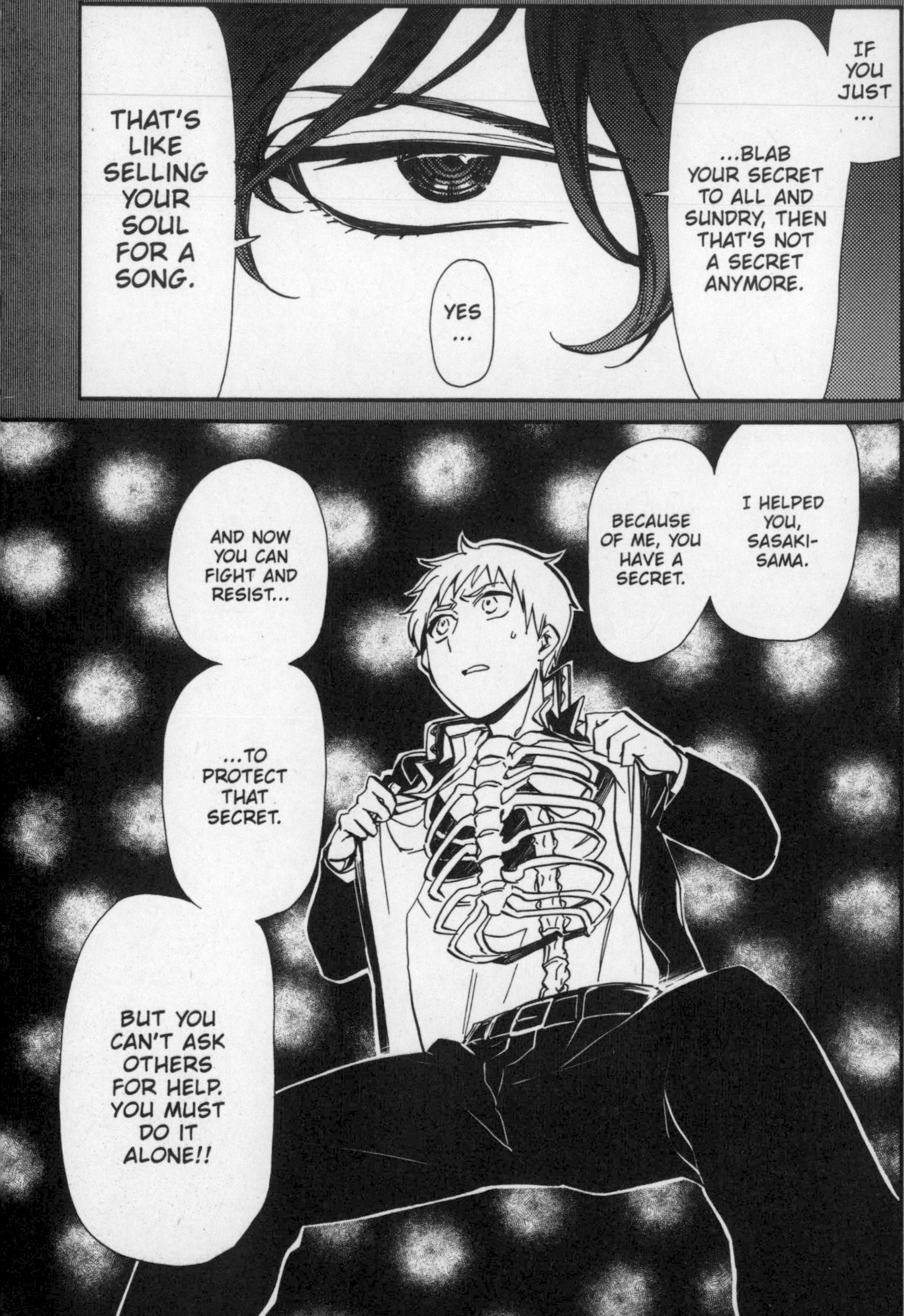
IF YOU JUST ...
...BLAB YOUR SECRET TO ALL AND SUNDRY, THEN THAT'S NOT A SECRET ANYMORE.
YES ...
THAT'S LIKE SELLING YOUR SOUL FOR A SONG.
I HELPED YOU, SASAKI-SAMA.
BECAUSE OF ME, YOU HAVE A SECRET.
AND NOW YOU CAN FIGHT AND RESIST...
...TO PROTECT THAT SECRET.
BUT YOU CAN'T ASK OTHERS FOR HELP. YOU MUST DO IT ALONE!!

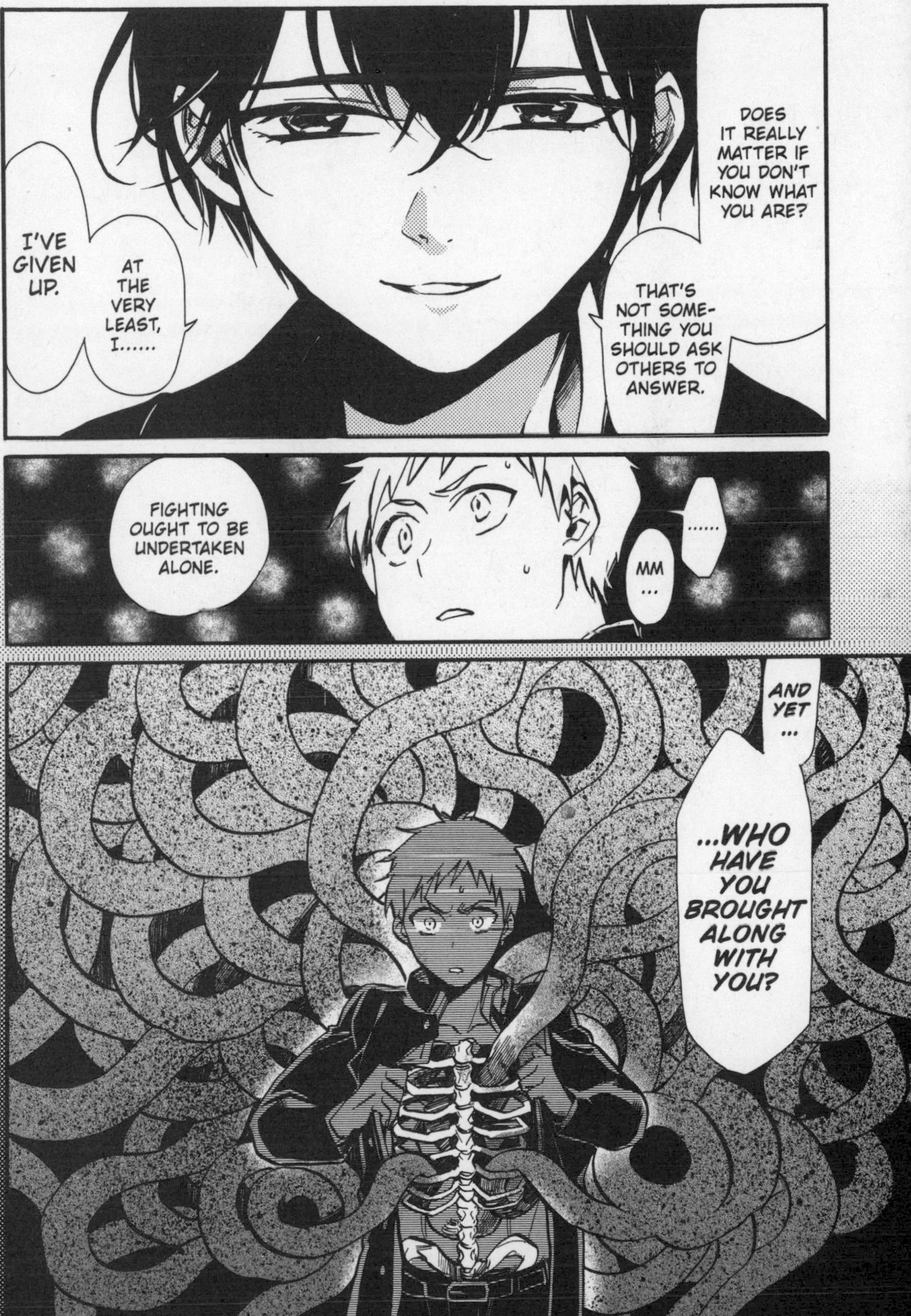
DOES IT REALLY MATTER IF YOU DON'T KNOW WHAT YOU ARE?
THAT'S NOT SOME-THING YOU SHOULD ASK OTHERS TO ANSWER.
AT THE VERY LEAST, I......
I'VE GIVEN UP.
......
MM...
FIGHTING OUGHT TO BE UNDERTAKEN ALONE.
AND YET...
...WHO HAVE YOU BROUGHT ALONG WITH YOU?

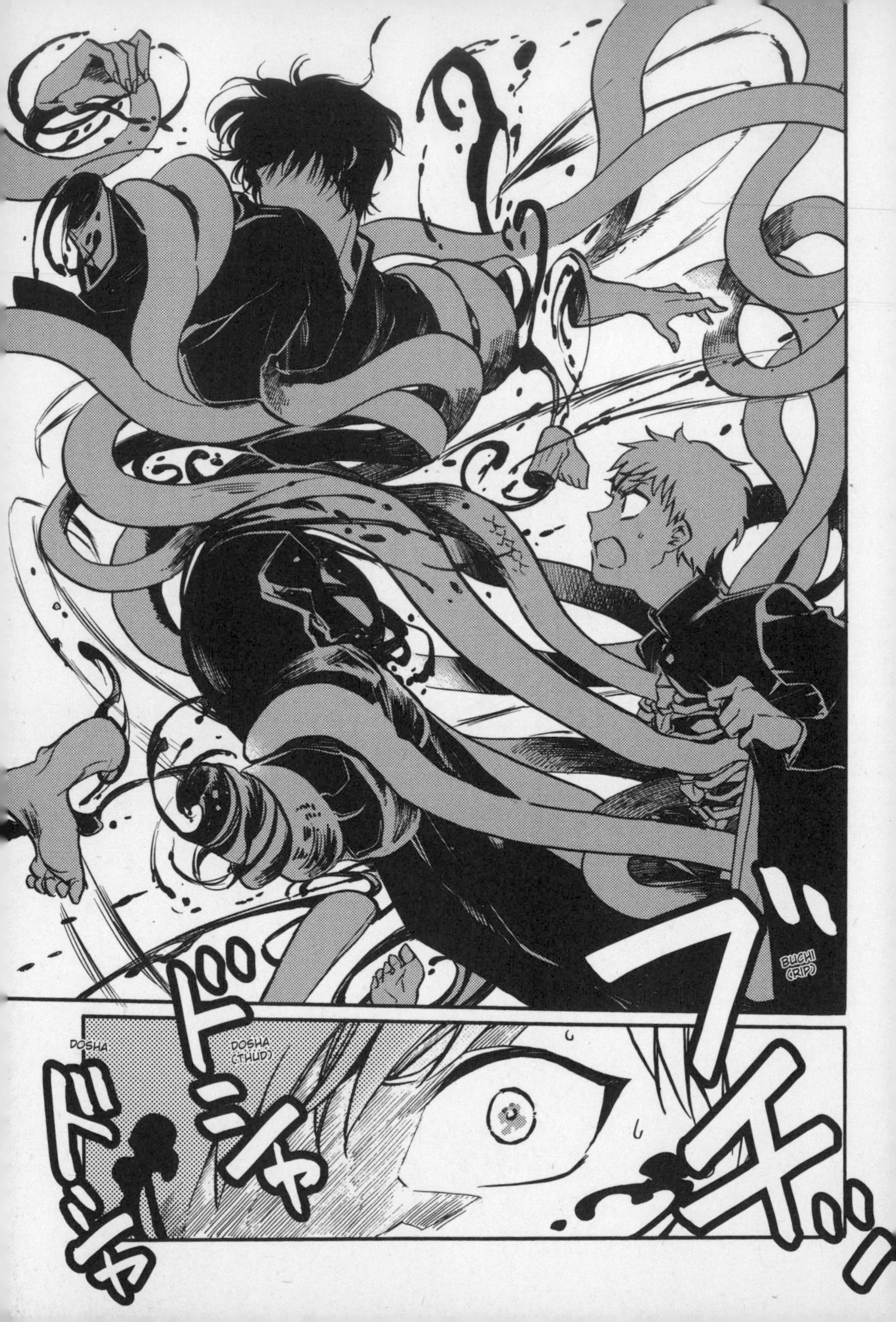
BUCHI (RIP)
DOSHA (THUD)
DOSHA

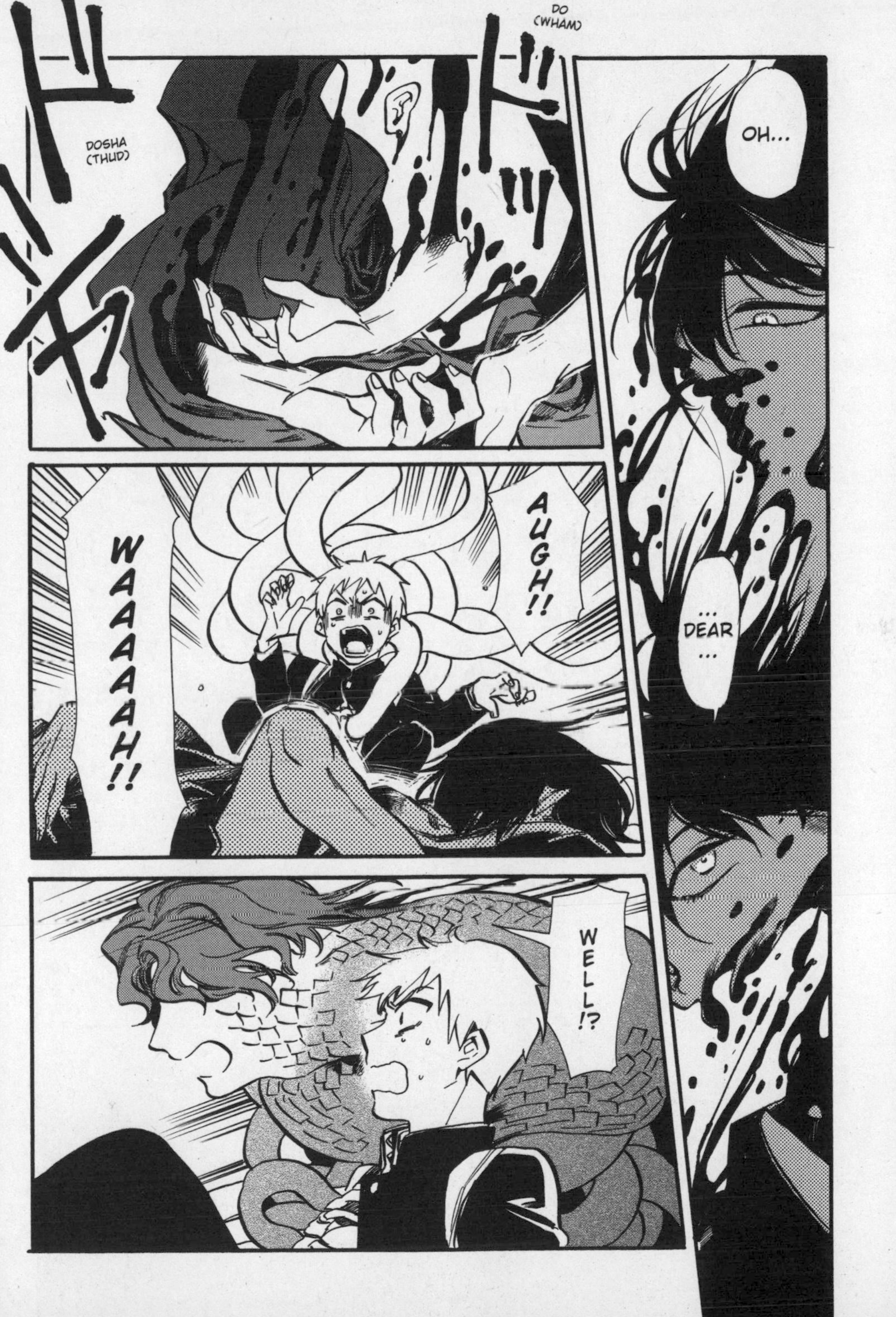
OH...
... DEAR ...
DO (WHAM)
DOSHA (THUD)
AUGH!!
WAAAAAAAH!!
WELL!?

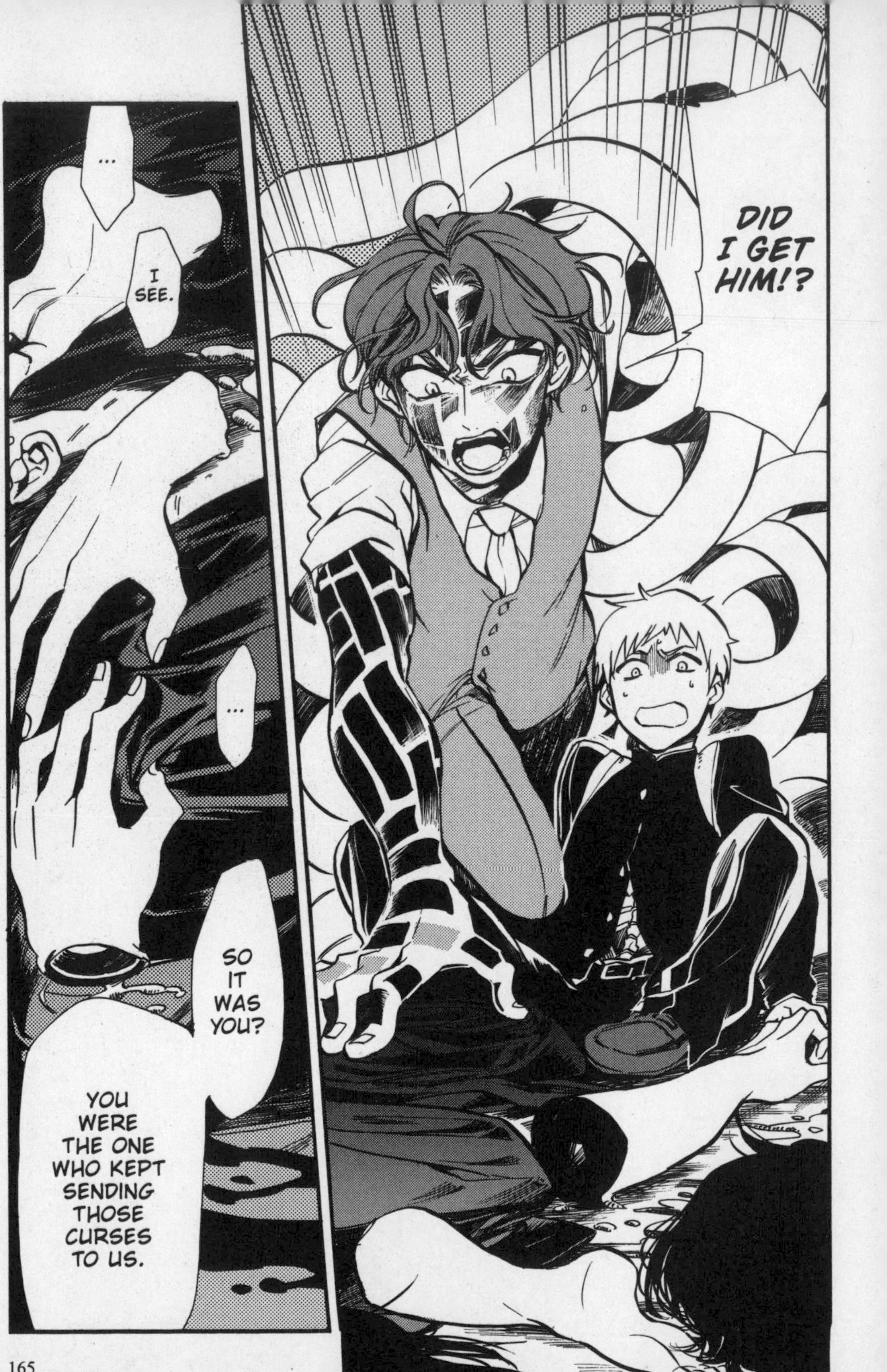
DID I GET HIM!?
...
I SEE.
...
SO IT WAS YOU?
YOU WERE THE ONE WHO KEPT SENDING THOSE CURSES TO US.

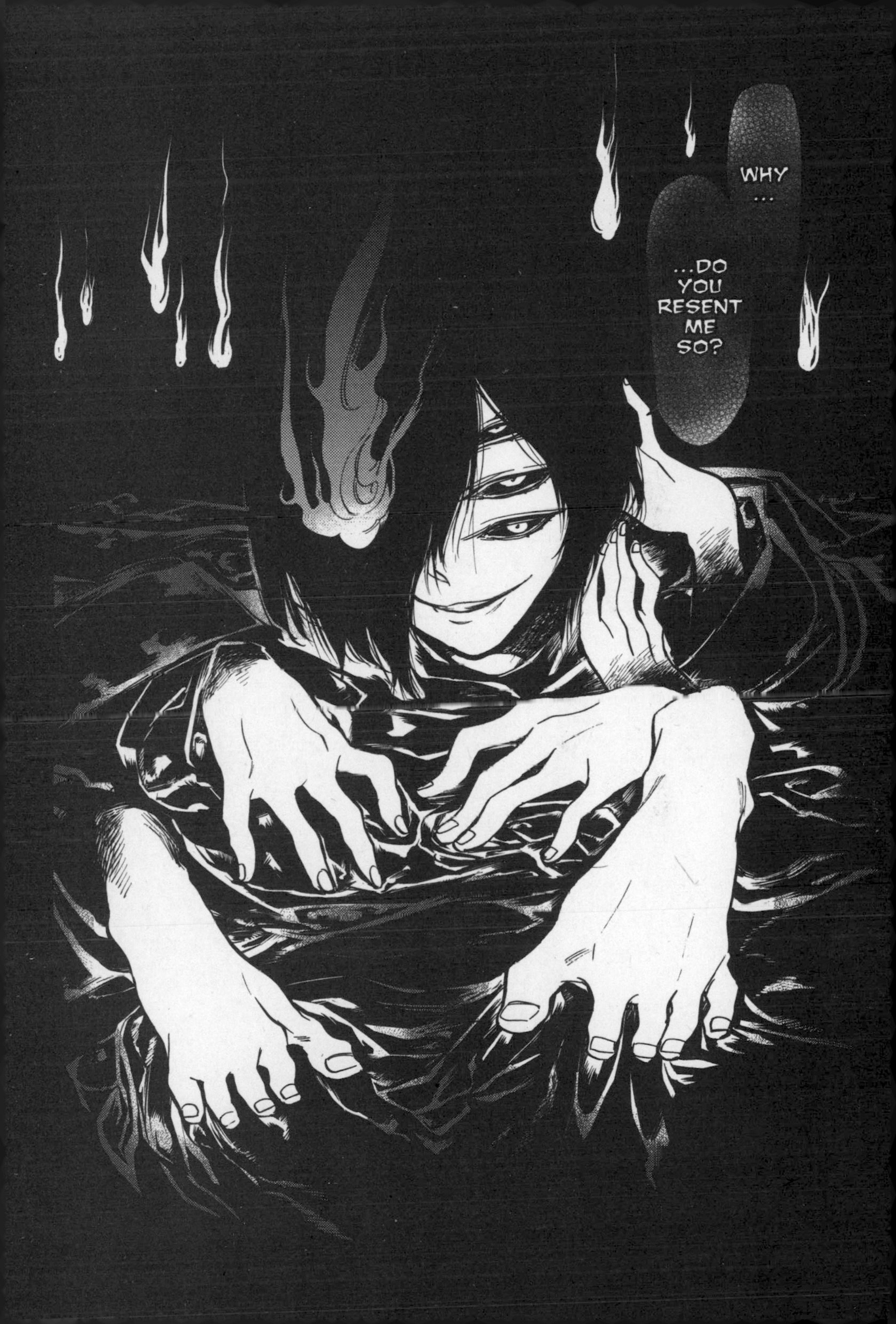
WHY ...
...DO YOU RESENT ME SO?

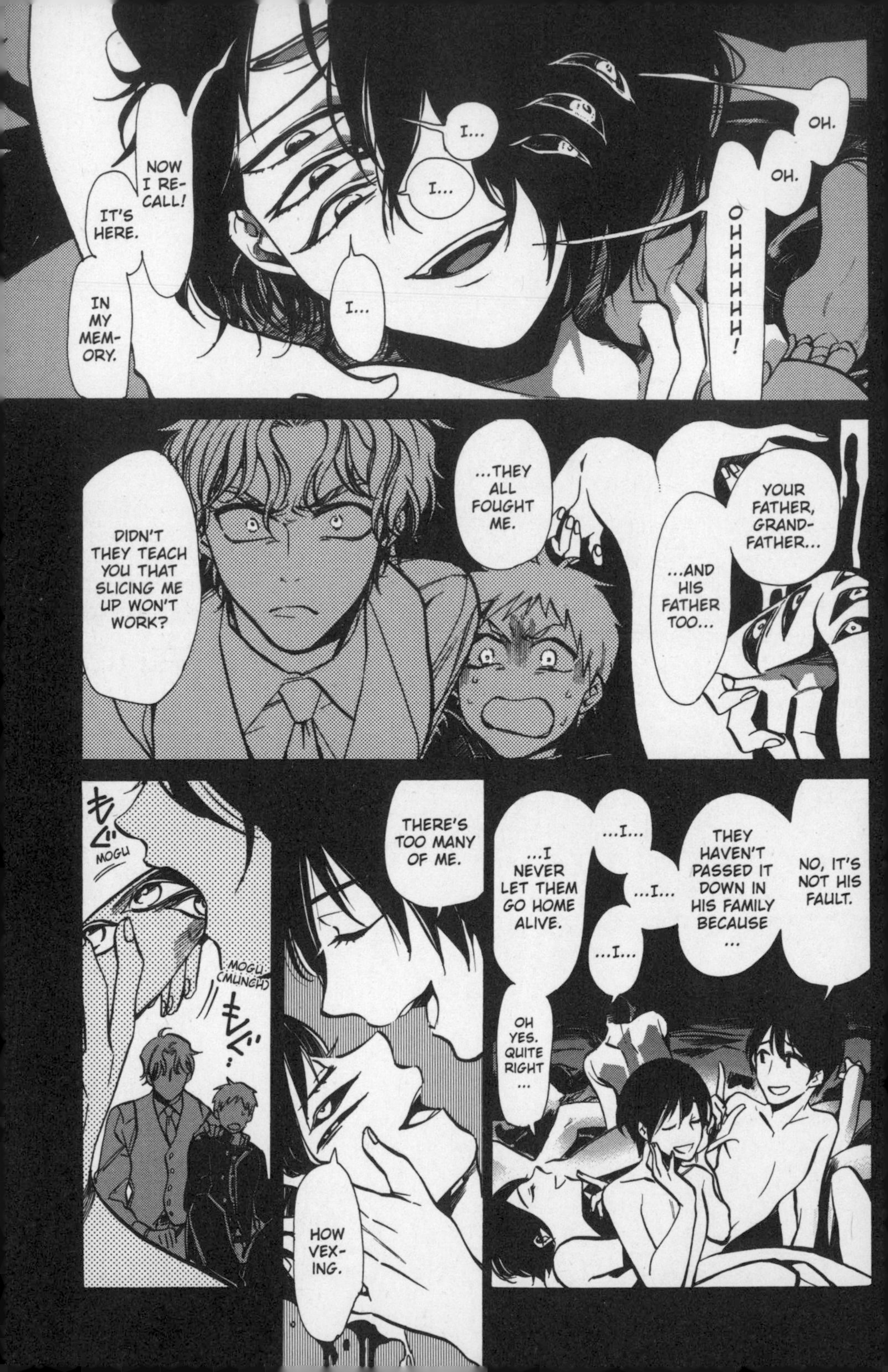
OH.
OH.
OHHHHHHH!
I...
I...
I...
NOW I RE-CALL!
IT'S HERE.
IN MY MEM-ORY.
YOUR FATHER, GRAND-FATHER...
...AND HIS FATHER TOO...
...THEY ALL FOUGHT ME.
DIDN'T THEY TEACH YOU THAT SLICING ME UP WON'T WORK?
NO, IT'S NOT HIS FAULT.
THEY HAVEN'T PASSED IT DOWN IN HIS FAMILY BECAUSE ...
...I...
...I...
...I...
...I NEVER LET THEM GO HOME ALIVE.
OH YES. QUITE RIGHT ...
THERE'S TOO MANY OF ME.
HOW VEX-ING.
もぐ
MOGU
MOGU (MUNCH)
もぐ...

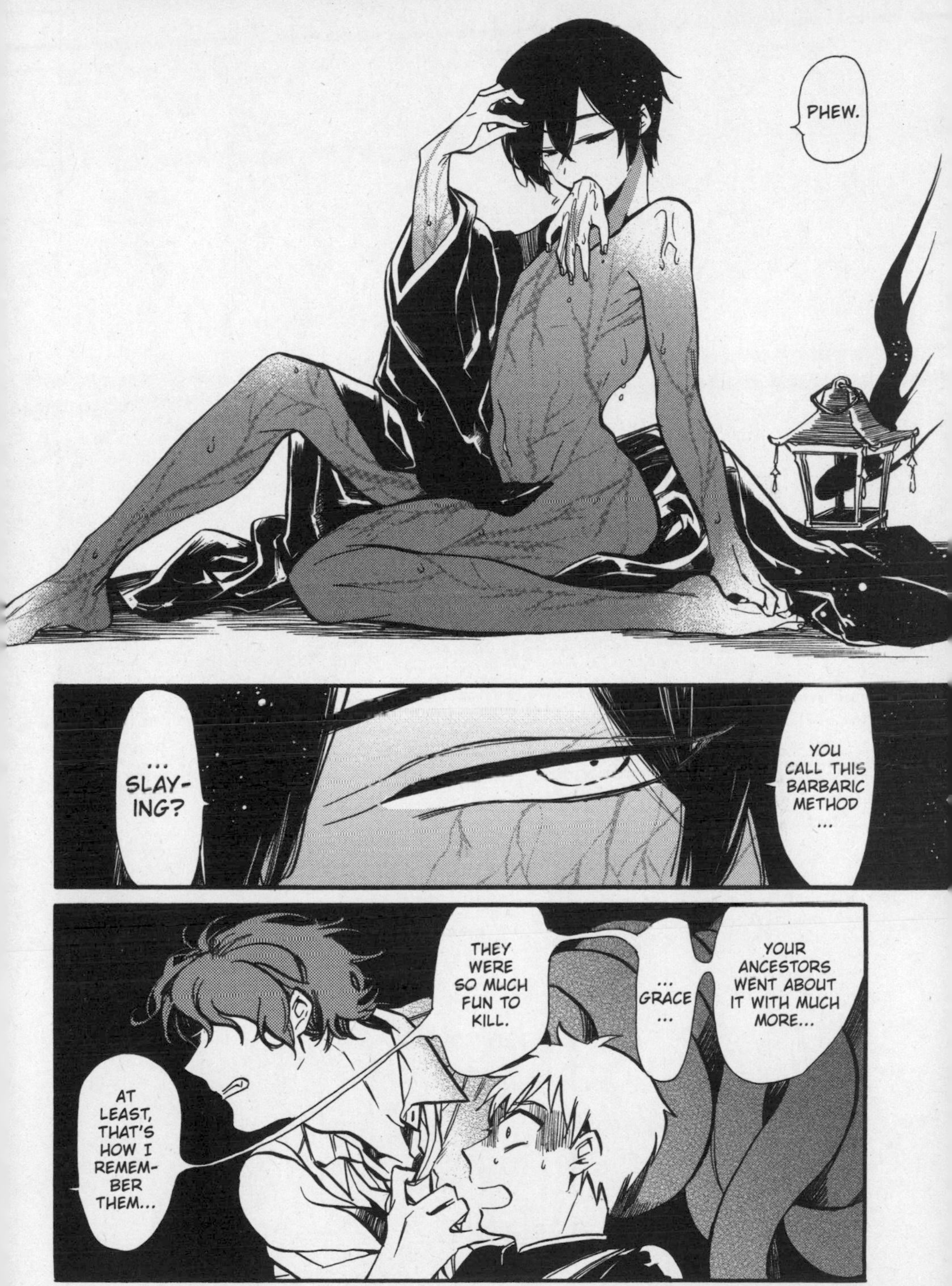
PHEW.
YOU CALL THIS BARBARIC METHOD ...
... SLAY-ING?
YOUR ANCESTORS WENT ABOUT IT WITH MUCH MORE...
... GRACE ...
THEY WERE SO MUCH FUN TO KILL.
AT LEAST, THAT'S HOW I REMEM-BER THEM...

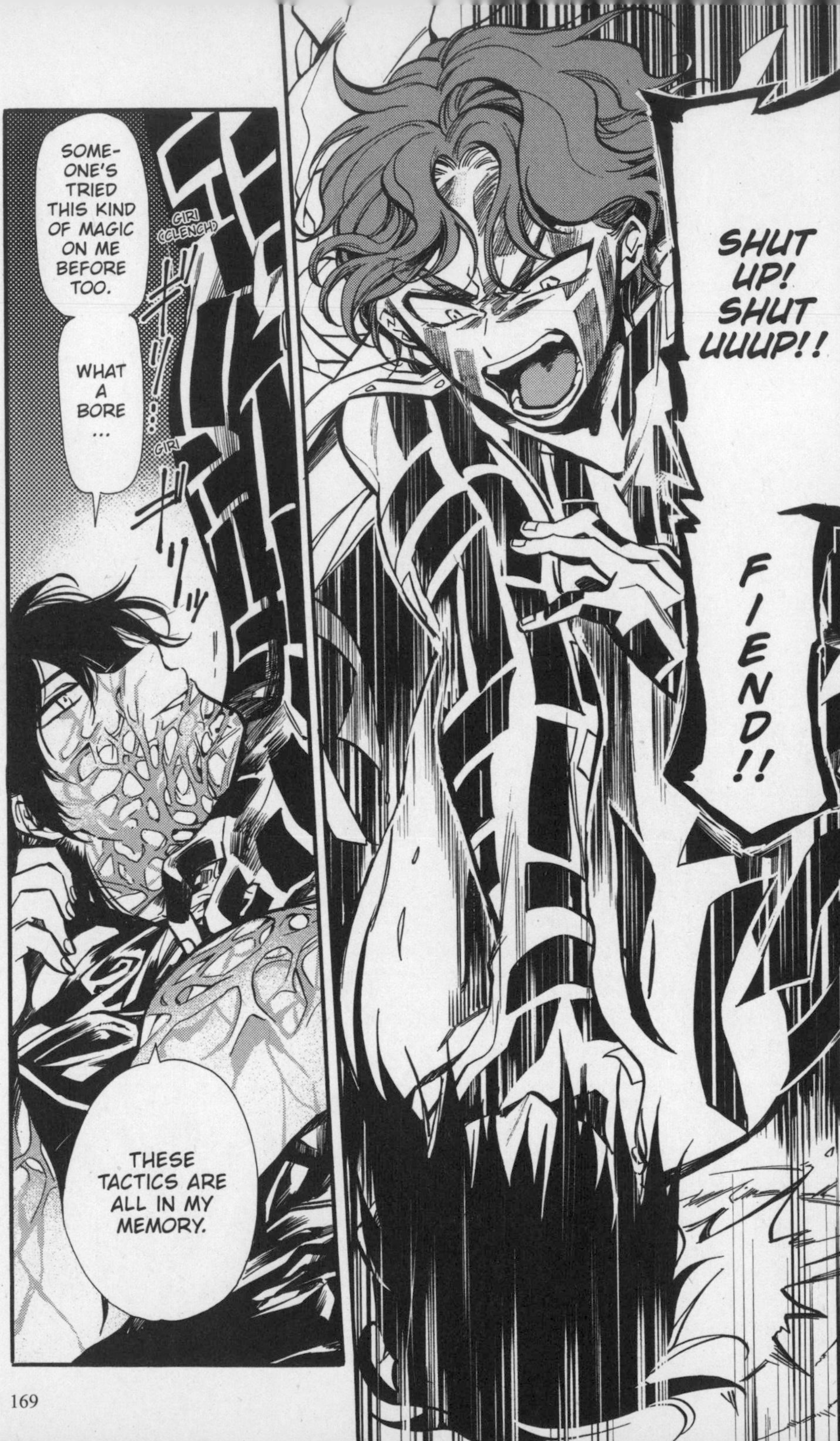
SHUT UP! SHUT UUUP!!
FIEND!!
SOME-ONE'S TRIED THIS KIND OF MAGIC ON ME BEFORE TOO.
GIRI (CLENCH)
WHAT A BORE ...
GIRI
THESE TACTICS ARE ALL IN MY MEMORY.

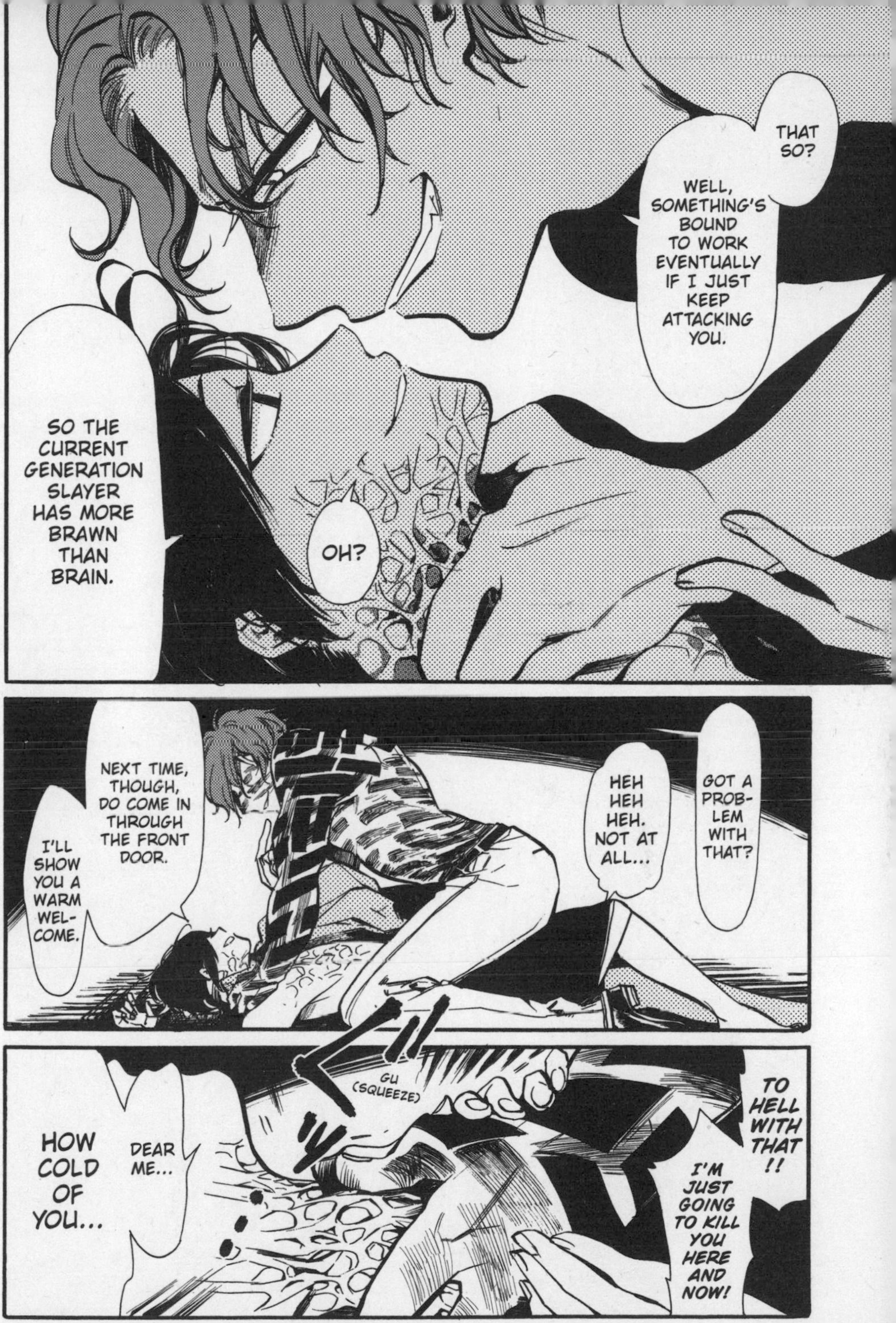
THAT SO?
WELL, SOMETHING'S BOUND TO WORK EVENTUALLY IF I JUST KEEP ATTACKING YOU.
OH?
SO THE CURRENT GENERATION SLAYER HAS MORE BRAWN THAN BRAIN.
GOT A PROB-LEM WITH THAT?
HEH HEH HEH. NOT AT ALL...
NEXT TIME, THOUGH, DO COME IN THROUGH THE FRONT DOOR.
I'LL SHOW YOU A WARM WEL-COME.
TO HELL WITH THAT!!
I'M JUST GOING TO KILL YOU HERE AND NOW!
GU (SQUEEZE)
DEAR ME...
HOW COLD OF YOU...

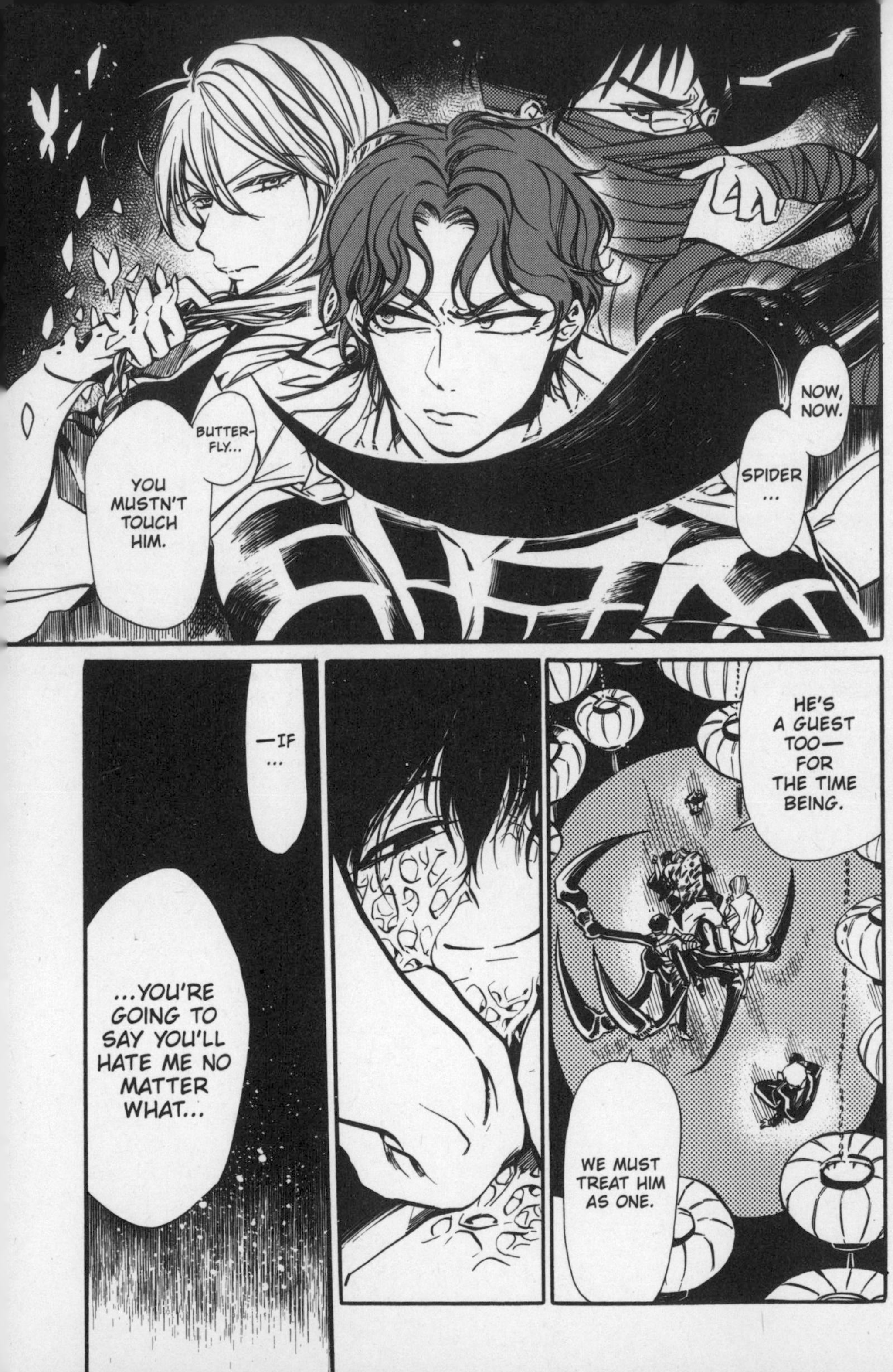
NOW, NOW.
SPIDER...
BUTTER-FLY...
YOU MUSTN'T TOUCH HIM.
HE'S A GUEST TOO—FOR THE TIME BEING.
WE MUST TREAT HIM AS ONE.
—IF...
...YOU'RE GOING TO SAY YOU'LL HATE ME NO MATTER WHAT...

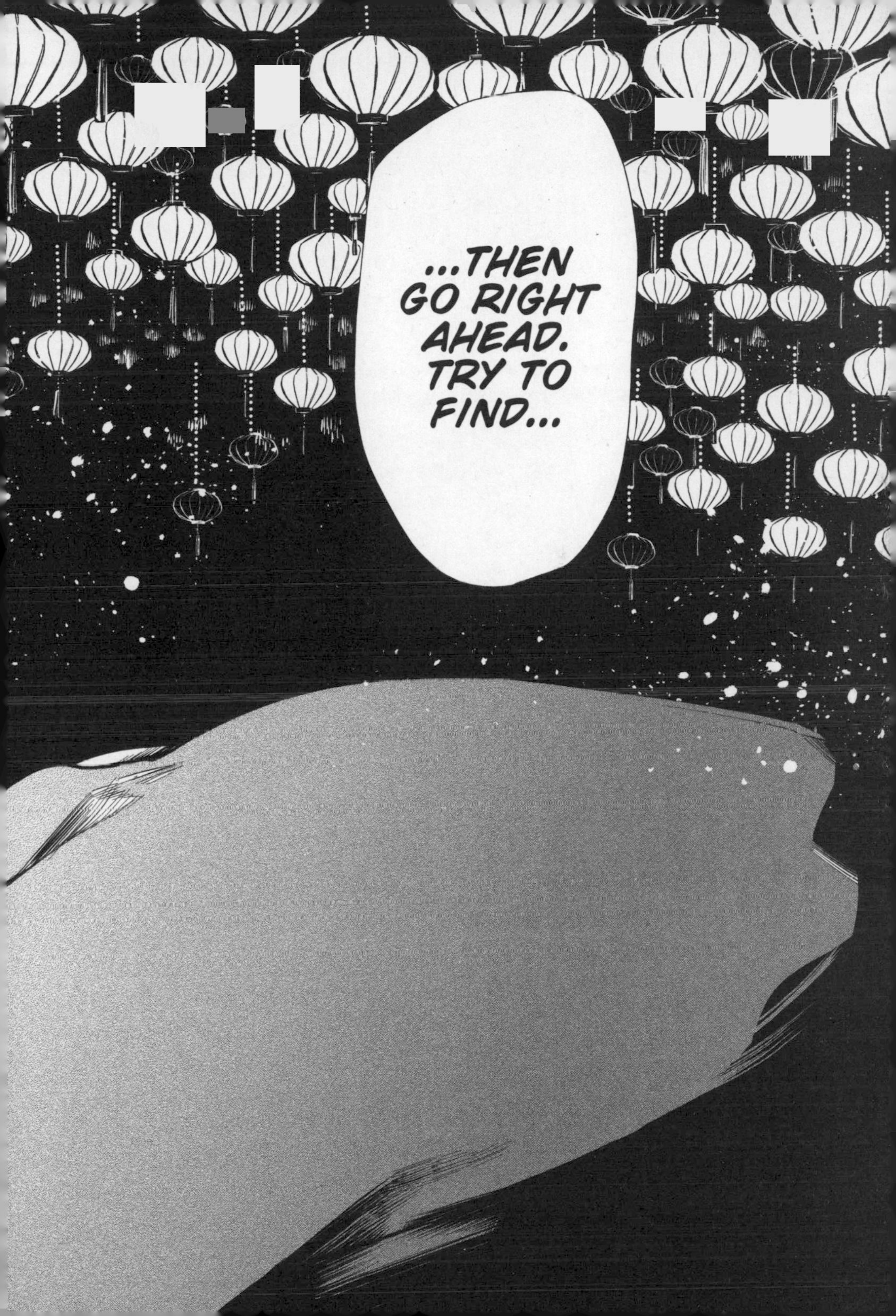
...THEN GO RIGHT AHEAD. TRY TO FIND...

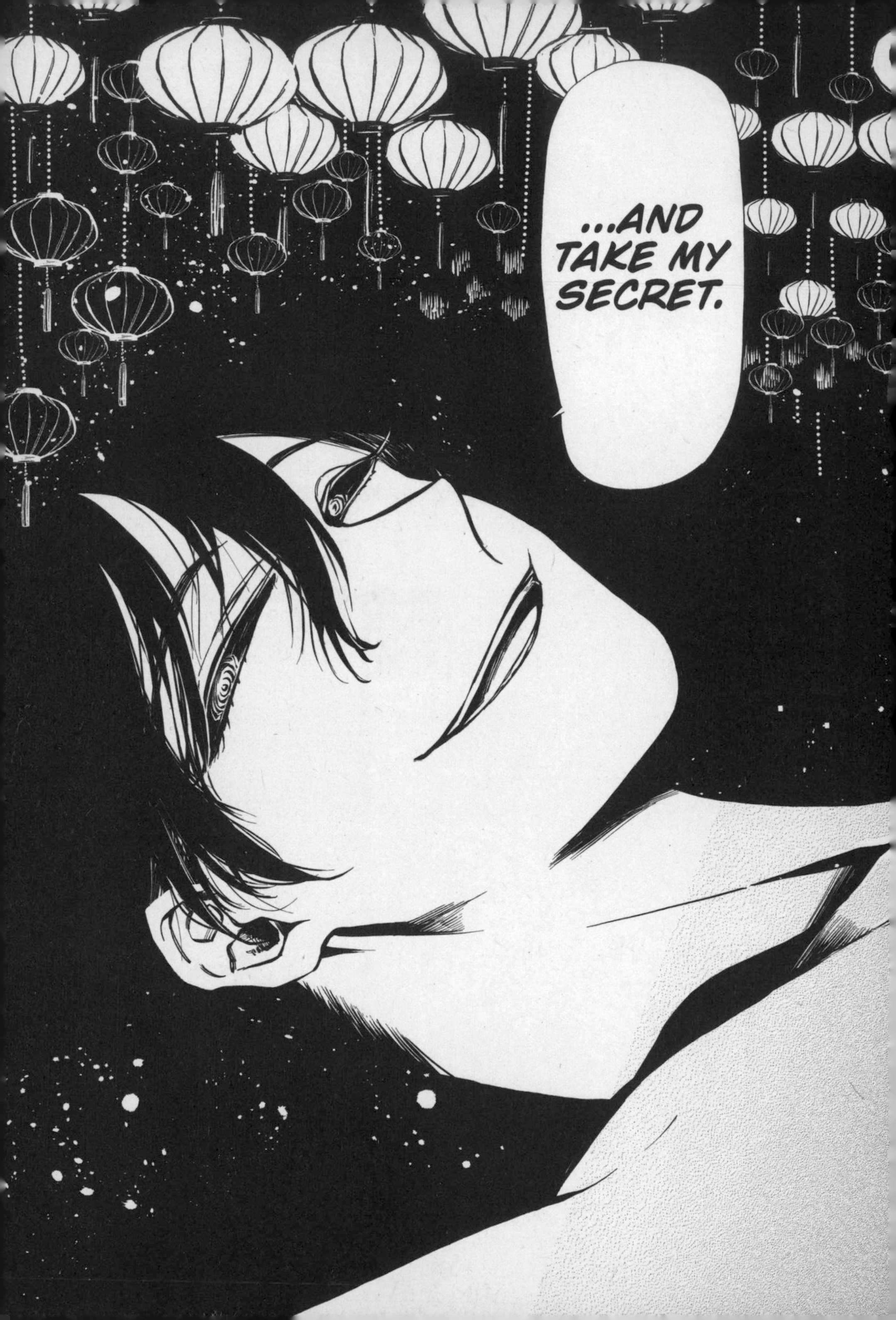
...AND TAKE MY SECRET.

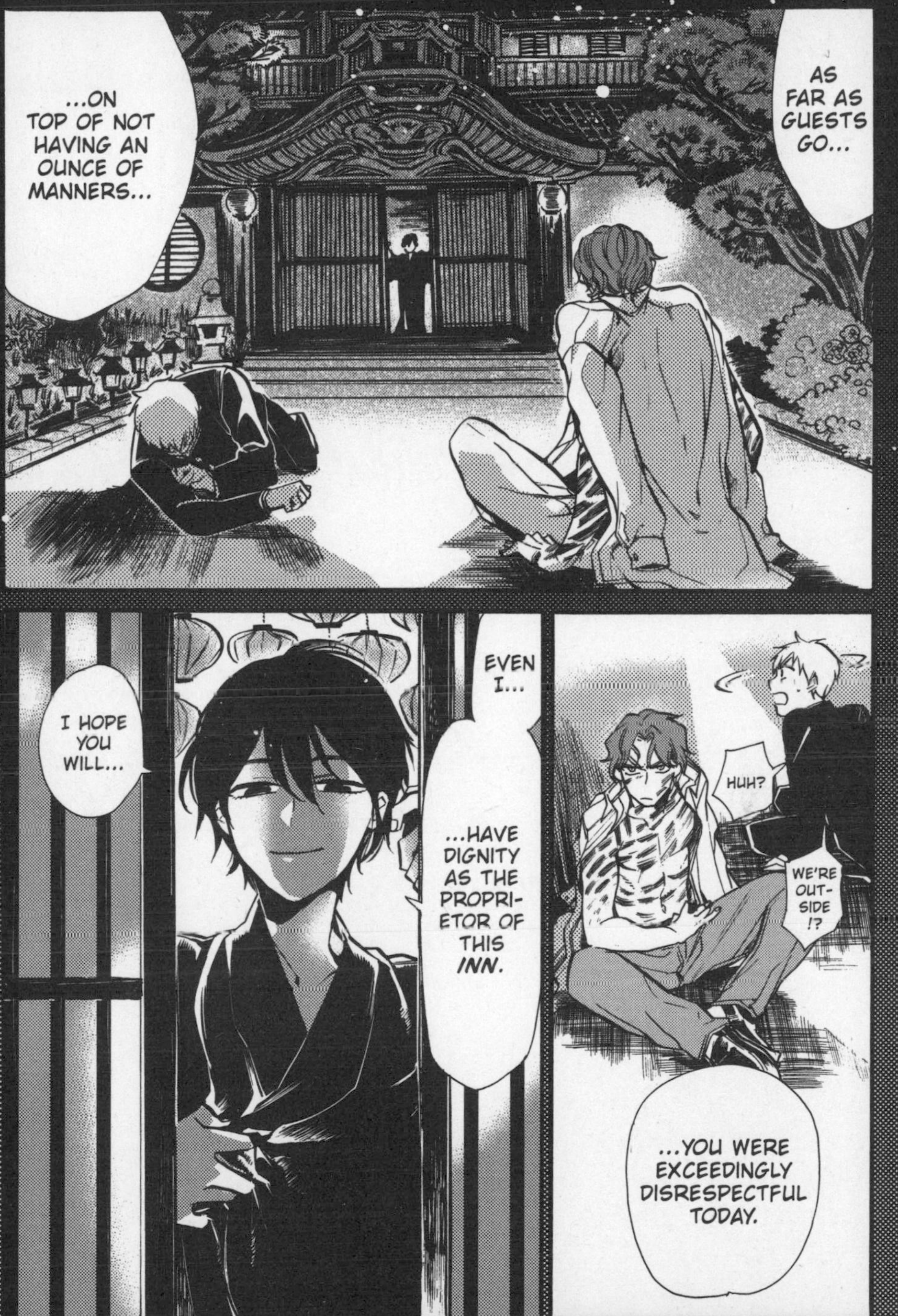
AS FAR AS GUESTS GO...
...ON TOP OF NOT HAVING AN OUNCE OF MANNERS...
HUH?
WE'RE OUT-SIDE !?
...YOU WERE EXCEEDINGLY DISRESPECTFUL TODAY.
EVEN I...
I HOPE YOU WILL...
...HAVE DIGNITY AS THE PROPRI-ETOR OF THIS *INN*.

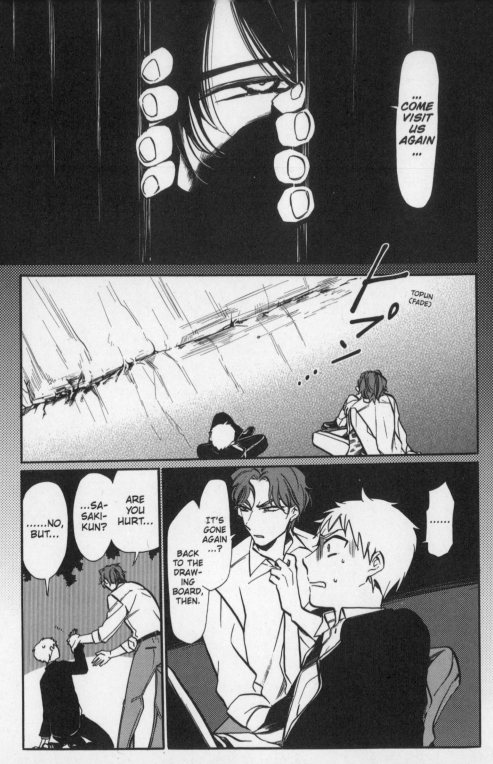

...COME VISIT US AGAIN...

TOPUN (FADE)

ARE YOU HURT...

...SA-SAKI-KUN?

......NO, BUT...

IT'S GONE AGAIN...?

BACK TO THE DRAWING BOARD, THEN.

....

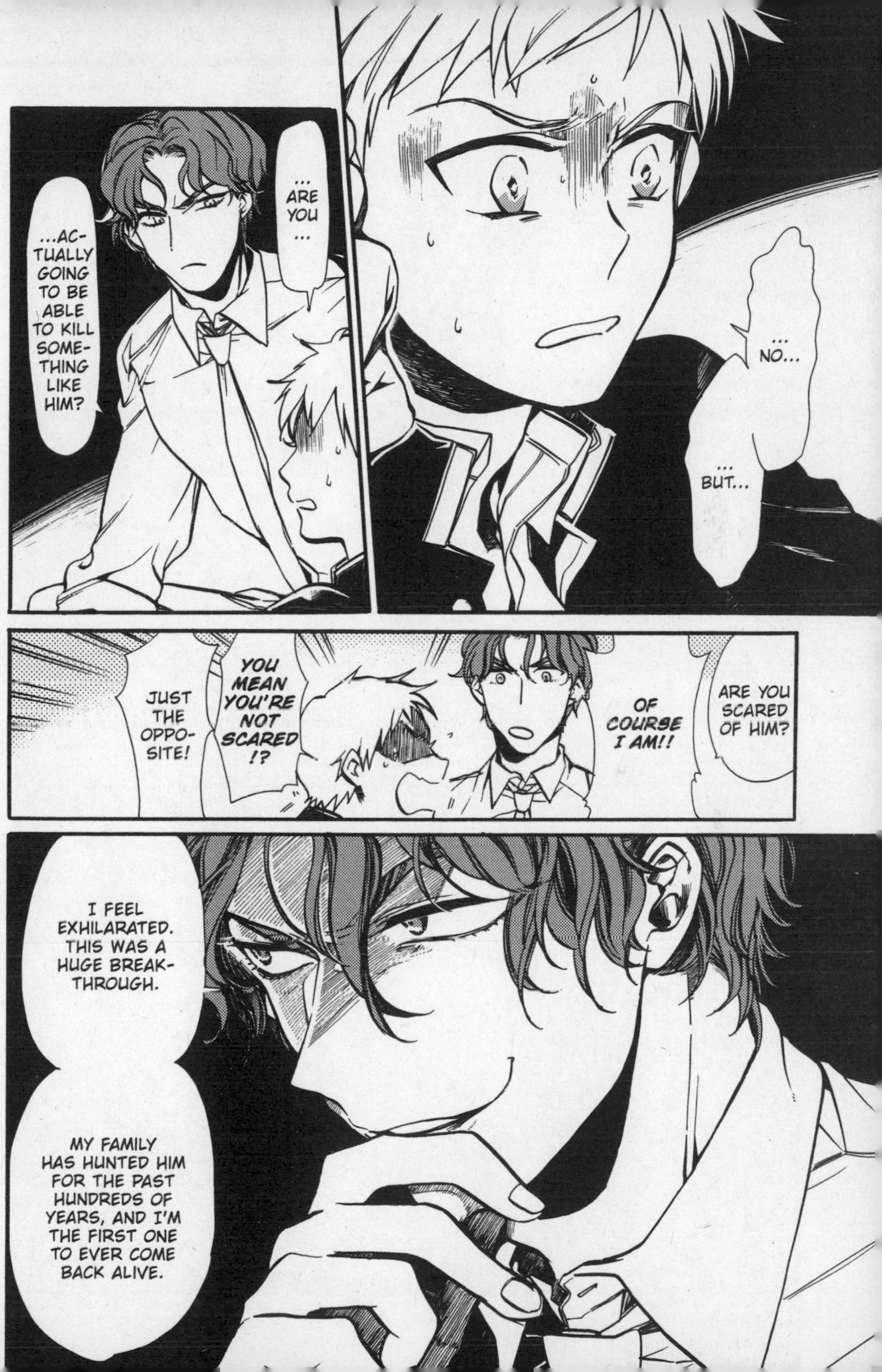
... NO...
... BUT...
... ARE YOU ...
...ACTUALLY GOING TO BE ABLE TO KILL SOMETHING LIKE HIM?
ARE YOU SCARED OF HIM?
OF COURSE I AM!!
YOU MEAN YOU'RE NOT SCARED!?
JUST THE OPPOSITE!
I FEEL EXHILARATED. THIS WAS A HUGE BREAKTHROUGH.
MY FAMILY HAS HUNTED HIM FOR THE PAST HUNDREDS OF YEARS, AND I'M THE FIRST ONE TO EVER COME BACK ALIVE.

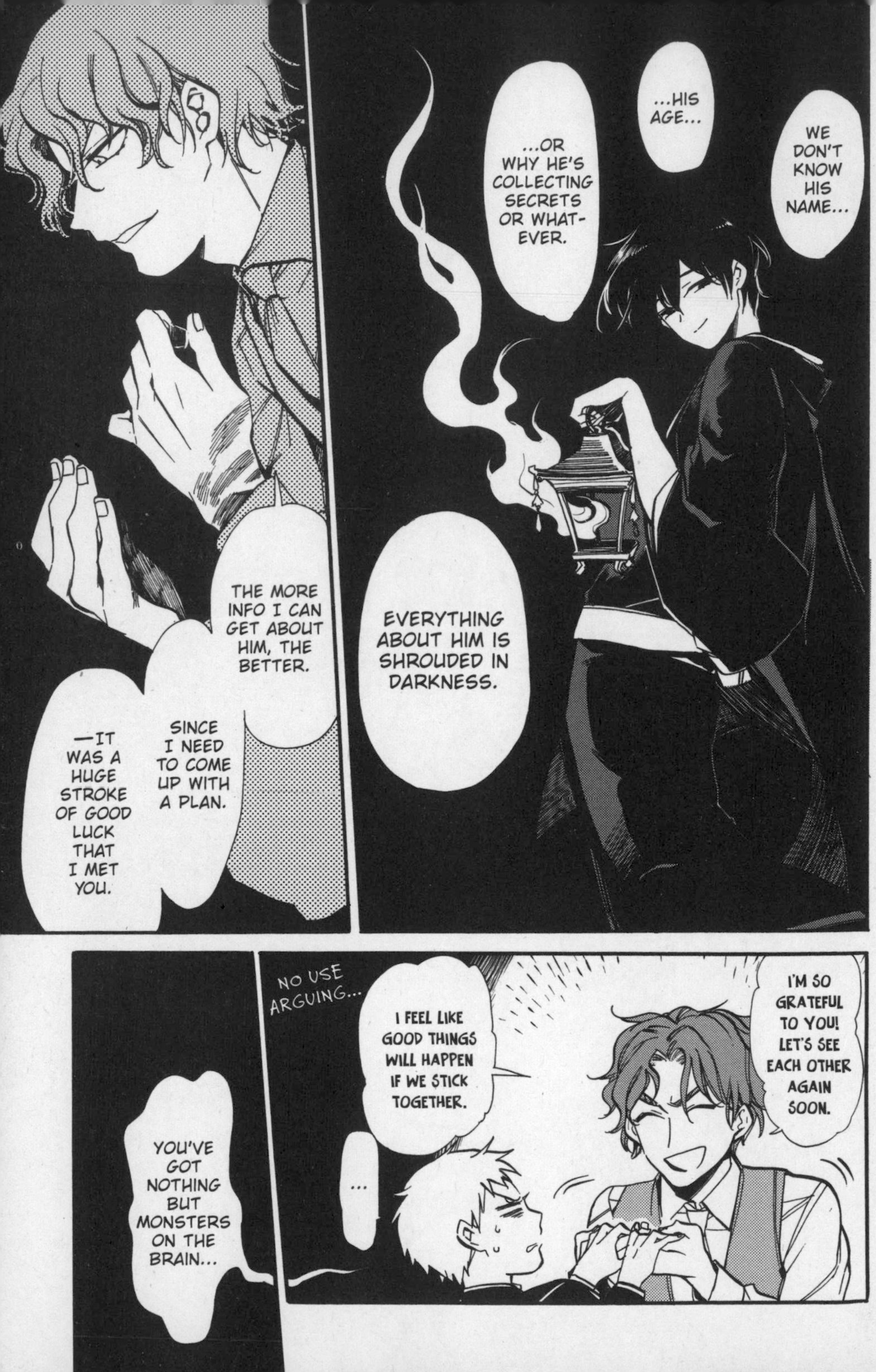
WE DON'T KNOW HIS NAME...
...HIS AGE...
...OR WHY HE'S COLLECTING SECRETS OR WHAT-EVER.
EVERYTHING ABOUT HIM IS SHROUDED IN DARKNESS.
THE MORE INFO I CAN GET ABOUT HIM, THE BETTER.
SINCE I NEED TO COME UP WITH A PLAN.
—IT WAS A HUGE STROKE OF GOOD LUCK THAT I MET YOU.
I'M SO GRATEFUL TO YOU! LET'S SEE EACH OTHER AGAIN SOON.
I FEEL LIKE GOOD THINGS WILL HAPPEN IF WE STICK TOGETHER.
NO USE ARGUING...
...
YOU'VE GOT NOTHING BUT MONSTERS ON THE BRAIN...

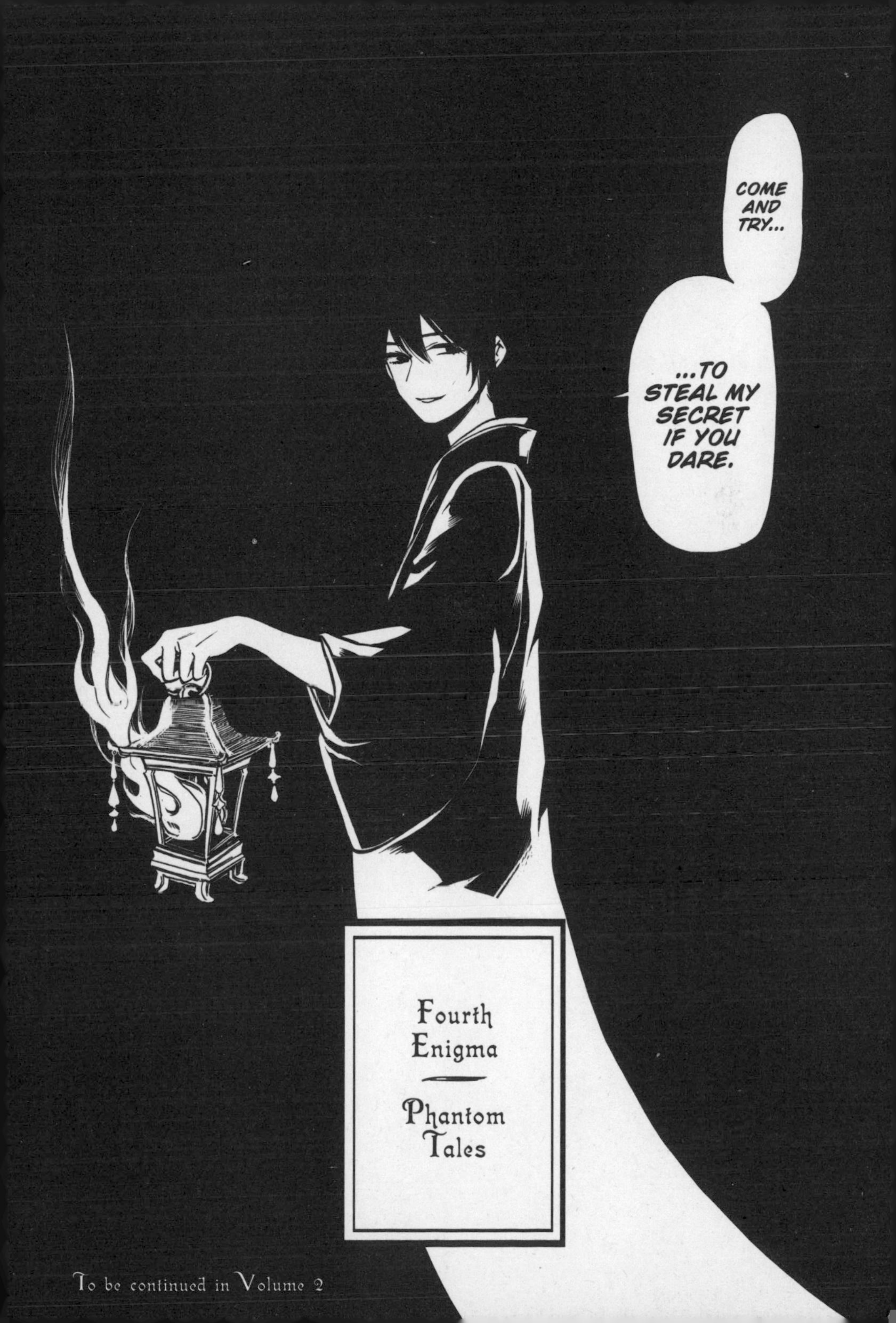
COME AND TRY...
...TO STEAL MY SECRET IF YOU DARE.
Fourth Enigma
Phantom Tales
To be continued in Volume 2

Translation Notes

Page 11
In Japanese, the **Owner** is called *Taishou*, a term used to refer to the owners of traditional Japanese restaurants and inns. It generally means "boss" or "chief." A *taishou*'s wife is usually called *okami-san*.

Page 22
Butterfly in Japanese is *chou*, and the character is referred to as such in Japanese.

Page 43
Spider in Japanese is *kumo*, and the character is also referred to as such in Japanese.

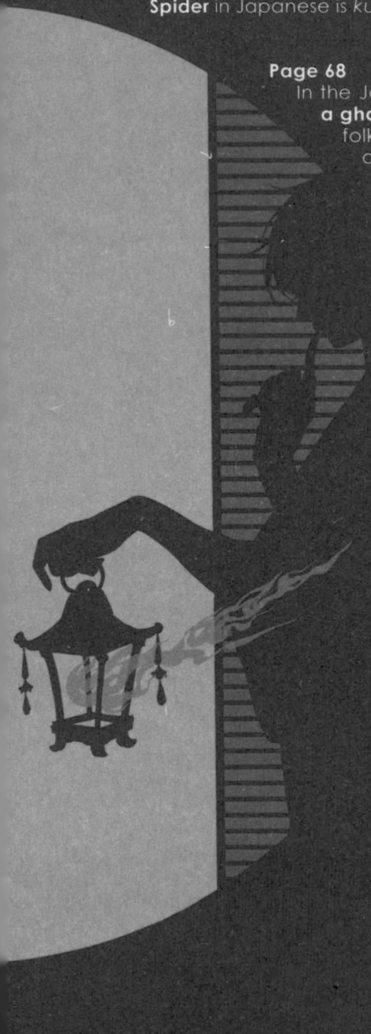

Page 68
In the Japanese version, instead of saying **"You look like you've seen a ghost,"** Butterfly greets Miho by saying *moushi* once. In Japanese folklore, spirits are unable to say *moushi* twice in a row, so greeting others with *moushi moushi* became a way to inform the other person, especially from a distance, that the speaker is human. In other words, it's a hint at Butterfly being supernatural. The use of *moushi moushi* as a long-distance greeting is why it became the de facto salutation for phone calls in Japanese.

Page 101
Murakumo means "gathering clouds" in Japanese.

Page 181
An **earth spider** (*tsuchigumo*) is a spider *youkai* (a kind of monster or spirit in Japanese folklore). The word can also refer to a nonsupernatural purseweb spider, with the idea that purseweb spiders that have lived long lives can grow to enormous size and eat humans.

Incarnate butterflies (*choukeshin*) are white butterfly *youkai* said to follow people who are nearing death.

Phantom Tales of the Night

BONUS MANGA HERE!

FIRST ENIGMA
ALL KINDS OF CUSTOMER SERVICE

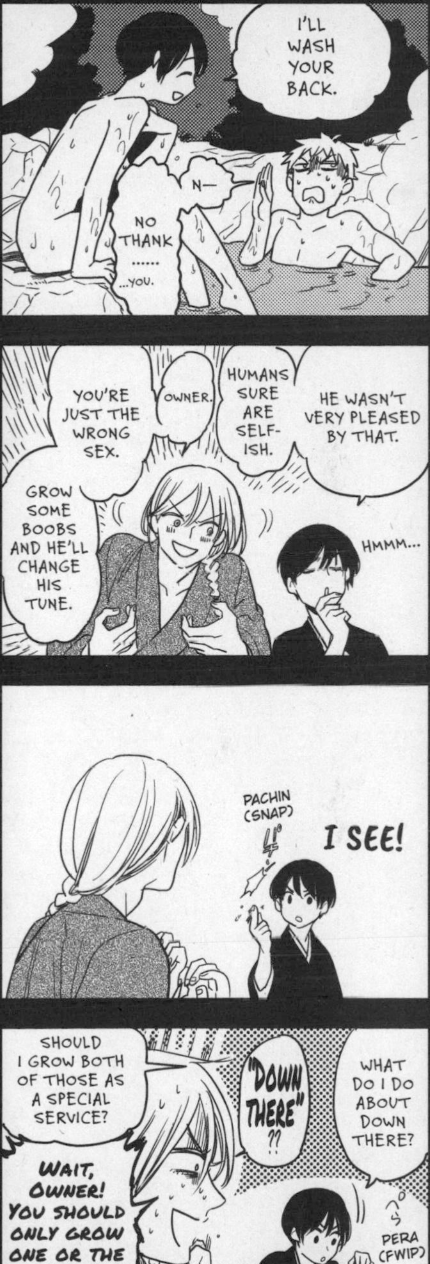
I'LL WASH YOUR BACK.
N—
NO THANK ....YOU.
HE WASN'T VERY PLEASED BY THAT.
HUMANS SURE ARE SELF-ISH.
OWNER.
YOU'RE JUST THE WRONG SEX.
GROW SOME BOOBS AND HE'LL CHANGE HIS TUNE.
HMMM...
I SEE!
PACHIN (SNAP)
WHAT DO I DO ABOUT DOWN THERE?
"DOWN THERE" ??
SHOULD I GROW BOTH OF THOSE AS A SPECIAL SERVICE?
WAIT, OWNER! YOU SHOULD ONLY GROW ONE OR THE OTHER!!!
PERA (FWIP)

TOO MUCH SPECIAL SERVICE

SECOND ENIGMA
ALL KINDS OF FOODSTUFFS

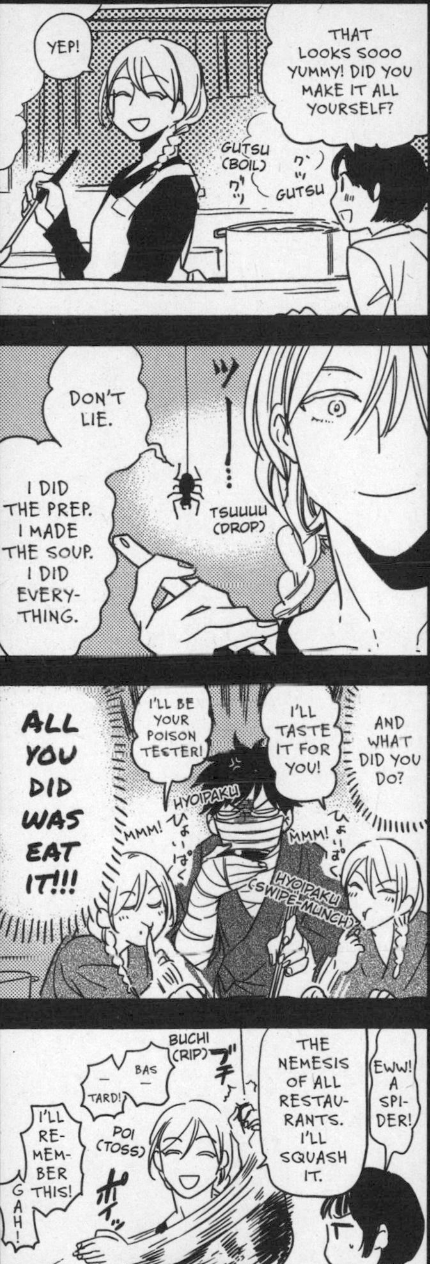
THAT LOOKS SOOO YUMMY! DID YOU MAKE IT ALL YOURSELF?
YEP!
GUTSU (BOIL)
GUTSU
TSUUUU (DROP)
DON'T LIE.
I DID THE PREP. I MADE THE SOUP. I DID EVERY-THING.
AND WHAT DID YOU DO?
I'LL TASTE IT FOR YOU!
I'LL BE YOUR POISON TESTER!
HYOIPAKU
MMM!
MMM!
HYOIPAKU (SWIPE-MUNCH)
ALL YOU DID WAS EAT IT!!!
EWW! A SPI-DER!
THE NEMESIS OF ALL RESTAU-RANTS. I'LL SQUASH IT.
BUCHI (RIP)
BAS — TARD!
POI (TOSS)
I'LL RE-MEM-BER THIS!
GAH!

THIRD ENIGMA
ALL KINDS OF PETTING

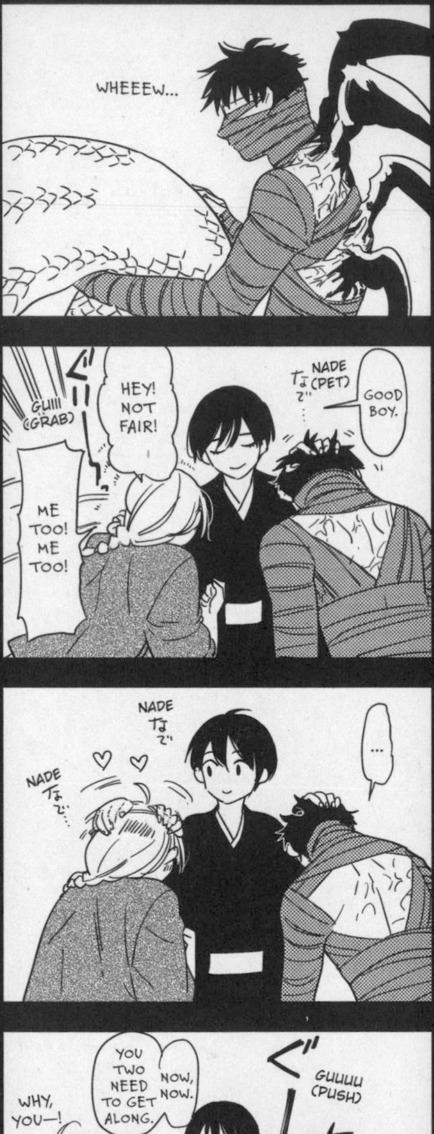
WHEEEW...
GOOD BOY.
NADE (PET)
HEY! NOT FAIR!
GUIII (GRAB)
ME TOO! ME TOO!
...
NADE
NADE
GUUUU (PUSH)
NOW, NOW.
YOU TWO NEED TO GET ALONG.
WHY, YOU—!

FOURTH ENIGMA
ALL KINDS OF PHANTOMS

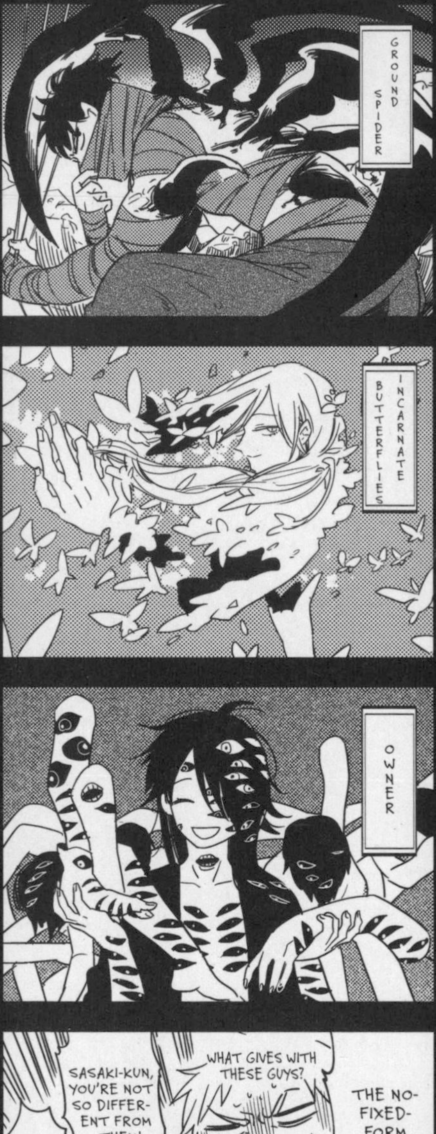
GROUND SPIDER
INCARNATE BUTTERFLIES
OWNER
THE NO-FIXED-FORM TRIO!! (HIS NAME FOR THEM)
WHAT GIVES WITH THESE GUYS?
SASAKI-KUN, YOU'RE NOT SO DIFFERENT FROM THEM!
SHUT UUUP! JUST SHUT UUUP!

Phantom Tales of the Night 1

Matsuri

Translation: Julie Goniwich
Lettering: Takeshi Kamura

This book is a work of fiction. Names, characters, places, and incidents are the product of the author's imagination or are used fictitiously. Any resemblance to actual events, locales, or persons, living or dead, is coincidental.

BAKEMONO YAWA ZUKUSHI vol. 1
© Matsuri 2016
First published in Japan in 2016 by KADOKAWA CORPORATION, Tokyo. English translation right arranged with KADOKAWA CORPORATION, Tokyo through TUTTLE-MORI AGENCY, INC., Tokyo.

English translation © 2019 by Yen Press, LLC

Yen Press, LLC supports the right to free expression and the value of copyright. The purpose of copyright is to encourage writers and artists to produce the creative works that enrich our culture.

The scanning, uploading, and distribution of this book without permission is a theft of the author's intellectual property. If you would like permission to use material from the book (other than for review purposes), please contact the publisher. Thank you for your support of the author's rights.

Yen Press
150 West 30th Street, 19th Floor
New York, NY 10001

Visit us at yenpress.com
facebook.com/yenpress
twitter.com/yenpress
yenpress.tumblr.com
instagram.com/yenpress

First Yen Press Edition: August 2019

Yen Press is an imprint of Yen Press, LLC.
The Yen Press name and logo are trademarks of Yen Press, LLC.

The publisher is not responsible for websites (or their content) that are not owned by the publisher.

Library of Congress Control Number: 2019942895

ISBNs: 978-1-9753-8521-7 (paperback)
978-1-0753-8522-4 (ebook)

10 9 8 7 6 5 4 3 2 1

WOR

Printed in the United States of America

CONTENTS

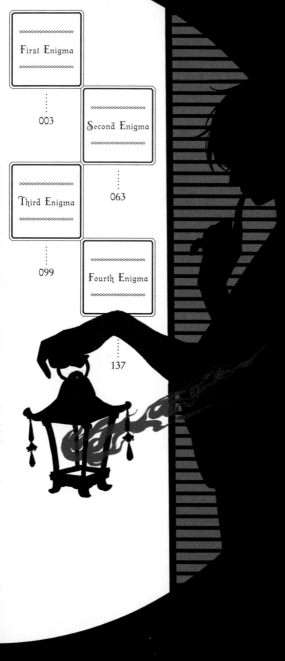

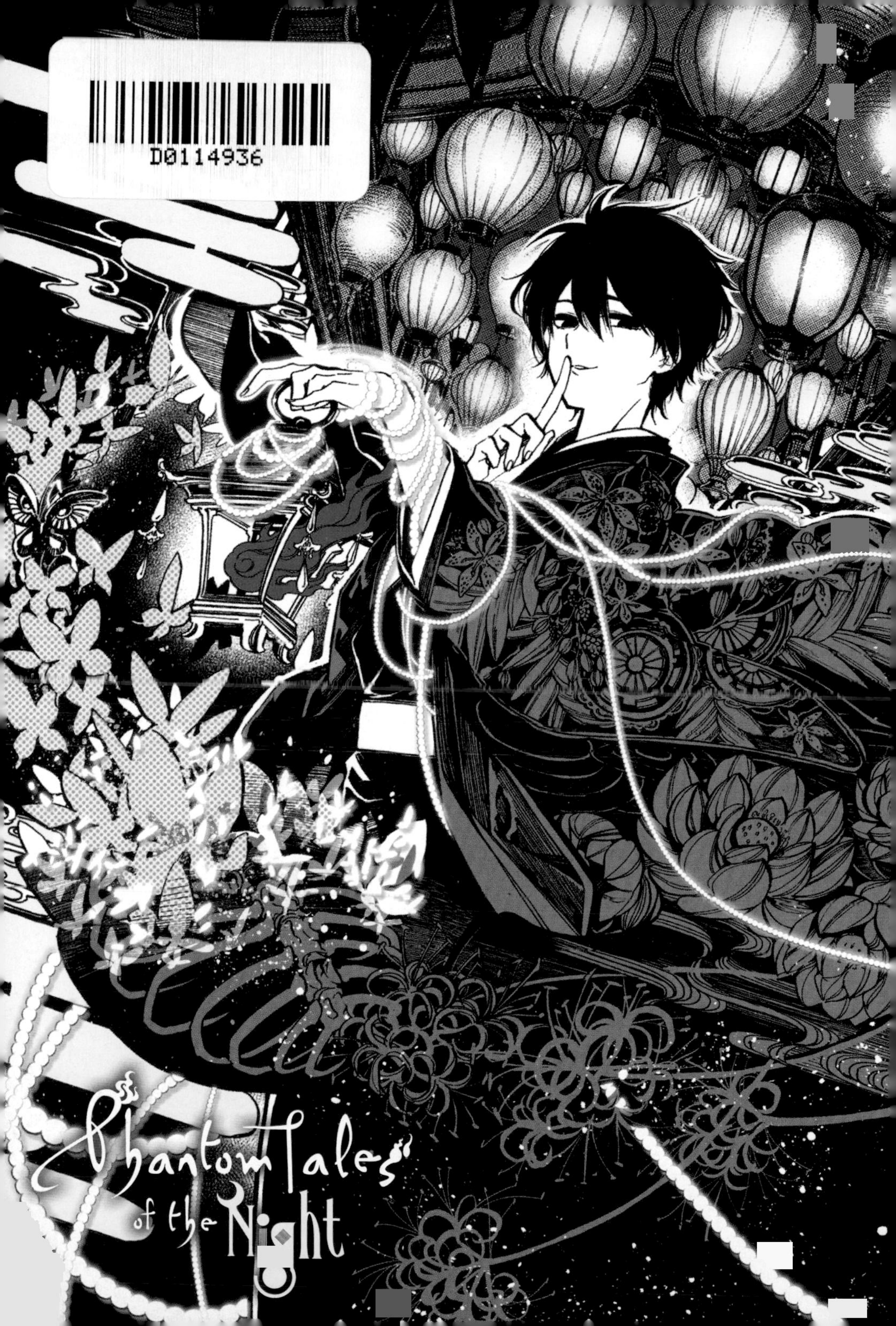
Phantom Tales of the Night